PARIS THEATRE AUDIENCES

in the
Seventeenth & Eighteenth
Centuries

UNIVERSITY OF DURHAM
PUBLICATIONS

J. B. PATAS. *La petite loge*

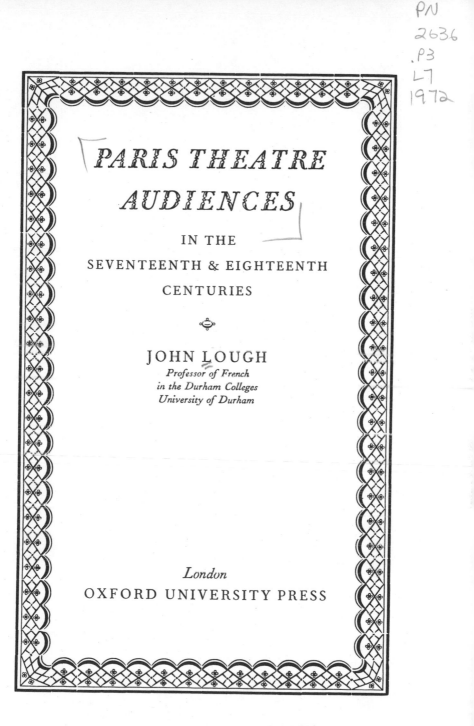

PARIS THEATRE AUDIENCES

IN THE
SEVENTEENTH & EIGHTEENTH
CENTURIES

❖

JOHN LOUGH

Professor of French
in the Durham Colleges
University of Durham

London
OXFORD UNIVERSITY PRESS

PN
2636
P3
L7
1972

Oxford University Press, Ely House, London W. 1

GLASGOW   NEW YORK   TORONTO   MELBOURNE   WELLINGTON
CAPE TOWN   IBADAN   NAIROBI   DAR ES SALAAM   LUSAKA   ADDIS ABABA
DELHI   BOMBAY   CALCUTTA   MADRAS   KARACHI   LAHORE   DACCA
KUALA LUMPUR   SINGAPORE   HONG KONG   TOKYO

ISBN 0 19 713112 3

First Published 1957
Reprinted 1965 and 1972

PRINTED IN GREAT BRITAIN

Preface

*T*HIS book does not claim to provide the impossible—a precise and detailed picture of the changing theatre audiences of seventeenth- and eighteenth-century Paris. Its purpose is more modest: to assemble the fragments of evidence available to us on this subject, and to offer a tentative interpretation of them.

It originated in the belief that in this field it was possible to discover some rather closer approximations to the truth than those contained in such vague formulae as 'aristocratic audience' or 'rise of the middle classes'. The material presented in these pages and the interpretation put upon it are the fruits of a good many years' research, carried on in English and French libraries; but the book also owes much to the preparation of lectures on French drama under the Ancien Régime as on many other aspects of French literature and thought in the seventeenth and eighteenth centuries, as well as to investigations into quite different problems of this period.

A wide variety of sources has been drawn upon, ranging from contemporary plays and prefaces to learned dissertations on the theatre, from legal documents to Furetière's dictionary, from the writings of Father Caffaro to the accounts of their travels in France left behind by foreigners like Thomas Platter and Dr. Burney.[1] Meagre as the results of all these investigations may appear to some readers, they have taken in every source of information, published or unpublished, which presented itself. Completeness would be a vain ideal in such a book; several lifetimes might be spent in groping for material. The time seemed ripe to publish the results of the investigation for what they are worth.

Many a weighty tome and many a more or less illegible manuscript which do not appear in the list of sources given in the bibliography, have been waded through without the slightest result. Rare books,

---

[1] Among the various travellers' accounts explored for this purpose Locke's Journal proved one of the most useless from the point of view of this book.

*

ancient and modern, and articles in obscure periodicals have been
tracked down after patient inquiry, only to yield precisely nothing.
Given the nature of the material available, it will be obvious that where
the views advanced in these pages happen to differ from those generally
accepted, they are put forward in no dogmatic spirit. That does not
mean that any apology is offered for describing the audiences in the
Paris theatres of the seventeenth and eighteenth centuries as they appear to me to have been. Sometimes the hypotheses with which I began
these investigations have been confirmed by the facts as they were collected; sometimes, too, they have had to be abandoned and replaced by
the conclusions which the available facts require. If occasionally disagreement is expressed with views put forward by scholars who have
worked in this field, it is with the humility engendered by a study of
the facts in all their complexity and rarity.

The debt of this book to innumerable works on the French theatre
in the seventeenth and eighteenth centuries, as to large numbers of
monographs on individual playwrights and actors in this period, is
immense. The greatest debt of all is to the bulky writings of the late
Professor H. Carrington Lancaster. Perhaps the clearest way of acknow-
ledging what I owe to his works on French drama of the seventeenth
and eighteenth centuries is to confess that where they were not there to
assist me, in particular with the history of comedy and dramatic forms
other than tragedy between 1715 and 1789 and with the history of the
Comédie Française between 1774 and the Revolution, they have been
sorely missed. Having made plain my debt, I may perhaps be allowed
in my findings to differ occasionally from my predecessors.

After considerable hesitation I have modernized the spelling and
punctuation of passages quoted from seventeenth- and eighteenth-
century sources. Although there is much to be said for reproducing
these as they stand, many of the passages come from editions in which
the spelling and punctuation have already been altered, and there seemed
no point in offering the reader a strange medley of quotations, some
modernized and some left in their original state.

I am grateful to the editors of the *Durham University Journal* and
French Studies for permission to reproduce wholly or in part articles
which appeared in those reviews. I should also like to acknowledge
here grants towards the cost of journeys to Paris to carry out these investigations from both the Ernest Cassel Educational Trust and the
Research Fund of the Durham Colleges; to the latter I am also in-
debted for a grant for the typing of the manuscript of this book.

It is also fitting that I should here express my gratitude to the Publications Board of the University of Durham which has turned the typescript of this work into a book, and offer my thanks to the Assistant Registrar, Mr. Ian E. Graham, for his assistance in seeing the book through the press.

I owe much to the librarians who have helped me to track down pieces of information which were hard to come by. In the preparation of this book I have received much assistance from the University Libraries of Cambridge and Durham, the British Museum, the Bibliothèque Nationale, and the Bibliothèque de l'Arsenal. I have also explored the rich resources of the Archives de la Comédie Française with the assistance of successive librarians—Monsieur L. Bourny, the late Jean-Jacques Olivier and, more recently, Monsieur Paul Gazagne.

As usual, my greatest debt of all in the preparation and writing of this book is to my wife.

J. L.

Durham
March 1956

Contents

Illustrations

Reproduced from photographs, provided by the Service Photographique of the Bibliothèque Nationale, Paris, of prints in the Cabinet des Estampes.

Introduction

*I*N the past occasional articles have been devoted to a study of the
Paris theatre audiences of the seventeenth and eighteenth centuries, and
here and there a few pages or even a whole chapter on this question can
be found in the standard works on French drama. So far no one has
thought the subject worthy of the detailed study which a whole book
devoted to such an inquiry demands. Yet most people would agree that
useful work could be done in this field, especially as it is on the border-
line between two quite distinct disciplines which only too often have
no dealings with one another—the history of literature and social
history.

Such a book may repel and even shock people who prefer to study
literary masterpieces in a complete vacuum and are content to register
the impact which great plays make on their refined sensibility without
even wishing to know anything about the vulgar details of the conditions under which they were first produced. However, experience of
lecturing on this subject has shown that audiences, both at the undergraduate level and well beyond it, are interested in the attempt to
discover something more precise about the spectators for whom
Corneille, Molière, and Racine, Voltaire, Marivaux, and Beaumarchais
wrote, and the influence exercised on their plays by the audiences of the
time. In such an investigation an incursion into the realm of social
history leads one back again to the masterpieces of drama produced in
France under the Ancien Régime.

All historians of the theatre recognize that there is a connexion
between theatre audiences of a given time and country, and the types of
drama which are produced for them. It is true that even if we had fifty
times more material available for a study of the audiences of the Paris
theatres under the Ancien Régime than we actually have, we should
still not be able to explain more than a limited amount about the plays
performed there. Other factors—aesthetic, dramatic, and psychological—must also be taken into account. Yet for the light which it

undoubtedly throws on the drama of the period, that relationship is worth at least an attempt at detailed study.

The choice of the whole of the seventeenth and eighteenth centuries as the field for this investigation perhaps requires some explanation. A long period such as this has the advantage that the two centuries between the end of the Wars of Religion and the outbreak of the Revolution in 1789 do form a coherent whole. Indeed, it is an age which it is extremely difficult to divide into two parts; in any but the strictly numerical sense it is almost impossible to determine where the seventeenth century leaves off and the eighteenth begins. Although the theatre, like the society around it, was in a constant state of evolution, these two centuries do present a certain organic unity which enables one to treat them as a whole.

It could be argued on the other hand that a detailed study of two or three important decades taken from either period would have led to more fruitful results, since a more restricted field would have permitted a more detailed examination of the problem. While there is something to be said for this argument, it is also true that the researches undertaken for this book have not led to the discovery for any one part of the period of a mass of evidence so great as to furnish material for a book on a more restricted field. Moreover, there is much to be said for studying Paris theatre audiences before the Revolution over a fairly long period. Even if the material had justified a detailed study of two or three decades out of these two centuries, such a limited investigation would lack perspective. It could give little idea of the constant evolution which was going on in this field as in all other spheres of French society in the two centuries before the Revolution.

These investigations have been limited to Paris, not only because a study of the not inconsiderable literature on the provincial theatre in this period provided a relatively small amount of material, but also for the more important reason that if we leave aside the first two or three decades of the seventeenth century, during these two centuries it was Paris that led the provinces in everything concerning the theatre. The best actors gravitated towards the capital; all the important playwrights lived there and wrote for the audiences of Paris and the court. Though not entirely absent from these pages, the provinces must inevitably sink into the background in any discussion of the relationship between the theatre audience and the drama of the Ancien Régime.

Even so far as the Paris theatre audience is concerned, certain restrictions have been necessary. In the period before the foundation of the Comédie Française in 1680, all the theatres which at different times in the century competed for the custom of the theatre-going public have been brought into the discussion: the Hôtel de Bourgogne where one company was at last permanently established in 1629, the company of the Théâtre du Marais which set up in Paris in 1630 and gave its first performance in its permanent quarters in 1635; the companies of Italian actors which visited Paris at different periods in the first half of the century until finally in 1660 the company of Scaramouche settled permanently there; and Molière's company which competed successfully with the Hôtel de Bourgogne between 1658 and 1673, and was merged at his death with the Théâtre du Marais to form the Théâtre Guénégaud.

In 1680 competition between the French companies of actors in Paris was brought to an end by Louis XIV. The Hôtel de Bourgogne and the Théâtre Guénégaud were merged to form the Comédie Française, and their only competitors, the Italian actors who now occupied the Hôtel de Bourgogne, were expelled from France in 1697. For nearly twenty years—until the recall of the Italians by the Regent in 1716—the Comédie Française had a monopoly of theatrical performances in Paris. Although the Théâtres de la Foire attempted to invade this monopoly, their contribution to drama, both then and later in the century, was negligible. It is even true that the Italians, while they were responsible for the production of most of the masterpieces of Marivaux, contributed relatively little to the production of worthwhile drama. Neither the Théâtre Italien nor the Théâtres de la Foire (the latter developed more and more as the eighteenth century went on) will be entirely neglected in these pages; but the fact remains that during the eighteenth century the Comédie Française was responsible for the production of almost all new plays of any importance. It was there that the tragedies of Voltaire and the comedies of Beaumarchais first faced the footlights. It is then not merely because we are better informed about this theatre than about any other of the time, but because in the eighteenth century the Comédie Française occupied a dominant position in the theatrical life of Paris, that in the pages which follow it will be given much greater prominence than any other.

Historians of French drama in the seventeenth and eighteenth centuries appear to agree on the whole[1] that the history of the relationship between the theatre audience and the drama of the period falls roughly

---

[1] For the seventeenth century Lancaster lends the weight of his authority to a rather different view which will be discussed below (pp. 49 f.).

into three periods. It is generally accepted that the audience of the first twenty or so years of the seventeenth century was an almost entirely plebeian one, lacking the refining influence of the aristocracy, learned men (*les doctes*), and especially respectable women. The crude tastes of such an audience are, it is held, reflected in the extremely low aesthetic and moral standards of French drama in the opening decades of the century. Then, it is argued, in the period between about 1625 and 1635 a revolution occurred in the composition of the audience; from being overwhelmingly plebeian it became preponderantly aristocratic. From being crude and salacious in its tastes, it became, partly under the influence of respectable women, much more refined, both from the aesthetic and the moral point of view. It was for this preponderantly aristocratic audience that Corneille, Molière, and Racine in the seventeenth century, and Voltaire and Marivaux in the first half of the eighteenth, composed their masterpieces. However, so the accepted view goes, in the course of the fifty or sixty years before the Revolution the rise of the middle classes had its effect in the theatre as in other spheres of culture; it gave rise to a more serious, moralizing type of comedy such as that of Destouches, then to the *comédie larmoyante* of Nivelle de La Chaussée, and finally, after 1750, to the *drame bourgeois* of writers like Diderot, Sedaine, and Beaumarchais.

Even if this view of the relationship between French drama and its audience were entirely acceptable, it would still require to be founded on a more generous supply of documents than has hitherto been vouchsafed by its supporters. Again, even if it may be held to be true in essentials, such an interpretation needs to be broadened before it can hope to do anything like justice to the extreme complexity of the facts; and on occasion the documents do, it will be seen, tend to modify and even at times substantially correct this view of the matter. Moreover, in order to come as near as possible to the truth, one must continually bear in mind that the Paris theatre audiences of the different periods of the seventeenth and eighteenth centuries came from a society which was itself in a slow, but none the less constant process of evolution. Despite outward appearances, the structure of French society on the eve of the Revolution was very different from what it had been at the end of the Wars of Religion nearly two centuries earlier. We must constantly attempt to relate the evolution of Paris theatre audiences to the changing state of the world outside the theatre. It is only then that we can hope to give some reasonably precise meaning in our context to such expressions as 'aristocratic audience' and 'rise of the middle classes'.

Among the difficulties with which this whole subject bristles not the least is to be encountered in the field of social history itself. It is notorious that an immense amount of work remains to be done before we can have any clear idea of the changing social structure of France in the seventeenth and eighteenth centuries. Although this book deals only with a tiny fraction of the population of France in these two centuries—for the theatre-going public formed a definite minority amongst the inhabitants of the capital—even with that relatively restricted section of society our total knowledge is very limited indeed. Again, not only is the contemporary evidence on theatre audiences disappointingly small and scrappy; it is occasionally contradictory and often difficult to interpret. For instance, a great many documents bearing on the theme of this book use the word *peuple*; inevitably in these cases the word is used in a variety of senses as it was, according to seventeenth-century dictionaries, in many other contexts. The difficulty is to decide what was the meaning attached to the word by contemporaries when they applied it to theatre audiences.[1]

In discussing the size of theatre audiences in our period use has naturally been made of such precise figures as happen to be available— that is, those for the Comédie Française from its foundation in 1680.[2] It may shock some sensitive souls to see a book on French drama in the seventeenth and eighteenth centuries polluted by vulgar statistics; but where they are available, there seems little point in attempting to discuss how many people attended the leading Paris theatre of the time, or how many people were able and willing to support a successful play during its first run, simply by recourse to one's imagination. The reader will, of course, be spared not only the tedious calculations necessary to compile such statistics, but also any more of the results than is necessary.

The nature of the investigations which have produced this book precludes any high flights of imaginative writing. The most valuable part of it is clearly the collection of contemporary documents which it offers; some of them are by no means new, but even those already familiar to historians of the theatre have been carefully checked from the original sources and studied in their context, occasionally with rather surprising results. Sometimes it is by no means easy to assign a

[1] See below, pp. 55 f.
[2] Published by Lancaster in *The Comédie Française, 1680–1701; Plays, Actors, Spectators, Finances* (Baltimore, 1941) and *The Comédie Française, 1701–1774; Plays, Actors, Spectators, Finances* (Philadelphia, 1951).

precise meaning to contemporary references to theatre audiences; at times the available documents contradict one another. In dealing with these delicate problems of interpretation the only proper method is to set forth all the contemporary evidence, to discuss it frankly and then to attempt to suggest what is its true meaning, without failing in one's duty to the reader by offering no solution, and yet without attempting to ride one's own hobbyhorse at the expense of the highly complex truth of the situation.

The arrangement of the material into chapters and into the appropriate section of each chapter has often presented considerable difficulties. The division of the two centuries treated here into three main periods— the age of Alexandre Hardy,[1] the period from Corneille to Lesage, and finally that from the beginning of Voltaire's long career as a dramatist to the *Mariage de Figaro*—is not wholly satisfactory; yet it seemed the best way of avoiding the repetition which would be inevitable if one divided the period from 1630 to 1789 into more than two parts.

Experience of discussing these questions in public, both in lectures and under less formal conditions, has shown that a more precise knowledge of Paris theatre audiences in these 200 years can give greater life to the study of French drama in this period. Above all, it is hoped that this investigation will have cast some light on the changes in French taste in these two centuries and on their influence on the drama of the time.

[1] Studies of early seventeenth-century French drama published in recent years have shown that the importance of Hardy was much less than was once supposed; yet even so he does remain the outstanding playwright of his age.

1. *The Age of Alexandre Hardy*

*T*HE seventeenth century—one of the greatest periods in the history of French drama, the age of Corneille, Racine, and Molière—began dismally enough in the theatre. One or two plays, such as Racan's *Bergeries* and Théophile de Viau's *Pyrame et Thisbé*, stand out in the early part of the century from the motley collection of works produced for the theatre before 1630; but they were not performed until the early 1620's, and it was not until well into the fourth decade of the century that French drama acquired its first undoubted masterpiece. Until Pierre Corneille emerged as a great playwright in 1637 with the striking success of *Le Cid*, seventeenth-century France had no dramatist to set beside Shakespeare in England or Lope de Vega in Spain.

In the first two or three decades of the century the provinces exercised a greater influence on the development of French drama than did the capital. In these years the theatre in Paris brought wealth to neither actors nor playwrights. Travelling companies—Italian and even English, as well as French—occasionally performed in Paris in converted *jeux de paume* or other improvised theatres, but a legal monopoly of all theatrical performances was enjoyed by the Confrères de la Passion who owned the only proper theatre, the Hôtel de Bourgogne. At the end of the sixteenth century the Confrères gave up acting plays and merely hired out their theatre to such companies of actors as happened to present themselves, having recourse to the law courts to restrain other groups of actors from performing elsewhere in Paris. Most of the visiting companies managed to remain in the capital for only a short period at a time. It was not until 1629 that a French company succeeded in establishing itself permanently at the Hôtel de Bourgogne, and it was only in the following year that a second permanent theatre, later known as the Théâtre du Marais, could be set up in Paris. Earlier in the century the lot of the series of companies founded by a well-known actor, Valleran Le Conte, was very different; his repeated attempts to establish himself in Paris, on which further light has been thrown by

Mme Deierkauf-Holsboer in her recent book on Alexandre Hardy,[1] always ended in failure.

A company formed by Valleran was in Paris in 1598, but it was not until January of the following year that it performed at the Hôtel de Bourgogne. Another company of French actors which had hired the theatre until Lent signed an agreement with Valleran to give performances in alternate weeks until the expiry of its lease. After Lent and a brief interlude when the theatre was occupied by some Italian actors, Valleran and his company continued to perform at the Hôtel de Bourgogne, without great profit, until February 1600. The arrival of another Italian company in that month made Valleran's situation still worse; his company was compelled to join forces with the Italians for three months. Before this contract had expired, he formed a new company and hired for a fortnight a courtyard in the Rue du Coq to give performances there. It is clear from the available documents that Valleran was struggling all the time with debts; he must finally have been compelled to leave Paris for the provinces, and it is not until the end of 1605 that we again learn of his presence in the capital.

In February and April of the following year Valleran took two short leases of the Hôtel de Bourgogne, but once again he ran into difficulties and could not even pay the rent for his first lease of the theatre. The second lease was only granted on condition that the debt for the first should be paid off in instalments of 15 livres, to be handed over at the end of each performance. Once again the company left the capital for the provinces and did not return to Paris until the following year. It is probable that his was the company which performed a farce at the Hôtel de Bourgogne in January 1607 before Henry IV and his court.[2] We know definitely that later in the same year Valleran's company hired the theatre for several months, but in January 1608 he and his new group of actors were compelled to bring to an end their performances at the Hôtel de Bourgogne which was let to a company of Italian actors. For another year, until March 1609, we lose sight of Valleran and his companions; shortly after he leased the Hôtel de Bourgogne from September until the Shrove Tuesday of 1610. This time Valleran and his fellow actors seem to have succeeded in fulfilling their obligations towards the Confrères de la Passion, but only by fusing with another company in January 1610. The new company stayed in Paris until May, and then left for the provinces until July,

---

[1] *Vie d'Alexandre Hardy, Poète du Roi* (Philadelphia, 1947).
[2] See below, p. 23.

when a new lease of the Hôtel de Bourgogne was taken. Yet all the time, even in the provinces, Valleran was pursued by his creditors who seized his stock of costumes at Orleans. When he returned to Paris, Valleran lost some of his best actors, and although he renewed his lease in February 1611, the company was shortly afterwards disbanded. However, a new company was at once formed, and in March another lease of the Hôtel de Bourgogne was taken, this time for the period from 1 August until the Lent of the following year. Yet by the beginning of September the company was compelled to sign an agreement with one of its creditors whereby he was to collect all the daily receipts except for those from the *parterre* (pit). In February 1612 the difficulties of Valleran were increased by the arrival of an Italian company in Paris; the two groups of actors finally agreed that each should give a play in its own language at every performance. These joint performances soon faded out, the Italians vanished from the scene, and Valleran's company disintegrated. In March he again formed a new company, which does not appear to have performed at the Hôtel de Bourgogne; it was in the provinces and abroad (in Holland, for instance) that Valleran now sought the success which had eluded him in Paris. His fourteen years of struggle to establish himself in the capital ended in debt-ridden failure; even the date and place of his death are unknown.

If it was some time yet until the *Comédiens du Roi* finally installed themselves permanently at the Hôtel de Bourgogne, conditions do seem gradually to have improved after the first dozen or so years of the seventeenth century. The records of the Hôtel de Bourgogne still present certain gaps, but such leases as are known to us for the period between 1612 and 1629 do show that gradually there was more competition among different French companies to take over the theatre until finally one company secured a monopoly of its use and settled there for good. Even so, it was not until 1630 that Paris could support simultaneously two companies of French actors, whereas in the opening decades of the seventeenth century London had quite a number of both public and private theatres. The contrast between the struggles of an actor like Valleran in the opening decade of the century and the popularity enjoyed by the theatre in the London of Shakespeare's day is striking.

At the beginning of the seventeenth century the Paris theatre was thus in an extremely backward state, compared with that of London or Madrid. In addition the plays performed were of extreme crudity, judged both from the aesthetic and moral point of view; not a single play of the first three decades of the seventeenth century has held the stage down to our own day.

The conventional explanation of this lamentable state of affairs is a simple one. The audience in these opening years of the century was, it is argued, largely, if not exclusively, plebeian. French drama lacked the refining influence of the aristocracy, learned men (*les doctes*), and especially respectable women. This is how Gustave Lanson once described a typical performance at the Hôtel de Bourgogne in the first part of the seventeenth century:

Une salle rectangulaire, deux rangs de loges, un parterre dallé, gras de fange, où les spectateurs se tiennent debout, une scène éclairée de quelques chandelles, qu'un valet mouche dans les entr'actes, des comédiens misérablement ou ridiculement accoutrés, à moins que la munificence d'un gentilhomme ou d'un prince ne les ait gratifiés de quelques habits encore propres, un public grossier et tumultueux, des marchands, des clercs, des écoliers, des artisans, des pages, des soldats, des spadassins et des filous: voilà le cadre offert à la sublime tragédie. Elle se produit, pour se faire accepter, en vulgaire compagnie. Un *prologue* la précède, facétieux, bourré de calembours et d'obscénités, pour mettre le public en belle humeur. Une farce la suit, brutale et crue, pour dissiper l'émotion triste; et le spectacle se termine souvent par des chansons ordurières.[1]

The prologues mentioned in this passage—those of the farce actor, Bruscambille, the first authorized edition of which probably appeared in 1610—provide the basis for an even more colourful paragraph, penned by another great authority on the period, Émile Magne, in describing the audience before which the farce actor, Gaultier-Garguille, performed in the opening decades of the seventeenth century:

Il est le pourvoyeur de divertissement d'une extraordinaire canaille. Ce que recèle le parterre de l'Hôtel de Bourgogne, c'est un ramassis grouillant, fétide, tumultueux de laquais, de pages, de soldats, de filous, de poètes crottés, d'étudiants en ribote et 'autres ordures du genre humain'. Ivres de bière et de pétun, ces mistoudins, ces écornifleurs d'honneur, ces magasins de sottises brament et braillent, rotent, pètent, toussent, crachent, reniflent, rient, s'injurient, se battent, ou bien avec des gestes simiesques, se grattent la tête et le cul.[2]

As for the women who attended such performances, to quote another well-known historian of the theatre: 'On imagine bien que les honnêtes

[1] *Corneille* (Paris, 1898), pp. 30–31.
[2] *Gaultier-Garguille, comédien de l'Hôtel de Bourgogne* (Paris, n.d.), pp. 24–25.

femmes ne fréquentaient point un tel milieu; aussi bien, lorsque l'ora-
teur de la troupe s'adressait à la partie féminine de l'auditoire, il le
faisait en termes qui ne convenaient qu'à des spectatrices dont le front
ne sait plus rougir.'[1]

Lest the reader suspect that in this chapter a dead horse is being
flogged, it might be well to take a description of early seventeenth-
century theatre audiences which comes from the pen of one of the most
distinguished living experts on the period. If we turn to Professor
Antoine Adam's monumental *Histoire de la littérature française au
XVIIe siècle*, a work which is still in process of publication, we find, it
is true, certain slight retouches to the familiar picture, but the general
effect remains unchanged. In the opening years of the seventeenth
century, Professor Adam maintains, the theatre

reste au niveau du bon peuple de Paris. L'aristocratie ne fréquente pas l'Hôtel,
et aucun mari raisonnable n'y mènerait sa femme. L'abbé d'Aubignac, comme
Tallemant, est formel. Une honnête femme, avant 1630, n'allait pas au
théâtre. . . . Le parterre était occupé par des clercs de la basoche, des pages,
des laquais, des militaires, pour ne rien dire des filous qui s'y introduisaient,
pour y exercer leurs talents. N'oublions pas pourtant les loges. De jeunes
nobles, d'humeur libertine, les fréquentaient et le bon Père Garasse appelle
Théophile et ses amis 'des amphibies de la taverne et de l'hôtel de Bourgogne,
vivant partie en l'un et partie en l'autre'. Le droit d'entrée est minime: cinq
sous au parterre, et dix sous aux loges, et fait du théâtre une distraction
éminemment populaire.[2]

Gradually, so the accepted view goes, in the years between about
1625 and 1635, as the theatre became much more popular in Paris and
could at last support two permanent French companies, a revolution
took place in the composition of the audience. It ceased to be essentially
plebeian and became predominantly aristocratic; its tastes were no
longer crude and salacious, and, partly under the influence of respectable women, the new plays performed at the Hôtel de Bourgogne and
the Marais theatre became much more refined, from both the aesthetic
and the moral point of view. 'Enfin', says Lanson, 'les dames ne crai-
gnirent plus de se montrer à la comédie. Il ne s'y débita plus rien qu'une
honnête femme ne pût entendre'; he hastens to add, however: 'c'est-
à-dire, selon les bienséances de 1630 qui ne sont pas, tant s'en faut,
celles de 1900'.[3] These prudent reservations will be appreciated by

---

[1] F. Gaiffe, *Le Rire et la scène française* (Paris, 1932), p. 86.
[2] Vol. i (Paris, 1948), pp. 173–4.
[3] *Corneille*, p. 31.

those who have studied, for instance, the text of the first editions of the early comedies of Corneille. In his first comedy, *Mélite*, probably performed in 1630, two lovers are allowed to indulge in a pastime soon to be banished from the French stage by the tyranny of the *bienséances* —kissing; in later editions this episode naturally vanishes. The earliest editions of the play reproduce the scene unblushingly:

> PHILANDRE: Cependant un baiser accordé par avance
> Soulagerait beaucoup ma pénible souffrance.
> CLORIS: Prends-le sans demander, poltron; pour un baiser
> Crois-tu que ta Cloris te voulût refuser?

What is more startling are the words put into the mouth of the girl's brother, who appears on the scene at this point:

> Voilà traiter l'amour justement bouche à bouche;
> C'est par là où vous alliez commencer l'escarmouche?

He is not content to make a discreet withdrawal after remarking, 'Two's company, three's none.' He expresses the idea in extremely crude terms:

> Je pense ne pouvoir vous être qu'importun,
> Vous feriez mieux un tiers que d'en accepter un.

In later editions of the play these lines are rendered in the harmless fashion:

> De moins sorciers que moi pourraient bien deviner
> Qu'un troisième ne fait que vous importuner.[1]

In a word, the observance of the *bienséances* about 1630 still had to make considerable progress before they held full sway over French drama, but already by about that date, we are told, there had emerged that more refined and fundamentally aristocratic audience for which Corneille, Molière, and Racine were in the course of the next half-century to produce their masterpieces.

It has thus become an article of faith among historians of the theatre that the undoubted aesthetic and moral crudity of all forms of French drama in the opening decades of the seventeenth century was a direct consequence of the coarse, plebeian nature of the audience which frequented the Paris theatre in this period. It is a misfortune that, although occasional discoveries, such as those set forth by Mme Deierkauf-Holsboer in her recent *Vie d'Alexandre Hardy*, serve to illuminate odd corners of the scene, the historian of the Paris theatre in the opening years of the seventeenth century must grope his way in

[1] Act I, Sc. 4 and 5.

almost total darkness. Not only were there no newspapers or periodicals to record for posterity what was going on in the contemporary theatre, but there is an almost complete absence of useful information in such letters, memoirs, and similar documents as have come down to us. Since our knowledge of the Paris theatrical world in these years is so scrappy, any generalizations about the theatre audience must remain extremely fragile. Even if one is not satisfied with the generally accepted interpretation of such fragments of knowledge as we possess, it would be foolish to attempt to substitute one set of dogmatic assertions for another.

Even so, a dispassionate examination of the available facts concerning several aspects of the Paris theatre in the early seventeenth century leads one inexorably to conclusions which differ from those which are generally accepted. It is, for instance, universally agreed that, as the theatre was not yet a flourishing industry and the actors were far from prosperous, the costumes in which they appeared on the stage must have been miserably poor. 'Des comédiens misérablement ou ridiculement accoutrés', is how Lanson speaks of them. The standard text in support of this view comes from the *Historiettes* of Tallemant des Réaux: the actors, he tells us, 'louaient des habits à la friperie' and were 'vêtus infâmement'.[1] Yet a rather different impression emerges from the documents concerning Valleran Le Conte and his company recently brought to light by Mme Deierkauf-Holsboer. In 1598 Valleran paid a second-hand clothes dealer in Paris a debt of 200 écus soleil (i.e. 600 livres, or over £40 in English money of the time) for supplying 'sept robes dont cinq de toile d'argent et de drap d'or et une de damas et une de taffetas changeant — dont cinq à usage de femme et deux à usage d'homme'. From another legal document we learn that eight years later Valleran had in his possession such costumes as 'deux robes de drap d'or faites à la turque, garnies de boutons à queues, une casaque de drap d'or sans manches, trois colletins à l'antique aussi de drap d'or, une casaque de velours cramoisi en broderie d'or et le colletin à l'antique de même étoffe' and so on.[2] While the actors and actresses of the early part of the century cannot have possessed such rich costumes as their successors when the theatre had become a fashionable and prosperous form of entertainment, and great noblemen or even the

---

[1] *Historiettes*, ed. G. Mongrédien (Paris, 1932–4), 8 vols., vol. vii, p. 121. Although they are generally quoted with reference to the opening decades of the seventeenth century, Tallemant's remarks do in fact concern a slightly earlier period.

[2] *Vie d'Alexandre Hardy*, pp. 385, 390.

King would provide them with valuable costumes, such documents as these scarcely confirm Tallemant's statement that they were 'vêtus infâmement'.

What concerns us here, however, is the audiences of the early seventeenth-century Paris theatre and the problem of establishing what sort of people frequented the still primitive auditorium with its *parterre* reserved for men, who had to remain standing during the whole performance, and its more expensive galleries or boxes. By comparison with the charges at the Comédie Française from 1680 onwards when a ticket to the *parterre* cost 15 sous and the most expensive seats 3 livres (prices which were roughly doubled during the first run of most new plays), the theatre in these years was undoubtedly an inexpensive form of entertainment. In 1609 (or 1619)[1] there appear to have been disturbances in the Paris theatres because it was considered that the actors were overcharging. The *Lieutenant civil* therefore forbade the actors to ask more than 'cinq sous au parterre et dix sous aux loges et galeries', adding, however, that 'en cas qu'ils y aient quelques actes à représenter où il conviendra plus de frais, il y sera par nous pourvu, sur leur requête préalablement communiquée au procureur du Roi'. While prices which the *Lieutenant civil* considered to be reasonable under normal circumstances appear very low compared with those which were to become usual in Paris later in the century, it should be pointed out that they seem to have been higher than those which were considered fair some thirty or forty years earlier. When in 1571 the first Italian company—that of the *Gelosi*—visited France, they charged for tickets at the public performances which they gave in Paris prices ranging from 3 to 6 sous.[2]

If the theatre was unquestionably a relatively cheap form of entertainment in the opening years of the seventeenth century, it does not necessarily follow that it was a low, plebeian audience that came to the performances. Our information on this point is tantalizingly small, but in the documents of the time we do catch occasional glimpses of people attending the theatre who were solid bourgeois or even higher in the social scale. In the 1620's Isaac Laffemas, one of Richelieu's most un-

---

[1] 1609 is the date usually assigned to this document, but while the first (along with the second) edition of the work from which it is taken—N. de Lamare's *Traité de la police*—gives in the text preceding the decree and in the marginal note the date '12 novembre 1609', the text itself is dated 'le douzième jour de novembre mil six cent dix-neuf' (see the 1st ed., Paris, 1705–38, 4 vols., vol. i, p. 440).

[2] A. Baschet, *Les Comédiens italiens à la cour de France sous Charles IX, Henri III, Henri IV et Louis XIII* (Paris, 1882), p. 20.

popular henchmen, was accused of having been an actor in his youth—
a dreadful charge to make in an age when actors in France were beyond
the pale. Various people gave evidence that they had seen him perform
in Valleran's company at the beginning of the century. Monsieur de
Loménie, who is described as 'père de Monsieur de la Ville-aux-Clairs,
secrétaire des commandements', gave evidence that on several occasions Isaac's father, Barthélemy Laffemas, who during the reign of
Henry IV held the important government post of *Contrôleur du commerce*, 'le pria instamment de venir aller voir jouer des tragédies et
comédies.où son dit fils était afin d'y prendre plaisir et récréation'. He
added that the father 'le mena au Sabot en la rue Saint-Antoine en un
jeu de paume, au faubourg Saint-Germain et à l'Hôtel de Bourgogne où
il vit jouer son dit fils, qui à la vérité jouait très bien et surpassait tous
les autres comédiens'. Another witness, this time an *avocat*, also gave
evidence that he had seen Isaac de Laffemas act when, twenty or twenty-
five years earlier, 'Valleran, célèbre comédien, étant à Paris, il allait
pour la réputation dudit Valleran et de ses compagnons souvent à
l'Hôtel de Bourgogne, au Sabot en la rue Saint-Antoine et au faubourg
Saint-Germain en un jeu de paume les voir jouer'.[1]

Historians of the theatre also maintain that the audience of these
years was a predominantly masculine one. For instance, in discussing
an extremely coarse early seventeenth-century comedy, Troterel's *Les
Corrivaux*, published at Rouen in 1612, Lancaster declares that the play
was written 'for an audience of men before the theater had been influenced by the more polished stratum of French society'. If one reads
only the play itself, this conclusion seems sound enough. Speaking
from his unrivalled knowledge of French drama of the period, Lancaster can declare: 'No play of the seventeenth century goes further in
the obscenity of its vocabulary or its situations.'[2] 'Rien de plus simple
que le thème des *Corrivaux*', wrote Félix Gaiffe in *Le Rire ot la scène
française.*

Le jeune Brillant et son amie Clorette ont passé la nuit ensemble; les
parents le découvrent, et l'on convient d'attirer de nouveau le jeune homme
à la maison, et, après flagrant délit, de le forcer au mariage: plan qui réussit
parfaitement. Mais dans les premiers actes, nous avons vu la jeune fille
accorder ses faveurs à un autre jeune homme du nom de Gaullard, et même,

---

[1] F. Lachèvre, *Les Recueils collectifs de poésies libres et satiriques* (Paris, 1914–22),
2 vols., vol. i, pp. 248–9.

[2] *A History of French Dramatic Literature in the Seventeenth Century* (Baltimore, 1929–
42), 9 vols., vol. i, p. 144.

sans avoir, il est vrai, reconnu son identité, à Almérin, valet de Brillant. C'est bien là le sujet d'une farce, où la vertu du beau sexe est traitée sans plus de ménagements que dans notre théâtre du moyen âge.[1]

It is difficult to imagine such highly indelicate situations being treated in a delicate fashion; in fact, the author makes no attempt to achieve such a *tour de force*, with the result that the language of his comedy is at times extremely crude.

Yet, curiously enough, the prologue of the play is addressed, not only to men, but to women, married and unmarried. It opens with the lines:

> Messieurs, Dieu vous doint joie; à vous aussi, mes dames,
> Et vous pareillement, belles filles et femmes.[2]

There is, of course, a simple answer to this objection: despite its coarse tone some women, it may be conceded, did attend the theatre in Paris or in other parts of France in the early part of the seventeenth century, but these were not respectable women.[3] Once again, the piece of contemporary, or rather near-contemporary, evidence most frequently quoted on this subject comes from Tallemant's *Historiettes*. The theatre, he declares, did not become a respectable form of entertainment until about 1630, when Richelieu began to take an interest in it: 'Avant cela les honnêtes femmes n'y allaient point.'[4] This sounds definite enough, it must be admitted, and yet one is left wondering how far Tallemant, who was not born until 1619, can be regarded as a reliable authority on the state of the Paris theatre in the early seventeenth century.

Some evidence on this point is to be found in documents of the 1630's, though it must be said that it is more difficult to interpret than

---

[1] p. 73.

[2] E. L. N. Viollet le Duc (ed.), *Ancien théâtre français* (Paris, 1854–7), 10 vols., vol. viii, p. 232.

[3] It is difficult to know what, if any, significance should be attached to the curious fact that in his *Introduction à la vie dévote* (1608), which consists of letters addressed in the first instance to a lady of the court, St. François de Sales does not, as one might expect, if the theatre really was shunned like the plague by all respectable women, condemn it root and branch. 'Les jeux, les bals, les festins, les pompes, les comédies en leur substance ne sont nullement choses mauvaises, ains indifférentes, pouvant être bien et mal exercées; toujours néanmoins ces choses-là sont dangereuses, et de s'y affectionner, cela est encore plus dangereux. Je dis donc, Philothée, qu'encore qu'il soit loisible de jouer, danser, se parer, ouïr des honnêtes comédies, banqueter, si est-ce que d'avoir affection à cela, c'est chose contraire à la dévotion et extrêmement nuisible et périlleuse' (3rd ed., Lyons, 1610, p. 99).

[4] Vol. vii, p. 122.

some historians of the theatre make out. In 1636 when Mairet published his comedy, *Les Galanteries du Duc d'Ossonne*, performed four years earlier, he was bold enough to maintain in the preface that this highly improper play had so raised the tone of the theatre that 'les plus honnêtes femmes fréquentent maintenant l'Hôtel de Bourgogne, avec aussi peu de scrupule qu'elles feraient celui du Luxembourg'. This claim was refuted in one of the anonymous pamphlets of the *Querelle du Cid*, the *Réponse à* . . ., which declares: 'Il a voulu par le même poème bannir les honnêtes femmes de la comédie, qui n'ont pu jamais souffrir les paroles, ni les actions de ses deux héroïnes.'[1] More bluntly Corneille said of his rival:

> Tout Paris ayant lu son cartel,
> L'envoie au diable et sa muse au bordel.[2]

Certainly Mairet's claim that his play was a highly moral one and of the kind likely to encourage respectable women to come to the theatre is completely absurd; yet his remarks are interesting from our point of view, as the words 'les plus honnêtes femmes fréquentent *maintenant* l'Hôtel de Bourgogne . . .' do seem to imply that there had been a time when they did not do so.

Rigal quotes in support of the theory that no respectable women frequented the Hôtel de Bourgogne in the opening decades of the seventeenth century an extract from the little pamphlet entitled *L'Ouverture des Jours Gras, ou l'Entretien du Carnaval*, which boosts in a somewhat facetious manner the plays performed at that theatre during the Carnival of 1634. In the passage which he quotes from the version given by Fournier in his *Variétés historiques et littéraires*,[3] it is claimed that the plays offered by the Hôtel de Bourgogne

sont autant d'aimans attractifs pour y faire venir non seulement les plus graves d'entre les hommes, mais les femmes les plus chastes et modestes, quy ne veulent plus faire autre chose maintenant que d'y aller; ce quy fait qu'on ne s'estonne pas si les maris, par un si long tems, avoient deffendu et interdict l'entrée de l'hostel de Bourgogne à leurs femmes, quy perdent presque la memoire de leurs loges quand elles ont veu représenter en ce lieu quelque pièce si belle, comme autrefois ceux quy avoient gousté une fois de lotes perdoient entierement la memoire de leur pays et de leur maison.

Rigal then concludes: 'Bien que le tour soit adroit et la raison donnée

---

[1] A. Gasté (ed.), *La Querelle du Cid* (Paris, 1898), p. 211.

[2] Gasté, *Querelle du Cid*, p. 70.

[3] (Paris, 1855–63), 10 vols., vol. ii, p. 352. (The passage quoted above is taken direct from Fournier; the spelling is left unaltered, as in the extract which follows.)

ingénieuse, le dire de Tallemant est confirmé. Les honnêtes femmes n'allaient point à l'Hôtel de Bourgogne. . . .'[1]

A close examination of the passage makes one less certain that this interpretation is the correct one. For one thing, there are reasons for doubting the accuracy of the version offered by Fournier. What, for instance, is the meaning of 'perdent presque la memoire de leurs *loges*'? The reading *logis* would seem more natural, and is in fact the one given in the only contemporary edition of the *Ouverture des Jours Gras* which I have been able to consult.[2] There are other slight differences in the passage quoted,[3] which reads in this text as follows:

pieces qui sont autant d'Aymants *attirans* pour y faire venir non seulement *les hommes les plus graues*, mais les femmes les plus chastes & modestes qui *ne veulent faire autre chose que d'y aller maintenant*: ce qui fait qu'on ne s'estonne pas si les maris par un si long temps avoient deffendu & interdit l'entrée de l'Hostel de Bourgongne à leurs femmes qui perdent presque la memoire de leurs *logis* quand elles ont veu representer en ce lieu quelque *belle pièce*: comme autrefois ceux qui auoient *vne fois gousté des lotes* perdoient entierement la memoire de leur pays & de leur maison.

It is almost impossible to assign a precise meaning to this passage, even when one carefully puts it back in its highly facetious context. If it would perhaps be naïve to interpret it in its literal sense, it is at least doubtful whether one can twist it into a clear and unambiguous confirmation of Tallemant's sweeping statement.

At first sight, however, his remarks do appear to be borne out by various works published in the second half of the century. Thus a violent diatribe against Molière and his *Dom Juan*, published in 1665 under the name of 'Sieur de Rochemont' (perhaps a pseudonym for a bitter opponent of the theatre, Barbier d'Aucour), also speaks of the improvement in the moral tone of drama for which Richelieu was responsible, and accuses Molière of having brought the theatre back to the immorality of the early part of the century, when 'son air lascif et ses gestes dissolus rebutaient tous les gens d'honneur, et l'on n'eût pas vu, en tout un siècle, une honnête femme lui rendre visite'.[4] In the

---

[1] *Le Théâtre Français avant la période classique* (Paris, 1901), p. 214.

[2] Bibliothèque Nationale, Réserve Li[19] 15. Fournier's version gives (p. 350) the title of one of Du Ryer's plays as *Rossyleon*, whereas the copy in the Bibliothèque Nationale gives the correct form of *Rosileon*.

[3] These are indicated by italics.

[4] *Observations sur une comédie de Molière intitulée le 'Festin de Pierre'* (reprinted in Molière, *Œuvres*, ed. E. Despois and P. Mesnard, Paris, 1873–1900, 13 vols., vol. v, p. 222).

following year Abbé d'Aubignac too speaks of the greater refinement introduced into the theatre by Richelieu. His words are invariably quoted by those who accept the view that respectable women did not frequent the theatre in the early part of the century, since they seem so clear and decisive: 'Il y a cinquante ans qu'une honnête femme n'osait aller au théâtre.' Such words indeed seem final, yet should one not take the trouble to copy out the second half of the sentence, even if it rather dims this clarity? 'Ou bien', he continues, 'il fallait qu'elle fût voilée et tout à fait invisible, et ce plaisir était comme réservé aux débauchées qui se donnaient la liberté de regarder à visage découvert.'[1] Thus, after an apparently categorical statement to the contrary, d'Aubignac concedes that some *honnêtes femmes* did attend the theatre in the opening decades of the century, even if they went veiled. Moreover, another contemporary, Charles Sorel, writing a few years later, is even farther from denying that respectable women were present in the theatre earlier in the century. 'Autrefois', he declares, 'toutes les femmes se retiraient quand on allait jouer la farce.'[2]

None of these pieces of information, which to some extent cancel one another out, could be as valuable as evidence derived from documents which date from the end of the sixteenth century and the beginning of the seventeenth. By a strange coincidence one of the most precise pieces of evidence on this question comes from exactly the same source as is invoked in a discussion of this problem as it affects the London theatres of the Elizabethan age—the Journal of a Basle doctor, Thomas Platter (1574–1628). It is interesting for purposes of comparison that many historians of the Elizabethan theatre argue that the number of women attending performances of the plays of Shakespeare and his fellow dramatists was very small. 'No respectable woman', declares one writer, 'might appear at a playhouse except with her face concealed under a mask.' Another states that 'the galleries were full of light women who found them a profitable haunt, but whose presence did not altogether prevent that of ladies of position, probably in the private rooms, and possibly masked'. In his *Shakespeare's Audience* Professor Harbage proves conclusively, by reference to such documents as Platter's *Travels in England*, that respectable women of different social strata did frequent the Elizabethan theatres.[3]

In 1599, between his departure from Montpellier where he had taken

---

[1] *Dissertation sur la condamnation des théâtres* (Paris, 1666), pp. 243–4.
[2] *De la connaissance des bons livres* (Amsterdam, 1672), p. 166.
[3] A. B. Harbage, *Shakespeare's Audience* (New York, 1941), pp. 74–78.

his doctor's degree and his arrival in this country, Platter spent some time in Paris and attended performances given at the Hôtel de Bourgogne by Valleran and his company. His description of the theatre and its seating arrangements includes a reference to the presence of ladies in the galleries:

> Les représentations ont lieu dans une grande salle, sur une estrade tendue de tapisserie; les gens du peuple ne paient que moitié prix, à la condition de rester debout. Mais les spectateurs payant place entière peuvent monter dans les galeries, où ils peuvent s'asseoir, se tenir debout ou s'appuyer sur une rampe, de façon à voir beaucoup mieux. C'est là où les dames ont l'habitude d'aller.[1]

Two years later, in 1601, L'Estoile noted in his Journal, in describing some of the acrobatics of an Italian company then visiting Paris, that 'beaucoup de dames, même des hommes, tournaient le dos, de peur qu'ils avaient de leur voir rompre le col'.[2] In 1607 there appeared the second part of John Barclay's Latin novel, *Euphormio*, which contains, under a transparent disguise, a variety of descriptions of life in early seventeenth-century Paris. The hero goes to the theatre in order to make the acquaintance of a married woman with whom he has fallen passionately in love. He goes into the *parterre* 'avec le commun', as the contemporary translator puts it,[3] so as to be able to see the lady arrive in the galleries, 'qui sont réservées', he adds, 'pour les seigneurs et les dames'. When the lady in whom he is interested takes off her mask, he hastens to join her in the gallery. The play, a tragi-comedy, has a great success in a packed theatre: 'Le théâtre était illustre à cause du poète et avait attiré le peuple; à peine les galeries étaient suffisantes pour les seigneurs, car nulle tragédie n'avait été plus ardemment désirée dans la ville.'[4]

It is true that none of these references to the presence of women in the theatre at the end of the sixteenth and the beginning of the seven-

---

[1] 'Description de Paris en 1599', *Mémoires de la Société de l'histoire de Paris* (1896), p. 196.

[2] *Mémoires-Journaux*, ed. G. Brunet and others (Paris, 1875–96), 12 vols., vol. vii, p. 300.

[3] What he understands by 'le commun' and later on by 'le peuple' is not altogether clear, as so often in the seventeenth century. (For a discussion of this point see below, pp. 55 f.)

[4] *Euphormionis Lusinini Satyricon*, pars secunda (Rouen, 1628), pp. 238–40. The above quotations are taken from the French translation by Jean Tournet (Paris, 1625), pp. 532–5. (A reference to this passage is to be found in G. Fagniez, *La Femme et la société française dans la première moitié du XVIIe siècle*, Paris, 1929, p. 231, in a chapter which offers an interesting discussion of this problem.)

teenth centuries furnishes the certificate of morality which historians of
the theatre apparently insist upon before they will allow of the presence of respectable women among the audience in this period. It must
even be conceded that, after devoting one chapter to an analysis of 'la
tragi-comédie d'*Hippophile et des Icoléontins*', Barclay continues his
novel with another entitled *Euphormion conduit sa dame en sa maison; il
jouit de ses désirs, mais si inconsidérément que les serviteurs d'Anemon* [the
husband] *le chassent avec menaces*.[1] Yet even without the additional
evidence which we shall consider in dealing with the attitude of the
court to drama, it would seem rather rash to conclude that respectable
women did not frequent the theatre in Paris in the opening decades of
the seventeenth century.

What of the theory that the audience in these years was overwhelmingly plebeian, with perhaps a sprinkling of aristocratic de-
bauchees? At first sight certain pieces of evidence—in particular the
notorious prologues of Bruscambille—point to this conclusion. Yet
Bruscambille, it must be said, remains an enigmatic figure. The first
authorized edition of his prologues was published in Paris; although the
title-page bears no date, the *privilège* is dated 27 July 1610. This edition
contains thirty-three prologues;[2] the very titles of some of these—
Prologue des parties naturelles des hommes et des femmes or *Prologue du
Cul*—indicate the scatological nature of much of the contents of this
volume. Yet filthy as Bruscambille's prologues often are, their smut is
at times curiously erudite.[3]

Neither 'Bruscambille', the name by which he was no doubt known
as a farce-actor, nor 'Des Lauriers', his professional name, was the real
surname of the author of these prologues. Consequently it has proved
impossible to identify him in any of the documents concerning the
various companies of actors which performed at the Hôtel de Bourgogne
in the opening years of the seventeenth century. It is therefore very
uncertain in what years and for how long he actually appeared at that
theatre, and how many of the prologues published in the various
editions of his *Prologues* and *Œuvres* were ever actually delivered there.
How far they were typical of the sort of entertainment normally

[1] Tournet translation, p. 561.
[2] The statement in the article by G. Mongrédien, 'Bibliographie des œuvres du facétieux
Bruscambille', *Bulletin du Bibliophile* (1926), p. 375: 'Le frontispice représente Bruscambille débitant un prologue sur la scène de l'Hôtel de Bourgogne aux applaudissements du
parterre', is pure imagination.
[3] See J. Vianey, 'Bruscambille et les poètes bernesques', *Revue d'histoire littéraire de la
France* (1901).

offered to audiences at this period of the century is not so easy to decide as seems to be imagined by various distinguished historians of the seventeenth-century theatre.[1]

In any case, the argument that if a play is coarse and badly written, it must have been composed for a plebeian audience is not wholly convincing. As we shall see, the taste in drama of Louis XIV's court, though it was famed throughout Europe for its polish and refinement, was far from being uniformly prudish or sophisticated, even if its standards had risen in most respects far above those which appear to have prevailed earlier in the century. Or again, what of the tremendous vogue enjoyed in the highly refined society of eighteenth-century Paris by those smutty little farces known as *parades*?

Moreover, there are scraps of evidence to show that from the very beginning of the seventeenth century the members of the French aristocracy did take some interest in the theatre.[2] It is true that while the Journal of a great nobleman of the time like Bassompierre is full of references to the performance of ballets, especially at court, it is for the most part provokingly silent on the subject of drama proper. Yet in 1608 we do find there a somewhat enigmatic allusion to an amateur performance of a play at a nobleman's house in Paris: 'On fit une grande assemblée chez le marquis de Cœuvres où il se joua une comédie qui était de toutes femmes blondes, parentes ou alliées du dit marquis.'[3] We have already seen that in his *Euphormio* John Barclay refers categorically to the presence of noblemen—not just one or two, but a whole crowd—in the galleries of the theatre.

More significant is the fact that, just as later in the period the different companies of professional actors frequently performed in the Paris mansions or the nearby country houses of the aristocracy, from the very beginning of the century such *visites* as they were called (they are frequently referred to by that name in the Register of Molière's company kept by the actor Lagrange) took place in and near Paris. In 1600

---

[1] See the quotations from such authorities as Lanson and Magne on p. 10.

[2] For what the information is worth, we may note that a number of plays published during the reign of Henry IV were dedicated to the King, princes and princesses of the blood, and members of the aristocracy. Pierre de Nancel dedicated his *Josué ou le Sac de Jéricho* (1607) to Henry IV; Montchrétien his *Hector* (1604) to the Prince de Condé; Claude Billard his *Polyxène* (1610) to the Princesse de Conti; Laudun d'Aigaliers his *Horace* (1596) to the Duc de Joyeuse; Du Souhait his *Radegonde* (1599) to the Duc d'Épernon; Guillaume de Chevalier his *Philis* (1609) to Bassompierre; and Isaac du Ryer his *Pastourelle* (1609) to the Duc de Bellegarde. See L. E. Dabney, *French Dramatic Literature in the Reign of Henri IV* (Austin, 1952).

[3] *Journal de ma vie*, ed. Marquis de Chantérac (Paris, 1870–7), 4 vols., vol. i, p. 196.

Valleran Le Conte's company made an agreement with a troupe of Italian actors to perform plays together 'tant en cette ville de Paris et faubourgs d'icelle qu'en maisons et visites où ils seront mandés'. Ten years later an agreement between the members of Valleran's company speaks of 'les deniers qui proviendront desdits jeux tant en public qu'en maisons particulières'.[1] In other words, from the very beginning of the century it was apparently customary for the wealthy members of the aristocracy to have professional actors come and perform in their mansions in Paris or in their nearby châteaux.

In any consideration of the problem of the theatre audience in this period, the attitude of the court to drama is crucial. This attitude cannot possibly have been as negative as is sometimes imagined. It is true that we suffer from a painful shortage of evidence on this point. Even so, meagre as our knowledge undoubtedly is, it suffices to prove that the court of Henry IV and the young Louis XIII did not regard drama as entirely beneath contempt, as an entertainment suited only for the plebs, for a horde of ruffians and dissolute women. No doubt in these opening years of the seventeenth century the theatre had not yet come to enjoy the favour and high prestige which it was later to win at the Versailles of Louis XIV, but it is clear that in this period the court already took some interest in drama.

The evidence cannot be said to be hidden away in remote and inaccessible documents. Most of it has long been published, and has even been commented on by various scholars in the last hundred years, though never in a systematic way, with precise reference to this particular question. The Journal of Pierre de l'Estoile, for instance, is a well-known document. It furnishes on one occasion the clearest possible evidence that the court of Henry IV—the King and great noblemen, the Queen and ladies—might even transport itself to the Hôtel de Bourgogne to be present at the sort of performance which, we are asked to believe, was so filthy and obscene that no respectable woman could possibly have gone near. 'Les honnêtes femmes n'y allaient point', Tallemant assures us. Yet in January 1607 L'Estoile wrote in his Journal: 'Le vendredi 26ᵉ de ce mois fut jouée, à l'Hôtel de Bourgogne, à Paris, une plaisante farce, à laquelle assistèrent le roi, la reine, et la plupart des princes, seigneurs et dames de la cour.'[2] Clear and unambiguous as it is in the vital respect that concerns us here, this entry is tantalizingly incomplete, since it mentions only one farce, which can

---

[1] Deierkauf-Holsboer, *Vie d'Alexandre Hardy*, pp. 389, 395.
[2] *Mémoires-Journaux*, vol. viii, p. 271.

scarcely have formed the whole of the programme. However, the long account which L'Estoile gives of the farce and of the King's attitude to it (he declared that it had made him laugh till he cried) shows that Henry IV and his courtiers enjoyed their visit to the Hôtel de Bourgogne and did not recoil in puritanical horror from attending this alleged house of ill fame. This will scarcely surprise anyone who is acquainted, however slightly, with the manners and morals of the court of Henry IV. While Marie de Médicis, as an Italian princess, naturally showed a great interest in actors from her own country, it is noteworthy that this performance of January 1607 was given by a French company, probably that of Valleran Le Conte.[1]

In this context it is perhaps of some significance that the title of 'Comédiens du Roi' seems to have existed at least as early as 1598. One ought not, it is true, to read more into this than the documents permit. There is no evidence that Henry IV showed a deep interest in the drama and in actors; there is not the slightest reason to suggest that he ever subsidized a French theatrical company in the way his successors were to do.[2] The title of 'Comédiens du Roi' during his reign probably meant no more than the high-sounding expression 'entretenu par Son Altesse Royale' (Gaston d'Orléans) applied by Molière and his fellow actors in the 1640's to the Illustre Théâtre, or the title of 'Troupe de Monsieur' (Louis XIV's younger brother, the Duc d'Orléans) assumed by his company on its return to Paris in 1658. How little the latter title meant is shown by Lagrange's Register, the first page of which informs us that Monsieur bestowed on Molière and his company 'l'honneur de sa protection et le titre de ses comédiens avec 300 ll. de pension pour chaque comédien', but a marginal note rapidly disillusions the reader: 'Nota que les 300 ll. n'ont point été payées.' Even so, if it had been a notorious fact that Henry IV and his court showed no interest whatever in drama, actors of the time would scarcely have flaunted the title of 'Comédiens du Roi'. In a legal document of 1598 Valleran Le Conte and various actors of his company are described as 'tous comédiens du roi'.[3] In a similar document which dates from the following year, he and his company are given the title of 'comédiens ordinaires du roi',[4] while Thomas Platter who was in Paris at that time

---

[1] There is a reference in L'Estoile's *Mémoires-Journaux* (vol. viii, p. 301) in May 1607 to 'Valleran (bouffon de l'Hôtel de Bourgogne)'.

[2] He behaved quite generously towards the companies whom he and his Queen invited from Italy.

[3] Deierkauf-Holsboer, *Vie d'Alexandre Hardy*, p. 384.

[4] E. Soulié, *Recherches sur Molière et sur sa famille* (Paris, 1863), p. 154.

speaks of Valleran as being 'engagé par le roi' and calls the actors of the Hôtel de Bourgogne 'les comédiens du roi'.[1] A petition addressed to Louis XIII in 1629 by the actors of the Hôtel de Bourgogne declares that they have used that theatre 'depuis qu'il aurait plu au feu roi, que Dieu absolve, et à vous, Sire, les retenir pour leur représenter, et au public, la comédie'.[2] A document of 1613 makes the young Louis XIII speak of members of a French company of actors as 's'étant acheminés pour nous venir trouver, suivant notre commandement', and declare that these men 'sont ordinairement près notre personne'.[3] The title of 'Comédiens du roi', for what it was worth, thus dates back at least as far as the year of the Edict of Nantes.

Most valuable information about theatrical performances at court in the first two decades of the seventeenth century is to be found in the Journal kept by Jean Héroard, the physician attached to the Dauphin, the future Louis XIII, who was born in 1601 and succeeded to the throne nine years later on his father's assassination. Substantial extracts from Héroard's Journal were published in 1868,[4] but further references to theatrical performances attended by Louis in the early part of his reign can be tracked down if one wades laboriously through the manuscript of his Journal which is preserved in the Bibliothèque Nationale.[5] In the midst of masses of trivial detail, such as endless descriptions of the diet, medicines, and motions of his charge, Héroard occasionally finds room for laconic references to the performance of plays at court. The manuscript of the Journal was made use of some seventy years ago by Armand Baschet in Les Comédiens italiens à la cour de France sous Charles IX, Henri III, Henri IV et Louis XIII, mostly, though not exclusively, with reference to the activities of the Italian actors at court; but neither the results of his investigations nor all the mentions of theatrical performances which are to be found even in the abridged version of Héroard's Journal seem to have been taken fully into account by subsequent historians of the theatre.

If nothing precise is known about court performances given by the company of Italian actors which was in Paris in April 1599[6] or by what

---

[1] 'Description de Paris en 1599', p. 195.

[2] C. and F. Parfaict, Histoire du Théâtre Français depuis son origine jusqu'à présent (Amsterdam and Paris, 1735–49), 15 vols., vol. iii, p. 266.

[3] E. Campardon, Les Comédiens du roi de la troupe française pendant les deux derniers siècles (Paris, 1879), pp. 279–80.

[4] Journal sur l'enfance et la jeunesse de Louis XIII (1601–1628), ed. E. Soulié and E. de Barthélemy (Paris, 1868), 2 vols.

[5] MS. français 4022–7.

[6] Baschet, Les Comédiens italiens, p. 102.

was presumably another company in February 1600 (an agreement between it and Valleran of that date is the only evidence which we possess about its presence in the capital and its activities there),[1] it is well known that Marie de Médicis and even Henry IV himself were keenly interested in the visits of the Italian actors. Before and after their marriage at Lyons in 1600 they had the company of the *Accesi* perform before them, and when the court returned to Paris in the following month, the Italian actors moved to the capital, where they remained until the autumn before going back to Italy. So keen had Henry been to secure a visit from these actors that he had written in person in December 1599 to Arlequin (Tristano Martinelli) to offer him and his company a most pressing invitation.[2] It is of this actor that Tallemant relates the well-known story:

> Arlequin et sa troupe vinrent à Paris en ce temps-là, et quand il alla saluer le roi, il prit si bien son temps, car il était fort dispos, que Sa Majesté s'étant levée de son siège, il s'en empara, et comme si le roi eût été Arlequin: 'Eh bien! Arlequin, lui dit-il, vous êtes venu ici avec votre troupe pour me divertir; j'en suis bien aise; je vous promets de vous protéger et de vous donner tant de pension, etc. etc.' Le Roi ne l'osa dédire de rien, mais il lui dit: 'Hola, il y assez longtemps que vous faites mon personnage; laissez-le-moi faire à cette heure.'[3]

In 1603 another Italian company, that of Francesco Andreini and his wife, Isabella, played at Fontainebleau and then moved with the court to Paris to perform at the Hôtel de Bourgogne. Isabella Andreini, who was to die at Lyons on the return journey to Italy in June 1604, published during her stay in France a second edition of her *Rime* which contains poems dedicated to members of the royal family from the King and Queen downwards, as well as to various courtiers of both sexes. It was in this same year, in September, that Héroard recorded in his Journal the first occasion on which the Dauphin, then a child of three, was present at a play. Curiously enough, the company which appeared at Fontainebleau on this occasion was neither French nor Italian, but English; in the opening years of the seventeenth century English strolling players were still in the habit of visiting France.[4] In his account of the Dauphin's activities on this particular day Héroard

[1] Deierkauf-Holsboer, *Vie d'Alexandre Hardy*, pp. 345, 389.
[2] Baschet, *Comédiens italiens*, p. 106.
[3] *Historiettes*, vol. i, p. 16.
[4] See Frances A. Yates, 'English Actors in Paris during the Lifetime of Shakespeare', *Review of English Studies* (1925), pp. 392–403.

writes: 'Mené en la grande salle neuve ouïr une tragédie représentée par des Anglais; il les écoute avec froideur, gravité et patience jusques à ce qu'il fallut couper la tête à un des personnages.'[1]

Our information as to theatrical performances at court during the next three years is very meagre. There is a tantalizingly vague allusion in a letter written by Henry IV in 1606 to his mistress, the Marquise de Verneuil; as the precise date of the letter is unknown, it is impossible to work out where the King was when he wrote it. Despite the gallant reservations of the second half of the sentence, it shows without question that the King was far from being completely uninterested in drama. 'J'ai ouï une fort belle comédie', he wrote, 'mais je pensais plus en vous qu'en elle.'[2] We have already noticed the presence of Henry IV and Marie de Médicis and their court at a performance given by a French company of actors at the Hôtel de Bourgogne in January 1607. In this and the following month Héroard refers to some rather rudimentary amateur theatricals at Court. The first performance of which he speaks took place on the very same day as the court went to the Hôtel de Bourgogne, and was given for the benefit of the five-year-old Dauphin by members of his entourage. On the following day the Dauphin, along with other children, took part in the performance of what is very laconically described as 'une comédie'. One evening in February the King himself was present at one of these amateur performances. Héroard notes somewhat cryptically: 'A huit heures et demie le roi y vient pour y voir jouer la comédie de quatre du bourg. A neuf heures et demie le roi s'en va.' A few days later another farce was performed before the Dauphin.[3]

There was renewed theatrical activity at court in 1608 when the Italian company of the *Accesi* arrived again in Paris. The negotiations for the dispatch of this company between the French court and the Duke of Mantua, the brother-in-law of Marie de Médicis, had lasted some eighteen months, despite pressing letters from both Henry and Marie de Médicis. At the end of June 1607, for instance, the Queen wrote to her brother-in-law:

Mon frère. Je vous écris encore celle-ci pour vous prier d'accomplir la promesse que vous nous avez ci-devant faite de nous envoyer une compagnie de comédiens italiens des meilleurs qui seront par delà. Le Roi mon seigneur

---

[1] *Journal*, vol. i, p. 88.
[2] *Recueil de lettres missives de Henri IV*, ed. Berger de Xivrey (Paris, 1843–76), 9 vols., vol. vii, p. 25.
[3] Héroard, *Journal*, vol. i, pp. 245, 251, 253.

les désire extrêmement, et serais bien aise qu'il[s] se rendissent à Lyon vers le mois de septembre afin qu'ils puissent passer l'hiver prochain en cette cour.[1]

It was not, however, until February of the following year that the company reached Paris, headed this time by the actor Fritellino. The Italian actors performed both at court and at the Hôtel de Bourgogne, and then followed the King and Queen to Fontainebleau. The French nobility certainly did not fail to frequent the Hôtel de Bourgogne during their visit, as we learn from the following picturesque incident which is described in a dispatch to the Duke of Mantua, to whom the company belonged, from his ambassador in Paris:

> Un gentilhomme français de grande maison, proche parent de M. le grand Écuyer [the Duc de Bellegarde], allant à la comédie, donna à Battistino un soufflet au lieu de l'argent que celui-ci réclamait, puis le bousculant, se rendit au rang des loges. Le comédien l'y suivit, se plaignant de ce qu'il l'avait frappé et lui réclamant le prix dû. A quoi le gentilhomme lui dit: 'Je t'ai payé avec la monnaie que tu mérites'; sur ce, Battistino, tout en colère, s'avançant sur lui: 'Puisqu'il en est ainsi, prenez ce qui vous revient'; et dans ce même temps il lui donna si fort du poing sur le nez que soudain le sang jaillit vivement. Le gentilhomme mit l'épée à la main; beaucoup firent comme lui; mais le comédien, appuyé de quelques Italiens qui se trouvaient là, se sauva.

Two nights later the nobleman and his followers tried to murder the offending actor, but he managed to escape and order was finally restored by the King.[2] The manners of French noblemen in the opening years of the century inclined to roughness.

The visit of the Italian actors to Fontainebleau is duly recorded by Héroard. Henry and Marie de Médicis were there with the court, and on five occasions in July the Dauphin, who was now nearly seven, was taken to see the company perform. While it is true that on one occasion the boy went somewhat unwillingly ('Ne veut point aller à la comédie', Héroard notes, 'ne s'y plaît point, ni aux bouffons'), the Italian actors appear to have made a considerable impression on him, as some weeks later he was still giving as the password the names of various members of the company.[3]

In this same month Louis twice amused himself by performing a play with children of his own age. In January 1609 Héroard also records a visit by the Dauphin to the apartment of the Duc de Verneuil, one of the illegitimate children of Henry IV, in order to 'y voir jouer une

---

[1] Baschet, *Comédiens italiens*, pp. 159–160.
[2] Ibid., pp. 169–70.
[3] *Journal*, vol. i, pp. 346–7, 351–3.

comédie par ses gens'. 'Y est attentif', his physician notes in his Journal.[1] In April of the same year Héroard gives the following account of a performance of part of Garnier's tragi-comedy, *Bradamante*, in which the Dauphin himself took part in the presence of the King and Queen: 'A neuf heures il va chez le roi, où quelques-uns de ses petits gentils-hommes se préparent de jouer quelques vers de la *Bradamante* devant le roi; il avait sept vers à dire de Charlemagne. A dix heures ils vont à la chambre de la reine, et en présence de Leurs Majestés ils jouèrent. Il dit: "J'ai oublié mon rôlet." '[2]

Far more significant, however, than these juvenile amateur dramatics at court is the fact that in the month of February 1609 the young Dauphin was three times taken to performances given in that place of perdition, the Hôtel de Bourgogne. On Saturday, 7 February, Héroard writes: 'A cinq heures mené à l'Hôtel de Bourgogne, à la comédie; ce fut la première fois. Ramené à six heures et demie, il en récite beaucoup devant Leurs Majestés.' On the following day Héroard adds: 'A trois heures trois quarts mené à l'Hôtel de Bourgogne, il se met à rire avec éclat et dit: "Monsieur de Souvré,[3] je ris ainsi, afin qu'on pense que j'entends l'italien." Ramené à six heures et demie.' Finally on the Saturday after this Héroard makes the following entry: 'A quatre heures mené à l'Hôtel de Bourgogne, ramené à huit heures.'[4] As there is an unfortunate gap in our collection of leases of the Hôtel de Bour-gogne between the departure of the Italian company in the summer of 1608 and the arrival of French actors in July 1609,[5] it is impossible to say what company was performing in this theatre in February of the latter year. However, that does not in the least detract from the signifi-cance of the three visits paid by the Dauphin to the Hôtel de Bourgogne in any study of the attitude of the court to drama in the opening decade of the seventeenth century.

Theatrical performances at court in 1610 were brought to an abrupt end by the assassination of Henry IV in May. Yet on two occasions in January of that year the Dauphin was taken to the King's apartments at the Louvre to see a play. That it was a company of French actors which performed on these dates is clear from Héroard's entry on the first of these two days concerning some words of the Dauphin at dinner: 'Commande à une comédiante française et lui dit: "Venez à

---

[1] Ibid., p. 377 (the last three words are added from the manuscript).
[2] Ibid., p. 392. [3] His *gouverneur*.
[4] *Journal*, vol. i, pp. 382–4.
[5] See G. Mongrédien, 'Chronologie des troupes qui ont joué à l'Hôtel de Bourgogne (1598–1680)', *Revue d'histoire du théâtre* (1953), p. 163.

huit heures, car je me couche à dix." "[1] The company in question must
have been that of Valleran Le Conte which returned to Paris in September 1609 and hired the Hôtel de Bourgogne until the following
March.

If we are better informed about the presence of Italian actors at the
court of Henry IV than about that of French actors, it does not
necessarily follow that the role of the latter was quite unimportant.
We know, for instance, that Henry was much amused by the famous
farce actor Gros-Guillaume (Robert Guérin), who performed in Paris
at various dates from 1598 onwards.[2] In his note on the Maréchal de
Roquelaure (1543–1625) Tallemant writes:

> Une autre fois, le Roi le tenait entre ses jambes, tandis qu'il faisait jouer à
> Gros-Guillaume la farce du Gentilhomme gascon. A tout bout de champ,
> pour divertir son maître, le Maréchal faisait semblant de se vouloir lever pour
> aller battre Gros-Guillaume, et Gros-Guillaume disait: 'Cousis, ne bous
> fâchez.' Il arriva qu'après la mort du Roi, les comédiens, n'osant jouer à
> Paris, tant tout le monde était dans la consternation, s'en allèrent dans les
> provinces et enfin à Bordeaux.[3] Le maréchal y était lieutenant de roi; il fallut
> demander permission. 'Je vous la donne, leur dit-il, à condition que vous
> jouerez la farce du Gentilhomme gascon.' Ils crurent qu'on les rouerait de
> coups de bâton au sortir de là; ils voulurent faire leurs excuses. 'Jouez, jouez
> seulement', leur dit-il. Le maréchal y alla; mais le souvenir d'un si bon maître
> lui causa une telle douleur qu'il fut contraint de sortir tout en larmes, dès le
> commencement de la farce.[4]

Before leaving the reign of Henry IV we must at least glance at the
information about theatrical performances at court which is to be
gleaned from Tristan L'Hermite's more or less autobiographical novel,
Le Page disgracié. This is clearly a much less reliable source than, say,
Héroard's Journal; yet a novel which appeared in 1643 could not
presumably offer completely false information on a point of this kind.
Tristan tells us that, while he was page to Henry IV's illegitimate son,
the Duc de Verneuil, he became friendly with 'une troupe de comédiens
qui venaient représenter trois ou quatre fois la semaine devant toute
cette cour'.[5] His circumstantial account of his relations with these

---

[1] *Journal*, vol. i, pp. 420, 423.

[2] Deierkauf-Holsboer, *Vie d'Alexandre Hardy*, p. 343.

[3] The new company of actors formed by Valleran Le Conte in March 1610 included
Gros-Guillaume. It left Paris for the provinces shortly after the assassination of Henry IV
(Deierkauf-Holsboer, *Vie d'Alexandre Hardy*, p. 349).

[4] *Historiettes*, vol. i, p. 27.

[5] *Le Page disgracié*, ed. A. Dietrich (Paris, 1898), p. 51. The key to the 1667 edition of
this work identifies two of the actors in question as Valleran Le Conte and François de

actors and with their *poète à gages* cannot be dismissed as pure fiction, and may be added to the scanty supply of documents concerning the interest of the court in drama generally and in French actors in particular during the opening decade of the seventeenth century.

The assassination of Henry IV caused only a temporary interruption in the theatrical performances given at court. In January 1611 the young Louis XIII was amused one evening during supper, Héroard informs us, by 'un comédien qui représentait seul plusieurs personnages'.[1] In June, just over a year after his father's death, he was present on three successive days at performances given at Fontainebleau by a company of French actors:

20 juin. Va chez la reine et revient à la galerie lambrissée où il voit jouer une tragédie française et une farce.

21 juin. Va en la galerie lambrissée où il voit jouer une pastorale française et une farce.

22 juin. Va en la galerie lambrissée où il voit jouer une farce.[2]

The actors concerned must again have been Valleran Le Conte and his company who signed leases of the Hôtel de Bourgogne in February and March of this year.[3] Shortly afterwards (on 29 July and 2 August) the young King, along with the Queen Mother and various court dignitaries, was present at performances of Garnier's *Bradamante*, given by the other children of the royal family.[4] At Saint-Germain, on 7 August, Héroard informs us, Louis 'va en la grande salle du château, avec la reine et sa suite, pour y voir jouer une farce par des valets de Messieurs'.[5]

What is much more significant is that in the following month the young King was taken no less than five times to the Hôtel de Bourgogne, where Valleran Le Conte was struggling with grave financial difficulties which compelled him to relinquish to one of his creditors the proceeds from all the tickets sold in his theatre except those for the *parterre*.[6] On three successive Sundays and on the two intervening

Vautrel, who were both members of the same company at the time of the assassination of Henry IV.

[1] *Journal*, vol. ii, p. 52.

[2] Ibid., p. 67 (the text given above is expanded from the manuscript).

[3] G. Mongrédien, 'Chronologie des troupes qui ont joué à l'Hôtel de Bourgogne', p. 165.

[4] *Journal*, vol. ii, pp. 71–72. References to these performances are also to be found in Malherbe, *Œuvres*, ed. L. Lalanne (Paris, 1862–9), 5 vols., vol. iii, pp. 240, 243, 247, and L'Estoile, *Mémoires-Journaux*, vol. xi, p. 135.

[5] *Journal*, vol. ii, p. 75.

[6] Deierkauf-Holsboer, *Vie d'Alexandre Hardy*, p. 351.

Wednesdays Louis was taken first to church, then straight on to this allegedly infamous theatre:

11 septembre (dimanche). A deux heures mené en carrosse à Picpus à vêpres; ramené à l'Hôtel de Bourgogne et à six heures trois quarts soupé.

14 septembre (mercredi). Mené en carrosse à Saint-Eustache, puis à l'Hôtel de Bourgogne; ramené à six heures et demie.

18 septembre (dimanche). A trois heures goûté, mené à la comédie à l'Hôtel de Bourgogne.

21 septembre (mercredi). Mené en carrosse à vêpres à Picpus, puis à la comédie à l'Hôtel de Bourgogne. Ramené à six heures et demie.

25 septembre (dimanche). Mené en carrosse aux Filles-Dieu et à quatre heures et demie à la comédie en l'Hôtel de Bourgogne. Ramené à six heures et demie.[1]

On the last Monday of the month, Héroard tells us,[2] the King 'entend les comédiens français dans sa chambre', while in November he repeated his dual expedition to vespers and the Hôtel de Bourgogne:

30 novembre (mercredi). Mené en carrosse à vêpres, à Saint-Eustache, puis à la comédie en l'Hôtel de Bourgogne.[3]

For most of 1612 there seems to have been little theatrical activity at court. In September of the previous year Marie de Médicis had begun negotiations with a view to obtaining a visit from an Italian company, headed once again by Arlequin (Tristano Martinelli), but he and his companions were not to arrive in Paris until September 1613.[4] The history of the Hôtel de Bourgogne during the year 1612 is very obscure. Valleran Le Conte, whose company was in occupation at the beginning of the year, was having a hard struggle to make ends meet. The situation was complicated by the arrival of an Italian company led by a certain Alfieri. In February the two companies agreed that they should each perform a play at every performance, but this arrangement did not succeed for long. The Italians disappeared from the capital, and at the end of March Valleran formed a new company which seems to have left for the provinces and ultimately for Holland.[5] It was not until August that another French company, headed by Robert Guérin (Gros-Guillaume), took a lease of the theatre for November and December; it was presumably this company which appeared before the young King in November.[6]

[1] *Journal*, vol. ii, pp. 78–80 (the text is expanded from the manuscript).
[2] Ibid., p. 80 (26 Sept.).   [3] Ibid., p. 91.
[4] Baschet, *Les Comédiens italiens*, p. 193.
[5] Deierkauf-Holsboer, *Vie d'Alexandre Hardy*, pp. 351–4.
[6] Héroard, *Journal*, vol. ii, p. 112.

This performance, given on 9 November 1612, inaugurated a period of exceptionally intense dramatic activity at court which lasted down to February 1614. For some reason it has received practically no attention from historians of the theatre except for the part played in these court entertainments by Arlequin and his company from September 1613 onwards. Yet in this period of almost exactly fifteen months French actors played an even more prominent part in these entertainments, both as regards the number of performances and the length of time over which they were given. In considering this spate of theatrical performances it is, perhaps, as well to bear in mind the political background of these years. The Regency of Marie de Médicis was a period of political disorder which at times degenerated into civil war. The great nobles, no longer restrained by the firm hand of Henry IV, took the opportunity to threaten to revolt and to blackmail the Regent into showering all sorts of pensions and favours on them. To keep the nobles occupied at court the Queen Mother indulged in a dizzy round of ballets and plays. It is significant that this exceptional period of dramatic activity came to an end in February 1614, when various great nobles, headed by the Prince de Condé, left the court and set up the standard of revolt in the provinces, ultimately compelling the Regent to summon the States General for its last meeting before 1789.

Deficient as they are in information about what was going on in the contemporary theatre, a number of journals and correspondences of the time, long since published, do throw some light on these activities at court. The Journal of Bassompierre, for instance, contains two brief references to plays being performed at court at the beginning of 1613; as Arlequin and his company did not reach Paris until September of that year, these can have been given only by French actors. On 12 January, in describing the reconciliation between the Regent, Marie de Médicis, and a discontented great nobleman, the Duc d'Épernon, he writes: 'La Reine lui fit donner un siège près d'elle, et le convia à la comédie.' Bassompierre himself was present at this performance, along with the Princesse de Conti.[1] A few pages later he adds, speaking of the same period: 'Il faisait lors pour moi fort beau à la cour, et y passais bien mon temps. La Reine jouait devant souper dans l'entreciel (qui est un petit cabinet au-dessus du sien); puis nous allions à la comédie, où une beauté grecque venait à cause de moi.'[2]

In themselves these vague allusions to theatrical performances at

---

[1] *Journal de ma vie*, vol. i, pp. 336–7.
[2] Ibid., p. 341.

court at the beginning of 1613 do not take us very far, but fortunately we may have recourse to an even better known source, the letters of Malherbe to Peiresc, which furnish rather more precise information. In the period before the arrival of Arlequin and his company in the month of September, Malherbe several times refers to performances of plays at court which can only have been given by French actors. On 8 January he adds in a postscript to a letter to Peiresc: 'Il y eut hier au soir comédie à la galerie.' On 11 February he observes: 'Nous n'avons nulles nouvelles en cette cour; il ne s'y parle que de comédies et de ballets.' A fortnight or so later (on the 28th) he adds some further interesting information: 'Les ballets sont cessés, mais les comédies continuent à l'entresol, où la reine a fait faire le plus agréable théâtre qui se puisse voir, avec des sièges pour environ quatre-vingts personnes.' He refers to the same subject again on 6 June in describing conditions in Paris: 'Au demeurant, avec toutes ces nouvelles et préparatifs de guerre, on ne laisse pas d'y jouer, d'ouïr des comédies, et de bien passer le temps.' When the Italian actors began their performances at court in September, Malherbe has quite a lot to say about their activities, although his comments are mostly unfavourable; but what is more interesting from our point of view is a sentence in a letter of 24 November in which he specifically refers to French actors. 'L'on a renvoyé quérir les comédiens français', he writes, 'le roi ne goûte point les Italiens.'[1] We can thus deduce from Malherbe's correspondence that French actors appeared at court at various dates throughout the year 1613, both before and after the arrival of Arlequin's company.

Further information on this point can be derived from the abridged version of Héroard's Journal published in 1868. For the period which concerns us here, there are references to French plays being given at court on the following dates: 9 November 1612, and 5 January, 2 and 13 March, 13 and 27 July 1613. What is more, the editors state in a footnote to an entry of March 1613: 'Il ne se passe guère de jour où il [Louis XIII] n'assiste à une comédie soit française, soit italienne, presque toujours chez la Reine.'[2] This note is not strictly accurate, as the Italian actors did not arrive at court until about six months later, and it perhaps gives an exaggerated idea of the number of plays given by French actors at court; but it is certainly an invitation to the curious reader to look for himself at the relevant volumes of the manuscript of Héroard's Journal which is preserved at the Bibliothèque Nationale.

---

[1] *Œuvres*, vol. iii, pp. 274, 290, 292, 311, 358.
[2] Vol. ii, p. 121.

Strangely enough, the only historian of the theatre to take the trouble to consult the original manuscript of the Journal for this period seems to have been Armand Baschet. In the preparation of his book, *Les Comédiens italiens à la cour de France*, he naturally made use of the manuscript mainly from the point of view of his study of the Italian actors at the court of Henry IV and Louis XIII, but he does mention in passing the presence of the young Louis XIII at performances of plays by French actors in December 1613.[1]

A close examination of the volumes of the manuscript of Héroard's Journal for the three years 1612, 1613, and 1614 gives us an entirely different picture of theatrical entertainments at court from the one which is generally accepted. We must bear in mind that Héroard's allusions to plays being given at court are both extremely laconic and buried away in a mass of tedious detail. Except when he is talking about amateur performances, Héroard mentions at the most the types of play performed, and most frequently contents-himself with such tantalizingly brief formulae as 'Va à la salle à la comédie française' or 'Va à la salle à la comédie italienne'. These are set forth in a handwriting which it is not always easy to decipher, so that it is not altogether impossible to miss a reference to a theatrical performance as one searches painfully through the pages of the manuscript. Moreover, Héroard was solely concerned with recording the activities of the young King; if, because of illness or for any other reason, Louis was not present at a performance, then presumably it went unrecorded.[2]

The Journal for 1612 mentions for the period up to November only four dramatic performances of any kind at which Louis was present. The first two of these (on 29 January and 5 February) appear to have been amateur performances. It was not apparently until three months later that he saw another play; on 16 and 17 May Héroard mentions two performances by Italian actors, presumably the company of Alfieri which, as we have seen, had shared the Hôtel de Bourgogne with Valleran Le Conte earlier in the year.

The summer apparently passed without a single theatrical perform- ance at court, but suddenly in early November things changed com- pletely. On 7 November a performance of 'la tragédie de Jephté'[3] was

[1] p. 247.

[2] An exception is provided by the entry concerning a performance of the Italian actors on 7 Dec. 1613: 'Vêtu, désirant d'aller voir la Reine à son retour de la Comédie italienne où elle était allée: elle tardait trop. Il avait envie de dormir.'

[3] A French translation of the Latin tragedy of Buchanan, such as that by André Mage de Fiefmelin (1601)?

given by 'des petits garçons'. Two days later began the long series of performances given by French actors which were to last until the arrival of the Italians in the following September. On 9 November Héroard records: 'Va en sa chambre voir jouer une comédie française et deux farces', and two days later: 'Entend une comédie française et deux farces.' On the 13th he mentions the presence of the Queen Mother at the evening's entertainment: 'A huit heures entend une comédie française et une farce: la Reine y assista', and on the 18th the young King saw performed 'la comédie française et farce'. After this the entries become even briefer and speak merely of 'comédie française' or 'comédiens français'; but altogether eight performances were given by professional actors in the course of this month.[1] That these performances were enjoyed by the King is made clear by the entry for 26 November: 'Va en son cabinet, en celui de la Reine où il se joue, et avec ses petits gentilshommes contrefont [sic] les comédiens français.'

December saw another amateur performance at court. On the 11th Héroard notes: 'Va chez la Reine où il fait jouer par ses petits une tragédie française de Priam'.[2] The main part of the theatrical activity at court in this month was carried on by French actors; on no fewer than twelve occasions (if we are to include the not very clear reference on 8 December to what may have been an amateur performance: 'Va chez la Reine où il fait jouer la farce') plays were given by professional actors.[3]

The new year saw a continuation of this series of performances by French actors. In January Louis was present at 'la comédie française' on nine occasions.[4] In addition, on the afternoon of Sunday, 6 January, he went to the gallery for a performance of what Héroard enigmatically describes as 'une comédie française de la folie et de l'amour aveugle'. Even this amount of detail, tantalizingly vague as it is, is unusual for Héroard. The only information of interest about the professional performances which can be gleaned from the manuscript of his Journal is contained in the entry for 24 January: 'Envoie prier la Reine de venir voir jouer la farce par des comédiens; il en entend deux.'

In February Héroard mentions ten occasions on which the French actors performed before Louis.[5] In addition, on 26 February, the King,

---

[1] 9, 11, 13, 18, 20, 24, 27, 29 Nov.
[2] Perhaps *Pryam, roy en Troye*, by François Bertrand (1605 ?).
[3] 1, 5, 6, 8, 10, 12, 15, 17, 19, 22, 17, 29 Dec.
[4] 2, 6, 12, 14, 16, 19, 24, 26, 31 Jan. Malherbe's letter of 8 Jan. refers to a performance on the previous evening which is not mentioned by Héroard.
[5] 4, 6, 11, 13, 14, 16, 18, 23, 25, 27 Feb.

he states, 'fait jouer dans sa chambre la tragédie de Emon, tiré de l'Arioste, par ses petits, la Reine présente'. The French company continued to perform at court in March; besides twice attending performances given by his 'enfants d'honneur',[1] Louis was present on seven occasions at plays given by the French actors.[2] This theatrical activity was no doubt interrupted by the approach of Easter; but already by 20 March the French company had performed before the King on at least forty-six occasions since November.

To judge from Héroard's Journal, April did not see a quick renewal of the court's interest in drama. The only two relevant entries for this month concern the King's presence, on the 28th, at a play performed by his 'enfants d'honneur', and, on the following day, at 'la comédie'. This latter performance should presumably be linked with three given in May,[3] the last two of which are specifically referred to as 'la comédie française'. In June the French company was kept busier, since, in addition to the King's presence on the 25th at a play given by his 'enfants d'honneur', the Journal mentions seven performances by French actors.[4] July saw further theatrical performances at court; not only were 'une comédie et une farce' given by the King's 'enfants d'honneur' on the 5th, but in addition on seven occasions he was present at 'la comédie française'.[5] Despite the heat mentioned by Héroard in August, these performances by French actors (seven altogether) continued into the first week of September.[6] Thus by the time that the Italian actors, headed by Arlequin, arrived to take over from them, the French actors had performed at least seventy-one times at court since November 1612.[7]

The first duty of the Italian company on their arrival in Paris was to the court. They began their performances at the Louvre on 10 September. The letters of Malherbe contain several interesting, though highly prejudiced, references to their reception at court,[8] but it is to Héroard's Journal that we must follow Baschet[9] for precise details about the number of performances which they gave there. After the Italian actors had appeared four times at the Louvre,[10] Louis and the Queen Mother moved to Fontainebleau. There Arlequin and his company gave

---

[1] 17 and 27 Mar.
[2] 2, 4, 9, 13, 14, 16, 20 Mar.
[3] 4, 18, 30 May.
[4] 1, 3, 5, 8, 15, 22, 26 June.
[5] 1, 6, 10, 13, 15, 22, 28 July.
[6] 8, 13, 17, 22, 26, 31 Aug.; 4 Sept.
[7] For a discussion of the problem of the identity of these French actors see my article 'French Actors in Paris from 1612 to 1614', *French Studies* (1955).
[8] *Œuvres*, vol. iii, pp. 329 f.
[9] *Les Comédiens italiens*, pp. 243–7.
[10] 10, 12, 14, 15 Sept.

a very large number of performances down to 21 November.[1] From the beginning of their stay at Fontainebleau to the end of September they gave seven performances, in October eighteen, and in November sixteen. According to a letter of Malherbe[2] the Italians began their public performances in Paris at the Hôtel de Bourgogne on 23 November, two days after their last appearance at Fontainebleau. This letter of 24 November also contains the interesting remark: 'L'on a renvoyé quérir les comédiens français; le roi ne goûte point les Italiens.'

This last statement should be treated with caution as Malherbe continually runs down Arlequin and his company in his letters; yet Héroard's Journal does confirm the reappearance of the French actors at court. On 5 December he notes that Louis 'va chez la Reine et aux comédiens français'. Two days later he indicates a performance at court by the Italian actors at which the King was not present.[3] Before he fell ill in the middle of the month, Louis was present at another four performances by the French actors;[4] in just over a year he had therefore been present at at least seventy-six performances of French plays.

The turn of the Italian actors came again in January 1614; in less than four weeks (between 15 January and 10 February) they performed another eleven times before the King.[5] The pressure of political events then temporarily brought to an end this round of dramatic entertainments at court which had lasted with scarcely a break since November 1612.[6]

This intense theatrical activity was no doubt exceptional during the early part of the reign of Louis XIII. Even so, it remains a fact that in a

---

[1] 21, 22, 23, 25, 28, 29, 30 Sept.; 1, 3, 5, 6, 7, 8, 12, 13, 14, 17, 22, 23, 24, 26, 27, 28, 29, 30 Oct.; 3, 4, 5, 6, 7, 9, 10, 11, 13, 14, 16, 17, 18, 19, 20, 21 Nov.

[2] *Œuvres*, vol. iii, p. 358. In his article 'Documents inédits sur l'Hôtel de Bourgogne', *Revue d'histoire littéraire de la France* (1927), p. 326, Fransen states that the Italians hired the Hôtel de Bourgogne from 1 Oct. 1613 to 31 Mar. 1614, but gives the date of the lease as 17 Oct. (p. 353). He rebukes Rigal for stating that the Italians began their public performances in Paris on 24 Nov., but the latter was only one day out.

[3] See p. 35, n. 2.   [4] 10, 11, 12, 14 Dec.

[5] 15, 21, 25, 26, 28, 30 Jan.; 4, 5, 6, 8, 10 Feb.

[6] For the rest of the year 1614 we find in the manuscript of Héroard's Journal the following mentions of dramatic entertainments at court at which the young King was present: three performances (26, 28, 29 June) given by the Italian actors before they left for home; during the court's absence from Paris between July and Sept. four performances by French actors at Tours (20, 21, 22, 24 July): a pastoral play given at the Jesuit school at Poitiers on 31 July; another performance by French actors at Loudun (5 Aug.); performances of a pastoral play, a tragedy and a comedy at the Jesuit school at La Flèche (all on 3 Sept.); after the court's return to Paris seven performances by French actors in Nov. (17, 19, 22, 24, 26, 27, 29) and nine in Dec. (1, 3, 4, 7, 15, 17, 18, 20, 29). On 21 Dec. Louis XIII once more went in person to the Hôtel de Bourgogne.

period of fifteen months, between November 1612 and February 1614, over 130 performances were given at court by professional actors. In this period at least fifty-seven performances, already recorded by historians like Baschet, were given by Arlequin and his company, and, what is more important for the history of French drama in the early part of the seventeenth century, in this same period of time at least another seventy-six performances were given by French actors at the court of Louis XIII, a fact which appears to be unknown to historians of the French theatre in this period.

It would be possible to follow out in detail, month by month, down to 1625 or 1630 all the mentions of performances of plays at court which one encounters in Héroard's Journal and the few other sources of information available to us. Yet for our present purposes such an investigation is unnecessary. Even if it must be conceded that this period of intense theatrical activity at court was exceptional, it still remains obvious that in the opening decades of the seventeenth century the French court did not by any means reject the theatre as a low and plebeian form of entertainment, utterly beneath contempt. Whether the performances which we have discussed were given at the Louvre or at Fontainebleau, or whether (this seems to have happened much less frequently) they took place at the Hôtel de Bourgogne, there can be no reasonable doubt that the King and his courtiers, male and female, saw the same plays—French and Italian—as were presented to the normal audience in the Paris theatre. It is unfortunate that neither Héroard's Journal nor the few other documents at our disposal give us any information about the titles of the plays performed; even so far as the types of plays given before the court is concerned, we must content ourselves with occasional references to farces, together with one to tragedy and one to a pastoral play. None the less it is obvious that, for the opening decades of the seventeenth century, we do not possess one set of crude plays written for the plebeian audiences of the Hôtel de Bourgogne, and another set of refined plays written to please the more sophisticated taste of the court.

It is, after all, notorious that the taste of the court during the reign of Henry IV and the early part of the reign of Louis XIII was far from elevated; it was not as if the outlook of the King and his courtiers of both sexes was separated by an abyss from that of his humbler subjects. A work like Magendie's *La Politesse mondaine et les théories de l'honnêteté en France au XVIIe siècle*[1] shows clearly from what lowly begin-

[1] Paris, 1925 (see especially pp. 1–15 and 63–87).

nings the polite society of seventeenth-century France raised itself towards its ideals of refinement and good taste. Certainly the moral tone, as well as the aesthetic value, of early seventeenth-century French drama often leaves much to be desired. Yet that is also true of many of the ballets which were so popular at the beginning of the century, in particular of what their historian, Henri Prunières, calls 'les ballets-mascarades' which are constantly referred to in such memoirs of the time as those of Bassompierre.[1] Some of the *libretti* of these ballets-mascarades have come down to us; the contents of these curious publications are described by the same author in the following terms:

Au début du XVIIe siècle, les vers imprimés dans le livret ont pour principal objet de représenter les discours que tiendraient les divers personnages s'ils rompaient le silence auquel ils étaient condamnés. Dans les *ballets-mascarades*, ce sont presque toujours les mêmes équivoques ordurières; aussi est-il difficile de citer des exemples.[2]

Henri Prunières confines himself to giving discreet page-references in a footnote, but here the reader can see for himself how some of the *libretti* collected by Paul Lacroix[3] offer interesting parallels with early seventeenth-century drama. Take, for instance, *Le Recueil des Ballets qui ont été joués devant la Majesté du Roi avec les personnages qui auraient présenté aux dames leurs airs, billets, dictons, vers et chants royaux par P.B.S.D.V.*, Historiographe du Roi, to which the editor assigns the approximate date of 1615. The *chant royal* which is addressed to the ladies by the dancer who took the part of the knife-grinder in the ballet, the Comte d'Auvergne, has one theme and one theme only—sexual intercourse.[4] Among other examples of crudity we may note the following passage from this text:

Le Sergent fut représenté par Monsieur Cécilien, qui faisait des contraintes aux dames en singerie:

> Si je porte un habit de singe,
> Sans braguette ni flageolet,
> Ce n'est pas que dessous mon linge
> Il n'y ait un bon pistolet,
> Qui tire trois coups sans amorce
> Tout par amour, sans qu'on le force.[5]

[1] *Le Ballet de cour en France avant Benserade et Lully* (Paris, 1913), p. 99.
[2] *Le Ballet de cour*, p. 101.
[3] *Ballets et mascarades de cour de Henri III à Louis XIV (1581–1652)* (Geneva, 1869), 6 vols.
[4] Ibid., vol. ii, p. 44.   [5] Ibid., p. 50.

In the same collection we find *Le Ballet des quolibets, dansé au Louvre et à la Maison de ville par Monseigneur, frère du Roi, le quatrième janvier 1627* (Paris, 1627), in which the following lines are addressed to the ladies:

> Je porte un bâton de mesure
> Dont quinze pouces de longueur
> Par les effets de la nature
> Amortiraient votre langueur.[1]

No date is assigned by Lacroix to *Le Ballet des Andouilles porté en guise de momon,* but it appears to belong at any rate to the first half of the seventeenth century. Here *andouille* is used in its strictly Freudian sense, as is made only too plain by the following verses, addressed to the ladies:

> Sachez que c'est un beau morceau;
> Belles, je crois que j'en vois l'eau
> Déjà vous monter à la bouche. . . .
> Mais pour faire un si bon repas,
> Dépêchez-vous de mettre bas
> Le cotillon et la chemise.[2]

The approximate date of 1640 is assigned by the editor to the *Boutade des Incurables du corps et de l'esprit,* but there is not much sign of refinement and scrupulous regard for the *bienséances* in these pages. A series of people are made to lament their impotence; the following words are put into the mouth of 'un châtré';

> Le beau sexe a pour moi des éternels dédains;
> Je ne porte à son gré qu'une bourse insolvable,
> Et pour être léger seulement de deux grains
> Me tient pour pièce irrecevable.[3]

So far as the first two or three decades of the century are concerned, Héroard's Journal furnishes many vivid examples of the coarseness of manners and outlook at the court of Henry IV and his successor. Among the more quotable examples is one which has some bearing on the court's taste in theatrical matters. In January 1607 the future Louis XIII was entertained with a farce performed by three members of his entourage—a 'soldat aux gardes', his 'joueur de luth', and the young son of the noblewoman, Mme de Montglat, who was responsible for his upbringing. Héroard does not give us the subject of the farce, but

---

[1] Ibid., vol. iii, p. 233.   [2] Ibid., vol. iv, pp. 57–58.
[3] Ibid., vol. v, p. 322.

his description of the parts taken by the different actors is sufficiently revealing. The soldier had the role of 'le badin mari', the boy that of 'la femme garce', and the lute-player was 'l'amoureux qui la débaucha'.[1] This was apparently considered, by Héroard and the other persons responsible for the Dauphin's welfare, to be suitable entertainment for a child of five.

We have already seen how the only two anecdotes in Tallemant's *Historiettes* which relate to Henry IV's interest in the theatre are concerned, characteristically enough, with his relations with actors who were particularly distinguished for their roles in farce—Arlequin and Gros-Guillaume.[2] His Queen, Marie de Médicis, took a keen interest in the Italian actors, but she also seems to have enjoyed performances by French actors, particularly in farce. After the murder of her Italian favourite, Concini, in 1617, she endeavoured in her exile at Blois to while away the time with visits from two well-known farce-actors. The accounts of her household show that in May 1618 the sum of 90 livres was paid to 'Robert Guérin, dit La Fleur', better known still as Gros-Guillaume. In December of the same year the Queen Mother gave 600 livres to 'Philippe Mondor, médecin' and to 'ceux qui l'ont assisté pour jouer les comédies qu'ils ont représentées diverses fois devant nous pour notre plaisir et service'. Philippe de Mondor (his real name was Philippe Girard) was the brother of a more illustrious personage, Antoine Girard, the famous farce actor, Tabarin. Both brothers are mentioned in another item from the Queen Mother's household accounts, dated February 1619; Marie de Médicis ordered her treasurer to pay 'Philippe de Mondor, docteur en médecine, et Antoine Girard, dit Tabarin, la somme de trois cents livres de laquelle nous leur avons fait don tant en considération de ce qu'ils ont représenté plusieurs comédies devant nous pour notre plaisir et service que pour leur faire sentir notre libéralité'.[3]

Tabarin, we remember, was shortly to make a name for himself in Paris in the Place Dauphine, where he helped to attract a crowd by his monologues, dialogues, and little farces and thus persuaded the populace to buy quack medicines. What sort of audience he appealed to is made clear by a contemporary comparison between his efforts and those of the farce actors of the Hôtel de Bourgogne:

---

[1] *Journal*, vol. i, p. 245.   [2] *Historiettes*, vol. i, pp. 16, 27.

[3] Bibliothèque Nationale, Cinq Cents Colbert, vol. 92, ff. 187, 201, 214. These most interesting documents were discovered by Émile Magne and published in *Le Plaisant Abbé de Boisrobert* (Paris, 1909), pp. 49–50.

L'on a vu un Gaultier-Garguille avec son loyal serviteur Guillaume, assisté de la dame Perrine, qui ont joué des plus fameuses facéties qu'on puisse désirer; mais je dirai qu'ils étaient trois personnes à représenter icelles; et Tabarin avec son chapeau en représente autant sans argent que les comédiens ne font à leurs assistants pour chacun cinq sols, et partant doit-il être plus aimé de ceux qui n'ont point d'argent et qui désirent de voir quelque chose de plaisant.[1]

It is obvious then that in the opening years of the seventeenth century there was no unbridgeable gulf between the taste of the court and that of the plebs.

It is indisputable that the theatre became much more fashionable in Paris by about 1630: the actors prospered, as two French companies were now permanently established in the capital. It is also an undoubted fact that gradually the theatre was to become much less coarse and that, from the aesthetic point of view, immense progress was to be made in the 1630's. To see this transformation one has only to contrast the surviving plays of Alexandre Hardy, the outstanding playwright of the first quarter of the seventeenth century, with a masterpiece like Corneille's *Cid*. Yet how far these changes in French drama were accompanied by, and to some extent caused by, a modification in the social composition of the Paris theatre audience is a very complex question. It may be that, as the theatre became more fashionable, the influence of the aristocracy and especially its female members became more important, and that the audience grew less plebeian. Yet, rare as are the documents at our disposal for a study of the Paris theatre in the first two decades of the seventeenth century, and although they are at times contradictory, they do prove beyond a doubt that even in that period the theatre was never an exclusively plebeian entertainment. The crude plays performed at the Hôtel de Bourgogne, farces included, appear to have found favour with both sexes at court. One is therefore tempted to put forward the suggestion that the improvement which took place in the type of play performed in the decade between 1625 and 1635 may have been due less (if at all) to a change in the social composition of the audience than to the greater refinement, both in manners and language, which was spread among the upper classes of French society by the development of social life in the salons. The cult of the *bienséances* with its rejection of every suggestion of impropriety either in situations or language and, more positively, the new and more

---

[1] *Les Fantaisies plaisantes et facétieuses du chapeau à Tabarin*, in Tabarin, *Œuvres complètes*, ed. G. Aventin (Paris, 1858), 2 vols., vol. ii, pp. 338–9.

sophisticated conceptions of the aims and technique of drama revealed in the acceptance of the famous 'rules', all these changes are undoubtedly connected with (though not, alas, necessarily explained by) the development of polite society which was to exercise such a dominant influence on French language and literature down to 1789.

In short, if in the first three decades of the seventeenth century—the age of Shakespeare and Lope de Vega—the French theatre failed to produce a single play which still holds the stage today, this cannot be explained away by putting the blame on the plebeian audience of the Hôtel de Bourgogne.

2. *From Corneille to Lesage*

O NE turns with relief from the almost totally dead drama of the opening decades of the seventeenth century in France to the brilliantly original and creative age which followed. If there is some interest in attempting to discover from the handful of available documents something about the influence exercised by the audience on a drama which few today read and no one can ever see performed, there is no doubt considerably more in applying the same methods of investigation to the period which produced some of the greatest masterpieces of French drama.

Our period begins with the appearance on the scene of a whole group of young writers of whom Corneille only gradually proved himself the most illustrious. They wrote for the two competing theatres of the Hôtel de Bourgogne and the Marais, and were supported by the patronage of various noblemen and, above all, of Cardinal Richelieu. The years which run from the date of Richelieu's intervention in theatrical affairs (about 1630) to the outbreak of the civil wars of the Fronde in 1648 are one of the two summits of dramatic achievement in seventeenth-century France. Not only was there a much more intensive production of plays—especially tragicomedies and tragedies and to a less degree comedies—than in the opening decades of the century, but in these years all Corneille's masterpieces from *Le Cid* to *Polyeucte* were given their first performance.

The second and even higher summit of dramatic achievement was attained in the period between Molière's return to Paris in 1658 and the performance of Racine's last secular tragedy, *Phèdre*, in 1677. If by this time the Marais theatre, except in its speciality of spectacular plays (*pièces à machines*), was in decline, from 1658 to 1673 Molière's theatre offered the audiences of the time a brilliant series of comedies, *comédies-ballets*, and farces which have never been equalled in any age, while in the rival theatre of the Hôtel de Bourgogne Racine was producing in the ten years between 1667 and 1677 the superb succession of tragedies which opened with *Andromaque*.

After Molière's death his company was merged by the King's command with that of the Marais, and finally in 1680 a second amalgamation, with the Hôtel de Bourgogne, led to the creation of the Comédie Française. Once again Paris had only one theatre, endowed with a monopoly of all performances of plays in French. Bad as this monopoly may have been in certain respects, particularly for the unfortunate playwrights who were left at the mercy of the one set of actors and actresses available to produce their plays, it had none the less certain advantages. It provided a large and varied company, capable of giving performances almost every day throughout the year (hitherto the different theatres had only been open three or at most four times a week) and at the same time able to carry out its duty of making a certain number of appearances at court without having to abandon its performances in Paris.

From 1680 until their expulsion in 1697 the Italian actors, now installed at the Hôtel de Bourgogne, offered more direct competition to the Comédie Française than they had done to earlier French companies, since they gradually tended to introduce an ever larger proportion of French scenes into the plays which they performed. Yet it must be said that the aesthetic value of the plays or scenes in French collected together by the actor Gherardi, and finally published in his *Théâtre Italien* (1700),[1] was not high, and as the Italian actors were expelled from France in 1697, leaving their theatre vacant until their recall by the Regent in 1716, it is mainly to the Comédie Française that we must look for such new plays of merit as were performed in the period from 1680 down to the death of Louis XIV. It is true that after the great achievements of Molière and Racine in the 1660's and 1670's, this was a period of decline. Yet though there is only slight injustice in Hugo's verdict on the successors of Racine in tragedy,

> Sur le Racine mort le Campistron pullule,

in comedy Molière was followed by writers who are by no means entirely negligible—Dancourt, Regnard, and finally Lesage.

In the period between 1630 and 1715 there was thus gradually built up a varied repertoire of established French plays which continued to be performed long after their first appearance on the boards and which

---

[1] E. Gherardi (ed.), *Le Théâtre Italien . . . , ou le Recueil général de toutes les comédies et scènes françaises jouées par les comédiens italiens du roi* (Paris, 1700), 6 vols.

formed one of the richest collections of masterpieces and good plays of the second class which any country has ever possessed. The situation of French drama by the beginning of the eighteenth century thus offers a striking contrast with its poverty a hundred years earlier in the age of Alexandre Hardy.

(i) *The Size of the Audience*

The main question to which this chapter seeks to provide an answer is this: to what extent is the term 'aristocratic audience' correctly applied to the spectators who frequented the Paris theatres between 1630 and the death of Louis XIV? It can obviously be used correctly of the audience which saw the first performance of Racine's *Iphigénie* (and probably also *Andromaque*) as of a considerable number of the plays of Molière, since these first faced the footlights in the presence of Louis XIV and his courtiers. This was clearly an exceptional honour for any new play in our period, and even those which were first given at court had subsequently to face the ordeal of being presented to the ordinary Paris audiences in the different theatres of the capital. How far can the term 'aristocratic audience' be applied to the spectators who congregated in the Hôtel de Bourgogne, the Marais, or Molière's theatre at the Palais Royal, or later in the Comédie Française?

'Aristocratic' can be interpreted in two senses, to mean either that the audience was restricted in numbers, or that it was confined wholly or at least mainly to persons of blue blood. We may begin by examining the question of the size of theatre audiences, before passing on to the more complex question of their social composition. The field over which we can explore this first problem is, of course, restricted. Neither for the Hôtel de Bourgogne nor for the Théâtre du Marais at which most of the plays of Racine and Corneille were first produced do we possess the slightest shred of evidence as to the size of the audience. Our ignorance for the Italian actors down to their expulsion from France 1697 is equally profound. From the Register of Lagrange we can tell, so far as Molière's company was concerned, what were the receipts for every performance from Easter 1659 onwards; but as we do not know how many tickets were sold for the different parts of the theatre, we have no means of calculating how many people were present at any one performance or how many paid for admission in the course of the year.

Only for the last year of Molière's career in Paris can we make any such calculations, thanks to the Register which was kept by another of his actors, Hubert, and is also preserved in the Archives of the Comédie Française.[1] In considering the figures which can be deduced from this Register one has to bear in mind a number of points. Molière's company did not perform every day of the week, even during the period when the theatres were normally open (i.e. from shortly after the Easter of one year to shortly before the Easter of the following year). Allowing for certain abnormal breaks and in particular for the period of a week after Molière's death when the theatre was closed, we find that between 29 April 1672 and 21 March 1673 131 performances were given—i.e. an average of rather less than three a week. Again, unlike the Comédie Française a few years later, Molière's company did not have a monopoly of the performance of French plays in Paris. It had to compete not only with the Italians who shared the same theatre and performed on the days when it was left free, but also with the Théâtre du Marais and especially with its more powerful rival at the Hôtel de Bourgogne. On the other hand, we must not forget that, if the Paris of that date was a much smaller place than it is today, it had a population of something like half a million, was the seat of the King and his court, and was, in addition, the Mecca of a horde of provincials and foreigners many of whom, as we know from their accounts of their stay in the capital, paid frequent visits to the theatre.

Yet in this last year in the life of Molière's company (in which we include such performances as were given by his company after his death down to the end of the theatrical season on 21 March) his theatre attracted only some 52,000 spectators. For a total of 131 performances this represents an average daily attendance of only about 400. Molière, moreover, was at the very height of his fame, and the theatrical year included the end of the first run of *Les Femmes savantes*, the first run of *La Comtesse d'Escarbagnas*, the first run of *Le Malade imaginaire* (sadly interrupted, it is true, by Molière's death after the fourth performance) and, in addition, the highly successful revival of *Psyché*, the *pièce à machines* which he had produced in 1671 with the collaboration of Quinault and Pierre Corneille. Its revival in 1672–3 reached 31 performances and accounted for just over 20,000 spectators out of the total of some 52,000 who paid for admission to his theatre in that year.

It is impossible to draw any very precise conclusions from such figures as can be established for attendances at Molière's theatre during the last year of its existence, since we can compare these figures neither

---

[1] See W. L. Schwartz, 'Molière's Theater in 1672–3: Light from *Le Registre d'Hubert*', *Publications of the Modern Languages Association of America* (1941), pp. 395 f.

with those for earlier years nor with those for the Hôtel de Bourgogne or the Théâtre du Marais for the same period. It is true that the registers of the Théâtre Guénégaud, from its foundation in 1673 after the death of Molière down to its fusion with the Hôtel de Bourgogne in 1680, are preserved in the Archives of the Comédie Française; unfortunately they still await the treatment accorded to the registers of the Comédie Française, which have been neatly summarized in recent years by Lancaster.[1] It is therefore only when we reach the year 1680 that we are able to get rather closer to a precise knowledge of the size of the theatre audiences of seventeenth-century Paris.

Our gratitude to Lancaster for these invaluable publications ought not to prevent us looking closely at the deductions which he draws from them. With all the authority conferred by an unrivalled knowledge of the seventeenth- and eighteenth-century French theatre he flatly rejects the accepted view that French drama of the Classical Age was written for an audience at once small in numbers and virtually restricted to the upper classes of a severely hierarchical society. He argues that the audience which frequented the Comédie Française in the period 1680–1701 cannot, from its very size, be called aristocratic. In the theatrical year 1682–3, for instance, over 150,000 spectators paid for admission, and a certain number were no doubt admitted free. He therefore concludes that, allowing for the fact that some spectators went more than once in that particular year, 'there must have been well over 100,000 different individuals who attended'.[2] He would thus have us discard the hoary notion that the theatre-going public in seventeenth-century Paris was a relatively small *élite*.

Before we accept this summary dismissal of an almost universally accepted belief, we might do well to examine rather more closely the figures on which this sweeping conclusion is based. First, how does the figure of 150,000 paying spectators in the theatrical year 1682–3 chosen by Lancaster compare with the figure for other years in the period from 1680 to 1701, which is the one on which his argument is based? In the very next year the attendance fell to only 109,000, and there were three other bad years (1691–2, 1693–4, and 1694–5) when it failed to reach 120,000. It is true that there were four years altogether (1682–3, 1695–6, 1698–9, and 1700–1) when it rose to over 150,000, reaching over 192,000 in the record season of 1698–9. Yet the average attendance for

---

[1] *The Comédie Française, 1680–1701*, and *The Comédie Française, 1701–1774*.
[2] *History*, part v, p. 5.

these years, as for the following period from 1701 down to the death of Louis XIV, was rather less than 140,000. However, even though the figure for the year chosen by Lancaster is rather above the average, it is a good round figure and may well be accepted for the sake of argument.

Some mention must be made of the spectators who were admitted free. The *règlements* of 1688 and 1697 laid down strict rules for their admission.[1] According to these new rules which were drawn up to prevent unauthorized persons from entering without payment and to 'empêcher que les gens de qualité ne se voient confondus avec toutes sortes de gens, et que le spectacle de la Comédie ne soit troublé et avili par ces désordres', actors and actresses were allowed one free ticket each for two persons on alternate days; extra tickets had to be paid for. Authors of new plays were allowed four tickets for five-act plays and two tickets for shorter ones; the cost of all others had to be deducted from their share in the receipts. A list was drawn up of all persons on whom the actors had conferred the privilege of free admission; in addition to a number of playwrights it included high officials, lawyers, doctors, tradesmen, and so on. The parents, wives, husbands, and children of actors and actresses also enjoyed the privilege of free admission, but were not allowed to bring anyone with them except 'des domestiques étant actuellement à leur service'. All other relatives, including brothers and sisters, were excluded from this privilege, unless they were given the free tickets which the actors had at their disposal on alternate days.

Even if these elaborate rules were strictly observed (this is more than doubtful), we have no means of telling how many of the persons who enjoyed the privilege of free admission actually made use of it in the course of a single year. The number may well have been fairly considerable, since only 30 persons at each performance would account for some 10,000 spectators in a year; but as we have no means of telling how numerous they were, they are best left out of our calculations. Even if there were as many as 20,000 (which seems improbable), they would not greatly affect calculations based on an average total attendance of 150,000 paying spectators a year.

As soon as we attempt to discover the approximate number of different individuals who made up this total, we find ourselves confronted by almost insuperable difficulties. The only absolutely safe conclusion is the not very helpful one that the solution to the problem

---

[1] J. Bonnassies, *La Comédie-Française, Histoire administrative (1658–1757)* (Paris, 1874), pp. 111–27.

is to be found somewhere in between two equally absurd suppositions: either that 150,000 different individuals went once each to the Comédie Française in that year, or else that approximately 426 people attended every one of the 352 performances given there in that period. Lancaster plunges boldly in and asserts that 'well over 100,000 different individuals' were present at these performances. It is, however, quite possible to account for these 150,000 attendances in rather a different manner.

At the 352 performances given at the Comédie Française in this period 9 new plays were put on, while 89 older plays—full-length tragedies and comedies as well as *petites pièces*—were performed. It is reasonable to assume that, given the choice of nearly 100 different plays, a certain number of enthusiasts went to the theatre a considerable number of times in the course of the year—say, for the sake of argument, 30 times in the year (roughly once a fortnight)—and that, among other less regular theatre-goers, some turned up 20 times and others 10. We might therefore assume, for example, that the figure of 150,000 attendances was made up as follows:

```
1,000 individuals attending 30 times would account for 30,000
1,500     ,,          ,,      20  ,,      ,,      ,,    ,,  30,000
3,000     ,,          ,,      10  ,,      ,,      ,,    ,,  30,000
5,000     ,,          ,,       5  ,,      ,,      ,,    ,,  25,000
10,000    ,,          ,,       2  ,,      ,,      ,,    ,,  20,000
15,000    ,,          ,,       1  ,,      ,,      ,,    ,,  15,000
```

On this hypothesis 35,500 individuals would thus account for these 150,000 attendances, which would represent an average of 4·23 performances each.

To see this figure in its true perspective we must bear in mind both the size of Paris by the end of the seventeenth century and the importance of its role as capital and international tourist centre. The only competitors of the Comédie Française at this period in its history were the Opéra and, down to their expulsion in 1697, the Italian actors. And yet, as we have seen, it is at least possible to account for a total of 150,000 attendances at the Comédie Française by postulating the presence of no more than some 35,000 individuals. In fact, given the wide choice of plays offered during the year, there is nothing wildly improbable in the assumption we have made that a mere 2,500 individuals might account for as many as 60,000 attendances; similarly 5,500 might have been responsible for a total of 90,000, and 10,500 for a total of 115,000. Thus the figure of 150,000 spectators who paid for admission in the course of one year is not necessarily as impressive as it appears at first sight. It means, in fact, an average daily attendance of well below 500 persons; and it might quite well mean that less than 40,000 people—provincials and foreigners as well as Parisians—were present at the Comédie Française in the theatrical year 1682–3.

It will, of course, be retorted that all this is pure guess-work, and it is no doubt not a sufficient answer to say that here one's own guess is as good as anyone else's. But it is at least clear that the current belief in the smallness of the theatre-going public in seventeenth-century Paris cannot be convincingly refuted simply by reference to the total attendance at the Comédie Française in any given year. One would require much more solid proofs before casting aside the accepted theory, which has plenty of precise evidence to support it. There is, for instance, a significant remark on the smallness of the theatre-going public in Voltaire's *Lettre à un premier commis*, written in 1733, at a date when, as we shall see, conditions in the Paris theatre had changed little since the period which we are now discussing: 'D'ailleurs, on ne va pas aux spectacles tous les jours, et, dans la multitude de nos citoyens, il n'y a pas quatre mille hommes qui les fréquentent avec assiduité.'[1]

Much more impressive is the evidence to be derived from the number of performances enjoyed by successful plays of our period. It is notorious that in the seventeenth century the run of even the most popular new plays was, by modern standards, ridiculously short. Then, and for many years afterwards, 10 to 15 performances represented a modest, but definite success; 15 to 22 or 23 was a very considerable figure. Twenty-four or so to 30 meant a very striking success, while figures in the 30's or 40's were altogether exceptional. In fact, only three new plays achieved the phenomenal success of 30 or more performances in the whole period from 1680 to 1701 and only two in the period from 1701 to 1715.

It is here, if anywhere, that we must look for some idea, however approximate, of the size of the theatre-going public in Paris in the last part of the seventeenth century. The number of persons attracted to the theatre during the first run of the average successful play can give us at least a rough idea of the number of people who were in the habit of frequenting the Comédie Française. For our purpose we can set aside such phenomenal successes as Dancourt's one-act plays, *Les Vendanges de Suresnes* (49 performances; over 33,000 spectators) and *La Foire de Bezons* (30 performances; over 24,000 spectators), as well as Boursault's

[1] *Œuvres complètes*, ed. L. Moland, 52 vols. (Paris, 1877–85), vol. xxxiii, p. 354.

five-act comedy, *Ésope* (43 performances; over 25,000 spectators) and the revival in 1682–3 of Corneille's *pièce à machines*, *Andromède* (45 performances spread over the year; over 27,000 spectators).[1] It is clear that the vogue of such plays was so great as to draw in people who did not normally attend the Comédie Française.

The number of spectators attracted to the remainder of the successful plays of the period should give some more precise notion of the total theatre-going public of the time. These plays fall conveniently into three main groups. At the other end of the scale from the comedies of Dancourt and Boursault mentioned above, come the plays of our period which enjoyed only a modest success: those which ran for 11 to 16 performances and drew from 6,000 to 8,000 spectators. This group includes such tragedies as La Chapelle's *Zaïde*, Genest's *Zélonide*, La Chapelle's *Ajax*, and Longepierre's *Médée*, and, among comedies, Campistron's *Amante amant*, Boursault's *Les Mots à la mode*, Champmeslé's *Parisien*, and the masterpiece of Brueys and Palaprat, *Le Grondeur*.

The most interesting group of all, from our point of view, consists of the average successful plays of the period, which reached from 15 to 25 performances and were seen by 10,000 to 12,000 or so spectators, since they give a very fair idea of the number of people whom, failing a quite outstanding success, the author of a new play could reasonably expect to draw to the Comédie Française. Regnard's *Le Joueur*, for instance, reached 18 performances and attracted some 12,000 spectators. Some 11,000 came to see Dancourt's *Moulin de Javelle* and his *Trois Cousines*, Campistron's *Tiridate*, Boyer's *Judith*, La Fosse's *Polixène*, and Robbe's comedy, *La Rapinière*. Some 10,000 spectators attended the first run of such tragedies as La Fosse's *Manlius*, Catherine Bernard's *Brutus* and *Laodamie*, Campistron's *Andronic*, and Péchantré's *Géta*. The same figure was reached by such comedies as Boursault's *Mercure Galant* and Champmeslé's *Coupe enchantée*.

Finally, we have a more select group: those plays which scored a really striking success, i.e. reached between 20 and 30 performances and attracted between 15,000 and 17,000 spectators. This group consists of three tragedies—Campistron's *Alcibiade*, Pradon's *Régulus*, and La Fosse's *Thésée*—all of which drew around 16,000 spectators; Baron's comedies, *L'Homme à bonnes fortunes* and *La Coquette*; and no less than six plays of Dancourt—*Le Chevalier à la mode*, *Les Bour-*

[1] With the exception of those for Corneille's *Andromède*, the figures for performances given here include only those for which the authors received royalties.

geoises à la mode, Les Vacances, Le Mari retrouvé, La Loterie, and *Les Curieux de Compiègne.*

From a study of these figures we can safely conclude that 10,000 to 12,000 people represented the largest number of spectators who could be expected to support a new play, unless it enjoyed an especially great vogue, when the total attendance would reach from 15,000 to 17,000; or, in other words, that the number of regular patrons of the Comédie Française at the end of the seventeenth century lay somewhere between a minimum of 10,000 and, at the outside, a maximum of 17,000.

The same conclusion is seen in miniature, if we study in detail the theatrical year 1682–3 which we have taken as a rough average for the whole period. We can, of course, put aside the revival of Corneille's *Andromède* with its 27,000 spectators—an altogether exceptional success which was no doubt largely responsible for the total attendance in this year being rather above the average. A study of the nine new plays put on during the year is more to the point. Of these four turned out to be failures, while three enjoyed a very moderate success—La Chapelle's *Téléphonte,* Champmeslé's *Les Joueurs,* and Campistron's *Virginie;* all of these attracted less than 6,000 spectators. Two comedies, however, achieved a good average success: both Robbe's *La Rapinière* and Boursault's *Mercure Galant* reached 18 performances and attracted to the theatre 11,203 and 10,029 spectators respectively. In other words, both had exhausted their success by the time they had been seen by 10,000 or 11,000 spectators and had then to be taken off.[1]

Far from disproving the smallness of the theatre-going public in Paris at that period, all the evidence which we can derive from a study of the figures for attendances at the Comédie Française in the years from 1680 to 1701 goes to confirm this generally accepted interpretation of the facts. Between 1680 and 1701 only three new plays could attract over 20,000 spectators. In twenty years only eleven new plays proved so strikingly popular as to attract between 15,000 and 17,000 spectators. All that the author of the normally successful play could expect was a total attendance of from 10,000 to 12,000 spectators; when that number had come to the Comédie Française, his play was taken off and his royalties ceased.[2]

---

[1] Six more performances of the *Mercure Galant* were given shortly afterwards, in May and June 1683, attracting another 2,762 spectators, but Boursault drew no royalties from them.

[2] It is unfortunate that we cannot compare with these figures similar ones for performances given by Molière's company during the last year of its existence (see Schwartz, 'Molière's Theater in 1672–3'). We do not find in this year any new plays which had a

Without entering into the same amount of detail about the period from 1701 to 1715, we can quickly see that the situation in these years remained very much the same. A number of plays achieved enough success to draw 10,000 or so spectators to the theatre. At the other end of the scale came two phenomenally successful plays which reached 30 or more performances during their first run and attracted over 20,000 spectators to the Comédie Française—Crébillon's tragedy, *Rhadamiste et Zénobie*, and, even more successful despite its totally ephemeral nature, Dancourt's one-act comedy, *Les Fêtes nocturnes du Cours*. In between these two extremes there came five plays which reached between 19 and 27 performances and which about 15,000 spectators paid to see: Mme Gomez's tragedy, *Habis*, Regnard's *Légataire universel*, and three one-act comedies, Legrand's *Usurier gentilhomme* and Dancourt's *Diable boiteux* and *Impromptu de Suresnes*. The new plays of this period thus achieved a pattern of success very similar to that achieved by those of the last two decades of the seventeenth century.

In a word, the old-fashioned notion that the audience in the seventeenth-century Paris theatre was a relatively small *élite* is seen to be confirmed by the statistics of attendances at the Comédie Française from its foundation in 1680 onwards—at least so far as the *size* of the audience is concerned.[1] Its social composition—the predominance or otherwise of persons of high social rank among the spectators before whom the masterpieces of Corneille, Molière, and Racine were first played—is another question with the complexities of which we must now attempt to grapple.

(ii) *The* Peuple *and the Theatre*

While historians of the seventeenth-century Paris theatre are almost unanimous in describing audiences at the beginning of the period as plebeian, they have on the whole little to say about the role of the plebs in the audiences of the Classical period. In his invaluable book *Le Théâtre et le public à Paris sous Louis XIV*,[2] M. Pierre Mélèse speaks of the occupants of the *parterre* at this period of the century as 'la foule

complete first run except for the rather minor *Comtesse d'Escarbagnaes* which drew only 4,450 spectators in 14 performances. The first 9 performances of *Le Malade Imaginaire*, which were interrupted for a fortnight by Molière's death, attracted 4,949 spectators. On the other hand, we have seen how the 31 performances of *Psyché*, which was revived in Nov. 1672, were attended by over 20,000 spectators.

[1] Further detailed evidence on this question is contained in my article, 'The Earnings of Playwrights in Seventeenth-Century France', *Modern Language Review* (1947), pp. 321–36.   [2] (Paris, 1934), p. 210.

des spectateurs moins fortunés, qui ne pouvaient payer que leurs quinze sols, ou même qui entraient sans payer, malgré les interdictions royales, officiers, poètes, lettrés, bourgeois, artisans, laquais même'. Clearly those people who bought the cheapest theatre tickets which were to be had must in general have had less money to spare than those who could afford the luxury of a seat in the boxes or on the stage; but if, as we shall see, 'officiers, poètes, lettrés, bourgeois' were prominent among the spectators in the *parterre*, this statement does not even attempt to define the place of more plebeian sections of the community, such as artisans and lackeys, in the audiences of Corneille, Molière, and Racine.

One voice, speaking with considerable authority, that of Lancaster, maintains with great force that the dramatists of the age did not write only for an *élite*. After arguing that large numbers of people were in the habit of frequenting the Comédie Française in the last part of the seventeenth century, he continues in words which deserve to be quoted and carefully weighed:

It is impossible that so large a number did not include persons of all classes. Subligny's reference to a *porteuse d'eau* who discussed *Andromaque* would hardly be found in a play acted at the Palais Royal[1] if such persons did not go to the theater. Nor did La Bruyère have a selected audience in mind when he wrote that 'le peuple écoute avidement, les yeux élevés et la bouche ouverte'. As it is said that in the first quarter of the century women of refinement did not go to the theater, we may suppose that it was then frequented by the unrefined, and there is no reason to suppose that the latter gave up the habit after the audience began to include respectable spectators. Nor is the question of expense a serious argument. Even when 'quinze sous' represented a day's pay, the man who earned no more than this amount may well have spent it once or twice a year at the theater. Dramatists knew that their plays would be seen by highly mixed audiences at Paris, that they would be carried to the provinces and abroad by strolling players, and that publication would further increase the number of persons for whom they were writing.[2]

There can, of course, be no question that, in contrast with the audience which was present at court performances of plays, that of the different Paris theatres must have been a mixed one; the very existence of different theatre prices, ranging from those paid for the expensive 'premières loges' and seats on the stage down to the more modest 'quinze sous' for the right to stand in the *parterre*, presupposes considerable differences in purse and possibly in rank among the spectators.

---

[1] Molière's theatre.   [2] *History*, part v, pp. 5–6.

Yet can we go beyond this and consider the audiences of the seventeenth-century Paris theatre to have offered a broad cross-section of the population of the capital, ranging from members of the royal family and princes of the blood down to their humblest fellow citizens? Even Lancaster does not suggest that the different classes of society were represented in the theatres of seventeenth-century Paris in direct proportion to their numbers, for that would, of course, have given an overwhelming preponderance to the lower classes in the contemporary theatre. Yet, if we reject as untenable the opposite alternative that the audience consisted only of persons of blue blood, it still remains to establish roughly in what proportion the different classes of society were represented in the theatres of the time, and whether in particular the lower classes—those beneath the status of, say, merchants, lawyers, teachers, and writers—came to the theatre in numbers that were at all significant.

The problem is full of complexities, and one can only regret that in the ten volumes which Lancaster wrote on French drama between 1610 and 1715, he devoted merely a few scattered references to it. One would feel happier if the two quotations with which he supports his theory of the importance of the lower classes in the seventeenth-century Paris theatre were really decisive. Subligny's reference to the question which he adduces in support of his interpretation is taken from his satirical attack on Racine's *Andromaque*—*La Folle Querelle*, performed by Molière's company in 1668. In the first scene Lise, a *femme de chambre*, is made to say of the success of Racine's play: 'J'en ai tellement la tête étourdie depuis hier que je crois que je n'entendrai parler d'autre chose. Cuisinier, cocher, palefrenier, laquais, et jusqu'à la porteuse d'eau, il n'y a personne qui n'en veuille discourir.' Lancaster solemnly concludes that such a remark 'could hardly be found in a play acted at the Palais Royal if such persons did not go to the theater'. But is there not such a thing as comic exaggeration? Must one take literally all references to contemporary life in the comedies of the age? Must one conclude from *Le Bourgeois gentilhomme*, for instance, that all wealthy bourgeois who aped the aristocracy would have been delighted to marry their daughters to 'le fils du Grand Turc'? Or must one take literally the very next sentence put into the mouth of the *femme de chambre*: 'Je pense même que le chien et le chat s'en mêleront, si cela ne finit bientôt'?[1]

---

[1] It is interesting that in this play the only representative of the lower orders who claims to have actually seen *Andromaque* performed is the *valet de chambre* of a nobleman.

Nor is the other piece of evidence adduced by Lancaster really convincing, although for different reasons. In a well-known passage in the chapter 'Des ouvrages de l'esprit' in *Les Caractères* La Bruyère wrote:

Certains poètes sont sujets, dans le dramatique, à de longues suites de vers pompeux qui semblent forts, élevés et remplis de grands sentiments. Le *peuple* écoute avidement, les yeux élevés et la bouche ouverte, croit que cela lui plaît et à mesure qu'il y comprend moins, l'admire davantage; il n'a pas le temps de respirer, il a à peine celui de se récrier et d'applaudir. J'ai cru autrefois, et dans ma première jeunesse, que ces endroits étaient clairs et intelligibles pour les acteurs, pour le parterre et l'amphithéâtre,[1] que leurs auteurs s'entendaient eux-mêmes, et qu'avec toute l'attention que je donnais à leur récit, j'avais tort de n'y rien entendre: je suis détrompé.

If we were sure that by the word *peuple* La Bruyère meant here 'the lower orders', then all would be clear and Lancaster's argument would be sound. Unfortunately, as anyone who has studied the question knows, in the seventeenth century the word *peuple* is used in a variety of senses which it is by no means easy to disentangle and to define with accuracy. While *peuple* is often synonymous with 'lower orders', it can have a wide variety of senses.

A mid-seventeenth-century play furnishes a rather astonishing example which shows straight away that the word could be used of people who were far from plebeian. In his comedy, *Les Songes des hommes éveillés*,[2] Brosse makes one nobleman offer another a performance of a play to cure him of his melancholy. The actors, he says, will be another nobleman from Paris together with his own sister and niece. Yet, speaking of an amateur performance given by noblemen and their womenfolk apparently before an aristocratic audience, he says of his niece's prowess as an actress:

Cette fille est adroite, et dans ses actions
Elle excite le *peuple* aux acclamations.

It is difficult here to see how the word *peuple* means anything more than 'audience, public'. A similar use of the word seems to occur in Chevalier's comedy, *Les Amours de Caotin*,[3] in which one of the characters, a *chevalier*, describes a visit to Molière's theatre to see *La Critique de l'École des Femmes*:

[1] 'Lieu élevé vis-à-vis du théâtre, d'où les spectateurs voient la comédie plus commodément' (*Dictionnaire de l'Académie*, 1694).
[2] (Paris, 1646) Act V, Sc. 2.
[3] (Paris, 1664) Act I, Sc. 2.

> Sombre et mélancolique,
> Pour me déchagriner je fus voir la *Critique,*
> Où je trouvai moyen de chasser mon ennui.
> Ce diable de Molière entraîne tout chez lui;
> Tout y crevait de *peuple,* et fort peu, je t'assure,
> Se purent exempter des traits de sa censure.

Contemporary dictionaries are not as helpful as they might be in determining the precise senses in which the word was used in the seventeenth century. The essential part of the definition in the 1694 edition of the Dictionary of the Academy consists of the following lines:

Il se dit aussi d'une multitude d'habitants qui vivent, ou dans une même ville, ou dans un même bourg ou village. *Il y a beaucoup de peuple dans Paris. Tout le peuple du bourg, du village accourut.*

Il se prend aussi quelquefois pour la partie la moins considérable d'entre les habitants d'une même ville, d'un même pays. *Il y eut quelque émotion parmi le peuple. Le peuple ne sait ce qu'il veut la plupart du temps.* En ce même sens on dit, *Le menu peuple, le bas peuple, le petit peuple.*

If the first paragraph possibly throws a remote light on the use of *peuple* to mean *public* in our period, the second does not take us very far, since the words 'la partie la moins considérable' do not even begin to attempt to define where, in descending the social scale, one came to the *peuple.*

Furetière's Dictionary perhaps throws a little more light on the question, but even so it does not take us very far:

Peuple, se dit encore plus particulièrement par opposition à ceux qui sont nobles, riches ou éclairés. *Le peuple est peuple partout,* c'est-à-dire, sot, remuant, aimant les nouveautés. *Cet homme est gâté de toutes les erreurs et opinions du peuple. Il est de la lie du peuple. Le petit peuple, le menu peuple, le commun du peuple est malin et séditieux. Il y a bien du peuple au quartier des halles.*

In the revised edition of his Dictionary published in 1701, this definition is expanded to the following:

Peuple, se dit encore plus particulièrement par opposition à ceux qui sont nobles, riches ou éclairés. *Qui dit peuple, dit plus d'une chose; c'est une vaste expression. Il y a le peuple qui est opposé aux grands; c'est la populace et la multitude. Il y a le peuple qui est opposé aux sages et aux habiles: ce sont les grands comme les petits.* La B. *Il y a bien de la différence entre populus* en latin et *peuple* en français. *Le mot de peuple ne signifie d'ordinaire parmi nous que ce que les Romains appelaient plebs.* Vaug. *Il faut être bien peuple pour se

.aisser éblouir par l'éclat qui environne les grands. Œ.M. Les gens de cour méprisent le *peuple*, et ils sont souvent *peuple* eux-mêmes. La B. En ce sens *peuple* signifie les manières basses et les sots préjugés du *peuple*. Tout le monde n'est pas *peuple*, c'est-à-dire, tout le monde n'est pas sot ou dupe. Le *peuple* est *peuple* partout, c'est-à-dire, sot, remuant, aimant les nouveautés. Cet homme est gâté de toutes les erreurs et opinions du *peuple*. Il est de la lie du *peuple*. Le petit *peuple*, le menu *peuple*, le commun du *peuple* est malin et séditieux. Il y a bien du *peuple* au quartier des halles, c'est-à-dire, de la populace, de la canaille.

Interesting as the opening definition is, it is somewhat blurred by what follows; and we are still left without any notion, however approximate, of where in the seventeenth century the line was drawn between the *peuple* and its betters.

Richelet's Dictionary is perhaps the least unhelpful in this respect:

PEUPLE. Ce mot en général signifie une multitude de personnes qui habitent dans un même lieu en y comprenant les personnes de qualité et autres. (Ainsi on dit, Il y a bien du peuple à Paris. Il y a une infinité de peuple à Paris.)

Ce mot se prend dans un sens moins vague pour dire tout le corps du peuple, sans y comprendre ce qu'on appelle les gens de qualité et les gens qui ont de l'esprit et de la politesse. (Et c'est en ce sens que d'Ablancourt a écrit que *le peuple était amoureux de la nouveauté*.) . . .

Le petit peuple. C'est toute la racaille d'une ville. C'est tout ce qu'il y a de gens qui ne sont pas de qualité ni bourgeois aisés, ni ce qu'on appelle honnêtes. (Le petit peuple de Londres est méchant.)

After all these different definitions of the word *peuple* as it was understood by seventeenth-century lexicographers, it will be seen that La Bruyère's use of the word with reference to part of the theatre audience is far from explicit. Where did the *peuple* leave off for La Bruyère? In his definition of the word *parterre* Furetière himself uses the word *peuple*: 'Parterre signifie aussi l'aire d'une salle de comédie où le peuple l'entend debout. . . . Parterre se dit figurément du peuple qui est contenu dans le *parterre*. Molière a fait dire à un marquis impertinent: "Ris, parterre", pour mépriser le jugement du peuple.' But, he continues: 'Le parterre est pourtant ce qui donne le plus d'applaudissement et de cours aux pièces. Ces messieurs ne veulent pas que le parterre ait du sens commun. Mol. Le parterre qui n'a d'autres lumières que celles de la nature, juge mieux que ceux qui embarrassent le théâtre. St.-Év.'

From a study of contemporary documents, both those concerned with the theatre audience and others drawn from a wider field, it does seem fairly clear that on occasion the term *peuple* was used in the seventeenth century in a wide sense which included people who were far from plebeian in the more modern sense of the term, and which consequently took in at least a proportion of the middle classes. There is an interesting example of this sort of use of the term in one of the *Factums* of Furetière. In attacking his former colleagues of the Academy for their treatment of proverbs in their Dictionary, he declares: 'Ils ont cru par ces beaux proverbes rendre leur dictionnaire utile au *peuple*, mais ils se sont lourdement trompés; car il n'y a point de bourgeois qui n'en sache davantage que toute l'Académie et qu'Antoine Oudin qui a pris à tâche de les recueillir.'[1]

One of the contexts in which the term *peuple* is constantly used throughout the seventeenth century with reference to the theatre audience is in contrast to 'la cour'. The anonymous introduction to Du Ryer's *Arétaphile* and *Clitophon*, performed about 1628,[2] states that they were received 'avec un applaudissement universel *du peuple et de la cour*'. In 1637 Chapelain declared in a letter to Balzac that the qualities of *Le Cid* 'ont mérité l'applaudissement *du peuple et de la cour* qui n'étaient point encore accoutumés à telles délicatesses',[3] while in a letter to Scudéry in the same year Balzac twice uses the same phrase in speaking of Corneille's success: 'Il a trompé *toute la cour et tout le peuple*. . . . Il est plus fin que *toute la cour et tout le peuple*.'[4] Corneille himself had used the same phrase in his *Excuse à Ariste*, which had set off the controversy over *Le Cid*: 'Je satisfais ensemble et *peuple et courtisans*', he proudly declares.

The same expression continued to be used later in the century. In the preface to his *Amaryllis* (1653), a revised version of Rotrou's pastoral play, *Célimène*, Tristan declares: 'C'est ici un tableau où deux différents pinceaux ont contribué et fait une union assez belle puisque généralement *le peuple et la cour* y trouvent beaucoup de divertissement.' Fifteen years later Abbé de Pure, in his *Idée des spectacles anciens et modernes*,[5] states that he uses the term *comédie* for all the different kinds of theatrical performances 'parce que l'idée vulgaire et universelle les confond ordinairement, et que les connaissances trop fines pour le

---

[1] *Recueil des Factums d'Antoine Furetière*, ed. C. Asselineau (Paris, 1859), 2 vols., vol. i, p. 191.
[2] Bibliothèque Nationale, MS. fr. 25496.
[3] *Correspondance*, ed. T. de Larroque (Paris, 1880–3), 2 vols., vol. i, p. 156.
[4] Gasté, *Querelle du Cid*, p. 454.
[5] (Paris, 1668), p. 162.

peuple et pour les gens de la cour, les embarrassent beaucoup plus qu'elles ne les instruisent, et qu'ils s'en rebutent plutôt que d'en profiter'. In 1676 Corneille again used the expression in the poem which he addressed to the King on the revival of several of his plays at Versailles; of his last plays he writes:

> Le *peuple*, je l'avoue, *et la cour* les dégradent:
> J'affaiblis, ou du moins ils se le persuadent.[1]

Two years later the *Mercure Galant*, in discussing Hauteroche's comedy, *Les Nouvellistes*, declares that this author 'n'a pas moins diverti *la cour* que *le peuple*'.[2] Many more examples of the use of this expression in the seventeenth century could be quoted, but the reader's patience is no doubt already exhausted.

If so many examples of this expression have been set forth here, it is because it seems to throw light on at least one of the meanings attached to the word *peuple* in the seventeenth century when it was applied to the theatre audience. It seems reasonably clear that when the expression 'le peuple et la cour' is used, the word *peuple* is given a very wide meaning. It is obviously used to take in a very large group of people— all those in fact who did not belong to the world of the court, the middle classes as well as the lower orders. That this is sometimes the meaning of the word is made clear by the fact that an alternative expression substitutes *bourgeois* for *peuple*. In the 1650's Loret, in his *Muse historique*, links *bourgeois* and *courtisans* several times in speaking of theatre audiences. Boisrobert's tragi-comedy, *La Comtesse de Barcelone*, he informs his readers in 1653,

> . . . contenta tout à la fois
> Le courtisan et le bourgeois.[3]

Six years later, in retailing a rumour, subsequently proved false, of the death of the famous Italian actor Scaramouche, he begins his lament:

> O vous, bourgeois et courtisans,
> Qui faites cas des gens plaisants,
> O tous amateurs du théâtre,
> Dont moi-même suis idolâtre,
> Sanglotez, pleurez, soupirez . . .[4]

If the reader may legitimately feel some slight doubt as to whether

---

[1] *Œuvres*, ed. C. Marty-Laveaux (Paris, 1862–6), 12 vols., vol. x, p. 312.
[2] Jan. 1678, pp. 295–6.
[3] *La Muse historique*, ed. C. Livet (Paris, 1857–78), 4 vols., vol. i, p. 428.
[4] Ibid., vol. iii, p. 114.

'bourgeois et courtisans', in these and other examples which could be quoted, is used in exactly the same sense as 'le peuple et la cour', these uncertainties will presumably be removed by a passage in the *Avis au Lecteur* of *La Cocue imaginaire* of F. Donneau (1660) which seems to equate the two expressions. Speaking of the success achieved by Molière after his return to Paris with *L'Étourdi*, *Le Dépit amoureux*, *Les Précieuses ridicules*, and *Le Cocu imaginaire*, he says: '. . . *La cour* les a non seulement approuvés, mais encore *le peuple*, qui dans Paris sait parfaitement bien juger de ces sortes d'ouvrages.' He then goes on to speak of the success achieved by *Le Cocu imaginaire* despite the King's absence from Paris: 'quoique Paris fût, ce semble, désert, il s'y est trouvé encore assez de *personnes de condition* pour remplir plus de quarante fois les loges et le théâtre du Petit Bourbon, et assez de *bourgeois* pour remplir autant de fois le parterre'.

In the severely hierarchical society of seventeenth-century France it would not be surprising if at times the term *peuple* were made to cover a very wide section of society, up to and including at least some sections of the middle classes—anyone who had no connexion with the world of the court. If that were always the sense in which the term is used, a discussion of its application to a portion of seventeenth-century Paris theatre audiences would be easy; unfortunately this is not the case.

In contemporary writings about the theatre there exist a host of allusions, like the passage from La Bruyère quoted by Lancaster, to the presence of *le peuple* in the theatre; seldom is there anything in them which enables one to give even an approximate interpretation of their real meaning. What is one, for instance, to make of Scudéry's remark that with his tragi-comedy, *Orante* (performed in 1633), 'je tirai cent et cent fois des larmes non seulement du *peuple*, mais des plus beaux yeux du monde'?[1] Or of his statement in the preface to *Didon* (1637):

> Après cela, il ne me reste plus qu'à vous confesser ingénument que cette pièce est un peu hors de la sévérité des règles, bien que je ne les ignore pas; mais souvenez-vous, je vous prie, qu'ayant satisfait les savants par elle, il faut parfois contenter le *peuple* par la diversité des spectacles et par les différentes faces du théâtre.

And yet the same Scudéry in his onslaught on *Le Cid* can also use the term *peuple* in a context which seems at least to include the middle classes:

> Tout ce qui brille n'est pas toujours précieux . . . Aussi ne m'étonnai-je

---

[1] Preface to *Arminius* (Paris, 1643).

pas beaucoup que le *peuple* qui porte le jugement dans les yeux, se laisse tromper par celui de tous les sens le plus facile à décevoir; mais que cette vapeur grossière, qui se forme dans le parterre, ait pu s'élever jusqu'aux galeries, et qu'un fantôme ait abusé le savoir comme l'ignorance, et la cour aussi bien que le *bourgeois*, j'avoue que ce prodige m'étonne.[1]

This interpretation of Scudéry's words seems to be supported by another pamphlet in the same controversy, *Le Souhait du Cid*, the author of which retorts: 'Pourquoi trouvera-[t-]on étrange que le parterre s'accorde avec les galeries, et si la cour approuve ce que le bourgeois n'a pas rejeté, c'est l'action et non pas le temps qui agrée au spectateur.'[2]

The pamphlets of the *Querelle du Cid* are a mine of information (often, alas, contradictory) on the theatre audiences of the time, and contain many references to the presence of *le peuple* at the theatre. The only difficulty is to interpret them correctly. The author of *Le Juge-ment du Cid, composé par un Bourgeois de Paris, marguillier de sa paroisse* (Charles Sorel?), twice speaks of 'nous autres qui sommes du peuple',[3] and declares that his judgement on *Le Cid* 'est, ce me semble, le sentiment des honnêtes gens d'entre le *peuple*'.[4] The anonymous *Discours à Cliton* also seems to include bourgeois among the *peuple*. 'Je ne me laisse guère surprendre aux acclamations du *peuple*', he declares, 'et même je ne suis pas la voix commune des honnêtes gens ni le plus grand nombre qu'à la charge de raisonner avec eux.' The applause given to a new play in the theatre, he argues, consists of two very different things—'un doux murmure et comme un juste concert des personnes de condition' and a 'rumeur populaire' which is the result of an appeal to the senses, and not the minds, of the spectators. But, the author continues (although he remains anonymous, we know he was a play-wright), 'je me suis trouvé une fois dans le parterre et une autre fois dans les galeries à la représentation de ce nouveau poème; et je suis témoin de ce qu'en disent encore les savants et les ignorants, la cour et le *bourgeois* . . .'.[5]

Yet that no very precise meaning was often attached to the word *peuple* in our period is shown by Georges de Scudéry's comments in his *Apologie du Théâtre*[6] on the place of this section of the community in the theatre audiences of the time. He divides the spectators of the

[1] *Observations sur le Cid*, in Gasté, *Querelle du Cid*, p. 71.
[2] Ibid., p. 165.
[3] Ibid., pp. 239–40.   [4] Ibid., p. 231.
[5] Ibid., pp. 243–4.   [6] Paris, 1639.

theatre of his day into three classes: 'savants, préoccupés [i.e. pre-judiced] et ignorants', subdividing the last class into 'ignorants des galeries' and 'ignorants du parterre'.[1] If 'quelques jeunes gens de la cour' who fall into the first of these two subdivisions are fairly severely chastised by Scudéry, it is for the 'ignorants du parterre' that he re-serves his severest strictures:

Mais il s'en va temps, pour finir, de descendre des galeries au parterre et de dire un mot en passant à cet animal à tant de têtes et à tant d'opinions qu'on appelle *peuple*. Quelqu'un demandait un jour à Simonide, poète comique, pourquoi il ne trompait point les Thessaliens aussi bien que les autres Grecs: 'Parce, dit-il, qu'ils sont trop grossiers pour être trompés par moi'. . . Et de là vient qu'une partie de cette multitude ignorante que la farce attire à la comédie, écoute avec si peu d'attention les poèmes qu'on représente, parce que ce lui est un obstacle qui l'empêche d'arriver plus tôt à la fin que sa stupidité s'est proposée. Et de là procèdent ces risées impertinentes qui sou-vent naissent de la plus grave, de la plus sérieuse et de la plus importante action d'une tragédie. Mais puisque ces centaures, demi-hommes et demi-chevaux, ou comme dit un Italien,[2] 'Mezo huomo, mezo capra, e tuto bestia', ne sont pas capables de goûter les bonnes choses, qu'ils imitent au moins les oies qui passent sur le Mont Taurus, où les aigles ont leurs aires, c'est-à-dire, qu'ils portent une pierre au bec, qui les oblige au silence.[3]

While it is true that Georges de Scudéry had an inflated notion of his aristocratic birth, it still remains clear that he regards at least certain elements in the contemporary *parterre* as being of the most humble extraction as well as of the dimmest intelligence.

And yet we find in the following year a writer like Chapelain using the word *peuple*, not as a term of abuse, but in its widest possible sense, to include all the general public, when he writes of the early perform-ances of Corneille's latest tragedy: 'Pour les Horaces, les comédiens . . . ne les ont encore représentés que trois fois au *peuple*.'[4] Again, in 1653, when Loret describes the tremendous crowd at the 'Ballet du Roi', on the day in which he was present at it, he speaks of

> . . . tout autant d'affluence
> Et de *peuple* aussi grand concours
> Que les autres précédents jours.

But a fortnight later, in referring to the last performance of the ballet,

[1] p. 89.
[2] 'Guarini, *Pastor Fido*' (marginal note by Scudéry).
[3] *Apologie du Théâtre*, pp. 96–98.
[4] *Lettres*, vol. i, p. 627.

he does not describe the audience in a way which would suggest any noticeable plebeian element:

> Vous, cardinaux, princesses, princes,
> Gens de Paris, gens de provinces,
> Ambassadeurs et résidents,
> Présidentes et présidents,
> Conseillers et maîtres des comptes,
> Femmes de ducs, marquis et comtes,
> Abbés, prieurs, bénéficiers,
> Directeurs, banquiers, financiers,
> Polis, galants, coquets, coquettes,
> Marchandes, bourgeoises, soubrettes,
> Qui, pour plus aisément passer,
> Vous laissiez un peu caresser;
> Vieilles, vieillards, puceaux, pucelles,
> Enfin, tous ceux et toutes celles,
> Et moi tout aussi bien que vous,
> Qui d'un plaisir tout à fait doux
> Eûmes l'aimable jouissance,
> Voyant ce ballet d'importance
> Dans un auguste et brillant lieu,
> Disons-lui pour jamais adieu.[1]

Indeed, if we leave aside the *soubrettes*, who no doubt came with their mistresses, the different sections of the community enumerated by Loret do not descend lower than the presumably prosperous section of the middle classes.

In his various writings on the theatre D'Aubignac is full of allusions to *le peuple*. In his *Pratique du Théâtre* he is continually using the expression. 'J'écris seulement', he writes for instance, 'pour faire connaître au *peuple* l'excellence de leur [the dramatists'] art, et pour lui donner sujet de les admirer.' A few pages later we meet another familiar use of the term—'les pièces modernes qui ont trouvé grâce devant le *peuple* et même à la cour'. Later on he speaks of 'ces décorations dont la variété ravit toujours le *peuple*, et même les habiles, quand elles sont bien faites'.[2] However, vague and unsatisfactory as these and other references are, on one occasion D'Aubignac does at least attempt to define what he means by *le peuple*. In the passage in question, which comes from his *Deux dissertations concernant le poème dramatique* (1663), he maintains that during the performance of Corneille's *Sophonisbe* the

---

[1] *La Muse historique*, vol. i, pp. 348, 353.
[2] *La Pratique du Théâtre*, ed. P. Martino (Paris, 1927), pp. 18, 28, 102.

audience remained almost the whole time 'froid et sans émotion'. He continues:

> Car c'est une preuve infaillible que les affaires de la scène languissaient; le *peuple* est le premier juge de ces ouvrages. Ce n'est pas que je les commette au mauvais sentiment des courtauds de boutique et des laquais; j'entends par le peuple cet amas d'honnêtes gens qui s'en divertissent, et qui ne manquent ni de lumières naturelles, ni d'inclinations à la vertu, pour être touchés des beaux éclairs de la poésie et des bonnes moralités; car bien qu'ils ne soient peut-être pas tous instruits en la délicatesse du théâtre pour savoir les raisons du bien et du mal qu'ils y trouvent, ils ne laissent pas de le sentir. Ils ne connaissent pas pourquoi les choses sont telles qu'ils les sentent; mais ils ne laissent pas d'avoir dans les oreilles et dans le fond de l'âme un tribunal secret qui ne peut tromper, et devant lequel rien ne se déguise.[1]

Thus D'Aubignac regards the *peuple* as a group more elevated than the lowest ranks of society and one for whose natural taste he has some respect.

On the other hand the attitude taken up by Boileau in his *Art poétique* in his famous lines on Molière is altogether different. There is no question that the term *peuple* is used in a highly pejorative sense when he writes:

> Étudiez la cour et connaissez la ville:[2]
> L'une et l'autre est toujours en modèles fertile.
> C'est par là que Molière, illustrant ses écrits,
> Peut-être de son art eût remporté le prix,
> Si, moins ami du *peuple*, en ses doctes peintures,
> Il n'eût point fait souvent grimacer ses figures,
> Quitté pour le bouffon l'agréable et le fin,
> Et sans honte à Térence allié Tabarin . . .
> Le comique, ennemi des soupirs et des pleurs,
> N'admet point en ses vers de tragiques douleurs;
> Mais son emploi n'est point d'aller, dans une place,
> De mots sales et bas charmer la populace.

For him *peuple* and *populace* seem to be pretty nearly synonymous.

Peuple in its more or less plebeian sense continued to be applied to part of the theatre audience right to the end of the century. In 1696, for instance, the *Lettres historiques de La Haye*[3] speaks of the Paris

[1] p. 3.
[2] The meaning of this expression is discussed by Professor Erich Auerbach in a stimulating essay, entitled 'La Cour et la Ville', in his *Vier Untersuchungen zur Geschichte der französischen Bildung* (Berne, 1951). He also offers an interesting discussion of many other points dealt with in this chapter, including the meaning of the term *peuple*.
[3] Mar. 1696 (quoted in Mélèse, *Le Théâtre et le public*, p. 220).

theatres as 'ces spectacles où le *peuple* se va délasser quelquefois de son travail, et tâcher d'oublier les fâcheuses affaires de son domestique'.

If the term is vague in the extreme, the same cannot be said, however, of other expressions which are sometimes applied by writers of the time to part of the theatre audience—terms like 'menu peuple', 'petit peuple', or even 'racaille'. That these meant quite definitely a lowly section of the community seems certain, even if we must constantly bear in mind that the social outlook of the upper classes of seventeenth-century France inevitably led to some exaggeration when describing people of the lower ranks of society. There seems little doubt what Chapelain meant when he wrote in 1630 in his *Lettre sur la règle des vingt-quatre heures*:

Je veux que le poète s'accommode à l'inclination de l'assistance, mais non pas à son vice, et ne conseillerai jamais à mon ami de se faire Tabarin plutôt que Roscius, pour complaire aux idiots et à cette *racaille* qui passe en apparence pour le vrai peuple et qui n'en est en effet que sa lie et son rebut.[1]

The same word, *racaille*, is used in Sorel's *Maison des Jeux* (1642), though the person who makes use of it is contradicted by another of the speakers. The first speaker dislikes the 'galeries' (i.e. boxes) of the theatre because in them the spectator sees the stage only from the side; but his complaints about the *parterre* are far more bitter:

Le parterre est fort incommode pour la presse qui s'y trouve de mille marauds mêlés parmi les honnêtes gens, auxquels ils veulent quelquefois faire des affronts, et ayant fait des querelles pour un rien, mettent la main à l'épée et interrompent toute la comédie. Dans leur plus parfait repos ils ne cessent aussi de parler, de siffler et de crier, et pource qu'ils n'ont rien payé à l'entrée et qu'ils ne viennent là qu'à faute d'autre occupation, ils ne se soucient guère d'entendre ce que disent les comédiens. C'est une preuve que la comédie est infâme, de ce qu'elle est fréquentée par de telles gens, et l'on montre que ceux qui ont de la puissance dans le monde en font bien peu de cas, puisqu'ils n'empêchent point que toute cette *racaille* y entre sans payer, pour y faire du désordre.[2]

Much more detailed and precise is the denunciation of 'le vulgaire' in the *Argument* to Desmaretz de Saint-Sorlin's comedy, *Les Visionnaires*, published in 1637. The author answers in the most downright terms the criticism that his play 'n'était pas propre pour toutes sortes de gens, et que ceux qui n'ont aucun savoir, n'en pouvaient entendre beaucoup de mots'. Since when, he indignantly asks, have the ignorant

---

[1] *Opuscules critiques*, ed. A. C. Hunter (Paris, 1936), p. 125.
[2] *La Maison des Jeux* (Paris, 1642), 2 vols., vol. ii, pp. 424–5.

become so worthy of respect in France that one must seek to please them? 'Pensez', he continues, 'que l'on doit bien du respect ou à la bassesse de leur condition, ou à la dureté de leurs esprits, ou au mépris qu'ils ont fait des lettres, pour faire que l'on songe à les divertir!' The playwright's aim must be to win 'l'estime des honnêtes gens. Le *peuple* à l'esprit si grossier et si extravagant qu'il n'aime que des nouveautés grotesques.' He must write for an *élite*; as for the rest of his audience . . . . 'Après que les personnes raisonnables seront satisfaites, il en restera encore assez pour les autres, et plus qu'ils n'en méritent.' The *Argument* ends with the contemptuous quatrain:

> Ce n'est pas pour toi que j'écris,
> Indocte et stupide vulgaire;
> J'écris pour les nobles esprits.
> Je serais marri de te plaire.

Four years later, in the preface to his tragedy *Méléagre*, Benserade took up a very different standpoint. In this as in all his other plays, he declares, 'je tâche de satisfaire à tout ce qu'il y a d'habiles et d'ignorants; je veux bien m'élever, mais je ne veux pas qu'on me perde de vue, et si je veux être estimé de quelques-uns, je veux être entendu de tout le monde.' His preface ends with a quatrain which is clearly the counterpart of Desmaretz's parting shot:

> En vain de ce que je compose
> Les doctes paraissent contents;
> A ma gloire il manque une chose,
> Vulgaire, si tu ne m'entends.

Both the two most important dramatic theorists of the age, La Mesnardière and D'Aubignac, have some interesting observations to make on the place of the lower orders in the theatre. In the preliminary *Discours* of his *Poétique* (1639) the former devotes several pages to a violent attack on the sixteenth-century Italian commentator, Castelvetro, for his denial that poetry has any moral aim. Castelvetro, he declares with horror, 'soutient qu'elle a été formée, non seulement pour divertir, mais pour divertir le *peuple*; et non seulement le peuple, mais la vile populace, grossière, ignorante et stupide'.[1] La Mesnardière declares that as the first volume of his *Poétique* is reserved for tragedy, he will confine himself to that field, but he undertakes to examine in due course all the different kinds of poetry and to prove that 'aucun n'est si abject que de prendre pour sa fin le plaisir d'un *peuple* stupide'.[2]

[1] p. H.   [2] p. L.

Tragedy, he proceeds to argue, is an elevated literary form which portrays the destruction of empires and the changes which have taken place in the world through the mistakes of kings and princes. It is 'un poème grave et magnifique, qui a pour sujet ordinaire la révolution des états, la récompense des bons princes et la punition des méchants'.[1] So great is the gap between the exalted characters and actions portrayed in tragedy and the world of the common herd that 'si le *peuple* a quelque part en ces spectacles illustres, c'est seulement par la vue'.[2] If the lower orders were to be touched by tragedy, it would have to treat 'des aventures populaires'; but as it does not do so, 'il est fort aisé de juger que si la vile populace a quelque accès auprès de lui, c'est de la même manière qu'elle en a auprès des monarques qui se laissent voir aux peuples afin d'en être admirés'.[3] Passing from a discussion of the moral aim of tragedy to that of the pleasure which it gives, La Mesnardière declares that 'la multitude grossière ne peut trouver aucun plaisir dans un discours sérieux, grave, chaste et vraiment tragique, et . . . ce monstre à plusieurs têtes ne peut connaître pour le plus que des ornements de théâtre'.[4]

So far La Mesnardière's onslaught on the ignorance and stupidity of the common herd has been confined to generalities, without any specific reference to the presence of such unworthy spectators in the theatres of the Paris of his day; but he seems at this point to become more explicit when he declares: 'Les approbations ignorantes dont il flatte ordinairement les plus imparfaites pensées, témoignent qu'il n'a de l'estime que pour les choses ridicules; et les clameurs tumultueuses dont il étourdit les acteurs au milieu des beaux mouvements, font voir que, pour le dégoûter, il suffit d'être habile homme et d'écrire parfaitement.'[5] He goes on to stress this point further in the following sentence: 'Le plaisir intérieur que le poème bien entendu produit à un honnête homme qui n'en a pas appris les règles, est même trop spirituel pour toucher les sentiments d'un animal si stupide; et pour ressentir les effets de la science théâtrale, it faut être fort élevé au-dessus de la populace.' The society of Greece and Rome was very different from that of seventeenth-century France; if in ancient times playwrights could write for the multitude, 'les saltimbanques d'Italie, les faiseurs de sauts périlleux, les Zanis, les Pantalons, et autres gens de cette étoffe sont des acteurs proportionnés à la capacité du *peuple*, selon qu'elle est aujourd'hui'.[6] In the ancient world generals, dictators, and consuls

[1] p. M.   [2] p. N.   [3] p. O.
[4] p. P.   [5] p. Q.   [6] p. R.

'étaient du nombre des bourgeois et de celui des laboureurs'. Today all that has changed. 'Maintenant que . . . les honnêtes gens', La Mesnardière declares, 'ne sont plus semeurs de lentilles, ni conducteurs de labourage, tout ce qu'il y a de bien né, de raisonnable et de savant dans les états bien policés, est séparé d'avec le *peuple*, qui n'a pour toutes connaissances que celle des arts mécaniques, qu'il exerce par usage plutôt que par théorie.'[1]

If these pages of indignant denunciation of the heresy of Castelvetro are mainly filled with generalities about the incapacity of 'la vile multitude' to enjoy and profit from the noble genre of tragedy, they do occasionally make precise reference to the society and theatre audiences of seventeenth-century Paris. D'Aubignac, the other outstanding dramatic theorist of the age of Richelieu, is much more explicit in his references to the presence of the lower orders in the theatre of his day. Although it was not published until 1657, his *Pratique du Théâtre* was conceived and apparently largely written between 1640 and the death of his patron in 1642.[2] While D'Aubignac makes frequent use of the term *peuple* in senses which, as we have seen, it is not often easy to define, in his *Pratique du Théâtre* and in the *Projet pour le rétablissement du Théâtre Français* which was published with it he also employs less ambiguous terms, such as *petit peuple* and *menu peuple*, which can only refer to the presence in the contemporary Paris theatres of spectators from low down the social scale.

Thus he declares that, while the court prefers tragedies to comedies, 'parmi le petit peuple les comédies et même les farces et vilaines bouffonneries de nos théâtres sont tenues plus divertissantes que les tragédies'. The reason for this state of affairs is a simple one:

Dans ce royaume les personnes, ou de naissance, ou nourries parmi les grands, ne s'entretiennent que de sentiments généreux, et ne se portent qu'à de hauts desseins, ou par les mouvements de la vertu, ou par les emportements de l'ambition; de sorte que leur vie a beaucoup de rapport aux représentations du théâtre tragique. Mais la populace, élevée dans la fange et entretenue de sentiments et de discours déshonnêtes, se trouve fort disposée à recevoir pour bonnes les méchantes bouffonneries de nos farces, et prend toujours plaisir d'y voir les images de ce qu'elle a accoutumé de dire et de faire.[3]

In his *Projet pour le rétablissement du Théâtre Français* he returns to this

[1] pp. R–S.
[2] *Pratique du Théâtre*, ed. P. Martino, pp. xi–xii.
[3] Ibid., pp. 74–75.

theme in discussing the immorality which had brought upon the
theatre the condemnation of Catholic writers.

Bien qu'elle ait été absolument bannie du théâtre de feu Monsieur le Cardinal de Richelieu, il en reste encore néanmoins quelque trace sur ceux du
public, non seulement dans les farces sales et déshonnêtes, mais encore dans
les poèmes où les auteurs, par un mauvais désir de plaire au petit peuple,
représentent des histoires impudiques et de mauvais exemple.[1]

Moreover, he declares, the physical disposition of existing theatres
drives away most of the *honnêtes gens*:

. . . Les galeries et le parterre sont très incommodes, la plupart des loges
étant trop éloignées et mal situées, et le parterre n'ayant aucune élévation, ni
aucun siège; si bien que la sûreté n'y étant point, les gens d'honneur ne veulent pas s'exposer aux filous, les dames craignent d'y voir des épées nues, et
beaucoup de personnes n'en peuvent souffrir l'incommodité. Ainsi, le théâtre
étant peu fréquenté des honnêtes gens, il demeure décrédité comme un simple
batelage, et non pas estimé comme un divertissement honnête.[2]

There is no doubt some exaggeration in this picture of the contemporary theatre, whether D'Aubignac is speaking of the state of
affairs in 1657 or even in 1640; but in the detailed reforms which he
proposes he once again refers specifically to the presence of the *menu
peuple* among the theatre audiences of his day. He urges that the *parterre*
should be arranged on an incline and not on the flat, and that it should
be provided with fixed seats, 'ce qui empêchera même que les assistants
ne s'y battent, n'ayant aucun espace pour le faire'. In the splendid new
theatre of his dreams things would be arranged so that 'les sièges des
spectateurs soient distingués, sans que les personnes de condition y
soient mêlées avec le menu peuple'.[3]

References to the presence at the theatre of the *menu peuple* or the
petit peuple become rarer as the century moves on. In 1682, according
to the *Mercure*,[4] 'l'affluence du petit peuple fut fort grande' at the
Théâtre Italien, 'parce que le quartier en est très rempli'; but this was
not for one of the ordinary performances at the theatre. It was a free
performance given in honour of the birth of the Duc de Bourgogne;
the theatre no doubt admitted on that occasion many people who did
not normally frequent it.[5]

Indeed, Father Caffaro maintained in his defence of the theatre in his

---

[1] *Pratique du Théâtre*, p. 388.   [2] Ibid., p. 394.
[3] Ibid., p. 397.   [4] Aug. 1682, p. 111.
[5] For a more detailed discussion of free performances in Paris theatres see below,
pp. 215 ff.

Lettre d'un théologien (1694) that the poorer sections of the community did not normally go there. He proceeds to draw from this fact an ingenious answer to the charge of immorality which was levelled against the theatre:

A l'égard des confessions, je n'ai jamais pu, par leur moyen, entrevoir cette prétendue malignité de la comédie. Car si elle était la source de tant de crimes, il s'ensuivrait qu'il n'y aurait que les riches et ceux qui ont le moyen d'y aller qui fussent les plus grands pécheurs, et nous voyons cependant que cela est bien égal, et que les pauvres, qui ne savent pas ce que c'est que la comédie, ne tombent pas moins dans les crimes de colère, de vengeance, d'impureté et d'ambition.[1]

So far, in discussing the plebeian elements in the theatre audiences of the Classical Age, we have confined ourselves to a study of the documents of the time which deal in general terms with the presence in the contemporary theatre of *le peuple* or *le menu peuple*. Confusing and to some extent contradictory as many of these pieces of evidence are, they are unfortunately more numerous than precise references to the presence of specific representatives of the lower classes among the theatre audiences of the age. The latter are extremely rare and are generally of little assistance in forming a precise picture of a representative theatre audience of the time. Thus, in the description of the audience given by Bordelon in *Les Coudées franches* (1712),[2] we are shown, among the spectators in the *amphithéâtre*, 'Monsieur Ptipa, pâtissier; Madame Ptipa, sa femme; Madame Croustille, blanchisseuse; Jeannette, sa fille; Monsieur Lucignon, chandelier', but all these have been given free tickets by actors of their acquaintance, no doubt in return for professional services rendered.

Some further precise evidence is furnished by the scandals caused at the Comédie Française in the 1690's by the craze which broke out for interrupting the performances with *sifflets*. The following contemporary *chanson* relates to an incident at that theatre which led to the culprit being locked up for three weeks:

Chanson nouvelle sur la raillerie du boucher qui a sifflé à la Comédie.

> Je mérite qu'on me raille,
> Moi, pauvre marchand boucher,
> D'avoir, comme une canaille,
> A la comédie sifflé.

---

[1] C. Urbain and E. Levesque (eds.), *L'Église et le théâtre* (Paris, 1930), pp. 100–1.
[2] Vol. ii, pp. 118–19.

> J'étais parmi le beau monde,
> En faisant le fanfaron,
> Avec les brunes et les blondes,
> Contrefaisant le gascon. . . .[1]

The petition which the offender addressed from prison to the Lieutenant de police, La Reynie, throws further light on his social status and on the circumstances of his escapade. He wrote:

> René Caraque, marchand boucher, vous remontre très humblement qu'ayant trouvé l'occasion vendredi dernier d'un billet pour la Comédie Française, il y aurait été pour la première fois de sa vie. Les gens du parterre dans un entr'acte crièrent à haute voix à l'occasion d'un homme qui avait ôté sa perruque, 'Cachez vos oreilles', et excitèrent beaucoup de bruit; qu'à ce sujet l'exposant se servit d'un instrument avec lequel il éveille ses garçons le matin.

He then petitions for his release in order to prevent his business from being ruined: 'Il faudrait que ses étaux restassent fermés, ce qui le mettrait en risque de perdre toutes ses habitudes.'[2] Even though this was the delinquent's very first visit to a theatre, he was apparently a tradesman of some substance, employing enough assistants to require a whistle to wake them in the mornings.

However relevant it may be to the point under discussion, one almost hesitates to reproduce once again the famous couplet from Boileau's ninth Satire (1668):

> Un clerc pour quinze sous, sans craindre le hola,
> Peut aller au parterre attaquer *Attila*.[3]

Like most other documents on the subject it yields little precise information, even if it is subjected to laborious analysis. If we may presume that Boileau meant a lawyer's clerk,[4] it is still not clear how low in the social scale such a person came in seventeenth-century Paris, whether Boileau meant to imply that that was the most plebeian type to be encountered in contemporary theatre audiences, and, if so, whether such people were frequently to be found amongst the spectators. There are also contemptuous references in documents of the time to the presence of shop assistants in theatre audiences: D'Aubignac and

---

[1] Bibliothèque de l'Arsenal, *Recueil de Tralage*, vol. iv, MS. 6544, f. 204.
[2] *Recueil de Tralage*, vol. iv, f. 171.
[3] Corneille's tragedy *Attila* was first performed in Mar. 1667.
[4] '*Clerc*, signifie encore plus ordinairement, Celui qui écrit et travaille sous un homme de pratique' (*Dictionnaire de l'Académie Française*, 1694).

Bordelon speak of *courtauds de boutique*[1] and Mme de Sévigné of *garçons de boutique*.[2]

Before leaving this not very satisfactory discussion of the place of the lower orders in Paris theatre audiences in the seventeenth century, we must stop to consider the relatively frequent allusions in contemporary documents to the presence among the spectators of such low-born fellows as lackeys. Every undergraduate who has read Molière's *Critique de l'École des Femmes* will remember the well-known passage in which one of the female characters makes fun of the grimaces of the *précieuses* at the spicier parts of *L'École des Femmes*:

> Il y avait l'autre jour des femmes à cette comédie, vis-à-vis de la loge où nous étions, qui par les mines qu'elles affectèrent durant toute la pièce . . ., firent dire de tous côtés cent sottises de leur conduite, que l'on n'aurait pas dites sans cela; et quelqu'un même des laquais cria tout haut qu'elles étaient plus chastes des oreilles que de tout le reste du corps.[3]

This is no isolated allusion; they are to be found in contemporary writings from one end of the century to the other. In describing her visit to the theatre to see Racine's *Bajazet*, Mme de Sévigné speaks of the audience in these terms: 'Monsieur le Duc était derrière, Pomenars au-dessus, avec les laquais, son manteau dans son nez, parce que le comte de Créance le veut faire pendre, quelque résistance qu'il y fasse;[4] tout le bel air était sur le théâtre.'[5]

Although of very different social origins, pages and lackeys are often bracketed together as potential trouble-makers in documents of the time. In 1611 the Châtelet forbade 'tous pages, laquais et . . . quelques [*sic*] personnes de quelque qualité et condition qu'ils soient de forcer et faire aucunes insolences aux portes dudit Hôtel de Bourgogne'.[6] There is a vivid passage in Bruscambille's *Prologue de l'Impatience* on the same mischief-makers. After rebuking the spectators for their impatient shouts of 'Commencez, commencez', he goes on:

> A-t-on commencé, c'est pis qu'antan; l'un tousse, l'autre crache, l'autre pète, l'autre rit, l'autre gratte son cul. Il n'est pas jusques à Messieurs les pages et laquais qui n'y veulent mettre le nez, tantôt faisant intervenir les gourmades réciproquées, maintenant à faire pleuvoir des pierres sur ceux qui n'en peuvent mais. Pour eux je les réserve à leurs maîtres qui peuvent au

---

[1] See pp. 67 and 88.   [2] See p. 77.
[3] Sc. 3.
[4] Because he had run off with the Count's daughter.
[5] *Lettres*, ed. Monmerqué (Paris, 1862–6), 14 vols., vol. ii, p. 471 (15 Jan. 1672).
[6] Soulié, *Recherches sur Molière*, p. 155.

retour, avec une fomentation d'étrivières appliquées sur les parties posté-
rieures, éteindre l'ardeur de leurs insolences.[1]

Why did the lackeys come to the theatre? Was it because they chose
of their own free will to join the ranks of the spectators, or simply, as
Bruscambille seems to hint, because they accompanied their masters?
That the latter interpretation is correct would seem to emerge from
a passage in the *Apologie de Guillot Gorju* (1634), in which this well-
known farce actor speaks of the rows which sometimes took place in
the theatre: '. . . L'intention des comédiens, vous attirant en ce lieu,
c'est pour vous y donner un agréable divertissement, car ils sont les
plus fâchés quand il se fait du bruit. Pour preuve de ceci, c'est que si
vous les vouliez croire, jamais vous n'y améneriez vos laquais. . . .'[2] The
Gazette of Théophraste Renaudot mentions in 1641 a recent edict of the
Lieutenant de police which forbids servants to

porter épées, dagues, ni pistolets à la suite de leurs maîtres, et particulièrement à l'Hôtel de Bourgogne, Marais du Temple et autres lieux où sont permis les divertissements publics de la comédie, enjoint à leurs maîtres de veiller
sur leurs actions et les désarmer à peine de répondre des insolences qu'ils
feront et des demandes adjugées à ceux qui seront offensés.[3]

The presence of lackeys in the Paris theatre is attested down to the
end of the century. Tallemant tells us that the actor Floridor was
ragged by them because, being of Protestant origin, he bore the
Christian name of 'Josias': 'Autrefois, quand il paraissait du temps de
Montdory, les laquais criaient sans cesse: Josias, Josias! Ils le faisaient
enrager.'[4] In the second part of the *Roman comique* (1657), in discussing
the rise in .the status of actors, Scarron declares that 'la comédie' (i.e.
the theatre) has been purged of all licence and adds: 'Il serait à souhaiter
qu'elle le fût aussi des filous, des pages et des laquais et autres ordures
du genre humain que la facilité de prendre des manteaux y attire encore
plus que ne faisaient autrefois les mauvaises plaisanteries des farceurs.'[5]

Molière's reference to the presence of lackeys among the spectators
in his theatre in his *Critique de l'École des Femmes*, first performed in
June 1663, may be linked with an incident at the Palais Royal in

[1] *Œuvres* (Rouen, 1626), pp. 71–72.
[2] p. 25 (quoted in Rigal, *Théâtre français*, p. 210).
[3] 1641, No. 9, p. 42.
[4] *Historiettes*, vol. vii, p. 126. There is some difficulty about dates here, as Floridor
joined the Théâtre du Marais only after the enforced retirement of Montdory in 1637. See
S. W. Deierkauf-Holsboer, *Le Théâtre du Marais*, vol. i (Paris, 1954), p. 74.
[5] *Roman comique*, ed. E. Magne (Paris, 1937), p. 198.

February of the previous year when his actors joined the Italian company who shared the same theatre in making a complaint to the authorities. The Italian actors alleged that shortly before the beginning of their performance their porter and his assistants had been assaulted by 'quelques particuliers à eux inconnus qu'ils ont appris depuis être laquais et valets de chambre, voulant entrer sans payer ...'.[1] The precise status of these ruffians is not altogether clear, though one witness declared that some of them were 'les valets de chambre de MM. de Béthune et de Roquelaure'.[2] In 1672, at the beginning of the war with Holland, Mme de Sévigné wrote to her daughter that the Paris theatres were empty, and quoted her *maître d'hôtel* as saying: 'Madame, il n'y a plus que des garçons de boutique à la comédie; il n'y a pas seulement des filous, ni des pages, ni de grands laquais; tout est à l'armée.'[3] At the very end of the century we learn of a minor diplomatic incident which was caused when the Ambassador of Savoy insisted that the two pages and a lackey who accompanied him to the Comédie Française should be admitted free. The Chancellor, Pontchartrain, wrote on this occasion to the Secretary of State for Foreign Affairs, Torcy: 'Vous savez qu'il y a une ordonnance précise qui porte défenses à toutes personnes d'y entrer sans payer: elle s'exécute très ponctuellement à l'égard des officiers et pages du roi; les autres de sa livrée n'y entrent point même en payant.'[4]

This last remark is interesting. To an eighteenth-century editor of Molière like Bret it was a matter for surprise that in the *Critique de l'École des Femmes* there should be an allusion to the presence of lackeys in the theatre. 'On voit dans cette scène', he writes, '... que les laquais n'étaient pas encore exclus de nos spectacles, puisque Molière les fait même parler haut dans la salle, à l'occasion des grimaces que faisaient quelques femmes, à certains endroits de son *École des Femmes*.'[5] It is not an easy task to establish precisely at what date lackeys in livery were banned from the Comédie Française. For the Théâtre Italien it is relatively simple, since when it was reopened in 1716 there was issued an *Ordonnance pour empêcher les désordres qui pourraient arriver à la Comédie Italienne* which contains the following clause: 'Défend aussi à tous domestiques portant livrées sans aucune réserve, exception, ni

---

[1] E. Campardon, *Documents inédits sur J. B. Poquelin Molière* (Paris, 1871), p. 11.
[2] Ibid., pp. 28–29.
[3] *Lettres*, vol. iii, p. 103 (6 June 1672).
[4] *Correspondance administrative sous le règne de Louis XIV*, ed. G. B. Depping (Paris, 1850–5), 4 vols., vol. ii, p. 764.
[5] Molière, *Théâtre*, ed. A. Bret (Paris, 1773), 6 vols., vol. ii, p. 507.

distinction d'entrer à ladite Comédie même en payant.'[1] It is probable that a similar ban was imposed even earlier at the Comédie Française, but it is unfortunately difficult to find the relevant *Ordonnance du Roi*. In the Collection Delamare at the Bibliothèque Nationale there is a gap in the collection of *Ordonnances du Roi* relating to the Paris theatres between that of 18 April 1703 and one issued on 10 April 1720. The latter, entitled *Ordonnance de Sa Majesté pour la tranquillité des spectacles*, no doubt reproduces an earlier edict; it contains the clause: 'Défend . . . à tous domestiques portant livrées, sans aucune réserve, exception ni distinction d'entrer à l'Opéra ou à la Comédie, même en payant.'[2]

Now that we have conscientiously set forth every allusion encountered in the course of these investigations to the presence in the seventeenth-century theatre of the lower orders of the time, we may, it is hoped, take the liberty of stating what seems to us the most reasonable interpretation of the documents, rare and contradictory as they are. If one starts with the assumption that at the beginning of the century the theatre in Paris was an overwhelmingly plebeian entertainment, then it is logical to hold, as Lancaster does, that it did not sud-

[1] E. Campardon, *Les Comédiens du Roi de la troupe italienne pendant les deux derniers siècles* (Paris, 1880), 2 vols., vol. ii, p. 238. There is a reference to this ban on lackeys in the prologue, entitled *L'Auteur superstitieux*, to Boissy's comedy *La Critique* (1732). Arlequin, the valet of a playwright who, in his suspense over the fate of his new play, has struck him, exclaims (Sc. 3):

> Que n'en puis-je au parterre aller prendre vengeance!
> A messieurs mes pareils pourquoi l'interdit-on?
> Je sifflerais alors, mais sur un joli ton!
> Quel plaisir, pour vingt sols, de huer comme un diable!

Lackeys were banned from the Opéra Comique when it was taken over by Jean Monnet in 1743. See his memoirs, published under the title of *Supplément au Roman comique* (London, 1772), 2 vols., vol. i, pp. 145–7: 'La livrée y était en possession du parterre; elle décidait des pièces, sifflait les acteurs, et quelquefois même ses maîtres, quand ils s'avançaient trop sur le devant de la scène. . . . Voulant y mettre de la décence et de l'ordre, je sollicitai et j'obtins une ordonnance du Roi qui défendait les entrées à la livrée.'

[2] Bibliothèque Nationale, Ms. fr. 21625, f. 243v. The absence of lackeys from at least part of the house is mentioned as early as 1690 in Furetière's dictionary which defines one of the meanings of the word *paradis* thus: 'en termes de comédie est le troisième et dernier rang des galeries qui sont autour de la salle, qui était autrefois occupé par les laquais et qu'on loue maintenant'. There are some puzzling references to the presence of lackeys at the Comédie Française in the early eighteenth century in Lancaster's *Comédie Française 1701–1774* (p. 594). In discussing the theatre audience of the period, he speaks of 'the lackeys and coachmen to whom Lesage refers as occupying the third tier of boxes', but without giving any reference. In a footnote he adds: 'According to the *Registres*, Mme Bouchu engaged a seat in this part of the house for her lackey on September 11, 1701'; but an examination of the Registers in the Archives of the Comédie Française produced no result, at least under that date.

denly cease to appeal to the lower orders, despite the fairly steep rise in theatre prices which took place. A ticket to the *parterre* cost normally at the beginning of the century only 5 sous, whereas by the middle of the century the price had risen to 15, indeed to 30 during the first run of most new plays. While the opening chapter of this book has sought to establish that not only the lower classes of society, but also their betters, from the King and court downwards, did enjoy theatrical performances in this early period of the century, no attempt was made there to define how plebeian the audience really was at this date, for the excellent reason that the available documents are too insignificant for one even to begin to produce an answer to this question.[1] As the century wears on, our knowledge, though still very far from adequate, does grow, as documents become slightly less rare. There can be no question that the audience of Corneille, Molière, and Racine was a very mixed one when their plays were first performed in the theatres of the capital. Undoubtedly the lower orders were not entirely unrepresented in the theatre of the time. Lackeys, shop-assistants, and lawyers' clerks, for instance, are specifically referred to in the documents of the time. If the term *peuple* as applied to part of the theatre audience has been shown to have a very elusive meaning and to have varied almost from writer to writer, there can be no question of what is meant by terms like *petit peuple* and *menu peuple*.

Yet the question is not wholly disposed of when this has been said. One wonders, first, whether such plebeian elements continued through-

---

[1] The only really precise document belongs to the period immediately prior to the one under discussion. In his *Remonstrances très humbles au Roy de France* (n.p., 1588) Rolland du Plessis denounces 'les ieux et spectacles publics qui se font lesdits iours de festes et Dimanches, tant par des estrangers Italiens que par des François, et par dessus tous ceux qui se font en une Cloaque & maison de Sathan, nommee l'hostel de Bourgongne, par ceux qui abusivement se disent Confraires de la Passion de Jesus-Christ.

'En ce lieu se donnent mille assignations scandaleuses au preiudice de l'honnesteté & pudicité des femmes et à la ruine des familles des pauvres artisans, desquels la salle basse est toute plaine, & lesquels plus de deux heures avant le jeu, passent leur temps en devis impudiques, en ieux de cartes & de dez, en gourmandise & yvrongnerie tout publiquement, d'où viennent plusieurs querelles & batteries . . .

'Par ce moyen Dieu est grandement offensé tant en ladite transgression des festes, que par les susdits blasphemes, ieux et impudicitez qui s'y commettent. D'avantage Dieu y est courroucé en l'abus et prophanation des choses sainctes, dont ils le servent. Et le public interessé par la des-bauche et ieux des artisans . . .

'Ceux qui deffendent telles choses disent une seule raison d'apparance, assavoir que tels ieux & spectacles sont bons pour le menu peuple, afin de le destourner des berlans & autres desbauches qu'il fait lesdits iours de festes, & qu'apres avoir travaillé toute la sepmaine en peine & tristesse, cela luy sert de resioüyssance & plaisir, & le retire d'autres vices plus grands.' (pp. 182–7.)

out the century to form part of theatre audiences. There is certainly no precise documentary evidence (except possibly in the case of lackeys) to suggest that their importance, such as it was, diminished after, say, the middle of the seventeenth century. But there is an interesting pointer, which can only be discussed fully in the following chapter in dealing with Paris theatre audiences in the eighteenth century:[1] there is, we shall then see, a considerable amount of evidence to show that in the last twenty or thirty years of the Ancien Régime the appearance in the theatre of more humble members of society was looked upon as a new phenomenon, one which put an end to a state of affairs of long standing. Judging from the evidence available, writers of the 1760's and 1770's seem to have felt that the appearance of these more plebeian spectators in the theatre was an encroachment upon the monopoly of such entertainments which had long been enjoyed by the upper classes of society, from the aristocracy down to the cultured sections of the middle class. If in the eighteenth century, down to at least 1750 or 1760, the theatre audiences were restricted in this way, it seems a fair assumption that, fifty or sixty years earlier, the place occupied in them by more plebeian elements must already have been small. This is, of course, a mere hypothesis in support of which no precise facts can for the moment be adduced.

More important is the point that, granted that the lower classes of society were not entirely unrepresented in the theatre audiences of the age of Corneille, Molière, and Racine, it still remains to determine what proportion of the audience they formed and what influence they exercised on the drama of the period. In general it is agreed that the literature of seventeenth-century France appealed in the first instance to a relatively narrow section of the community—to the 'honnêtes gens', to the polite society of Paris and the court. This did not mean that the literature of the period was read only by the upper classes of society; it no doubt also reached middle and lower middle-class households. Books penetrated to people of all classes who happened to be able to read—to lackeys and servant-maids as well as to princes and duchesses. But the fact remains that they were written primarily to appeal to a more restricted public, to those sections of society which moved in the orbit of the court of the French kings in or near Paris.

Unquestionably the Paris theatre audiences of our period were much more mixed than one might at first imagine; even the lower orders of society were not entirely unrepresented there. Yet their influence on

[1] See below, pp. 206 f.

the general level of taste in drama would seem to have been negligible; when their presence in the audience is mentioned at all by playwrights and critics, it is with the profoundest contempt. Moreover, a close study of the available documents would suggest that, at any rate from about 1630 onwards, the numbers of such people were small. The *parterre* of the different Paris theatres of this age was composed, not of plebeian groundlings, but for the most part of solid bourgeois, with at least a sprinkling of noblemen.

(iii) *The Middle Classes and the Theatre*

In considering the place of the middle classes in the theatre audiences of seventeenth-century Paris we may begin with the well-established fact that it was quite common for playwrights or aspiring playwrights to stand among the crowd in the *parterre*, at least until the success of their plays entitled them to free admission to the theatre. Pierre Corneille sat in a box at the first performance of his younger rival's *Britannicus*.[1] Twenty-five years earlier, in *La Suite du Menteur*,[2] he made Dorante and his servant, Cliton, discuss putting their new adventures on the stage as in *Le Menteur*:

CLITON: Mais peut-on l'ajuster dans les vingt et quatre heures?
DORANTE: Qu'importe?
CLITON: A mon avis, ce sont bien les meilleures;
         Car, grâces au bon Dieu, nous nous y connaissons;
         Les poètes au parterre en font tant de leçons,
         Et là cette science est si bien éclaircie
         Que nous savons que c'est que de péripétie,
         Catastase, épisode, unité, dénoûment,
         Et quand nous en parlons, nous parlons congrûment.

We have already quoted the passage in Sorel's *Maison des Jeux* in which one of the speakers denounces the presence of the *racaille* in the *parterre*;[3] his statements are, however, contradicted by another character who replies to his objections about the unsuitability of existing theatres:

Mais je me souviens que vous avez déclaré que le lieu où se fait l'assemblée vous déplaît, et que vous ne vous trouvez pas bien aux loges, pource qu'il n'y a que les premières qui soient bonnes et qu'aux autres l'on ne voit les acteurs que de loin et de côté. L'on s'approche comme l'on veut au parterre,

[1] Boursault, *Artémise et Poliante* (Paris, 1670), p. 3.
[2] Act V, Sc. 5. (This passage was dropped after the 1656 edition.)
[3] See above, p. 68.

mais j'ai vu des gens qui se tenaient si mal à propos sur la gravité qu'ils eussent cru être déshonorés de se placer en ce lieu-là, d'autant qu'ils disaient que ce n'était que pour les gens de pied, comme s'il n'était permis de s'asseoir qu'aux gens de cheval ou de carrosse. S'ils entendaient aussi quelque rencontre de bouffon qui ne leur plut pas, ils disaient dédaigneusement que c'était des railleries à faire rire le parterre. Cependant l'on y voyait quelquefois de fort honnêtes gens, et même la plupart de nos poètes qui sont les plus capables de juger des pièces, n'y vont point ailleurs.[1]

In 1655 the *gazetier* Jean Loret tells us how he frequented the *parterre* of the Hôtel de Bourgogne 'en payant des sols quinze ou trente' (the higher price, of course, during the first run of new plays); and in 1657 he mentions that he had seen Thomas Corneille's *Timocrate* 'pour trente sous'. When the *Précieuses ridicules* had begun its triumphant run at Molière's theatre with prices doubled, 'j'y portai trente sous', Loret tells us.[2]

The same weight cannot be attached to the not very convincing, but rather amusing story of how Racine's rival, Pradon, went and joined the crowd in the *parterre* when one of his plays was being performed in order to discover the public's reactions to it. The play, so the story goes, was 'sifflée' from the very first act, but, despite his anger, Pradon took the advice of a friend and joined in these expressions of disapproval. This landed him in a quarrel with one of the spectators who said to him angrily: 'Pourquoi sifflez-vous, monsieur? La pièce est belle; son auteur n'est pas un sot, il fait figure et bruit à la cour.' Finally the episode ended in a free fight.[3] A very picturesque tale, but scarcely one that can be readily believed.

More importance is obviously to be attached to such documents as we have encountered for the end of the seventeenth and the beginning of the eighteenth centuries. In the preface to his tragedy, *Gabinie* (1699), Brueys complains that at its first performance 'on vit dans le parterre deux ou trois auteurs, qu'on ne connaîtrait pas, quand même je les nommerais, qui cabalaient ouvertement de tous côtés pour faire tomber cette tragédie, et qui en disaient tout haut eux seuls ce que le public a dit de leurs ouvrages, qu'on ne revoit plus sur le théâtre'. The presence of writers in the *parterre* is commented on amusingly in Regnard's *Critique du Légataire universel* (1708). The *poète* of this little play, M. Boniface, complains:

[1] *La Maison des Jeux*, vol. ii, pp. 472–3.
[2] *La Muse historique*, vol. ii, pp. 108, 292; vol. iii, p. 137.
[3] Vigneul-Marville, *Mélanges d'histoire et de littérature* (Paris, 1725), 3 vols., vol. ii, pp. 89–90.

Pour moi, j'étais dans le parterre à la première représentation; il ne m'en a jamais tant coûté pour voir une mauvaise comédie; une moitié de mon justau-corps fut emportée par la foule, et j'eus bien de la peine à sauver l'autre, au milieu des flots de laquais qui m'inondèrent de cire en sortant, et me brûlè-rent tout un côté de ma perruque.

His aristocratic hearers do not waste any sympathy on his misfortunes. The Countess in the play retorts: 'Les auteurs qui ont les habits aussi mûrs que le vôtre, Monsieur Boniface, ne doivent point se trouver dans le parterre à une première représentation.' The Marquis then joins in: 'Madame la Comtesse a raison. Vous êtes là un tas de mauvais poètes cantonnés par pelotons (je ne parle pas de ceux qui sont avoués d'Apol-lon, dont on doit respecter les avis), vous êtes là, dis-je, comme des âmes en peine, tout prêts à donner l'alarme dans votre quartier, et à sonner le tocsin sur un mot qui ne vous plaira pas.'[1] In the following year, in his *Critique du Turcaret*, Lesage also refers to the presence of cabals of authors in the *parterre* at the first performance of his play.[2] It remained the custom for authors to frequent the *parterre* of the different Paris theatres throughout the eighteenth century.

It may be objected that in the seventeenth century there was too much poverty among the mass of writers, that there were too many 'poètes crottés', to use the language of the time, for the presence of authors in the *parterre* to throw much light on its social composition and in particular to prove that it contained many solid bourgeois. The argument has some force; there is, however, sufficient evidence from other sources to prove that the middle classes were strongly represented in the *parterre*.

We have already seen[3] how the expression *peuple* which was applied to part of the theatre audience often included in the seventeenth century members of the middle class. On many occasions indeed con-temporaries speak of the audience as consisting of *nobles* and *bourgeois*. For instance, in his *Apologie pour Malefas* (1633), in which he alleged that Richelieu's henchman, Barthélemy Laffemas, had once been an actor, Paul Hay du Châtelet wrote jeeringly:

Le sort encore un coup t'appelle au théâtre.
Ton visage blanchi de farine et de plâtre
Fera rire bientôt le noble et le *bourgeois*.[4]

---

[1] Sc. 3.
[2] See both scenes of the *Critique*.
[3] See above, pp. 55 f.
[4] Lachèvre, *Recueils collectifs de poésies libres et satiriques*, vol. i, p. 247.

Again, Loret informs us in his *Muse historique*,[1] in 1659, that at Molière's theatre Magnon's tragedy, *Zénobie*,

> S'y joue une seconde fois
> Pour le noble et pour le *bourgeois*.

More often still, the bourgeois are mentioned in their own right as an important section of the audience. An anonymous pamphlet attacking Corneille, *L'Anatomie du Cid*, speaks of duels on the stage as 'des jeux d'enfants pour faire rire les *bourgeois*'.[2] The *Affiche pour les Comédiens* which Scarron wrote for his comedy, *Jodelet souffleté*, performed about 1645, addresses first officers, courtiers, and ladies, and then goes on:

> Conseillers, financiers, *bourgeois*,
> Accourez au Marais vous donner au cœur joie,
> Seuls, deux à deux, ou trois à trois,
> Mais tous avec belle monnaie.[3]

In his controversy with Corneille in the 1660's Abbé d'Aubignac makes several mentions of bourgeois among the audience of the time. 'Il y a bien de la différence', he informs Corneille, 'entre un honnête homme qui fait des vers et un poète en titre d'office. . . . Mais le poète qui fait profession de fournir le théâtre et d'entretenir pendant toute sa vie la satisfaction des *bourgeois* ne peut souffrir de compagnon.'[4] A few pages later he expresses the hope that Pierre Corneille's younger brother, Thomas, will not produce any more plays like his *Camma* and *Démétrius* which, he declares, 'n'ont été que des escroqueries pour nos *bourgeois*'.[5]

In the same year in his *Zélinde*, a satirical comedy directed against Molière after the success of *L'École des Femmes*, Donneau de Visé makes one of his characters speak of the popularity of the theatre at this time: 'Les personnes de qualité l'aiment passionnément, et les *bourgeois* ne l'aiment pas moins.'[6] In announcing Molière's *Dom Juan* in his *Muse historique* in 1665, Loret says of the spectacular effects which it contains:

> Pour les changements de théâtre
> Dont le *bourgeois* est idolâtre,
> Selon le discours qu'on en fait,
> Feront un surprenant effet.[7]

---

[1] Vol. iii, p. 140.

[2] G. L. van Roosbroeck, 'Un document inconnu sur la Querelle du Cid: *L'Anatomie du Cid*', *Revue d'histoire littéraire de la France* (1925), p. 249.

[3] *Œuvres* (Paris, 1786), 7 vols., vol. vii, p. 345.

[4] *Quatrième dissertation servant de réponse aux calomnies de M. Corneille* (Paris, 1663), p. 119.   [5] Ibid., p. 131.

[6] Sc. 7.   [7] Vol. iv, p. 312.

Three years later, in his *Idée des spectacles anciens et modernes*, Abbé de Pure complains bitterly of the disorders caused in the different Paris theatres by a lot of swashbucklers who forced their way in without paying and by their unruly conduct drove away 'les vrais curieux et les bons *bourgeois*'. He also suggests that the actors ought in their own interest to begin their performances earlier, at half past three in winter and at half past four in summer. 'Les *bourgeois* et les *bourgeoises*', he goes on, 'qui ordinairement craignent plus les filous que le serein, y courraient en foule dans les deux saisons, surtout si cette première règle était suivie de la sûreté dont nous avons parlé, de quelque soin de leur commodité, et de leur faire tenir des sièges dans le parterre.'[1]

The importance of the bourgeois in the contemporary audience is underlined by Chappuzeau in his *Théâtre Français* (1674). If the different theatres avoid performing on Wednesdays and Saturdays, it is, he declares, because they are 'jours de marché et d'affaires où le *bourgeois* est plus occupé qu'en d'autres'; Thursday is another blank day, 'étant comme consacré en bien des lieux pour un jour de promenade, surtout aux académies et aux collèges'.[2] He also assures us that the Marais theatre, thanks to its actors, the support of prominent authors, and its spectacular plays (*pièces à machines*), easily overcame 'le dégoût que l'éloignement du lieu pouvait donner au *bourgeois*, surtout en hiver'.[3] Like de Pure, he refers to the presence of rowdies in the theatre, 'ce qui causait souvent à la porte ou au parterre d'étranges désordres, qui dégoûtaient les *bourgeois* de la comédie'. However, the royal edict of 1673 has restored order, so that now 'le *bourgeois* peut venir avec plus de plaisir à la comédie'.[4]

Shortly afterwards, in his attack on the new vogue of the opera in his *Épître à M. de Niert* (1677), La Fontaine tells us something of the place of the middle classes in the audience of his period. He speaks, first, of the temporary appeal made by the spectacular *pièces à machines*:

> Des machines d'abord le surprenant spectacle
> Éblouit le *bourgeois* et fit crier miracle:
> Mais la seconde fois il ne s'y pressa plus;
> Il aima mieux le *Cid, Horace, Héraclius*.

But now the opera enjoys a quite different vogue:

---

[1] pp. 172–3.
[2] *Le Théâtre Français*, ed. P. L. Jacob (Brussels, 1867), p. 60.
[3] Ibid., p. 100.
[4] Ibid., pp. 90, 120.

Il a l'or de l'abbé, du brave, du commis,
La coquette s'y fait mener par ses amis;
L'officier,[1] le marchand tout son rôti retranche,
Pour y pouvoir porter tout son gain le dimanche.

Ten years later, when the Comédie Française was compelled to seek a new home and, wherever it turned, encountered opposition from the people of the district where it had chosen a site for its new theatre, Racine wrote to Boileau to tell him of the opposition of the inhabitants of the parish of Saint André to its establishment in their midst:

L'alarme est grande dans le quartier, tous les bourgeois, qui sont gens de palais,[2] trouvant fort étrange qu'on vienne leur embarrasser leurs rues. M. Billard[3] surtout, qui se trouvera vis-à-vis de la porte du parterre, crie fort haut; et quand on lui a voulu dire qu'il en aurait plus de commodité pour s'aller divertir quelquefois, il a répondu fort tragiquement: 'Je ne veux point me divertir.'[4]

From this one may conclude that it would not have been unheard of for a distinguished lawyer to have frequented the *parterre* of the theatre.

In the *Théâtre Gherardi*, that is in scenes in French performed at the Théâtre Italien between about 1680 and 1697, there are a number of references to the presence of *bourgeois* in the audiences of these years. Thus in Regnard's *Critique de l'Homme à bonnes fortunes*, performed in 1690, one of the characters is a *procureur-fiscal*[5] who declares: 'Tenez, voilà tout ce que j'ai pu sauver de mon manteau, j'ai laissé le reste au parterre.'[6]

In the final scene of *Les Chinois*, a comedy by Regnard and Dufresny which was performed in 1692, Colombine criticizes the Comédie Française, while Arlequin is made to defend it. Colombine attacks the habit of the rival theatre of doubling its prices during the first run of new plays, to which Arlequin replies: 'Est-ce qu'un *bourgeois* doit plaindre trente sols pour être logé pendant deux heures dans l'hôtel le plus magnifique et le plus doré qui soit à Paris?' Colombine then ridicules the iron railing which at the Comédie Française separated the stage from the *parterre*, and contrasts the practice of the Italians, providing

---

[1] The context does not make the meaning altogether clear; the word might here be used in the seventeenth-century sense of holders of *offices*, official posts.

[2] 'Lawyers.'

[3] A famous *avocat*.

[4] Racine, *Œuvres*, ed. P. Mesnard (Paris, 1865–73), 9 vols., vol. vi, pp. 590–1.

[5] 'L'officier qui a soin des intérêts d'un seigneur et des vassaux de sa terre, dans l'étendue de cette terre' (*Dictionnaire de l'Académie*, 1694).

[6] Sc. 1.

incidentally a very vivid picture of the spectators on the stage and those below in the pit:

Les Italiens donnent un champ libre sur la scène à tout le monde. L'officier vient jusques sur le bord du théâtre étaler impunément aux yeux du marchand la dorure qu'il lui doit encôre. L'enfant de famille, sur les frontières de l'orchestre, fait la moue à l'usurier qui ne saurait lui demander ni le principal, ni les intérêts. Le fils, mêlé avec les acteurs, rit de voir son père avaricieux faire le pied de grue dans le parterre pour lui laisser quinze sols de plus après sa mort.

A similar glimpse of the middle-class members of the audience is afforded by Dufresny's *Départ des Comédiens*, performed at the Théâtre Italien in 1694, in a scene in which the actors address the audience and Colombine exclaims:

> Adieu, bons *bourgeois* de Paris,
> Qui veniez nous voir le dimanche.[1]

More significant and precise is a statement of the *Lieutenant de police*, D'Argenson, about the composition of the *parterre* of the Comédie Française in 1700. He speaks of the greater part of the large number of spectators present in the *parterre* on a day when disorders took place at that theatre as being 'gens de collège, de palais ou de commerce'.[2] Even more significant perhaps is the fact that in the *règlements* of the Comédie Française of 1688 and 1697 the choice of parts of the theatre offered to 'Messieurs les Commissaires du quartier et Monsieur le Commissaire Labbé', who were among those admitted free, was 'au parterre et amphithéâtre et théâtre à leur choix', which surely proves that there was nothing socially degrading in standing in the *parterre*.[3]

A vivid picture of the audience at the Comédie Française at the end of our period is provided by Abbé Bordelon's satirical work, *Les Coudées franches* (1712). Some of the middle-class spectators whom he describes are in boxes. There is, for instance, the stupid 'bon bourgeois' with the whole of his stupid family and appendages, all of whom have crowded into one box—a wife, two daughters, his son together with his tutor, his nephew, as well as a maid and a lackey.[4] We are also shown in another box two daughters of an *avocat*, who are later joined, much against their will, by two 'femmes de maltôtiers'.[5] We are then invited to 'entendre les discours de quatre marchandes, qui sont placées

[1] Sc. 9.
[2] *Notes*, ed. L. Larchey and E. Mabille (Paris, 1866), p. 20.
[3] Bonnassies, *La Comédie Française. Histoire administrative*, pp. 113, 119.
[4] Vol. ii, p. 84.   [5] Vol. ii, pp. 74, 78.

dans la cinquième loge des premières'. These could scarcely be regarded as regular theatre-goers, and their husbands even less so. One of the four complains of the bad lighting, and exclaims: 'Il m'arrive une pauvre fois l'an de venir à la comédie. . . . Mon mari qui doit se trouver au parterre sera bien fâché, quand il verra qu'on ne remarquera point sa chère petite femme.' A second exclaims: 'Pour le mien il n'a pas cette curiosité', and the third adds: 'Ni le mien aussi; il aime mieux aller jouer à la boule.' None of the four women knows what play is to be performed, but then, as one of them puts it, 'Ni moi aussi; que m'importe? Je ne viens à la comédie que pour montrer que j'y vais.'[1]

The husband of one of these women had, as we have seen, a ticket for the *parterre*. Other glimpses of this section of the audience are provided by Bordelon. He shows us, first, a scene in which appear two *petits maîtres presque ivres*, an *abbé* and a painter. The first *petit maître* exclaims: 'Burlon, mon ami, nous sommes ici au milieu de bien des *bourgeois*! Que ne restions-nous là . . . là . . . où nous étions?' His friend replies: 'Cela est . . . oui, cela est vrai. Ah! ah! mes jambes sont drôles! . . . il faut que je m'appuie sur un de ces *bourgeois* pour les soulager; allons, tenons ferme' (it is actually the *abbé* who enjoys the favour of being leant upon).[2] In another scene Bordelon presents a '*bourgeois* qui se pique de bel esprit' and two writers, one of whom is the author of the play which is about to be performed. The latter has a grievance:

N'a-t-elle point été sifflée la première fois par quelque *bourgeois* ou par quelques courtauds de boutique, à cause que les acteurs n'avaient pas d'assez beaux habits; ou par quelques malendurants, lassés de se tenir longtemps sur leurs jambes, avant qu'on la commençât? Il ne faut rien pour mettre ces sortes de gens en mauvaise humeur.[3]

Although these scraps of information about the audience of the Comédie Française at the beginning of the eighteenth century are tantalizingly incomplete, they do give us some notion of the audience of the time, particularly of its bourgeois members.

It is a curious fact that, so far as evidence concerning the presence of the middle classes in the theatre in our period goes, the richest supply of precise contemporary documents should be those referring to the 'marchands de la rue Saint-Denis'. 'Marchands' is a vague term, and it is therefore important to be quite clear that the 'marchands de la rue Saint-Denis' who are referred to in contemporary documents as assiduous spectators in the *parterre*, were not small shopkeepers. It is

---

[1] Vol. ii, pp. 80–81.   [2] Vol. ii, pp. 126–7.
[3] Vol. ii, p. 137.

true that in the course of the seventeenth century the fashionable shopping centre of Paris tended to shift from the Rue Saint-Denis to the neighbourhood of the Louvre, the Tuileries, and the Palais-Royal, with the result that by the beginning of the eighteenth century trade there had become largely wholesale. The *Livre commode des adresses de Paris* (1694) lists among the inhabitants of the street, in addition to actors like Scaramouche and Raymond Poisson, two *échevins*, several bankers (including the notorious Samuel Bernard), and a number of drapers, mercers, and hosiers. In his *Curiosités de Paris* (1716) Saugrain describes the Rue Saint-Denis as one of the finest in Paris and adds: 'C'est là que se tiennent les boutiques des plus grands négociants de Paris. On y débite les étoffes de laine, de soie, de draps d'or et d'argent, le fer, la quincaillerie, l'épicerie. Ces maisons vendent partout en gros et font leurs principales affaires avec la province et l'étranger.'[1]

In the period which particularly concerns us—the 1660's—the Rue Saint-Denis was still rather the centre of an active retail trade in luxury goods. The action of Donneau de Visé's *Zélinde*, one of the plays attacking Molière which followed the success of *L'École des Femmes*, takes place 'dans la rue Saint-Denis, dans la chambre d'un marchand de dentelles'. In the second scene the merchant, Argimont, receives a visit from the servant of another merchant in the same street who has been sent by his master to ask him to book a box for the following Sunday so that they and two ladies can see Molière's *Critique de l'École des Femmes*. Argimont agrees to do so, but, when the servant has gone, he adds:

> Ce n'est pas que je ne l'aie déjà vue plusieurs fois. La plupart des marchands de la rue Saint-Denis aiment fort la comédie, et nous sommes quarante ou cinquante qui allons ordinairement aux premières représentations de toutes les pièces nouvelles; et quand elles ont quelque chose de particulier et qu'elles font grand bruit, nous nous mettons quatre ou cinq ensemble, et louons une loge pour nos femmes, car pour nous, nous nous contentons d'aller au parterre. Nous y menons dimanche quatre ou cinq marchandes de cette rue, avec la femme d'un notaire et celle d'un procureur.[2]

These words are addressed to a young noblewoman whom he treats as a potential customer, although in fact her aim is merely to 'amuser le marchand' until her lover makes his appearance at this *rendez-vous*. The girl asks the merchant for his opinion of Molière's *Critique* since he has already seen it so many times. He replies: 'Il y a quinze ou seize mar-

[1] M. Vimont, *Histoire de la Rue Saint-Denis* (Paris, 1936), 3 vols., vol. i, pp. 321–4.
[2] Sc. 3.

chands dans cette rue qui vous en diraient bien des nouvelles, puisque depuis trente ans ils ont vu toutes les comédies que l'on a jouées, et tout ce qu'il y a d'illustres bourgeois à Paris se rapporte au sentiment de ces messieurs.' What follows is no doubt the modesty of a bourgeois who 'knows his place' when talking to a member of the aristocracy:

> Il faut que je vous avoue une chose qui me surprend: je ne les ai jamais vu condamner une pièce dès la première représentation qu'elle ne soit tombée, ni dire qu'une réussirait, qu'elle n'ait eu beaucoup de succès; et ce qui m'étonne est qu'ils se sont toujours trouvés du sentiment des gens de qualité, et que toutes les pièces qu'ils ont fait réussir au parterre, ont toujours réussi aux loges et au théâtre.

The obsequious shopkeeper then goes on to relate how another merchant was asked his opinion of a play by a lady of quality before the company in her house, and how he surprised everyone present by his reply, which showed 'que l'on sait bien juger d'une pièce de théâtre à la rue Saint-Denis'.

This is no isolated reference to the presence of these merchants in the *parterre* of the theatres of the time. There is no need therefore to drag in the remarks of Grimarest in his *Vie de Molière* (1705) who tells us that 'à la quatrième représentation du *Misanthrope*'[1] Molière was compelled to support the play by putting on *Le Médecin malgré lui* 'qui fit bien rire le bourgeous de la rue Saint-Denis'.[2] In the very same year as Donneau de Visé was attacking Molière in his *Zélinde*, Abbé d'Aubignac was belabouring Corneille in his dissertations on *Sophonisbe* and *Sertorius*. To Corneille's haughty remark that in order to be able to judge his plays critics should produce better ones, D'Aubignac replies with a long diatribe. The *parterre*, he declares, has become so filled with this notion that

> cette erreur commence à monter sur le théâtre et dans les loges, et vous pourriez bien vous y entretenir par l'opinion de beaucoup de gens de qualité qui vous approchent. Mais, premièrement, je ne sais pourquoi ceux qui remplissent le parterre de nos théâtres se laissent abuser par un si mauvais discours, car ils n'ont qu'à faire réflexion sur eux-mêmes; ils ne sont pas tous capables de faire un habit, un soulier, ni un chapeau, et néanmoins ils en jugent tous les jours quand les artisans leur en apportent. Ils connaissent bien s'ils sont proportionnés à leur taille, ils sentent bien s'ils sont trop larges ou trop étroits,

---

[1] As usual, Grimarest is not to be relied upon. *Le Misanthrope* ran for twenty-one performances between 8 June and 1 Aug. 1666, and it was only when it was put on again in September that it was supported by *Le Médecin malgré lui*, which was given for the first time on 6 Aug.

[2] *Vie de M. de Molière*, ed. L. Chancerel (Paris, 1930), p. 58.

s'ils les incommodent, ou s'ils leur laissent la liberté de tous les mouvements de leur corps, ils discernent ceux qui sont bien ou mal fabriqués, et sans être instruits en tous ces arts que par leur lumière naturelle et par leur propre sentiment, ils les approuvent ou les rebutent; et ce serait une extravagance assez mal reçue si les ouvriers nous voulaient tous obliger de mieux faire quand nous ne voulons pas recevoir leurs ouvrages.

Although in the following passage he uses the word *peuple* in applying this principle to drama, the picture of the audience which he gives above and the reference to the 'marchands de la rue Saint-Denis' which follows make it clear that D'Aubignac has in mind here a *parterre* consisting of bourgeois rather than plebeian spectators:

Ainsi, lorsqu'il s'agit d'un poème dramatique, ceux du peuple qui n'ont aucune étude, s'en rendent les premiers juges; ils éclatent aux belles choses qui les touchent, et demeurent languissants et muets aussitôt que les intrigues de la scène s'affaiblissent ou souffrent quelque confusion ou quelque obscurité; ils ne consultent que leur propre sentiment, ils regardent ce qui leur plaît et ce qui leur déplaît, et décident hardiment de la bonté d'une pièce sans avoir lu Aristote, ni Scaliger. Il ne faut donc pas qu'ils condamnent si témérairement ce qu'ils font, ni qu'ils approuvent comme une règle certaine le contraire de ce qu'ils pratiquent tous les jours. Quand ils ont donné tant d'applaudissements aux poèmes de M. Corneille, les a-t-il obligés à mieux faire auparavant que d'en goûter la joie? et voudrait-il suspendre sa réputation tant que tous les marchands de la rue Saint-Denis eussent fait des comédies meilleures que les siennes? Car la même règle qu'il veut établir pour condamner, doit être aussi établie pour approuver, et les mêmes lumières doivent servir au discernement du bien comme du mal; et quand ils ont abandonné, après les premières représentations, le *Démétrius* du jeune Corneille comme une pièce indigne de leur attention, eût-il été bien fondé de les faire appeler en justice, pour faire mieux ou pour rétracter leur jugement?[1]

In his *Quatrième dissertation*, published in the same year, D'Aubignac returns to the 'bourgeois de la rue Saint-Denis', but this time he speaks of them with a lofty contempt when he tells Corneille: 'On vous connaît pour un poète qui sert depuis longtemps au divertissement des bourgeois de la rue Saint-Denis et des filous du Marais, c'est tout; mais je ne voudrais pas mettre en compromis avec cette qualité la moindre de celles qui m'ont fait connaître aux personnes de mérite et de condition.'[2]

There is a similar pejorative note in the writings of the critic Gabriel Guéret. In *Le Parnasse réformé* (1669) he makes Tristan l'Her-

---

[1] *Deux dissertations*, pp. 28–29.
[2] *Quatrième dissertation servant de réponse aux calomnies de M. Corneille*, p. 184.

mite speak of his successors among playwrights in somewhat disparaging terms, and then add:

> Ma plainte ne tombe que sur quelques jeunes gens sans connaissance, dont les comédiens, avides de nouveautés, prennent tout ce qu'ils leur présentent, et qui mettent leurs noms à des poèmes dont ils sont plutôt les héritiers que les auteurs. Ces poètes que révère[nt] l'Hôtel de Bourgogne et le Marais, et qui passent pour de grands hommes dans l'esprit des marchands de la rue Saint-Denis, ne connaissent pas davantage la *Poétique* d'Aristote et de Scaliger que le Talmud.[1]

There is a similar unfavourable reference to the same section of the community in Guéret's next work, *La Guerre des auteurs anciens et modernes* (1671), in which Vaugelas is made to speak slightingly of the authors of the time: 'Qu'un poète, par exemple, ait pour lui les marchands de la rue Saint-Denis, et qu'il trouve un libraire assez facile pour acheter ses folies, le voilà devenu auteur pour le reste de ses jours.'[2]

Perhaps the best known and the most interesting of these passages about the worthy shopkeepers of the Rue Saint-Denis is to be found in Boursault's *Artémise et Poliante* (1670), in which he relates his impressions of the first performance of Racine's *Britannicus*. The *parterre*, where he expected to find a crowd, was empty, he tells us, because of the counter-attraction of an execution, that of the Marquis de Courboyer:

> Je m'étais mis dans le parterre pour avoir l'honneur de me faire étouffer par la foule. Mais M. le Marquis de Courboyer . . . ayant attiré à son spectacle tout ce que la rue Saint-Denis a de marchands qui se rendent régulièrement à l'Hôtel de Bourgogne pour avoir la première vue de tous les ouvrages qu'on y représente, je me trouvai si à mon aise que j'étais résolu de prier M. de Corneille que j'aperçus tout seul dans une loge d'avoir la bonté de se précipiter sur moi, au moment que l'envie de se désespérer le voudrait prendre.[3]

It is interesting, as giving some indication of the sort of spectators whom one could encounter in the *parterre* of seventeenth-century Paris theatres, that Boursault quotes the opinions on the play expressed

---

[1] p. 83. In the same work (p. 87) there is an interesting reference to the middle-class element in contemporary theatre audiences in some words put into the mouth of the actor Montfleury (he died in 1667 after his exertions in the rôle of Oreste in *Andromaque*): 'Nous sommes bien fols de nous mettre si avant dans le cœur des passions, qui n'ont été qu'au bout de la plume de Messieurs les poètes; il vaudrait mieux bouffonner toujours et crever de rire en divertissant le *bourgeois* que crever d'orgueil et de dépit pour satisfaire les beaux esprits.'   [2] pp. 172-3.

[3] p. 3.

by 'des connaisseurs auprès de qui j'étais incognito et de qui j'écoutais les sentiments'.[1]

Before leaving the question of the place occupied by the middle classes of the time among the spectators of the *parterre*, it is interesting to see what part of the theatre foreign travellers in this period would normally frequent. Useful information on this point in accounts left behind by foreign visitors to Paris is not easy to come by, but two interesting references of this kind can be quoted, both of them concerning English travellers in the 1660's. In 1664 Edward Browne, the son of Sir Thomas Browne, the author of *Religio Medici*, visited Paris as part of his grand tour. At this time he was only twenty-two; he was in due course to follow in his father's footsteps and become a doctor. When he went to the Palais Royal to see a performance by Molière's company, he felt no compunction about buying a ticket to stand in the *parterre*: 'In the afternoon I heard a Comedy at Palais royall. They were Monseir's Comedians; they had a farce after it. I gave Quinze Solz to stand upon the grounde. The name of it was *Cœur de Mari*. They were not to be compared to the Londoners.'[2] Two years later Philip Skippon, the son of Cromwell's Major-General, a young Cambridge graduate who not long afterwards was to become a M.P. and a knight, saw both the Italian actors and Molière's company perform at the Palais Royal, and once again neither he nor his companion (or companions)[3] made any difficulty about standing in the *parterre*:

Palais Cardinal is a fair palace with handsome walks. Here Madame Henrietta, the dutchess of Orleans, lives. At one side of this house is a publick stage where the Italian and French comedians act by turns. I saw here *Il maritaggion d'una Statua*, a merry play where the famous buffoon, Scaramuccio, acted. Three antick dances pleased the spectators. The *Quattre Scaramuccie* was another pleasant Italian comedy. We stood in the parterre, or pit, and paid 30 sols apiece for seeing the first, and but 15 sols for the last.

We saw a French comedy entitled *L'estourdye* which was better acted than we expected. We paid for seeing this, and standing in the pit, 15 sols a man.[4]

In discussing what sort of spectators frequented the *parterre* in the

[1] p. 7.
[2] *A Journal of a Visit to Paris in the year 1664*, ed. G. Keynes (London, 1923), p. 16. The plays given in Lagrange's Register for this date (25 May) are *L'École des Maris* and 'la farce de la Casaque'.
[3] Skippon was in Paris with the famous naturalist John Ray and Dr. Martin Lister. See C. E. Raven, *John Ray Naturalist. His Life and Works* (Cambridge, 1942), p. 138.
[4] *An Account of a Journey through Part of the Low Countries, Germany, Italy and France* in *A Collection of Voyages and Travels* (London, 1732), vol. vi, p. 731.

seventeenth-century Paris theatres, we have gradually risen up the social scale from the *menu peuple* or even *racaille* to the solid middle class of merchants and professional men. It remains to say a word about the sprinkling of noblemen who on occasion frequented the *parterre*. No doubt it was altogether exceptional for a *grand seigneur* to stand in such lowly company to see a play; his place was in a box or on the stage.[1] Even a minor nobleman had to produce the money for a box when he took his wife or lady friend to the theatre; but when he was on his own or with male companions, he might well go and stand in the *parterre*.

This was particularly the case with the troops of the King's household, who were at this time nearly all noblemen. Abbé de Pure, who discusses the disorders which they frequently caused in the theatres of the period by forcing an entry without paying and then interrupting the performances, states quite explicitly: 'Aujourd'hui surtout que les gardes du corps, les mousquetaires et les autres officiers du roi sont presque tous gentilshommes et de qualité, il n'est rien de plus aisé que de régler leur entrée.'[2]

In his *Vie de Molière* Grimarest gives a long and circumstantial account of the trouble which Molière had with these gentlemen. Coming as it does from so suspect a source, the story must be treated with considerable reserve, but such a detailed account of the matter is perhaps worth quoting. Grimarest tells us that 'les mousquetaires, les gardes du corps, les gendarmes, les chevaux légers entraient à la comédie sans payer, et le parterre en était rempli'. Molière, he declares, obtained a royal decree forbidding the troops of the King's household to enter the theatre without paying, whereupon the soldiers forced their way into his theatre, killing the porter. The King ordered the punishment of the offenders, and Molière harangued the *gendarmes*, telling them

que ce n'était point pour eux, ni pour les autres personnes qui composaient la maison du roi qu'il avait demandé à Sa Majesté un ordre pour les empêcher d'entrer à la comédie; que la troupe serait toujours ravie de les recevoir quand ils voudraient les honorer de leurs présences, mais qu'il y avait un nombre infini de malheureux qui, tous les jours abusant de leurs noms et de la bandoulière de Messieurs les Gardes du corps, venaient remplir le parterre et ôter injustement à la troupe le gain qu'elle devait faire; qu'il ne croyait pas

---

[1] The playwright Boyer boasted of the success of his tragedy, *Agamemnon* (1680), in the following terms: 'Jamais pièce de théâtre n'a eu un succès plus avantageux. Les assemblées furent si nombreuses, et le théâtre si rempli, qu'on vit beaucoup de personnes de la première qualité prendre des places dans le parterre. Quel succès a été honoré d'une circonstance aussi singulière et si glorieuse?' (See the preface to his *Artaxerce*, 1683.)

[2] *Idée des spectacles anciens et modernes*, p. 171.

que des gentilshommes qui avaient l'honneur de servir le roi, dussent favo-
riser ces misérables contre les comédiens de Sa Majesté; que d'entrer à la
comédie sans payer n'était point une prérogative que des personnes de leur
caractère dussent si fort ambitionner jusqu'à répandre du sang pour se la
conserver; qu'il fallait laisser ce petit avantage aux auteurs et aux personnes
qui, n'ayant pas le moyen de dépenser quinze sols, ne voyaient le spectacle
que par charité, s'il m'est permis, dit-il, de parler de la sorte. Ce discours fit
tout l'effet que Molière s'était promis; et depuis ce temps-là la maison du roi
n'est point entrée à la comédie sans payer.[1]

Fortunately we are not compelled to rely on such a discredited source
for information about the presence of this type of spectator in the
parterre. We know from unimpeachable documents that twice during
the last few months of Molière's life there were disorders in his theatre.
On Sunday, 9 October 1672, during a performance of *La Comtesse
d'Escarbagnas* and *L'Amour médecin* 'plusieurs gens de livrée et autres
firent insulte à un homme d'épée auquel ils donnèrent quantité de coups
de bâton desquels il est grièvement blessé, et même jetèrent plusieurs
pierres aux acteurs qui jouaient la comédie'.[2] While Molière himself
was on the stage, 'il fut jeté du parterre le gros bout d'une pipe à fumer
sur le théâtre'.[3] Witnesses who gave evidence about the incident all
agreed that the culprits were pages; their victim, described as 'un homme
d'épée', might or might not have been an officer. On 13 January 1673,
just over a month before Molière's death, further disorders took place
at the Palais Royal during a performance of *Psyché*. A *commissaire du
Châtelet* was fetched to the theatre by the news that 'dans le parterre
il y avait quantité de gens d'épée entrés sous prétexte d'entendre la
comédie, . . . lesquels composaient entre eux, contre la volonté de
sadite Majesté . . ., un désordre et une sédition comme il a été ci-devant
fait à l'Hôtel de Bourgogne'.[4] The *commissaire* went on to the stage,

d'où aussitôt que la première entrée s'est faite, avons aperçu dans ledit parterre, à la faveur de la clarté des chandelles, quelques gens d'épée à nous inconnus qui se seraient approchés dudit théâtre, lesquels murmuraient et
frappaient du pied à terre, et quand la machine de Vénus est descendue, le
chœur des chanteurs de cette entrée récitant tous ensemble *Descendez, mère des
Amours!* lesdits gens d'épée, autant qu'avons pu remarquer être au nombre
de vingt-cinq ou trente, de complot, auraient troublé lesdits chanteurs par
des hurlements, chansons dérisionnaires et frappements de pied dans le parterre et contre les ais de l'enclos où sont les joueurs d'instruments.[5]

The uproar caused by these rowdies finally brought the performance to

---

[1] *Vie de Molière*, pp. 42–45.   [2] Campardon, *Documents inédits*, pp. 31–32.
[3] Ibid., p. 34.   [4] Ibid., p. 66.   [5] Ibid., pp. 68–69.

a standstill; when they were offered their money back, they refused and demanded instead that the play should start all over again. When this was done, they apparently behaved themselves; at least the *commissaire's* report breaks off at this point.

Once again we have no means of telling what was the rank of these *gens d'épée*, but if this was conduct unworthy of an officer and a gentleman, we cannot necessarily conclude that they were 'other ranks'. At the Comédie Française in 1691 a performance of *La Devineresse*, a *pièce à machines* by De Visé and Thomas Corneille, was brought to an end by the disorders created by a gang of rowdies, led by a drunken officer with the delightful name of Sallo. This officer, 'capitaine au régiment de Champagne', the documents in the case relate, 'força la garde et entra dans le parterre', followed by other members of his company. Sallo climbed up on to the stage from the *parterre* and shouted: 'Connais-tu ce bougre qui est à la porte de la Comédie? Je lui viens de foutre un bon coup d'épée dans le ventre. Je suis un capitaine qui ai vingt amis dans le parterre.'[1] This incident was followed by yet another royal edict (as so often under the Ancien Régime, it was not observed) in which the King

fait très expresses inhibitions et défenses à toutes personnes, de quelque qualité et condition qu'elles soient, même aux officers de sa maison, ses gardes, gendarmes, chevaux légers, mousquetaires, et tous autres, d'entrer auxdites comédies sans payer, comme aussi à tous ceux qui y seront entrés d'y faire aucun désordre ni interrompre les comédies de quelque manière que ce soit.[2]

Despite successive royal edicts trouble still continued from this quarter. In November 1700 the *Lieutenant de police*, D'Argenson, describes the following incident at the Comédie Française in which a *mousquetaire* was involved:

Avant-hier il arriva du bruit à la Comédie, à l'occasion d'un chien danois que M. le marquis de Livry, le fils, y avait mené. Ce chien se mit à faire le manège sur le théâtre et à faire voir son agilité en cent manières différentes. Messieurs du parterre firent pour l'encourager tous les bruits de chasse dont chacun put s'aviser, et l'un de ceux qui affecta le plus de s'y distinguer, ce fut le sieur de Creil, mousquetaire de la seconde compagnie, fort sujet à troubler la tranquillité du spectacle, aimant le désordre et l'excitant en toute rencontre, également prompt à critiquer et à applaudir, pourvu que ce soit avec éclat et qui regrette fort le temps des sifflets.[3]

Less than two months later further disturbances in the theatre are men-

[1] Campardon, *Comédiens du Roi de la troupe française*, pp. 290–7.
[2] A. Jal, *Dictionnaire critique de biographie et d'histoire*, 2nd ed. (Paris, 1872), p. 408.
[3] *Notes*, p. 41.

tioned by D'Argenson: 'Les sieurs Matas et de Salins ou de Sallegourne, qui interrompirent ces jours passés la Comédie par le bruit d'une bassinoire, sont mousquetaires de la 2ᵉ compagnie de la brigade de Chalais.'[1] Before the year was out, there was trouble about *mousquetaires* trying to force their way into the theatre without paying. 'MM. de Creil, de Berci et de Quervasi, mousquetaires de la seconde compagnie, voulurent entrer dimanche à la Comédie sans payer', D'Argenson notes in November 1701.

Les deux premiers mirent pour cela l'épée à la main et parlèrent des ordres du Roi dans des termes peu convenables. Il est vrai que le vin eut beaucoup plus de part à cette insulte que la réflexion. Cependant M. le Marquis de Vins, à qui j'en écrivis sur-le-champ, les a tous fait mettre en arrêt, et j'espère que ce premier exemple de sévérité aura son effet pendant tout le reste de l'hiver.[2]

While it is true that neither the rank nor the birth of all these delinquent members of the troops of the royal household is clearly established (it must be remembered that not only were most of the officers noblemen in this branch of the army, but also that many young noblemen served in the ranks), we have here so many allusions in contemporary documents to the presence—drunk or sober—of soldiers of this kind that at any rate a high proportion of them must have been noblemen, which shows that such people did not disdain to stand in the *parterre*, along with less elevated members of the community. Moreover, their presence was by no means always unwelcome to the actors of the different theatres. Their absence was lamented when in war-time they had to return to the front with the opening of the campaigning season in spring. In Dufresny's *Départ des Comédiens*, a little comedy performed at the Théâtre Italien in 1694, Arlequin laments the fact that at this season of the year 'il n'est officier qui ne parte' and that spring 'dépeuple de plumets théâtres et ruelles'. He goes on:

> Qu'êtes-vous devenus, jeunes foudres de guerre,
> Qui triomphiez jadis dans ce vaste parterre?
>   Hélas! je n'y vois plus
>   Ce doux flux et reflux
>   De têtes ondoyantes,
> Qui rend en plein hiver nos moissons abondantes,
> Quand le troupeau guerrier et terrestre et marin
>   Vient piétiner notre terrain;
>   En y semant quelques paroles,
>   Nous recueillons force pistoles . . .[3]

[1] Ibid., p. 54   [2] Ibid., p. 62.   Sc. 1.

There is also evidence that noblemen who were not necessarily army or naval officers frequented this part of the theatre. In Bordelon's *Coudées franches* (1712) two coquettes are depicted as vainly awaiting the arrival of some men in their *loge*. Suddenly the following dialogue ensues:

Ah! regarde: est-ce que je me trompe? Voilà assurément notre jeune marquis dans le parterre. — Où donc? — Là-bas dans ce coin. — Oui, vraiment; c'est lui. — Nous voir seules ici, et ne pas venir nous tenir compagnie! Cela m'étonne.

The explanation of the mystery is that the *marquis*'s aunt is in the box above, so that he is afraid to join the two coquettes.[1] Another reference to the presence of nobles in the *parterre* in our period is to be found in an epigram in *Le Poète sans fard*[2] of Gacon; it is said to have been inspired by the haughty tone of the prefaces of Lagrange-Chancel, one of the leading authors of tragedies at the end of the century:

Contre quelques jeunes gens d'épée qui se sont ingérés de donner des pièces de théâtre

Les petits-maîtres et les pages,
Peu connaisseurs en bons ouvrages,
Ennuyaient en sifflant les vers les mieux reçus;
Mais, depuis qu'au bon sens continuant la guerre,
Ils sont auteurs devenus,
Ils incommodent encore plus
Sur le théâtre qu'au parterre.

We have now surveyed the different sections of the community which contributed their quota to the all-male group of spectators who stood in the *parterre* of the different Paris theatres which were in existence between about 1630 and 1715. The result is not by any means a clear picture, since the documents are so rare, scattered, and difficult to interpret that it is impossible to make out of them anything like a precise cross-section of this part of the audience. We must also bear in mind that there may well have been changes in the course of this long period; what was true of the *parterre* when Corneille began his career in 1630 may well not have been true of the spectators in that part of the theatre seventy years later when Lesage was writing plays for the Comédie Française. We have examined the meaning of the ambiguous term *peuple* as applied to a section of the theatre audiences of seventeenth-century Paris. We have noted the presence among the spectators

[1] Vol. ii, pp. 102–3.   [2] 2nd ed. (n.p., 1701).

in this part of the theatre of representatives of the *menu peuple*, but only to conclude that they were neither numerous nor of any real importance in determining the sort of plays which were produced in the theatres of the time. We have found that the middle classes, the merchants and professional men, including writers and aspiring writers, formed at any rate a considerable part of the audience in the *parterre*, and we have seen that even a sprinkling of noblemen did not disdain to stand in a crowd to see a play. It now remains to examine the influence which the all-male audience in this part of the theatre exerted on the success or failure of new plays.

(iv) *The Importance of the* Parterre

A number of contemporary documents testify to the important part played by the spectators in the *parterre* in the life of the seventeenth-century Paris theatres; but before we attempt to assess their influence, we must first endeavour to establish what proportion of the audience stood in this part of the theatre. Before 1673, the year of the foundation of the Théâtre Guénégaud, we have absolutely no means of calculating what this proportion was, except for the last year of the existence of Molière's theatre at the Palais Royal. As we have seen, no records have survived for the other Paris theatres up to that date. Even Lagrange's Register, essential document though it is for any study of the activities of Molière and his actors, is useless for our present purpose, as it confines itself to recording the total receipts and the actor's share for each performance. Fortunately the preservation of the more detailed register of Hubert for the theatrical year 1672–3 and the summary and analysis of it given by Dr. Schwartz[1] enable us to form a clear idea of the proportion of the spectators at Molière's theatre who stood in the *parterre*.

As Dr. Schwartz points out, the *parterre* 'was the mainstay of Molière's popularity'.[2] At 113 out of a total of 131 performances given in this theatrical year more than half the audience stood in this part of the theatre.[3] The number of tickets to the *parterre* sold in 1672–3 ranged from 36, at a performance of De Visé's comedy, *Les Maris infidèles*, to 514, at a revival of *Psyché*; but on both occasions the occupants of the *parterre* accounted for more than half the total number of spectators (68 and 925 respectively). If we add together the largest

[1] 'Molière's Theater in 1672–1673', *PMLA* (1941), pp. 395f.
[2] Ibid., p. 397.
[3] Most of the occasions when the proportion of spectators in the *parterre* fell to less than half were during the revival of *Psyché*.

number of tickets sold on any one occasion throughout this year for all the other parts of the theatre, we find that the total exceeds that for the largest number of spectators in the *parterre*—534 against 514; none the less in all but a small number of cases the spectators in this part of the theatre formed the majority of Molière's audience.

On the other hand it must be observed that, where new plays were concerned (and here the reactions of the audience at the opening performances were particularly important as they largely determined the length of the first run), the doubling of prices which was practised had a considerable effect on the size of the audience as a whole and on the number of the spectators in the *parterre*.

When the season opened, Molière's comedy, *Les Femmes Savantes*, was still enjoying its first run, but, as the play had already been given 11 times before Easter 1672, prices in the *parterre* were reduced to 15 sous for the last 8 performances which it received at the opening of the new season. Consequently the *parterre* furnished very nearly three-quarters of the spectators who paid to see these 8 performances. In July *La Comtesse d'Escarbagnas* was given its first performance, and on the first 4 occasions, with prices doubled (30 sous in the *parterre* instead of 15) the proportion of spectators in that part of the theatre fell to just over 60 per cent., rising for the remaining 15 performances, when prices had been lowered, to nearly 70 per cent. At the first 4 performances of Donneau de Visé's *Les Maris infidèles*, a poorly attended play, the usual double prices kept the proportion of spectators in the *parterre* down to just below 55 per cent.; after these 4 performances the play had to be taken off, so that we cannot pursue the comparison farther. During the first run of *Le Malade imaginaire* in February and March 1673 (4 performances of it were given before Molière's death and 9 after) the proportion of the spectators in the *parterre*, with prices doubled, fell on 5 occasions to less than half.[1]

Lancaster's two books on the history of the Comédie Française from 1680 to 1774 permit one to offer a few further generalizations on this subject.[2] The custom of doubling prices during the first run of new plays was not finally abolished at that theatre until 1753; but it was carried on with all manner of variations into which we cannot enter

---

[1] The proportion of the receipts of the theatre contributed by the *parterre* will be examined below, p. 108.

[2] Ideally one ought to spend several months working on the series of registers preserved in the Archives of the Comédie Française analysing, performance by performance, the proportion of spectators in the different parts of the theatre from 1673 to 1789; but life is short.

here.[1] In the theatre occupied by the Comédie Française between 1689 and 1770 in the Rue des Fossés-Saint-Germain the largest number of spectators who paid for admission on any one day was 1,586 in March 1704, while on one occasion in 1690, when Boursault's new comedy, *Ésope*, was played at reduced prices, the record number of 777 spectators (out of a total of 1,300) stood in the *parterre*.[2] The *parterre*, as Lancaster puts it, was the most popular part of the theatre except when prices of admission were doubled. From the specimen figures which he gives for the period from 1680 to 1701[3] some interesting conclusions may be drawn, which fit in with the figures offered by Dr. Schwartz for Molière's theatre in the year 1672–3.

On 9 out of 11 occasions when prices were normal (including one during the first run of a play after prices had been reduced), the spectators in the *parterre* formed at least half the total audience and sometimes very substantially more than half. The 2 occasions when this was not the case were in some measure special ones: less than half the spectators were to be found in the *parterre* for the first performance of Dancourt's little play, *Les Curieux de Compiègne* (1698), and also at the last performance given at the Comédie Française before Easter 1701, even though on neither occasion had the prices been doubled. On the other hand, on all 3 occasions for which we are given detailed figures when prices were doubled—the first performances of La Tuillerie's tragedy, *Soliman* (1680), and of Baron's comedy, *La Coquette* (1686), and the second performance of La Fosse's tragedy, *Polixène*, (1696)—this brought the proportion of spectators in the *parterre* down to less than half the total audience.

We may thus conclude that the spectators standing in the *parterre* were extremely important from the numerical point of view. Under ordinary conditions they represented a majority among the audience in the seventeenth-century theatre whenever older plays were revived or during the first run of new plays, once the prices had been reduced to normal. Obviously there were exceptions to this rule even under those conditions, and when prices were raised during the opening performances of a new play, the *parterre* often ceased to enjoy its majority among the spectators. Even so, as new plays generally produced a good attendance, at any rate for the opening performances, even if they

[1] *The Comédie Française 1680–1701*, pp. 16–17, and *The Comédie Française 1701–1774*, pp. 594–5.
[2] *The Comédie Française 1701–1774*, p. 594.
[3] *The Comédie Française 1680–1701*, p. 18n.

quickly proved a failure, there would on such occasions be at least three
or four hundred spectators in the *parterre*, and this mass of men, packed
together like sardines, were obviously in a position to express their
reactions in a way which had a considerable effect on the fate of
the play.

Flattering references to the good taste of the *parterre* do not seem to
have been made before 1660. We have quoted many examples of rude
remarks made in the period roughly from 1630 to 1660 about the taste
of the *peuple* and even the *menu peuple*, who were presumably represented in the *parterre* of the various Paris theatres, but it is not until
we come to Molière's little play, *La Critique de l'École des Femmes*
(1663), that we find praise given to this section of the audience. There
we see perhaps the actor-manager who knew on which side his bread
was buttered, and was very conscious of the fact that the spectators who
bought tickets for the *parterre* generally represented more than half his
audience. However, even after that date critics like Rapin and Bouhours
continued to look with suspicion on the taste of the *peuple* as represented
in the *parterre* of their day. Why is it, Rapin asks Bussy-Rabutin in
a letter of 1672,[1] that the plays of Sophocles and Euripides are still
admired after 2,000 years, while the plays of modern authors do not
outlast a winter in Paris? 'Est-ce que le peuple qui en fait la réputation
par le concours du parterre n'est pas un bon juge?' He continues with
another question:

Ne trouvez-vous pas que les comédies de nos poètes (je ne nomme personne, car Molière est de nos amis) font tous les objets plus grands qu'ils ne
sont, et qu'elles ne copient presque point au naturel comme fait Térence?
Il en est de même des satires: on veut plaire au peuple par les uns et par les
autres, et pour lui frapper l'esprit, on grossit les choses: on fait un misanthrope plus misanthrope qu'il n'est; un tartufe plus hypocrite qu'il n'est.

From all this he concludes: 'Le génie du peuple est grossier: il faut de
grands traits pour le toucher.' In his reply[2] Bussy defends Molière,
pointing out that comedy must indulge in some exaggeration since its
aim is 'de plaire et de faire rire'. Father Rapin soon came back with
another question:

si vous croyez qu'on puisse plaire au peuple dans une comédie ou dans
une tragédie, c'est-à-dire, dans une pièce de théâtre, contre les règles? La
difficulté est que les actions publiques, surtout dans l'éloquence, sont principalement du ressort du jugement du peuple, *in eloquentia provocabatur ad*

---

[1] Bussy-Rabutin, *Correspondance*, ed. L. Lalanne (Paris, 1858-9), 6 vols., vol. ii, p. 147.
[2] Ibid., p. 156.

populum; mais il se trouve que souvent dans ces actions le parterre est d'un sentiment différent des honnêtes gens.[1]

Once again in his reply Bussy shows himself less affirmative and more sceptical than Rapin. The reputation of plays as of men, he declares, is to some extent a matter of chance, 'car quelquefois les pièces de théâtre naturelles, de bon sens et dans les règles plaisent au peuple, quelquefois non'. A good play can have its reputation destroyed by a single person who is hostile to it and succeeds in prejudicing other people against it; at another time 'une pièce plaira, parce que quelque sot de qualité l'aura louée hardiment'.[2] Thus on the one hand Bussy, the nobleman, although immensely proud of his rank, does not join Rapin in his condemnation of the taste of the *parterre*, while, even if the latter takes an unfavourable view of the taste of this section of the theatre audiences, he certainly attributes to it a considerable influence on contemporary drama.

A similar attitude of mistrust of the *parterre* is to be found in *La Manière de bien penser dans les ouvrages de l'esprit* (1687) of Father Bouhours. In this work Harpagon in *L'Avare* and the bluestockings in *Les Femmes Savantes* are criticized as going beyond nature. 'Il est vraisemblable', says Philanthe, 'que Philaminte et Armande sont ravies de voir Vadius parce qu'il sait du grec; mais il ne l'est pas qu'on chasse Martine parce qu'elle a fait une faute de grammaire.' In the interesting passage which follows, the other speaker, Eudoxe, is made to agree and to attribute this exaggeration to the influence of the *parterre*:

> Je suis de votre sentiment, dit Eudoxe: c'était assez pour la vraisemblance que la maîtresse du logis grondât sa servante d'avoir dit un mot condamné par Vaugelas; mais ce n'était pas assez pour le parterre. Les pièces comiques, dont le but est de faire rire le peuple, doivent être comme ces tableaux que l'on voit de loin, et où les figures sont plus grandes que le naturel. Ainsi un de nos poètes dramatiques qui connaît si bien la nature, et qui en a exprimé les sentiments les plus délicats dans son *Andromaque* et dans son *Iphigénie*, va, ce semble, un peu au delà dans ses *Plaideurs*; car il faut pour le peuple des traits bien marqués, et qui frappent d'abord. Il n'en va pas tout à fait de même des autres ouvrages d'esprit, qui sont plus pour les honnêtes gens que pour le peuple. Le raffinement ne vaut rien; et s'ils ne sont naturels, ils ne sauraient contenter les personnes raisonnables.[3]

In between these two works, it is hardly necessary to remind the reader, had appeared Boileau's *Art Poétique* with its condemnation of the more

---

[1] *Correspondance*, vol. ii, p. 173.   [2] Ibid., p. 177.
[3] *La Manière de bien penser* (Paris, 1705), pp. 337–8.

popular side of Molière's comedy. As Baillet puts it in his *Jugements des Savants* (1686), after Molière's death Boileau 'remarqua plus facilement ce qui avait tant imposé au monde, c'est-à-dire, ce caractère aisé et naturel, mais un peu trop populaire, trop bas, trop plaisant, et trop bouffon'.[1]

This was not, however, the attitude of those more closely connected with the theatre. In his *Vie de Molière* (1705) Grimarest pays tribute to the taste of the *parterre* both of that date and of the period when Molière returned to Paris from the provinces. There is for once every probability that Grimarest was correct in attributing to Molière, on his return to Paris in 1658, some uneasiness as to his ability to succeed as well in the capital as he had done in the provinces: 'Il appréhendait de trouver dans ce parterre, qui ne passait rien de défectueux dans ce temps-là non plus qu'en celui-ci, des esprits qui ne fussent pas plus contents de lui qu'il l'était lui-même.'[2]

Grimarest's attitude towards the taste of the *parterre* was, of course, in the pure tradition of Molière. In his *Critique de l'École des Femmes*[3] the foolish *marquis* whose critical judgement is limited to saying of *L'École des Femmes*, 'Elle est détestable, parce qu'elle est détestable', is made to condemn the play simply because it has amused the *parterre*: 'Il ne faut que voir les continuels éclats de rire que le parterre y fait. Je ne veux point d'autre chose pour témoigner qu'elle ne vaut rien.' In reply the young nobleman, Dorante, Molière's mouthpiece (if it is not going too much against the prevailing trend in Molière criticism to suggest that he could have had a mouthpiece under any circumstances, even in a polemical play), launches forth into an eloquent defence of the *parterre* which takes us straight back into the atmosphere of a seventeenth-century Paris theatre:

Tu es donc, marquis, de ces messieurs du bel air, qui ne veulent pas que le parterre ait du sens commun, et qui seraient fâchés d'avoir ri avec lui, fût-ce de la meilleure chose du monde? Je vis l'autre jour sur le théâtre un de nos amis, qui se rendit ridicule par là. Il écouta toute la pièce avec un sérieux le plus sombre du monde; et tout ce qui égayait les autres, ridait son front. A tous les éclats de rire, il haussait les épaules, et regardait le parterre en pitié; et quelquefois aussi le regardant avec dépit, il lui disait tout haut: *Ris donc, parterre, ris donc.* Ce fut une seconde comédie, que le chagrin de notre ami. Il la donna en galant homme à toute l'assemblée, et chacun demeura d'accord qu'on ne pouvait pas mieux jouer qu'il fit. Apprends, marquis, je te prie, et les autres aussi, que le bon sens n'a point de place déterminée à la comédie;

---

[1] *Jugements des Savants* (Amsterdam, 1725), 8 vols., vol. iv, p. 309.
[2] *Vie de Molière*, p. 14.   [3] Sc. 5.

que la différence du demi-louis d'or[1] et de la pièce de quinze sols ne fait rien du tout au bon goût; que debout et assis, on y peut donner un mauvais juge-ment; et qu'enfin, à le prendre en général, je me fierais assez à l'approbation du parterre, par la raison qu'entre ceux qui le composent, il y en a plusieurs[2] qui sont capables de juger d'une pièce selon les règles, et que les autres en jugent par la bonne façon d'en juger, qui est de se laisser prendre aux choses, et de n'avoir ni prévention aveugle, ni complaisance affectée, ni délicatesse ridicule.

This defence of the taste of the *parterre* against the contempt of at least certain elements of the aristocracy of the time is characteristically balanced by a eulogy, later in the play, of the taste of the court. It is also noticeable that it is no more than a defence; we have to wait until later still in the century before we find anyone putting forward the notion that it is the *parterre* which should be the final judge of both actors and plays.

It is the comic author, Regnard, who in the last decade of the cen-tury first expresses this idea. In his comedy, *La Coquette*, performed at the Théâtre Italien in 1691, he makes Colombine say to a Marquis: 'Vous avez beau pester, le parterre fait du bien à tout le monde; il re-dresse les auteurs, il tient les comédiens en haleine; un fat ne se campe point impunément devant lui sur les bancs du théâtre.'[3] Flattery of the *parterre* is carried much further in *Les Chinois*, a comedy written by Regnard in collaboration with Dufresny and performed at the Théâtre Italien in the following year. In the last scene the *Parterre* enters to act as judge in the debate between Colombine, representing the Théâtre Italien, and Arlequin, who represents the Comédie Française. Arlequin is made to greet the arrival of the *Parterre* with the words: 'Malepeste! il faut lui ouvrir la porte à deux battants, c'est notre père nourricier. Qu'il entre, en payant, s'entend.' The *Parterre* puts forward sweeping claims as to its functions in the theatre: 'Ne savez-vous pas que je suis seul juge naturel, et en dernier ressort, des comédiens et des comédies? Voilà avec quoi je prononce mes arrêts (*Il donne un coup de sifflet*).' When Colombine speaks of 'son Excellence, Monseigneur le Par-terre', Arlequin protests at such flattery, but she retorts with comic enthusiasm:

Non, ce n'est point la flatterie qui me dénoue la langue; je rends simple-

---

[1] 5 livres 10 sous, the price of a seat on the stage or in the first row of boxes in Molière's theatre.

[2] 'Beaucoup, quantité, grand nombre' (*Dictionnaire de l'Académie*, 1694).

[3] Act III, Sc. 3. For the last remark see Molière's description of the antics of a nobleman with a seat on the stage in *Les Fâcheux* (quoted below, pp. 115–16).

ment les hommages dus à ce souverain plénipotentiaire. C'est l'éperon des auteurs, le frein des comédiens, l'inspecteur et curieux examinateur des hautes et basses loges, et de tout ce qui se passe en icelles; en un mot, c'est un juge incorruptible, qui, bien loin de prendre de l'argent pour juger, commence par en donner à la porte de l'audience.

When the *Parterre* finally gives its judgement, Arlequin exclaims in horror: 'O tempora! O mores! J'appelle de ce jugement-là aux loges', to which the former replies: 'Mon jugement est sans appel.'

The same attitude is taken up in a much later play of Regnard, his *Critique du Légataire universel*, performed at the Comédie Française in 1708. Here a *Chevalier*, obviously a copy of the foolish *Marquis* in Molière's *Critique de l'École des Femmes*, insists, in his criticisms of Regnard's comedy, on the independence of his judgement. 'Je ne me laisse jamais entraîner au torrent', he declares; 'je fais tête au parterre, et quand il approuve quelque endroit, c'est justement celui que je condamne.' So far he is merely echoing the *Marquis* in Molière's little comedy, but the answer given him here by 'le Comédien' goes far beyond Dorante's defence of the taste of the *parterre* in the *Critique de l'École des Femmes*: 'Je vous dirai, monsieur, que nous autres comédiens, nous sommes d'un sentiment bien contraire. C'est de ce tribunal-là que nous attendons nos arrêts, et quand il a prononcé, nous n'appelons point de ses décisions.'[1]

No doubt one would be very unwise to take literally these passages from comedies of Regnard. We must attempt to allow, not only for comic exaggeration in general, but also for the effect that such paradoxes must have had on theatre audiences drawn from the profoundly aristocratic society which existed in France in the reign of Louis XIV. Yet if we couple these with less interested statements about the importance of the *parterre* which we encounter in later decades of the eighteenth century and also compare them with earlier scathing references to the taste of the *peuple* and *menu peuple*, we do seem to catch at least a glimpse of an evolution in the course of our period in the attitude of actors and playwrights towards that part of its audience which was of more modest social origins and status than the aristocratic or wealthy spectators in the dearer parts of the house.

(v) *Aristocratic Audience*

If the average theatre audience in Paris between 1630 and 1715 undoubtedly contained a strong middle-class element, and probably even

_____
[1] Sc. 2.

a plebeian one, that does not mean that the role of the upper classes of society in the theatre was unimportant. Given the social structure of seventeenth-century France where, although it was not impossible for commoners of wealth to rise into the aristocracy by acquiring a title or an official post which conferred noble rank on the holder, a gulf continued to divide the nobleman from the *roturier*; given the prevailing worship of rank and social position, it was inevitable that the outlook and ideals of the aristocracy should exercise a considerable influence on the drama of the age. That influence on the theatre was by no means confined to performances given before the King and court at the Louvre or Versailles, Fontainebleau or Saint Germain. The section of the aristocracy which gravitated around the King in Paris and later Versailles was powerfully represented in the different theatres which served Paris in the course of the seventeenth century.

When we think of the audiences which first saw the plays of Corneille, Molière, and Racine or later those of Dancourt, Regnard, and Lesage, we obviously cannot attempt a precise definition of what parts of the theatre were frequented by nobles and *roturiers*. The simple division between *loges* or *galeries* and *parterre* which existed at the Hôtel de Bourgogne at the beginning of the seventeenth century gradually became much more complicated. In the last year of Molière's career the Palais Royal theatre offered the following range of seats, in addition to the *parterre*: *Théâtre* (i.e. seats on the stage), *Loges* (i.e. the first row of boxes, hired as units or as single seats), *Amphithéâtre*, *Loges hautes* (second row of boxes), and *Loges du 3ᵉ rang*. At the Comédie Française from 1680 onwards the arrangement of seats was roughly the same, although there were various minor differences into which we need not enter here. No doubt the *parterre* was largely patronized by the middle classes, but the bourgeois who took his wife and family to the theatre would on such occasions take seats in one of the cheaper boxes or in the *amphithéâtre*, since the *parterre* was an exclusively masculine preserve. All the women who belonged to the aristocracy or to the wider circle of polite society obviously went to the better seats, along with their male companions of equivalent rank and status; yet it was certainly not unknown for minor noblemen, particularly officers, to stand in the *parterre*.

However, if we can establish no absolutely clear-cut line of demarcation between the different ranks of society and their place in the theatre, it is obvious that the more expensive seats were occupied by persons of rank or wealth. Theatre prices rose fairly steeply in the course of the

century. At the beginning the disparity between prices for the *parterre*
and *galeries* was not very considerable: 5 and 10 sous respectively were
the prices asked from patrons of the theatre. The price of admission to
the *parterre* rose to 15 sous about the middle of the century, and at the
opening performances of most plays to double that sum; at the end of
the century, with the imposition of a tax for the benefit of the poor,
prices rose still higher, reaching 18 sous by the end of the reign of
Louis XIV. By the second half of the century the normal prices for the
best seats in the theatre were very much more than double those of the
parterre. At Molière's theatre in the season 1672–3 the price of a seat on
the stage or in the first row of boxes was 5 livres 10 sous, i.e. 110 sous
as against 15 in the *parterre*. The *amphithéâtre* cost 3 livres, the
loges hautes 1 livre 10 sous, and the *loges du 3ᵉ rang* 1 livre.[1] The disparity in prices was considerably less at the Comédie Française: there
seats on the stage and in the first row of boxes cost to begin with
3 livres, or only four times the price of a ticket to the *parterre*, with
lower prices for seats in the less attractive boxes. By the end of the
reign of Louis XIV taxes had raised all theatre prices, so that a seat on
the stage or in the first row of boxes now cost 3 livres 12 sous, i.e.
72 sous against the 18 now charged in the *parterre*—still the same
proportion of four to one—with the prices of the less attractive seats
in between these two extremes. At the opening performances of a new
play these prices were, of course, approximately doubled.

A study of these prices in relation to the takings of seventeenth-
century Paris theatres leads one to the obvious conclusion that while
numerically the *parterre* might be extremely important, its contribution
to the total receipts from each performance was much smaller than its
numbers might at first suggest. The disparity between the number of
spectators in the *parterre* and the total takings at any one performance
was particularly marked in Molière's theatre in the only year for which
we have detailed accounts; this was because the best seats were always
very expensive, so much so that when other prices were increased
during the first run of a play, they were left unchanged. At ordinary
prices a seat in the first row of boxes or on the stage at 5 livres 10 sous
cost over seven times the price of a ticket to the *parterre*, and even when
the prices in the latter part of the theatre were doubled, the best seats
were nearly four times as expensive.[2]

It follows, therefore, that those who sat in the dearest seats in

---

[1] Schwartz, 'Molière's Theater in 1672–1673', pp. 400–1.
[2] Ibid., p. 400.

Molière's theatre were individually much more valuable clients than those who paid their 15 or even 30 sous for a ticket to the *parterre*. If when prices were raised for the first run of a new play, the most expensive seats in the Palais Royal were rather less than four times as dear as a ticket to the *parterre*, even so at the first performance of *Le Malade imaginaire* in 1673, although 394 out of 682 spectators stood in the pit, tickets for the part of the theatre account for less than a third of the total receipts (591 livres out of 1,892), while seats on the stage and in the first row of boxes contributed alone 682 livres to the total. At the second performance, the receipts of which amounted to 1,459 livres, the proportion of spectators in the *parterre* to the total audience fell considerably to 222 out of 482 spectators; the sale of tickets for this part of the theatre (333 livres) was responsible for an even smaller proportion of the total receipts, while the seats on the stage and in the first row of boxes brought in 484 livres.

When the play given at Molière's theatre was not a new one and prices were normal, the disparity between receipts from the *parterre* and the dearest seats could be even greater. When *Psyché* was revived in November 1672 the first performance brought in 1,442 livres 10 sous and attracted 872 spectators to the theatre. 482 of these stood in the *parterre*, but at 15 sous a head they contributed only 361 livres 10 sous to the total receipts—almost exactly a quarter. On the other hand, seats on the stage and in the first row of boxes brought in 440 livres on this occasion; it is noticeable, as Dr. Schwartz points out, that this revival of *Psyché* was most popular with the medium range of patrons of Molière's theatre—those who bought seats in the *amphithéâtre* or higher rows of boxes. Another example of the disparity between the numerical place of the *parterre* in the audience and its contribution to the total receipts is furnished by the performance given on 28 October 1672, when the young actor Baron appeared in the rôle of Alceste in *Le Misanthrope*, and the receipts for the day came to 974 livres 15 sous. Out of the 644 spectators present 399 stood in the *parterre*; they contributed just under 300 livres to this total, whereas the seats on the stage and the first row of boxes brought in 385 livres.

Too much importance should not be attributed to these figures, since, at least during the last year of its existence, Molière's company charged very heavily for the best seats in its theatre, if we compare the prices there with those which obtained at the Comédie Française from 1680 onwards.[1] Here, as we have seen, the normal ratio between the

---

[1] The Théâtre Guénégaud, at its foundation in 1673, continued to charge the same

prices of the best seats and of tickets to the *parterre* was 4 to 1; when prices were doubled for new plays, the ratio fell from that figure to 11 to 3. If we take first some figures for performances at which the lower prices were charged, we arrive at highly significant results. When the theatre was nearly empty, as on 4 September 1685 for a performance of *Cinna*, on 23 August 1695 for Quinault's *Mère Coquette*, and on 22 September 1699 for *L'École des Maris* and *George Dandin*, the *parterre* contributed approximately 50 per cent. of the total receipts. But these were exceptionally poor performances which attracted only 130, 56, and 48 spectators. Generally speaking, in these years at the Comédie Française its contribution to the total receipts was much smaller. While at the first performance of Dancourt's *Chevalier à la mode* on 24 October 1687 (it was given at the ordinary prices) the 565 occupants of the *parterre* contributed about 45 per cent. of the total receipts, the proportion was generally considerably lower. Thus on 19 February 1690 a performance of Boursault's new comedy, *Ésope* (given at reduced prices), attracted 773 spectators to the *parterre*, but they contributed only 579 livres 15 sous to the total receipts of 1,481 livres 15 sous, while the 393 occupants of the better seats (at 3 livres and 1 livre 10 sous) paid 766 livres 10 sous for admission. On occasion, the contribution of the *parterre* could fall even lower. Thus on 8 February 1692, at a very successful performance of *Bérénice* which brought in 1,903 livres 3 sous, the 671 spectators in the *parterre* contributed 503 livres 15 sous, a considerably smaller sum than the 732 livres paid for admission by the 244 occupants of the stage and the first row of boxes at 3 livres each. An even more striking example of what could on occasion happen is provided by the performance of *Polyeucte*, given on 11 March 1701 to mark the end of the theatrical year: to the total receipts of 2,134 livres the 616 occupants of the *parterre* contributed only 515 livres 18 sous, while the 289 persons who occupied seats on the stage or in the first row of boxes, together with the spectators who had hired fourteen whole boxes in the first row, contributed 1,388 livres 3 sous, thus reducing the *parterre*'s contribution to the total receipts to just under a quarter.

The same trend is even more marked in the records of attendances and receipts for those occasions when prices were doubled, so that a ticket to the *parterre* cost 30 sous and the best seats 5 livres 10 sous. At

prices as Molière's theatre, but before its fusion with the Hôtel de Bourgogne in 1680 it had already adopted the lower prices (3 livres) for seats on the stage or in the first row of boxes which were paid at the Comédie Française.

the first performance of La Tuillerie's *Soliman,* on 11 October 1680, of the total receipts of 1,521 livres 10 sous well below a quarter (333 livres) came from the 222 spectators in the *parterre*; this sum was nearly equalled by the 308 livres which came from the letting of seven whole boxes and quite eclipsed by the 610 livres paid by the 111 spectators on the stage. At the performance of Corneille's *Andromède* given on 21 July 1682 the share of the receipts of 2,191 livres furnished by the *parterre* was rather higher (440 tickets were sold for 660 livres), but even so 100 seats sold at 5 livres 10 sous and five whole boxes at 44 livres brought in a higher proportion of the total takings (770 livres). The proportion shrank again for the first performance of Baron's comedy, *La Coquette,* on 28 December 1686: the 330 spectators in the *parterre* contributed only 495 livres to the total receipts of 2,085 livres, whereas the tickets sold at 5 livres 10 sous brought in no less than 918 livres 10 sous. A similar situation is revealed by an examination of the Registers for the second performance of La Fosse's tragedy, *Polixène,* on 5 February 1696:[1] 480 spectators in the *parterre* contributed only 720 livres to the total receipts of 2,731 livres 10 sous, whereas the sale of the dearest seats, at 5 livres 10 sous, brought in no less than 1,160 livres 10 sous.

It is clear then that, from the point of view of the actors, although the often unruly band of male spectators, crowded together in the *parterre,* were an important section of their audience, their numerical preponderance was not matched by a corresponding contribution to the box-office receipts. Even if the society of the time had not accorded the respect which it did to birth and money, the men and women of blue blood or wealth who sat in the first row of boxes or on the stage had an importance, from the financial point of view, which far outweighed their numbers. And, of course, both actors and playwrights did bestow upon the upper classes of the society of their age the respect which the prevailing social outlook demanded.

The best seats in the theatre were no doubt the province of the more aristocratic or at least wealthier sections of society. Some notion of the upper ranks of the audience of the time is given in Scarron's mildly

---

[1] Lancaster gives the total receipts for this performance as 4,343 livres and describes this performance as 'the most remunerative recorded for the century'. He does not explain, however, that the receipts were swollen by a visit of the Dauphin. The Register for that date, after listing sales of tickets totalling 2,731 livres 10 sous, adds: 'Monseigneur nous a honorés de sa présence . . . et a donné cent louis d'or à la compagnie 1400 ll.; quatre loges basses 176 ll., une loge des secondes 24 ll.' It is, of course, the lower total for receipts which is taken here.

burlesque picture of the sort of people who might be attracted to the theatre, in his *Affiche pour les comédiens* for his comedy, *Jodelet souffleté*, performed at the Théâtre du Marais about 1645:

> Vous qu'on voit l'hiver à Paris,
> Ou pour votre plaisir, ou pour vos subsistances,
> *Id est*, pour y voir des Cloris,
> Ou pour faire la cour aux puissances:
> Guerriers tant à pied qu'à cheval,
> Dont l'hiver tous les ans purge bourgs et villages,
> Pour les guérir d'un certain mal,
> Qu'on appelle les brigandages.
> Courtisans, qui vos jours passez
> A souffrir des rebuts et faire révérences:
> Damoiseaux aux canons plissés,
> Grands débiteurs d'impertinences.
> Dames adorables ou non,
> Visibles déités ou franches marmousettes:
> Mais à nous tout argent est bon,
> Tant des prudes que des coquettes.
> Conseillers, financiers, bourgeois,
> Accourez au Marais vous donner au cœur joie,
> Seuls, deux à deux, ou trois à trois,
> Mais tous avec belle monnaie.[1]

Women, from the *grandes dames* in the *premières loges* to their humbler sisters in the higher boxes or the *amphithéâtre*, were undoubtedly an important element in the theatre audience from 1630 onwards. If there is some disagreement over the presence of respectable women in the Paris theatre before that date, there is unanimity for the period which concerns us here. In 1630, in the preface to his novel, *Les Spectacles d'horreur*, Bishop Camus declares that the subject of his book is sanguinary, but 'nos plus délicates dames ne font point de difficulté de se trouver aux lieux où se représentent les tragédies qui sont les images des plus sanglantes cruautés qui se sont exercées'. In the following year the actors of the Hôtel de Bourgogne stated in a petition to the King that they wished to rebuild their theatre, which was still the property of the Confrères de la Passion, 'en dôme ou autrement, à la façon des bâtiments qui sont en Italie, afin qu'en toute liberté les honnêtes gens et principalement les dames y puissent jouir du divertissement des comédies, sans appréhension des volontaires[2] et des mauvais

---

[1] *Œuvres*, vol. vii, p. 345.

[2] '*Volontaire* signifie aussi, Libertin qui ne veut s'assujettir à aucune règle, ni dépendre de personne, qui ne veut faire que sa volonté' (*Dictionnaire de l'Académie*, 1694).

esprits qui se portent aux insolences'.[1] An anonymous pamphlet of the Querelle du Cid, allegedly written five or six years earlier, advises the actors to change the tone of their farces by banishing for ever from them 'le déshonnête pour n'y laisser que le ridicule'. If they were to do so, 'les sots et les badauds ne les iraient pas voir en plus petit nombre, les honnêtes femmes souffriraient par coutume et par occasion leurs bouffonneries, et peut-être que les dévots mêmes, et les plus sérieux, en useraient comme d'un remède contre la mélancolie'.[2]

Great attention is paid in these years to the scruples of respectable women attending the theatre. As Lanson pointed out, the *bienséances* of 1630 were not quite the same as those of 1900, and an examination of certain passages, later suppressed, in the early comedies of Corneille has shown that the ladies of the time were not unduly squeamish. But earlier in the century they had been even less fastidious in their tastes. Writers in the middle of the century continually stress the improvement which has taken place in the moral tone of drama and which has made it a suitable entertainment for respectable women. In 1646, in dedicating his comedy, *Les Songes des hommes éveillés*, to the Demoiselles de Vincelotte, de Brosse writes:

> Rien ne vous peut empêcher de lire les compositions de ce genre; elles ne sont plus ce qu'elles étaient il y a trente ans. La comédie est devenue belle en vieillissant, et sa beauté est aujourd'hui d'accord avec son honneur. Aucune de ses actions n'est licencieuse, aucune de ses paroles déshonnête. Au contraire, la licence et l'infamie sont les sujets de ses censures, et je ne crains point de dire qu'elle est tellement épurée qu'une fille la peut voir avec moins de scandale qu'elle ne parlerait à un capucin à la porte de son couvent.

We need not take too literally these protestations (the last remark is a curious one), since in these matters standards are naturally relative, and even in the second half of the century, in the comedies of Molière and his contemporaries, there are passages which Dr. Bowdler would certainly not have passed if he had felt called upon to edit such plays. Yet writers continue to stress the modesty and purity of their own and other people's plays; for instance, in Dorimond's *La Comédie de la Comédie*, performed in 1660 or 1661, one lady is made to say to another:

> Pour moi, je vous le dis, jamais la comédie
> N'eut tant d'attraits charmants et tant de modestie,

[1] *Remontrance au Roi . . . pour l'abrogation de la Confrérie de la Passion en faveur de la Troupe royale des Comédiens* (Paris, 1631), p. 47.
[2] Gasté, *Querelle du Cid*, p. 280.

Le théâtre n'a rien que d'honnête et de beau,
Chaque jour il produit un prodige nouveau.
Les vestales pourraient avec bienséance
Ouïr la comédie, elle n'est qu'innocence.

She declares indeed that she intends to bring her daughter to the theatre
for the good of her morals, and the other lady agrees with her eulogy.[1]

There are, it is true, in the documents of the time certain things which
rather jar upon one and tend to destroy this picture of vestal purity.
There is the curious remark of D'Aubignac in his analysis of Sophocles'
Ajax, published as an appendix to his *Pratique du Théâtre* in 1657.
Women 'se mêlent de juger de tout', he declares; 'elles ónt aussi
souvent à la bouche Euripide que Malherbe; et . . . elles parlent aussi
hardiment des comédies de Plaute que des prologues de Bruscambille'.[2]
Bruscambille, whose obscene prologues are frequently adduced by
historians of the theatre as a proof that no respectable woman could
have frequented the Hôtel de Bourgogne in the opening years of the
seventeenth century! Even more disconcerting are two letters in
Bussy-Rabutin's correspondence on the behaviour of some of the
ladies of the court of Louis XIV who frequented the *loges* of the seventeenth-century Paris theatres. Mme de Montmorency wrote to Bussy
(both her letter and his reply lack dates): 'Madame de Longueville a
fort grondé mesdames de Saulx et de la Trimouille d'avoir satisfait à
quelques besoins à la Comédie, et puis, pour ôter la méchante odeur
de leurs loges, jeté le tout dans le parterre, d'où on leur a dit tant d'injures
qu'elles furent contraintes de partir.' Bussy replied: 'C'est une fort sotte
débauche que celle de ces dames, qui ont fait leur affaire dans leurs loges.
Vraisemblablement il n'y en a qu'une à qui le mal de ventre a pris et les
deux autres ont fait la sottise par complaisance. Madame de Longueville
a eu grande raison de gronder ces dames, et le parterre de leur chanter
pouille.'[3]

If the ladies of the aristocracy, with their male escorts, chiefly
frequented the *premières loges*, another part of the theatre which sometimes counted among its spectators illustrious personages of both sexes
was the *amphithéâtre*. Thus in 1663 the Duc de Mazarin owed Molière's
company 77 livres for seats in this part of the theatre at a performance

[1] Sc. 2.

[2] *Pratique du Théâtre* (ed. P. Martino), p. 366.

[3] Bussy-Rabutin, *Correspondance*, vol. iii, p. 456. These letters must have been written
not later than 1679, the year of the death of Mme de Longueville, the sister of le Grand
Condé.

of the *École des Femmes* and the *Critique*; while in December 1672 Louis XIV's brother, Monsieur, accompanied on one occasion by his second wife, the German princess Charlotte Elizabeth, was twice present at performances of *Psyché* and occupied with his suite 'deux bancs de l'amphithéâtre'.[1]

The other part of the theatre which contained a high proportion of aristocrats—this time men only[2]—was the stage. The practice of seating spectators on the stage grew up in the various Paris theatres in the first half of the seventeenth century and was to last until 1759 when these seats were abolished at the Comédie Française. Writers too—Corneille and Molière, for instance—are shown by contemporary documents to have gone on occasion to this part of the house,[3] but it seems mainly to have been frequented by the young bloods of the aristocracy. In 1657 Tallemant speaks of the disagreeable consequences of the custom:

> Il y a à cette heure une incommodité épouvantable à la comédie; c'est que les deux côtés du théâtre sont tout pleins de jeunes gens assis sur des chaises de paille; cela vient de ce qu'ils ne veulent pas aller au parterre, quoiqu'il y ait souvent des soldats à la porte, et que les pages ni les laquais ne portent plus d'épées. Les loges sont fort chères, et il y faut songer de bonne heure; pour un écu ou pour un demi-louis on est sur le théâtre; mais cela gâte tout, et il ne faut quelquefois qu'un insolent pour tout troubler.[4]

For a vivid, if somewhat exaggerated, picture of the behaviour of some of the aristocratic fops of the time when they sat on the stage, we need only turn to the famous description given by one of the characters in Molière's *Fâcheux* (1661):

> J'étais sur le théâtre, en humeur d'écouter
> La pièce, qu'à plusieurs j'avais ouï vanter;
> Les acteurs commençaient, chacun prêtait silence,
> Lorsque, d'un air bruyant et plein d'extravagance,

[1] Schwartz, 'Molière's Theater in 1672–1673', pp. 419–20.

[2] It is related as a most unusual occurrence that when Boyer's *Judith* was performed in 1695, the play was so popular with women that, according to Lesage, 'les hommes furent obligés de leur céder le théâtre et de se tenir debout dans les coulisses. Imaginez-vous deux cents dames assises sur des banquettes où l'on ne voit ordinairement que des hommes et tenant des mouchoirs étendus sur leurs genoux, pour essuyer leurs yeux dans les endroits touchants! Je me souviens surtout qu'il y avait au quatrième acte une scène où elles fondaient en pleurs et qui à cause de cela fut appelée "la scène des mouchoirs". Le parterre, où il y a toujours des rieurs, au lieu de pleurer avec elles, s'égayait à leurs dépens.' See *La Valise trouvée* (n.p., 1740), pp. 283–4.

[3] For Corneille see *Segraisiana* (Paris, 1721), p. 58, and for Molière see De Visé, *Réponse à l'Impromptu de Versailles*, Act I, Sc. 3.

[4] *Historiettes*, vol. vii, p. 128.

Un homme à grands canons est entré brusquement
En criant: 'Holà! ho! un siège promptement!'
Et, de son grand fracas surprenant l'assemblée,
Dans son plus bel endroit a la pièce troublée. . . .
Tandis que là-dessus je haussais les épaules,
Les acteurs ont voulu continuer leurs rôles;
Mais l'homme pour s'asseoir a fait nouveau fracas,
Et traversant encor le théâtre à grands pas,
Bien que dans les côtés il pût être à son aise,
Au milieu du devant il a planté sa chaise,
Et de son large dos narguant les spectateurs,
Aux trois quarts du parterre a caché les acteurs.
Un bruit s'est élevé, dont un autre eût eu honte;
Mais lui, ferme et constant, n'en a fait aucun compte,
Et se serait tenu comme il s'était posé,
Si, pour mon infortune, il ne m'eût avisé.
'Ah! marquis! m'a-t-il dit, prenant près de moi place,
Comment te portes-tu? Souffre que je t'embrasse.'
Au visage sur l'heure un rouge m'est monté,
Que l'on me vît connu d'un pareil éventé. . . .
Il m'a fait d'abord cent questions frivoles,
Plus haut que les acteurs élevant ses paroles.
Chacun le maudissait: et moi, pour l'arrêter:
'Je serais, ai-je dit, bien aise d'écouter.
—Tu n'as point vu ceci, marquis? Ah! Dieu me damne!
Je le trouve assez drôle, et je n'y suis pas âne;
Je sais par quelles lois un ouvrage est parfait,
Et Corneille me vient lire tout ce qu'il fait.'
Là-dessus de la pièce il m'a fait un sommaire,
Scène à scène averti de ce qui s'allait faire;
Et jusques à des vers qu'il en savait par cœur,
Il me les récitait tout haut avant l'acteur.
J'avais beau m'en défendre, il a poussé sa chance,
Et s'est devers la fin levé longtemps d'avance;
Car les gens du bel air, pour agir galamment,
Se gardent bien surtout d'ouïr le dénouement. . . .[1]

It is a pity that neither Molière nor any other writer of the time has left behind an equally vivid, if caricatural, picture of the other sections of the seventeenth-century theatre audience, particularly the ladies and their male companions in the *premières loges* and the crowded ranks of the masculine spectators standing in the *parterre*.

[1] Act I, Sc. 1.

Ô bien don Ie fuis ton feruuteur

J. LE PAUTRE. *Spectators on the stage*

Another lively account of the behaviour of spectators on the stage, once again to be accepted with some reserve since it also comes from a comedy, is to be found in Campistron's *L'Amante amant* (1684). One of the characters in it is a nobleman who describes how he intends to go to the theatre in order to prevent a new play which is being performed there from being successful. He explains how this is to be done:

Nous nous plaçons sur le théâtre, trois ou quatre de chaque côté, à quelque distance l'un de l'autre. Nous parlons; nous prenons du tabac; nous nous mouchons souvent; nous passons d'un côté à l'autre; nous venons reprendre notre première place; et dans les endroits les plus pathétiques nous faisons ou disons quelque plaisanterie, bonne ou mauvaise, n'importe. Nous en rions aussitôt. La moitié du parterre en rit aussi; l'autre en enrage. Tout cela en-semble fait du bruit. L'acteur s'arrête; il se rebute; tout son feu se perd; il ne joue plus rien qui vaille: voilà la pièce au diable.[1]

Yet a third comedy of the period offers a description of the behaviour of the young fops of the aristocracy on the stage—this time Regnard's *Coquette*, performed at the Théâtre Italien in 1691. The Marquis of the play boasts of his exploits when he sits on the stage, and Colombine rebukes him thus: 'Mais, de bonne foi, Monsieur le Marquis, croyez-vous que ce soit pour vous voir peigner votre perruque, prendre du tabac, et faire votre carrousel sur le théâtre, que le parterre donne ses quinze sous?' In the same scene, in answer to Colombine's question: 'Que ne vous mettez-vous dans les loges; on ne vous examinera pas de si près', the Marquis gives the fatuous reply: 'Moi dans les loges? Ho! je vous baise les mains. Je n'entends point la comédie dans une loge, comme un sansonnet; je veux, mordi, qu'on me voie de la tête aux pieds; et je ne donne mon écu que pour rouler pendant les entr'actes et voltiger autour des actrices.'[2]

The importance of the aristocratic section of the audience—both male and female—is constantly stressed in the dedications and pre-faces to plays as in contemporary critical writings and other works connected with the theatre of seventeenth-century France. In his old age, it is true, Alexandre Hardy speaks contemptuously of the taste of the court, of 'les délicats esprits de cour, qui désirent voir une tragédie aussi polie qu'une ode ou quelque élégie'.[3] 'Le vrai style tragique', he declares, 'ne s'accorde nullement avec un langage trivial, avec ces délicatesses efféminées qui, pour chatouiller quelque oreille courtisane,

---

[1] Act III, Sc. 1.
[2] Act III, Sc. 3.
[3] Dedication of vol. iii of *Théâtre* (Paris, 1626).

mécontentent tous les experts du métier.'[1] In verses published along with his *Tableau tragique* in 1633 Joyel makes the dead playwright declare:

> Mes œuvres voleront sous la voûte lunaire
> Malgré les courtisans
> Plus longtemps que les rais du monarque solaire
> Ne seront paraissants.[2]

Hardy, however, was behind the times in this last part of his life. The new playwrights who began their career around 1630 all proclaim that they write for 'la cour' and 'les honnêtes gens'. 'Je me range au jugement des honnêtes gens et ris de celui des autres', declared Rayssiguier in the preface to his *Aminte* (1632). Scudéry maintains that his tragi-comedy, *Le Prince déguisé*, probably first performed in 1634, 'fut si longtemps la passion et les délices de la cour . . .; toutes les dames en savaient les stances par cœur'.[3] Mairet's *Sophonisbe* (1634), the first regular Classical tragedy, was a success, Saint-Évremond was to declare some thirty years later, 'pour avoir rencontré le goût des dames et le vrai esprit des gens de la cour'.[4] It is in the salons of polite society, Mairet tells Corneille, that writers must seek to refine their taste:

> Vous savez, dis-je, que l'obligeante curiosité que les personnes d'esprit et de condition témoignent avoir pour les choses que nous faisons, m'appelle quelquefois, comme beaucoup d'autres, dans les plus dignes cabinets de Paris, qui sont les véritables écoles où vous et moi pourrions apprendre la politesse des mœurs et de la langue avec la bienséance des choses et des paroles que nous oublions si souvent en nos chefs-d'œuvre.[5]

We have already seen[6] how in another pamphlet of the *Querelle du Cid* a distinction is drawn between the applause of the 'personnes de condition' and the 'rumeur populaire' of their inferiors in the theatre audience.

The writers of the second half of the century are equally lavish in their praise of the taste of the court in drama. In a well-known passage in his *Critique de l'École des Femmes* Molière matches his defence of the *parterre* with an eloquent eulogy of the taste of the court. Lysidas, the jealous playwright, is told by Dorante:

> Achevez, Monsieur Lysidas. Je vois bien que vous voulez dire que la cour

---

[1] Dedication of vol. v of *Théâtre* (Paris, 1628).
[2] Quoted in Lancaster, *History*, vol. i, p. 41.
[3] *Arminius* (Paris, 1643), Preface.
[4] *Œuvres*, ed. R. de Planhol (Paris, 1927), 3 vols., vol. i, p. 200.
[5] *Épître familière* in Gasté, *Querelle du Cid*, pp. 288–9.
[6] See above p. 64.

ne se connaît pas à ces choses; et c'est le refuge ordinaire de vous autres, Messieurs les auteurs, dans le mauvais succès de vos ouvrages, que d'accuser l'injustice du siècle et le peu de lumière des courtisans. Sachez, s'il vous plaît, Monsieur Lysidas, que les courtisans ont d'aussi bons yeux que d'autres; qu'on peut être habile avec un point de Venise et des plumes, aussi bien qu'avec une perruque courte et un petit rabat uni; que la grande épreuve de toutes vos comédies, c'est le jugement de la cour; que c'est son goût qu'il faut étudier pour trouver l'art de réussir; qu'il n'y a point de lieu où les décisions soient si justes; et sans mettre en ligne de compte tous les gens savants qui y sont, que, du simple bon sens naturel et du commerce de tout le beau monde, on s'y fait une manière d'esprit, qui sans comparaison juge plus finement des choses que tout le savoir enrouillé des pédants.[1]

Molière's statement that the court is not lacking in 'gens savants' and that its members possess a specially refined taste, is echoed in the *Entretiens sur les tragédies de ce temps* (1675) of Abbé de Villiers. 'Si l'on plaît aux savants', one of his characters declares,

on plaira bientôt à la cour, où il y a des savants aussi bien qu'ailleurs; et je puis dire que les savants de la cour valent bien les autres, puisqu'avec la science ils joignent un certain caractère d'esprit fin et délicat qui sert admirablement pour bien juger. Ce n'est plus le caprice qui distribue les louanges et les applaudissements de la cour, c'est le bon sens.[2]

Similar though more directly interested praise of the taste of the aristocracy and the court is to be found in the preface to La Tuillerie's tragedy, *Soliman* (1680): 'Cette pièce n'a pas été tout à fait malheureuse dans ses représentations. Bien des gens de la première qualité, qui ont le discernement juste, l'ont applaudie; et ce qui me flatte bien davantage, c'est qu'elle n'a point déplu à la cour, où le goût est si fin et si délicat.' Finally, in speaking of the success of Dancourt's *Chevalier à la mode* (1687), which had already been given twice at court, the *Mercure* declares: 'Il ne faut point d'autre marque de la bonté d'un ouvrage, puisqu'il est certain que la cour a un certain bon goût qui ne se trouve point ailleurs, non pas même parmi les personnes qui ont le plus de savoir et d'esprit.'[3]

So far everything seems clear: 'la cour', in its wide sense, that of the aristocracy who gravitated round the French kings, and who formed an important element in the Paris theatre audiences of the time, included among its members a considerable number of *savants*, of men

---

[1] Sc. 6.
[2] Abbé P. de Villiers, *Entretiens sur les tragédies de ce temps* (Paris, 1675), pp. 89–90.
[3] *Mercure*, Nov. 1687, pp. 303–4.

learned enough to offer an expert judgement on a play, and those of its members who did not enter into this class possessed a refined taste which made them competent judges in such matters. Yet when we look closely at other contemporary statements about the nature of the theatre audience, we find that the situation was not in fact as clear-cut as that. At the beginning of our period the taste of the court was not particularly refined: Saint-Évremond tells us that in his youth (he was born in 1616) 'on admirait Théophile malgré ses irrégularités, qui échappaient au peu de délicatesse des courtisans de ce temps-là'.[1] As we shall see, throughout the century there were writers who did not offer so flattering a picture of the taste of the court as the one which we have outlined above.

Contemporary classifications of the theatre audience into nobles and plebeians, learned and ignorant, tend to be ambiguous. In his astonishment at the success of such a monster as *Le Cid* Scudéry wrote, as we have seen, in his *Observations*:

Tout ce qui brille n'est pas toujours précieux. . . . Aussi ne m'étonnai-je pas beaucoup que le peuple qui porte le jugement dans les yeux, se laisse tromper par celui de tous les sens le plus facile à décevoir; mais que cette vapeur grossière, qui se forme dans le parterre, ait pu s'élever jusqu'aux galeries, et qu'un fantôme ait abusé le savoir comme l'ignorance, et la cour aussi bien que le bourgeois, j'avoue que ce prodige m'étonne. . . .[2]

Is the intellectual classification which separates 'le savoir' from 'l'ignorance' intended to coincide with the social categories of 'la cour' and 'le bourgeois'? Such at first sight would seem to be Scudéry's meaning, as it appears to be that of Mareschal when he wrote in the preface to *Le Véritable Capitan Matamore* (published in 1640) that his aim had been to 'peindre au naturel ce vivant matamore du théâtre du Marais, cet original sans copie, et ce personnage admirable qui ravit également et les grands et le peuple, les doctes et les ignorants'.

On the other hand, certain writers of the time avoid this double classification in which intellectual and social categories are made to coincide. They divide the audience instead into three groups: 'la cour' (or 'les grands'), 'le peuple' (or 'les bourgeois'), and 'les savants' (or 'les doctes'). 'Savoir les règles, et entendre le secret de les apprivoiser adroitement avec notre théâtre', wrote Corneille in the famous dedication to his comedy, *La Suivante* (1637),

ce sont deux sciences bien différentes; et peut-être que pour faire réussir une

---

[1] *Œuvres*, vol. i, p. 238.   [2] Gasté, *Querelle du Cid*, p. 71.

pièce, ce n'est pas assez d'avoir étudié dans les livres d'Aristote et d'Horace. ... Puisque nous faisons des poèmes pour être représentés, notre premier but doit être de plaire à la cour et au peuple, et d'attirer un grand monde à leurs représentations. Il faut, s'il se peut, y ajouter les règles, afin de ne déplaire pas aux savants, et recevoir un applaudissement universel; mais surtout gagnons la voix publique.

In his *Vie de Molière* Grimarest declares that 'Molière connaissait les trois sortes de personnes qu'il avait à divertir, le courtisan, le savant et le bourgeois', and he goes on:

La cour se plaisait aux spectacles, aux beaux sentiments, de la *Princesse d'Élide*, des *Amants magnifiques*, de *Psyché*, et ne dédaignait pas de rire à *Scapin*, au *Mariage forcé*, à la *Comtesse d'Escarbagnas*. Le peuple ne cherchait que la farce, et négligeait ce qui était au-dessus de sa portée. L'habile homme voulait qu'un auteur comme Molière conduisît son sujet, et remplît noblement, en suivant la nature, le caractère qu'il avait choisi, à l'exemple de Térence. ... Tous les savants ont porté à peu près le même jugement sur les ouvrages de Molière; mais il divertissait tour à tour les trois sortes de personnes dont je viens de parler; et comme ils voyaient ensemble ses ouvrages, ils en jugeaient suivant qu'ils en devaient être affectés, sans qu'il s'en mît beaucoup en peine, pourvu que leurs jugements répondissent au dessein qu'il pouvait avoir, en donnant une pièce, ou de plaire à la cour, ou de s'enrichir par la foule, ou de s'attirer l'estime des connaisseurs.[1]

It would no doubt be unwise to accept at its face value Grimarest's account of Molière's relationship to the three different sections of his audience. In particular, there seems little likelihood that Molière wrote his different plays to please in turn specific sections of the audience. Yet the analysis which Grimarest makes of the different types of spectators who came to Molière's theatre is interesting both for the three sections into which he divides the audience and for his realistic appraisal of the tastes of the aristocracy in drama.

That the level of taste among at least a considerable part of the aristocracy was by no means high is an obvious truth which emerges from a study of contemporary documents. While many writers of the time offer an all-embracing eulogy of the court as the centre of good taste, there are occasional voices which speak in very different terms of some members of the aristocracy. In one of the pamphlets of the *Querelle du Cid* Claveret pointed out to Corneille that it was idle to boast of the approval which the *galeries* had given to his play, since that part of the audience was not necessarily impeccable in its taste:

[1] *Vie de Molière*, pp. 94–95.

Quant aux acclamations des galeries sur lesquelles vous faites tant de force, ils [les honnêtes gens] jugèrent bien que la bassesse de votre esprit, ébloui de cet éclat, ne considérait jamais qu'elles sont le plus souvent remplies de riches sots, et que depuis que la faveur ou l'argent ont ouvert le chemin aux dignités pour en exclure le mérite, l'ignorance se couvre de toutes sortes de robes et de toutes sortes de manteaux.[1]

In his *Apologie du Théâtre*, if Scudéry turns all his aristocratic scorn on the 'ignorants du parterre', he is also compelled to admit the existence of the aristocratic 'ignorants des galeries' and to offer them suitable chastisement. These ignorant 'jeunes gens de la cour' are, he declares, only a minority, but even a writer so imbued with aristocratic prejudice as Scudéry feels compelled to lash out at their vices:

. . . Lorsqu'ils se contenteront de dire qu'une pièce est belle, sans approfondir les choses, leur bonne mine, leur castor pointu, leur belle tête, leur collet de mille francs, leur manteau et leurs belles bottes feront croire qu'ils s'y connaissent; mais, lorsque, pour condamner un ouvrage, par une lumière confuse, ils feront un galimatias de belles paroles, et voudront parler de règles, d'unité d'action et de lieu, de vingt-quatre heures, de liaison de scène et de péripétie, qu'ils ne trouvent pas étrange que ceux qui savent l'art s'en moquent, et si leur opinion n'est point suivie. Ce n'est pas que je veuille dire que tous ceux de cette condition soient atteints de cette ignorance; j'en connais de trop spirituels pour avancer une proposition si fausse; mais aussi faut-il qu'ils me confessent que tous ceux de leur cabale ne sont pas d'égale force en cette matière, et qu'il y en a (s'il faut ainsi dire) qui n'ont que l'épée et la cape. Et ce sont eux que j'exhorte à pratiquer un beau silence, afin que si quelqu'un d'eux ne peut pas être habile homme, il en soit au moins le portrait.[2]

A not dissimilar attitude is to be deduced from a letter which Racan wrote to Ménage in 1654 on the subject of the application of the rules to drama. He deplores the hampering effect of the unities and argues that a masterpiece like *Le Cid* would be ruined if one attempted to make it conform to the unity of place; 'et cependant', he goes on, 'il a été approuvé de toute la cour, où sont les juges compétents en cette matière'. Yet despite this concession to the orthodox view that the court is the final arbiter in matters of taste, Racan goes on to suggest that in the theatre too strict observance of the unities destroys the pleasure of the overwhelming majority of the audience, whatever their social status:

L'unité de lieu, du temps et de l'action y sont sans doute nécessaires; mais cette trop grande rigueur que l'on y apporte met les plus beaux sujets dans

---

[1] Gasté, *Querelle du Cid*, pp. 307–8.   [2] *Apologie du Théâtre*, pp. 94–95.

les gênes, et est cause que les comédies ne sont pas aussi agréables aux esprits médiocres qui remplissent le plus souvent les trois parts de l'Hôtel de Bourgogne,[1] et qui sont ceux, à mon avis, que l'on doit le plus considérer si l'on veut acquérir de la réputation en ce genre d'écrire.[2]

Strictly contemporary descriptions of Molière's audience in Paris do not give an altogether flattering account of the aristocratic section of it. It is not easy to decide precisely how much importance we should attach to the sneering account given by Donneau de Visé of the success of Molière's company after its arrival in Paris and the reception given to two of his plays already performed in the provinces, *L'Étourdi* and *Le Dépit amoureux*. 'Après le succès de ces deux pièces', he tells us,

son théâtre commença à se trouver continuellement rempli de gens de qualité, non pas tant pour le divertissement qu'ils y prenaient (car l'on n'y jouait que de vieilles pièces) que parce que, le monde ayant pris l'habitude d'y aller, ceux qui aimaient la compagnie et qui aimaient à se faire voir, y trouvaient amplement de quoi se contenter. Ainsi l'on y venait par coutume, sans dessein d'écouter la comédie et savoir ce que l'on y jouait.[3]

However, there is no ambiguity about the lines in Boileau's *Épitre à M. Racine* (1677) in which he describes in vivid terms the obstacles which Molière had to overcome in his struggle for recognition. Here sections of the aristocracy are presented in a most unfavourable light, as hostile to the masterpieces of Molière:

> L'ignorance et l'erreur à ses naissantes pièces,
> En habits de marquis, en robes de comtesses,
> Venaient pour diffamer son chef-d'œuvre nouveau,
> Et secouaient la tête à l'endroit le plus beau.
> Le commandeur voulait la scène plus exacte;
> Le vicomte indigné sortait au second acte;
> L'un, défenseur zélé des bigots mis en jeu,
> Pour prix de ses bons mots le condamnait au feu.
> L'autre, fougueux marquis, lui déclarant la guerre,
> Voulait venger la cour immolée au parterre.[4]

In his *Réflexions sur la poétique* (1674) Rapin distinguishes between Plautus 'qui voulait plaire au peuple' and Terence 'qui voulait plaire aux honnêtes gens'; the former, he declares, exaggerated traits of

---

[1] The expression 'les trois parts' is not altogether clear; Racan presumably meant the *loges, théâtre*, and *parterre*.

[2] Racan, *Œuvres complètes*, ed. T. de Latour (Paris, 1857), 2 vols., vol. i, p. 354.

[3] *Nouvelles nouvelles* (Paris, 1663), 3 vols., vol. iii, pp. 221–2.

[4] Presumably an allusion to the satirical treatment of foolish *marquis* in certain of Molière's comedies.

character, whereas the latter 'se renfermait dans les bornes de la nature, et il représentait les vices sans les grossir et sans les augmenter'. Applying these principles to the theatre audiences of his own day, he is compelled to conclude: 'Toutefois ces caractères outrés, comme celui du gentilhomme bourgeois et du malade imaginaire de Molière, n'ont pas laissé de réussir depuis peu à la cour où l'on est si délicat; mais tout y est bien reçu, jusques aux divertissements de province, quand ils ont quelque air de plaisanterie, car on y aime à rire plus qu'à admirer.'[1]

Another interesting reflection on the taste of the aristocracy is furnished by Palaprat, one of the two authors of the famous comedy, *Le Grondeur* (1691). In his *Discours sur le Grondeur*, he states that it is a curious fact that when this comedy was first put on at the Comédie Française, 'elle fut sifflée par le théâtre et protégée par le parterre'. While he refuses to enter into a discussion as to which set of spectators make the better judges of drama, he declares: 'Disons seulement qu'en vérité, prix pour prix, il y a souvent autant de marchandise mêlée sur le théâtre que dans le parterre.' In the seats on the stage, he maintains, one finds people who insist on deciding the value of everything and imposing their decisions on other people; these are people 'que la jeunesse incertaine, qui entre toute neuve dans le monde, croit bonnement devoir prendre pour ses modèles'. There follows a vivid description of the reactions of the spectators on the stage to the first performance of *Le Grondeur*:

Il plut à quelques-uns de ceux-ci de venir à la première représentation du *Grondeur*, et de n'y pas venir de sang-froid. Il n'y eut sorte de singerie qu'ils ne fissent contre la pièce, sans malice et sans dessein peut-être, mais par la seule gaieté qui les animait. Tous les yeux se tournèrent de leur côté. Grichard[2] eut beau se démener, on le laissa crier tant qu'il voulut; et l'on n'eut plus d'attention pour l'ennuyeux spectacle d'un furieux et d'un enragé (car c'est ainsi qu'on l'appelait.) Le théâtre gronda à son tour d'avoir payé demi-pistole et se livra volontiers aux plaisanteries des jeunes gens enjoués, qui voulaient bien l'en dédommager en se donnant gratis eux-mêmes en spectacle.

La pièce fut enfin décriée à tel point dans l'esprit des gens du monde qu'à quelques jours de là feu M. le Prince, voulant aller à la comédie, demanda qu'on ne lui donnât pas le *Grondeur*, tant il en avait ouï dire de mal.

However, he finally agreed to come to the play and was so pleased with it that it was put on at court, where it was well received, with the result

---

[1] *Réflexions sur l'éloquence, la poétique, l'histoire et la philosophie* in *Les Comparaisons des grands hommes de l'antiquité* (Paris, 1684), 2 vols., vol. ii, p. 156.
[2] The chief character in the play.

that henceforth it was successful at the Comédie Française. 'Ce même théâtre qui l'avait vilipendée, par l'habitude outrée des Français de passer d'un excès à l'autre, commença à la porter beaucoup plus haut qu'elle ne méritait.'[1]

In considering the place of the aristocracy in the world of the seventeenth-century French theatre, we must also take into account the reactions to contemporary drama of the court proper—that is to say, of the King and the other members of the royal family and the lords and ladies of their immediate circle. It is not our intention to attempt in this book a systematic study of the interest taken by the court of the French kings in drama from 1600 to 1789, a subject which has never yet been studied in detail and which, despite many gaps in our sources of information, would yield valuable results if it were ever investigated. Here we are merely concerned with the general attitude to drama of Louis XIII and Louis XIV and their courtiers, since it overlaps to some extent with a study of the Paris theatre audiences of this century. Although the reactions of the Louvre or Versailles towards plays of the time might on occasion be different from those of the more mixed audiences in the various Paris theatres, no doubt many of the nobles and ladies who attended court performances were also assiduous spectators at the Hôtel de Bourgogne or the Comédie Française. Members of the royal family often attended performances in the ordinary theatres; Louis XIV's brother, Monsieur, and Madame were frequent spectators there, as were the Dauphin and his wife. If we know little of Louis XIII's visits to the Hôtel de Bourgogne after his early youth, it is an interesting fact that the young Louis XIV did not disdain to attend the Paris theatres before he took over the reins of power in 1661 and even for some time afterwards. In 1656, at the age of eighteen, he attended with his court a performance of Thomas Corneille's highly successful *Timocrate* at the Théâtre du Marais; according to Loret, he gave the actors a handsome present of 120 pistoles and

> Tint à l'auteur sur son ouvrage
> Un obligeant et doux langage.[2]

Two years later Louis and his court went to the Hôtel de Bourgogne for a performance of a lost tragedy, *Astyanax*, and shortly afterwards saw a performance given by the Italian actors.[3] At the beginning of 1659 they went to see Pierre Corneille's latest tragedy, *Œdipe*.[4] On

---

[1] Brueys, *Œuvres de Théâtre* (Paris, 1735), 3 vols., vol. ii, pp. viii–x.
[2] *Muse historique*, vol. ii, pp. 275–6.   [3] Ibid., vol. ii, pp. 431, 458.
[4] Ibid., vol. iii, p. 18.

9 July 1663 Lagrange recorded a visit by Louis to Molière's theatre to
see *L'École des Femmes* and *La Critique*: 'Le Roi nous honora de sa
présence en public'; and, six months later, on 10 January 1664, we find
the following entry: 'Joué dans notre salle au Palais Royal pour le Roi
la *Bradamante ridicule*.' Two years later, in January 1666, another
gazetier[1] records the presence of Louis, along with Monsieur and
Madame, at a performance at the Marais of Boyer's *pièce à machines*,
Jupiter et Sémélé.

Such visits to the Paris theatres were no doubt the exception during
the whole of our period, and long before Louis XIV gave up attending
performances at court, he seems to have ceased to attend the ordinary
theatres, although other members of the royal family continued to do
so. Performances given before the court in the various royal palaces in
and around Paris were clearly much more important. For details of
these our information is for the most part very scanty until we have
the Register of Lagrange to rely upon, and finally the Registers of the
Comédie Française. For the whole period down to 1680 our information is incomplete, since although, thanks to Lagrange's Register, we
know of at least most of the occasions when Molière and his company
performed at court and what plays they gave on nearly all these dates,
we have no such precise and virtually complete information about the
performances given by the other companies of the time, including the
very important Hôtel de Bourgogne. For the period before Molière's
return to Paris our information is even scrappier, and although a
clearer picture of theatrical activities at court in the seventeenth century could be pieced together from contemporary documents, this task
has not yet been undertaken.

Our present information about performances given at court during
the reign of Louis XIII is still fragmentary and for the early part of the
period we do not know the titles of plays performed there by professional companies.[2] We know that Théophile de Viau's *Pyrame et
Thisbé* was given before Louis XIII and his court, probably early in
1621.[3] Scudéry says of his tragi-comedy, *Ligdamon et Lidias*, which
was probably first performed in 1630: 'Toute la cour le vit trois fois à
Fontainebleau.'[4] It was about this date that Richelieu began to interest
himself in the drama and to give pensions to dramatists; he was even-

---

[1] La Gravette de Mayolas, *Lettres en vers*, 17 Jan. See *Les Continuateurs de Loret*,
ed. Baron James de Rothschild (Paris, 1881–9), 3 vols., vol. i, p. 613.
[2] See above, pp. 31 f.
[3] Adam, *Histoire de la littérature française au XVIIe siècle*, vol. i, p. 199.
[4] Preface to *Arminius*.

tually to have numerous plays performed at the Palais Cardinal. Although he was no doubt a much more important patron of the drama than his master, Louis XIII himself was not wholly without interest in the drama. We see him actively intervening in the theatrical life of Paris in 1635. 'La bonté de Sa Majesté', declared the *Gazette* of 6 January 1635, 'est telle qu'il veut entretenir trois bandes de comédiens: la première à l'Hôtel de Bourgogne, la seconde au Marais du Temple . . . et la troisième au faubourg Saint-Germain.'[1] The third company concerned did not long succeed in maintaining itself in Paris, but the interesting thing is that Louis should have intervened in this year in the distribution of actors among the existing companies in order to reinforce the Hôtel de Bourgogne with six performers. We learn also that in 1642 six actors and actresses of the Théâtre du Marais joined together with those at the Hôtel de Bourgogne to form a new company to exploit the latter theatre—'par le commandement de sa Majesté' as the legal agreement puts it.[2] Plays were dedicated to Louis XIII, for instance Rotrou's comedy, *La Bague de l'oubli* (published in 1635). Even if one must always treat with caution the praise contained in dedications, there must be a certain number of grains of truth in the following lines:

Sire,

Puisqu'enfin la comédie est en un point, où les plus honnêtes récréations ne lui peuvent plus causer d'envie, où elle se peut vanter d'être la passion de toute la France et le divertissement même de Votre Majesté, je ne trouve plus de honte à paraître, et je fais gloire d'avoir aidé à la rendre belle comme elle est. Les excellentes qualités de votre esprit font assez juger que tout ce que vous estimez est estimable; et ma muse serait une fille trop honteuse, si elle craignait la vue du peuple, après avoir été caressée par le plus grand roi de la terre. . . .

During the regency which followed, Anne of Austria continued to take an interest in the drama. In the dedication to his comedy, *Les Songes des hommes éveillés*, published in 1646, but probably performed two years earlier, Brosse declares that his play has had 'le bonheur de paraître assez glorieusement devant Leurs Majestés. . . . Les esprits de cour qui sont sans contredit les meilleurs et les [plus] délicats de Paris, ont parlé à son avantage en sept diverses représentations que la troupe royale en a données de jour à autre.' To the period of Mazarin belongs another reference to the court's interest in drama, this time in Quinault's

---

[1] Quoted in Deierkauf-Holsboer, *Le Théâtre du Marais*, vol. i (Paris, 1954), p. 39.

[2] Deierkauf-Holsboer, *Théâtre du Marais*, p. 83.

play, *La Comédie sans Comédie*, published in 1657. In this comedy a merchant is not at all pleased with the idea of having two actors as sons-in-law, for like many seventeenth-century French bourgeois he is convinced of the immorality of the theatre

> dont l'art dangereux n'a pour but que de plaire
> Aux désirs déréglés de l'ignorant vulgaire.

To these attacks on the theatre one of the actors replies that now the theatre is a highly moral institution, though things were earlier very different:

> Touchant la comédie, on peut dire avec vous
> Qu'elle fut autrefois l'art le plus vil de tous,
> Et qu'en vos jeunes ans elle était encore pleine
> De mille impuretés dignes de votre haine.

His insistence on the high morality of his art is taken up by the other prospective son-in-law:

> De ce qu'il fut jadis, il est bien différent,
> Son but n'est point de plaire au vulgaire ignorant;
> Il ne destine plus ses beautés sans égales
> Qu'aux esprits élevés et qu'aux âmes royales.

There follows praise of Louis XIV, the Queen Mother, and Mazarin as patrons of the drama.[1]

It was, however, during the period between Louis XIV's assumption of power in 1661 and his estrangement from the theatre in his years of piety that the drama saw its most brilliant period at the French court in the seventeenth century. There is no need to recount here the favour shown by *Le Roi Soleil* to Molière and especially Racine, the sumptuous fêtes of his years of splendour in which the drama played a prominent part, and the frequent performances of plays given by the various Paris companies in the brilliant setting of the royal palaces and gardens. It must not be forgotten, however, that from the time of the death of his Queen in 1683 and his attachment to Mme de Maintenon Louis began to lose interest in the drama. We can trace in Dangeau's Journal the King's gradual abandonment of theatre-going. In October 1684 he writes that the King went to see the Italian actors perform: 'C'était la seule comédie qu'il eût vue depuis la mort de la reine; il trouva la comédie fort mauvaise et s'y ennuya fort.'[2] Three weeks later,

---

[1] Act I, Sc. 5.
[2] Dangeau, *Journal*, ed. E. Soulié and others (Paris, 1854–60), 19 vols., vol. i, p. 60.

Dangeau informs us, 'le soir il y eut comédie française, le roi y vint et l'on choisit *Mithridate*, parce que c'est la comédie qui lui plaît le plus'.[1] After this date his appearances at theatrical performances become rarer and rarer until reference to Dangeau's Journal shows that they finally petered out altogether. Yet this did not happen quite so early as is suggested by Abbé de Choisy in his memoirs when he writes under the date of 1686: 'Il y avait tous les jours à Fontainebleau des comédies; mais le roi commença à n'y plus aller; on croyait d'abord que c'était affaires: on reconnut que c'était scrupule; et chacun admira qu'un prince à son âge eût la force de renoncer aux plaisirs.'[2] Dangeau's day-to-day account of happenings at court is here no doubt more reliable; it is not until 15 November 1691 that he notes in his Journal: 'Le soir il y eut comédie; le roi n'y va plus du tout.'[3] Louis's renunciation of theatrical performances was indeed a very gradual one. Until as late as 1702 he continued to attend amateur performances in which such members of the royal family as the Duchesse de Bourgogne and the Duc d'Orléans, the future Regent, played a prominent part; these amateur performances were mainly of religious plays such as Racine's *Athalie* or Duché's *Absalon*, but they could contain a farce as part of the entertainment. Moreover, as late as February 1702 Dangeau[4] and the *Mercure* record that Louis accompanied the Duchesse de Bourgogne to a performance, given by the actors of the Comédie Française, of a new tragedy, Ferrier's *Montézume*, followed by a comedy, *Le Grondeur*.

Theatrical performances still continued at court in these years despite the King's abstention from them. In 1702 his sister-in-law, Madame, in a letter to the Duchess of Hanover, wrote scathingly of the official attitude of Church and King to these entertainments. At the back of her mind—her reference to 'M. de Meaux' shows it clearly—was the thunder of Bossuet's *Maximes et Réflexions sur la Comédie* which had appeared eight years earlier:

Le malheur pour les pauvres comédiens, c'est que le roi ne veut plus de comédies. Tant qu'il y allait, ce n'était pas un péché; c'en était un si peu que les évêques y allaient journellement; il y avait une banquette pour eux, et elle

---

[1] *Journal*, vol. i, p. 67.

[2] *Mémoires* in *Nouvelle collection des Mémoires pour servir à l'histoire de France*, ed. J. F. Michaud and J. J. F. Poujoulat (Paris, 1836–9), 34 vols., 3rd ser., vol. vi, p. 618.

[3] Vol. iii, p. 431. See also the entry for 11 Jan. 1692: 'Le soir il y eut comédie italienne. Le roi ne va plus à aucune comédie' (vol. iv, p. 9).

[4] Vol. viii, p. 335.

était toujours bien garnie. M. de Meaux y était toujours. Depuis que le roi n'y va plus, c'est devenu un péché.[1]

It is, however, a curious fact that in the last three years of his life the old King, chastened by family and national misfortunes, was led by Mme de Maintenon to seek some comfort in the performance of comedies, especially those of Molière. The first entry on the subject in Dangeau's Journal is dated 21 December 1712: 'Le soir, chez Madame de Maintenon, il y eut grande musique, et le roi fit jouer par quelques-uns de ses musiciens des scènes du *Bourgeois gentilhomme*.' Three weeks later, on 13 January 1713, Dangeau noted a second performance, this time of the whole play; the King, says the Journal, 's'y divertit fort'. These and the other performances which followed down to 2 August 1715, to within a month of the King's death, were not, as Dangeau is careful to point out,[2] regular performances by the actors of the Comédie Française; the comedies were all performed by Louis's musicians in the privacy of Mme de Maintenon's apartment. Dangeau does not always give the title of the plays performed; when he does, we see that most of them were by Molière, such plays as the *Bourgeois gentilhomme*, *Le Médecin malgré lui*, and *Le Mariage forcé* being given several times, although comedies by other authors were also performed, for instance, *Le Grondeur*, *Crispin muscien*, and *Le Baron d'Albikrac*. Such were the tastes of the old King in the last three years of his life.

What was the general level of taste at the court in our period in the matter of the drama? So far as we are able to form an opinion on this question from the very scattered material at our disposal, it would seem fairly safe to conclude that it was very much the same as that of the much more mixed audiences of the Paris theatres, at least if we have in mind the average theatre-goers of the time, those who did not lay any claim to belong to the select band of connoisseurs known as 'les doctes' or more frequently 'les savants'. True, there were occasional divergences between the taste of the court and that of the Paris theatres, but where information about these has come down to us, they seem rather accidental and due to more or less inexplicable whims, except when, as occasionally happened, social prejudices were aroused. Thus in the preface to his *Plaideurs* Racine tells us that some people who saw the play at the Hôtel de Bourgogne 's'imaginèrent qu'il était bienséant à eux de s'y ennuyer, et que les matières de Palais ne pou-

[1] Charlotte-Élisabeth d'Orléans, *Correspondance*, transl. E. Jaeglé (Paris, 1890), 3 vols., vol. i, p. 277.
[2] 4 Sept. 1713.

vaient pas être un sujet de divertissement pour des gens de cour'. However, the subject-matter of the play—its satire upon the contemporary legal world—did not prevent it from being a success at Versailles, and, as Racine puts it, 'ceux qui avaient cru se déshonorer de rire à Paris furent peut-être obligés de rire à Versailles pour se faire honneur'.

Some interesting and significant clashes between the taste of the Paris theatre audience and that of the court do appear to have taken place towards the end of our period; as we shall see, they were to become much more common in the eighteenth century. In his manuscript notes[1] De Tralage has some remarks to make on this question: 'Depuis quelque temps on s'est mis en tête à la cour de trouver mauvais ce que l'on avait approuvé à Paris. Par exemple, la tragédie de *Judith* en 1694,[2] où tout Paris avait été avec empressement, a été méprisée à la cour.' It is true that he provides a rather curious reason for this state of affairs: 'La brigue de M. Racine et de M. Despréaux y a beaucoup contribué; il y a des gens qui aiment à se laisser mener. Ils ne voient ni n'entendent que par autrui.' He also notes a similar phenomenon with regard to the latest *dancourade*, *La Foire de Bezons*: 'En 1695 la petite comédie de *La Foire de Bezons*, qui a valu 20,000 francs aux comédiens français,[3] a été rebutée à Fontainebleau devant la cour, et l'on a dit hautement qu'on s'étonnait comment elle n'avait point été sifflée dans le commencement.' De Tralage adds the significant comment: 'Les gens de cour, et surtout les dames, affectent de mépriser ce que les bourgeois ont estimé. Cela a plus l'air de qualité et marque un génie supérieur; à peine le bourgeois a-t-il le sens commun.'

An interesting comment on the differences between the taste of the court and of Paris audiences is to be found in the discussion of two early comedies of Lesage in the *Histoire du Théâtre Français* of the Parfaict brothers.[4] It must be borne in mind in considering these comments that although the two plays in question, *Don César Ursin* and *Crispin rival de son maître*, enjoyed their first run together at the Comédie Française in 1707, the observations of the Parfaict brothers were made much later in the eighteenth century, at a time when the outlook on such matters

---

[1] Bibliothèque de l'Arsenal, vol. iv (MS. 6544), f. 221.

[2] Boyer's *Judith* was given at the Comédie Française in Mar. and Apr. 1695. It had seventeen performances in its first run. On seven occasions it brought in over 1,000 livres in receipts.

[3] This play scored a phenomenal success at the Comédie Française in Aug. and Sept. 1695. It was given thirty times in that period and on seventeen occasions brought in receipts of over 1,000 livres.

[4] Vol. xiv, pp. 442–3.

appears to have evolved considerably. We are told that while the longer comedy, *Don César Ursin*, was a failure at the Comédie Française (it ran for only six performances and was never revived) and the little one-act play, *Crispin rival de son maître*, was a success, exactly the opposite happened at court:

> On parut assez satisfait de *Don César Ursin*, et la comédie de *Crispin rival* fut regardée comme une farce. Il ne serait pas difficile de concilier ces jugements, qui paraissent si contraires, en observant qu'en général à la Cour on porte un tout autre esprit qu'à la Ville. *Don César Ursin* est bien écrit, l'intrigue soutenue et singulière. C'en était assez pour mériter l'indulgence des auditeurs. *Crispin rival* ne présente qu'un petit événement, et qui ne peut intéresser que par la force du comique, qui règne dans cette pièce du commencement à la fin; et de là cet événement et ce comique parurent déplacés au ton mesuré, qui était alors le dominant. A la Ville le vrai et le sentiment l'emportent sur la politique; ainsi ces deux pièces furent jugées avec équité. Et depuis l'auteur en convenait avec ses amis.

So far as we can judge from the penury of documents at our disposal, it does appear as if in our period there was no great gulf between the taste of the spectators at the court and the more mixed audiences of the Paris theatres in which, as we have seen, the aristocracy was powerfully represented. It is tempting at first to take at their face value the numerous pieces of praise lavished by contemporaries on the court as 'le centre du bon goût'. No doubt there were among the courtiers of the time a certain number of people who qualified for the title of 'savants'; more numerous still were people who possessed a good general culture and the ability to appreciate intelligently great works of drama. One thinks, for instance, of men and women of the aristocracy like La Rochefoucauld or Bussy-Rabutin, Mme de Sévigné or Mme de La Fayette, and no doubt there were many more. Even so, the attempt made by writers of the period to distinguish between the taste of the court and that of the rest—of *le peuple* or *le bourgeois*—is seldom convincing. We are reminded irresistibly of the famous passage on *les grands* in La Bruyère: 'Ces hommes, si grands ou par leur naissance, ou par leur faveur, ou par leurs dignités, ces têtes si fortes et si habiles, ces femmes si polies et si spirituelles, tous méprisent le peuple, et ils sont peuple.' Or if this is going too far, if we wish to find a more appropriate description of the attitude of the aristocracy to the theatre, compared with that of wider circles of the society of the time, we can take the earlier words of La Bruyère:

> Qui dit le peuple dit plus d'une chose: c'est une vaste expression, et l'on

s'étonnerait de voir ce qu'elle embrasse, et jusques où elle s'étend. Il y a le peuple qui est opposé aux grands: c'est la populace et la multitude; il y a le peuple qui est opposé aux sages, aux habiles et aux vertueux: ce sont les grands comme les petits.[1]

To say this is not to suggest that in the absolutist and aristocratic society of seventeenth-century France the court and the more or less exclusive circles associated with it did not exercise a tremendous influence on both the content and the form of the drama of the age. It is simply to maintain that the gulf between the taste of the court and the taste of the *peuple* which is described in several contemporary documents did not in fact exist, and that farce, for instance, was not something put on simply to amuse 'le petit peuple' or 'la racaille'. Although the history of French drama in the opening decades of the seventeenth century remains obscure, it does seem quite clear that no such gulf between the taste of the aristocracy and the lower orders existed in those years. The upper classes of French society from the King and court downwards enjoyed, as we have seen, the antics of the great farce actors of the early seventeenth century—Gros-Guillaume or Gaultier-Garguille; and the same upper classes continued to do so, whether in the circles of the court or in the high society of Paris.

Tallemant relates in his portrait of la Présidente Perrot that, when a group of people were going to perform Racan's *Bergeries* in the house of a *Greffier du Parlement*, 'il prit une fantaisie à un vieux garçon, parent du Président, nommé Montgazon, garçon qui avait vu tout le beau monde de Paris, de proposer de jouer une farce après cette pastorale; on ne fit que rire de cette pensée'. Finally the proposal was taken up, and the cast was arranged as follows: the part of 'la fille à marier' was taken by Madame la Présidente—or rather Madame la Conseillère as she then was, while Monsieur le Conseiller Perrot contented himself with the minor role of 'quatrième amoureux'. The father was played by the Président's cousin, the well-known translator, Perrot d'Ablancourt, and the famous lawyer, Patru, took the part of 'premier amoureux'. Another Conseiller was given the role of the 'écolier,' while that of Gros-Guillaume was allotted to 'un gentilhomme de Brie, nommé Meneton'. Tallemant's comments on the performance are very illuminating: 'D'Ablancourt, au jugement de tous, passa de bien loin Gaultier-Garguille, dont il avait imité l'habit. Il chanta aussi une chanson comme lui. En un endroit de la pièce Meneton surpassa aussi Gros-

---

[1] *Les Caractères*, chap. ix, No. 53. (The second passage was added in the 4th ed., the first in the 6th ed.)

Guillaume, car ils paraissaient l'un et l'autre aussi naturels que ces deux excellents acteurs, et avaient bien plus d'esprit.' The first performance was such a success that another was given at the house of the Présidente's mother.[1]

D'Ablancourt, we have seen, scored a great success by singing one of Gaultier-Garguille's songs. In the *privilège* for a collection of these songs, dated 4 March 1631, the chaste Louis XIII is made to state that

notre cher et bien aimé Hugues Guéru dit Fléchelles, l'un de nos comédiens ordinaires, nous a fait remontrer qu'ayant composé un petit livre intitulé *Les nouvelles chansons de Gaultier-Garguille*, il le désirerait mettre en lumière et faire imprimer, mais il craint qu'autres que celui à qui il donnerait charge de l'imprimer ne le contrefissent et n'ajoutassent quelques autres chansons plus dissolues que les siennes, s'il ne lui était sur ce par nous pourvu de nos lettres nécessaires. . . .[2]

Poor Gaultier-Garguille! One could scarcely ask for 'chansons plus dissolues que les siennes'. It is true that out of the sixty-six pieces in the volume entitled *Les Chansons de Gaultier-Garguille* (1632), piously reproduced by Émile Magne in his *Gaultier-Garguille, comédien de l'Hôtel de Bourgogne*, two seem strangely out of place in such a collection. One is reminded at once of the rather artificial sentiments and form of so much of the society verse of the age in such songs as

> Que je me plais sous votre loi,
> Cloris, sitôt que je vous vois,
>   Ma joie est sans seconde,
> Car vous avez je ne sais quoi
>   Qui charme tout le monde.[3]

or

> Je ne sais que j'ai au cœur,
> Toute la nuit je soupire,
> Je sens une vive ardeur
> Qui sans cesse me martyre.
> Une bergère d'ici
> Est cause de mon souci.[4]

The tone of the remaining sixty-four songs, however, amply fulfils the promise of the *privilège*. Their subject-matter and style are clearly revealed in such opening lines as

---

[1] *Historiettes*, vol. v, pp. 17–19.
[2] The privilège is printed in the two editions published in Paris in 1632 and 1636 (Bibliothèque Nationale, Rés. Ye. 2651 and 2652).
[3] xv.   [4] xxxii.

> Un jour en me promenant
> Dans l'épais d'un vert bocage,
> Trouvai Philin et Philis,
> Qui faisaient un beau ménage.[1]

or

> Fillettes, ne faites point
> Comme cela les honteuses,
> Lorsqu'on vous parle du point
> Qui vous rend toutes heureuses.[2]

or again

> Catin dormait dessus l'herbette,
> Colin leva sa chemisette . . . .[3]

Such songs naturally vary in indelicacy both of subject-matter and form, but it is difficult to imagine any of them being sung today before a mixed audience of at any rate reasonable respectability. Yet in the *Stances à Gaultier Garguille sur ses chansons*, which a poet who hides modestly under the initials 'D. M.'[4] addressed in the fashion of the time to the author, these songs are described in the following terms:

> Ce sont des airs de cour que Paris idolâtre,
> Qui sont les passetemps qu'on rencontre au théâtre,
>   Et les délices de nos jours;
> En un mot, leur beauté ne peut être exprimée
>   Que par la bouche des Amours
> Et par le bon récit qu'en fait la Renommée.

These 'airs de cour' could, we are further told, 'charmer l'oreille d'un Monarque'; indeed, the author continues,

> Gaultier aura l'honneur que les plus belles dames
> Emprunteront ses vers pour décrire leurs flammes.

No doubt one must take such remarks with a suitable quantity of salt, and yet not only did D'Ablancourt, later *de l'Académie Française*, and his circle admire Gaultier-Garguille; this farce-actor, along with others, undoubtedly entertained the King and his court on many occasions down to his death in 1632.

A generation later the King and court enjoyed equally thoroughly the farce of their time. In his youth and early manhood Louis XIV laughed as heartily as anyone at the antics of farce actors, French or

---

[1] i.   [2] xxix.   [3] xlii.

[4] Émile Magne suggests (op. cit., p. 82 n.) that these initials stand for Philippe de Mondor, the brother of the illustrious Tabarin.

Italian. In 1654, when the young King was in his sixteenth year, Loret inserted the following item in his rhymed news-sheet:

> Mais, à propos de comédie
> Il faut qu'en cet endroit je die
> Qu'un des jours passés Jean Doucet,
> Franc nigaud, comme chacun sait,
> Pensa faire pâmer de rire
> La Reine et le Roi notre sire,
> Et même tous les courtisans,
> Par les mots niais, mais plaisants,
> Que proféra sa propre bouche,
> Étant valet de Scaramouche,
> Sur le théâtre italien,
> Où ce simple et naïf chrétien,
> Sans avoir masque ou faux visage,
> Joua fort bien son personnage.

More interesting still, in the lines which follow Loret stresses the continuity of this tradition of farce actors performing at court right back to the opening decades of the seventeenth century.

> Jamais Mezzetin ni Scapin,
> Ni Trivelin, ni Turlupin,
> Ni Colombine, ni Briguelle,
> Ni le rare Polichinelle,
> Ni Gorju, le pédant gaillard,
> Ni Jodelet, le nasillard,
> Ni Garguille, ni Gros-Guillaume,
> Les plus grands bouffons du royaume,
> Ne divertirent mieux la cour
> Qu'elle le fut en cedit jour.[1]

In 1659, in relating a rumour (soon to be proved false) of the death of the famous Italian actor Scaramouche, Loret stresses his success with the higher ranks of society. 'Sanglotez, pleurez, soupirez', he tells all theatre-lovers, both 'bourgeois et courtisans', and in his epitaph of Scaramouche he declares:

> Alors qu'il vivait parmi nous,
> Il eut le don de plaire à tous,
> Mais bien plus aux grands qu'aux gens minces,
> Et on le nommait en tous lieux
> Le prince des facétieux
> Et le facétieux des princes.[2]

---

[1] *Muse historique*, vol. i, p. 465.   [2] Ibid., vol. iii, pp. 114–15.

The court's passion for the Italian actors continued into the personal reign of Louis XIV. In 1665 Robinet tells us of the success of the actress Brigida Bianchi with the King:

> Olaria, comédienne,
> Traita ces jours passés avec beaucoup d'apprêt
> Le Roi dans son cabaret.
> Et les amours de cette Italienne
> Parmi ses pintes et ses pots
> Divertirent beaucoup ce glorieux héros.[1]

The success of the Italian actors, particularly of Scaramouche (Fiorelli) and Arlequin (Dominique), at the court of Louis XIV is the subject of innumerable anecdotes which, if not all of complete authenticity, do prove that their favour was considerable.

If it is true, as Tallemant alleges,[2] that at the time when Molière returned to Paris from the provinces farce was extinct at the Hôtel de Bourgogne and survived at the rival theatre of the Marais only because of Jodelet, it remains a fact that Molière's success with the King at his first performance in Paris was achieved as a farce actor. He and his company appeared before the King and court at the Louvre on 24 October 1658; all that Lagrange can say about the reception given to their performance of Corneille's tragedy, *Nicomède*, is that 'ces nouveaux acteurs ne déplurent point, et on fut surtout fort satisfait de l'ajustement et du jeu des femmes'. But when they ended the proceedings with *Le Docteur amoureux*, one of the little farces which Molière had brought with him from the provinces, their success was complete. 'M. de Molière faisait le Docteur; et la manière dont il s'acquitta de ce personnage le mit dans une si grande estime que Sa Majesté donna des ordres pour établir sa troupe à Paris.'[3]

During the rest of Molière's career in Paris, down to his death in 1673, his company frequently performed at court—at the Louvre, at Saint Germain, at Versailles, at Chambord and also at other places at which the King was entertained. In considering the statistics of these performances derived from Lagrange's Register,[4] we must bear in mind not only that they are incomplete, but also that the number of times a play of Molière could be performed before Louis and the court during the author's lifetime depended to some extent on the date of

---

[1] *Continuateurs de Loret*, vol. i, p. 473.
[2] *Historiettes*, vol. vii, p. 126.
[3] Preface to the 1682 ed. of Molière's works, reproduced in *Œuvres*, ed. E. Despois and P. Mesnard (Paris, 1873–1900), 13 vols., vol. i, pp. xiv–xv.
[4] *Œuvres*, vol. i, pp. 539–57.

its first performance. It is obvious that, unless it had been performed at
court before its first run in Paris, *Le Malade imaginaire* could not have
been seen there, as Molière died after the fourth performance at the
Palais Royal. It is also clear that an early play like *L'Étourdi* or *Le
Dépit amoureux* stood a better chance of being performed at court
than, say, *Tartufe* or *Le Misanthrope*. Again, we do not know who was
responsible for the choice of the plays which Molière and his company
performed before the King. Yet even bearing all these reservations in
mind, one is still faintly astonished at the number of times certain plays
were performed at court and the absence of others from the list:

10 performances	*Fâcheux.*	
9	„	*Cocu imaginaire, Princesse d'Élide.*
8	„	*École des Maris, École des Femmes.*
7	„	*Dépit amoureux.*
6	„	*Étourdi, Mariage forcé.*
5	„	*Précieuses ridicules.*
4	„	*Impromptu de Versailles, George Dandin.*
3	„	*Dom Garcie de Navarre, Critique de L'École des Femmes, Amour médecin, Tartufe, Avare.*[1]
2	„	*Comtesse d'Escarbagnas.*
1 performance		*Médecin malgré lui, Mélicerte, Sicilien, Amphitryon, Pourceaugnac, Amants magnifiques, Bourgeois gentilhomme, Psyché, Femmes savantes.*
no performance		*Dom Juan, Misanthrope, Fourberies de Scapin, Malade imaginaire.*

That slight comedies like *Les Fâcheux* and *Le Cocu imaginaire* should
have been given so often at court is perhaps not quite so surprising
as it appears at first sight, since they were early plays. *L'École des
Femmes*, another relatively early play, is quite honourably placed, but
Tartufe and *L'Avare* seem very low on the list. It is surprising to see
such a masterpiece as *Le Médecin malgré lui* given only once at court
during Molière's lifetime, when we see the success enjoyed by *Les
Fâcheux* or *Le Cocu imaginaire*. Knowing as we do that *Dom Juan*
encountered considerable hostility in devout circles and had to be
taken off in the middle of its first run at the Palais Royal, it is scarcely to
be wondered at that it should not figure in this list. Among other plays
never performed at court during Molière's lifetime *Les Fourberies de
Scapin*, it must be remembered, came late in his career (it was first
performed in May 1671). That still leaves one play in this category to

[1] A third performance of *L'Avare* is mentioned in Hubert's register for Sept. 1672. See
Schwartz, 'Molière's Theater in 1672-3', p. 414.

account for, if one can—*Le Misanthrope*. It is true that its first performance in Paris in June 1666 occurred at an inauspicious moment: the death of the Queen Mother in January of that year had sent the court into mourning, and it does not appear to have been until December that the King called upon the services of Molière's company again, and even then it was only to play a part in the *Ballet des Muses*. Yet when all is said and done, it does remain an astonishing fact that *Le Misanthrope* was not performed before the court during Moliere's lifetime.

It is instructive to compare with these figures the number of performances given by Molière and his company in their Paris theatres from Easter 1659 to Easter 1673 (including the few performances given immediately after the death of Molière). Here we are, of course, dealing with an absolutely complete list, but the same reservations are necessary with regard to the differing periods of time during which each separate play could be performed. The following is a list of Molière's plays performed in these years in descending order of popularity:

Cocu imaginaire	122	performances
École des Maris	108	,,
Fâcheux	106	,,
École des Femmes	88	,,
Tartufe, Psyché	81	,,
Dépit amoureux	65	,,
Étourdi, Amour médecin	63	,,
Misanthrope, Médecin malgré lui	59	,,
Précieuses ridicules	56	,,
Amphitryon	53	,,
Pourceaugnac	49	,,
Avare	47	,,
Bourgeois gentilhomme	44	,,
George Dandin	39	,,
Mariage forcé	37	,,
Critique de l'École des Femmes	36	,,
Princesse d'Élide	25	,,
Femmes savantes	24	,,
Impromptu de Versailles, Le Sicilien	20	,,
Comtesse d'Escarbagnas	19	,,
Fourberies de Scapin	18	,,
Dom Juan	15	,,
Malade imaginaire	13	,,
Dom Garcie	9	,,

There are some fairly close similarities between the two lists: *Les Fâcheux*, *Le Cocu imaginaire*, *L'École des Maris*, and *L'École des Femmes* were among the five most popular plays both in Paris and at the court. On the other hand, *Tartufe*, *L'Avare*, and especially *Le Misanthrope* were given much more frequently for the general public than for the King. Even when every allowance has been made, the comparison is all to the advantage of the more mixed audiences of the Petit-Bourbon and the Palais Royal. Certainly, to put it no more strongly, there is no sign whatsoever that the King and the lords and ladies of the court possessed a more refined taste than did the much less homogeneous audiences which patronized the performances given by Molière and his company in Paris.

For the period from Molière's death down to the foundation of the Comédie Française in 1680 we have no means of telling how often his plays were performed at court. However, we have almost complete figures for the thirty-five years which followed; they form an interesting basis of comparison with those for the years from 1659 to 1673, provided one bears in mind that we are dealing here with a much longer period of time, and also that all the plays concerned were available for performance throughout the whole period, and not, as previously, according to the date at which they were written and produced:

26 performances	*Médecin malgré lui*, *Femmes savantes*.
23	„	*Comtesse d'Escarbagnas*.
21	„	*Mariage forcé*.
20	„	*Cocu imaginaire*, *Tartufe*.
19	„	*Misanthrope*.
17	„	*École des Femmes*.
15	„	*Précieuses ridicules*, *George Dandin*, *Avare*.
13	„	*Étourdi*, *École des Maris*, *Amphitryon*.
12	„	*Fâcheux*, *Amour médecin*, *Bourgeois gentilhomme*.
9	„	*Pourceaugnac*.
6	„	*Dépit amoureux*.
5	„	*Malade imaginaire*.
4	„	*Sicilien*.
3	„	*Fourberies de Scapin*.
2	„	*Dom Juan* (Thomas Corneille's version).
1 performance	*Critique de l'École des Femmes*.
no performance	*Dom Garcie de Navarre*, *Impromptu de Versailles*, *Princesse d'Élide*, *Mélicerte*, *Amants magnifiques*, *Psyché*.

This list does, it is true, contain a number of surprises; one wonders at the popularity of *La Comtesse d'Escarbagnas*; but it will be seen that *Le Misanthrope* had completely recovered from its neglect during Molière's lifetime, and if various farces appear to enjoy perhaps undue prominence, this is no doubt partly explained by the custom of putting on a short comedy or farce as *petite pièce* after the main dish of a five-act comedy or tragedy.

On the other hand, if we compare with the above list the per-formances of Molière at the Comédie Française in the years from 1680 to 1715, we find some interesting discrepancies. The ten most popular Molière plays at the Comédie Française in this period were:

Tartufe	332	performances
Avare	288	,,
George Dandin	280	,,
Médecin malgré lui	277	,,
Misanthrope	265	,,
Amphitryon	248	,,
Cocu imaginaire	237	,,
Dom Juan (Thomas Corneille's version)	217	,,
Comtesse d'Escarbagnas	211	,,
École des Femmes	210	,,

If there are one or two peculiar features about this list (for instance, the relative unpopularity of *Les Femmes savantes*, which was given only 184 times), it does maintain a certain balance between longer and shorter comedies which is absent from the list of court performances in the same period. Yet it is the list of performances given at court during Molière's lifetime which—for all the reservations one must make in attempting to interpret it—that causes one the greatest surprise and raises the most serious doubts about the taste in drama of Louis XIV and his court. It was, after all, relatively easy to be wise after the event, to pick out for performance at court the most important plays of a dead author. This was done at court on the whole with fair success in the period between 1680 and the end of the reign. But when all is said and done, the acid test of the taste in drama of Louis XIV and his court is the reception which they afforded to Molière's plays during the years of struggles and triumphs in Paris; and when every allowance is made for the incompleteness of our information and other technical difficulties, it is clear that they come out of it rather poorly.

To conclude that in its dealings with the theatre the aristocracy of seventeenth-century France did not exhibit any particular refinement of taste, is not to seek to deny that it exercised an influence on drama

commensurate with its exalted place in the society of the age. We have
seen how playwrights and other writers of the time tended, if anything,
to exaggerate the importance of the aristocracy in the theatre world
of the time. However conscious one must be of the part played in the
Paris theatres of the time by spectators drawn from less elevated sections of society, one must none the less subscribe to the view that the
aristocracy did play an important part in moulding the taste of the day
in the theatre as in other forms of literature. The term 'aristocratic
audience' is certainly misleading if it is taken to imply that the overwhelming proportion of the audience were men and women possessed
of blue blood; that was simply not true of the Paris theatre audiences
of our period. The middle classes of the time undoubtedly provided a
large quota of theatre-goers, and it is probable that the lower orders of
society were not entirely unrepresented, though not, of course, in relation to their true numbers. Yet not only did the aristocracy provide a
substantial proportion of the audience in the different theatres of the
time; not only did the aristocratic spectators, by occupying a great part
of the more expensive theatre seats, furnish a higher proportion of the
daily box offices receipts than their mere numbers would suggest; in
addition, it must never be forgotten, they formed what was the social
élite of their age, held in respect by their inferiors in a way which it is
difficult for us to imagine today.

One small detail which brings out very clearly the importance of the
aristocracy in theatre audiences of the time is to be observed in the
little polemical plays which were written to defend a new play against its
enemies or occasionally to attack a successful play. The model of this
minor genre is Molière's *Critique de l'École des Femmes*, performed in 1663
after the success of his recent comedy. It was he who set the example,
which was to be so closely followed, of giving the main parts in a play
of this kind to members of the aristocracy; it is taken as self-evident
that it is their opinions which count most, even though Molière puts
into the mouth of one of the noblemen a warm defence of the taste of
the *parterre*. Ignoring the lackey, who takes no part in the discussion,
we find that the only character in the play who is not obviously an
aristocrat is Lysidas, the professional writer, who incidentally receives,
along with his fellows, a severe drubbing when Dorante attacks the
foibles of authors—'leurs grimaces savantes et leurs raffinements ridicules, leur vicieuse coutume d'assassiner les gens de leurs ouvrages,
leur friandise de louanges, leurs ménagements de pensées, leur trafic de
réputation, et leurs ligues offensives et défensives, aussi bien que leurs

guerres d'esprit et leurs combats de prose et de vers'.[1] Among the other characters Dorante is described as a *chevalier*, and his opponent as chief critic of Molière is a *marquis*; all three female characters, the *précieuse* Climène and the two cousins Uranie and Élise, obviously belong to the ranks of the aristocracy. It is true that neither the Marquis nor Climène gives a flattering notion of the taste of the nobility of Molière's day, but both Dorante and the two cousins, who are admirers of *L'École des Femmes*, are represented as the embodiment of common sense. We feel here very clearly how Molière deliberately appeals over the heads of the so-called 'savants' to the great mass of his audience—whether it be the spectators of the *parterre* whose taste is defended, or the representatives of the aristocracy who, even when they are not 'savants', have acquired, thanks to 'le simple bon sens naturel et le commerce de tout le beau monde . . . une manière d'esprit, qui, sans comparaison, juge plus finement des choses que tout le savoir enrouillé des pédants'. All these musty discussions about rules should be left to the pedants, Dorante argues; and, although he declares that perhaps in no other play have the rules been more closely observed than in *L'École des Femmes*, he maintains that the supreme test of a play is whether or not it has given pleasure. 'Laissons nous aller de bonne foi aux choses qui nous prennent par les entrailles, et ne cherchons point de raisonnements pour nous empêcher d'avoir du plaisir.' While Molière does not disdain the *parterre* and even goes out of his way to defend its taste, it is clearly the outlook of the *honnêtes gens* of his time which stands forth most clearly in this little play.

In his second contribution to the controversy aroused by the success of *L'École des Femmes*, his *Impromptu de Versailles*, Molière deserts the aristocratic drawing-room of the *Critique* for 'la salle de la comédie' at Versailles, and brings on the stage not noblemen and noblewomen, but his own actors and actresses. But the example set in the *Critique* was followed by his enemies. The first reply to his little play came in Donneau de Visé's *Zélinde, comédie, ou la véritable Critique de l'École des Femmes et critique de la Critique*. The characters of *Zélinde* are definitely of more mixed social origins than those of Molière's play. There is the inevitable *poète*, but in addition to three aristocratic characters—father, daughter, and her lover—there is a *femme savante* (Zélinde), a 'bourgeois de Paris', and, more important, Argimont, 'marchand de dentelle de la rue Saint-Denis', whose acquaintance we have already made.[2] The part played by Argimont in the discussion of

[1] Sc. 6.   [2] See above, pp. 89–90.

the play is an important one: he denounces a great many faults in both *L'École des Femmes* and the *Critique*. On the other hand, we have seen what an obsequious role he is made to play when he is invited by a young noblewoman to give his opinion of the play. It is true that his first remark is not so modest as it appears at first sight. Donneau de Visé repeatedly attempts to embroil Molière with the aristocratic members of his audience by stressing the unheard-of insolence of an actor who dares to make fun of foolish *Marquis* in his comedies. That is why Argimont is made to say: 'Ah, madame, ce n'est pas à moi à porter jugement d'une pièce de cette nature; les gens de qualité en pourraient mieux parler que moi, et dire s'ils y sont bien ou mal dépeints', and Oriane to retort: 'Ah, que vous me plaisez de parler de la sorte. N'est-ce pas une chose étrange que des gens de qualité souffrent qu'on les joue en plein théâtre?'[1] But Argimont's attitude later in this scene is undoubtedly obsequious when, after stressing how the other bourgeois spectators of the *parterre* follow the lead given by 'quinze ou seize marchands de cette rue', he hastens to add that, of course, surprising as it may sound, 'ils se sont toujours trouvés du sentiment des gens de qualité'. Obviously what better proof could be offered of the discernment of his fellow shopkeepers?

The relatively important place given to a mere bourgeois in Donneau de Visé's play is, however, the exception which proves the rule that in plays of this type the greatest prominence should be given to members of the aristocracy. In the next play in the controversy, Boursault's *Le Portrait du Peintre ou la Contre-Critique de l'École des Femmes*, we have a close imitation of Molière's choice of characters—a Baron, a Count, a *chevalier*, a *marquise*, two other noblewomen, and the inevitable *poète*. It is significant that in his second contribution to the controversy, his *Réponse à l'Impromptu de Versailles ou La Vengeance des Marquis*, Donneau de Visé adopted the same formula of a discussion in a drawing-room among aristocrats of both sexes. Indeed, all his characters are nobles (there is not even an author in the play) except for the valet who is represented as going 'trois ou quatre fois la semaine' to the theatre with his master, a *marquis*, and who is brought on to the stage[2] to furnish a not very amusing answer to Molière's statement that in comedy the 'marquis ridicule' had taken the place of 'le valet bouffon'.[3]

The most virulent of all the attacks on Molière in this controversy, Montfleury's *Impromptu de l'Hôtel de Condé*, has a rather different setting. Instead of a drawing-room we are shown, as in Corneille's

---

[1] Sc. 3.   [2] Sc. 7.   [3] *Impromptu de Versailles*, Sc. 1.

Galerie du Palais some thirty years earlier, the famous shopping-centre of seventeenth-century Paris, the gallery of the Palais de Justice. However, although, in addition to two actors of the Hôtel de Bourgogne, we are shown on the stage a *solliciteur de procès* and a *marchande de livres*, nearly all the discussion of Molière and his comedies is conducted among a foolish *marquis*, a *marquise* (not his wife) who has a law-suit which she wins, Alcidon, another nobleman, and a second *marquis*, Cléante, who appears towards the end of the play. In other words, despite the setting the prominent roles in the play, whether the persons concerned be for or against Molière, are given to members of the aristocracy.[1]

Not all the plays in this controversy were hostile to Molière. An actor of the Marais theatre, Chevalier, produced a sort of prologue to a comedy called *Les Amours de Calotin*, which is largely favourable to Molière. It is true that Molière and all his works are bitterly attacked by a foolish Baron, but the rest of the spectators who are shown seated on the stage of the Marais theatre, a *Marquis*, a *Chevalier*, and a *Comte*, take up a very different attitude towards the whole dispute. In the second half of this prologue we are also introduced to such figures as the Baron de la Crasse (of Poisson's play), Mascarille (of *Les Précieuses ridicules*), and Monsieur de la Souche (Arnolphe of *L'École des femmes*), who all leave the theatre in disgust at the satirical remarks of the actors on the stage; but once again all the more or less serious discussion of Molière and his plays is put into the mouths of members of the aristocracy.

Later in the century other little plays of this type continued to follow in the tradition of Molière's *Critique de l'École des Femmes*. Subligny's *La Folle Querelle ou la Critique d'Andromaque*, which was performed at Molière's theatre in 1668, has in its opening scene a conversation between a *valet de chambre* and a *femme de chambre*, but they do little more than inform the spectator that their master and mistress, who are engaged to each other, have had a quarrel about Racine's tragedy. It is the four members of the aristocracy—a young noblewoman, her lover, his more successful rival, and a *vicomtesse*—who argue over the merits of the play. In the following year, after the success at the Hôtel de Bourgogne of his comedy, *La Femme juge et partie*, Montfleury produced a little play, *Le Procès de la Femme juge et partie*;

---

[1] Although Lancaster includes them in his list of extant plays, neither Robinet's *Panégyrique de l'École des Femmes* nor La Croix's *La Guerre comique* seems to deserve the title of play; however, in both works the aristocratic characters, male and female, play a preponderant part.

the characters in it are exclusively aristocratic—three noblemen who frequent the court, and four ladies, who are dressed up as judges and offer their verdict on Montfleury's comedy.

The use of this type of play was taken up by two writers who furnished scenes and plays in French for the Italian actors in the last two decades of the seventeenth century—Delosme de Monchesnay and Regnard. The former produced in 1688 his *Critique de la Cause des Femmes*, a defence of a comedy performed at the Hôtel de Bourgogne in the previous year. The action of the *Critique* takes place in the house of Cinthio, an elderly bourgeois with a flighty young wife, named Isabelle, who gads around at the theatre and elsewhere with noblemen and women acquaintances; Isabelle has returned from the theatre along with Colombine, a *baronne*, Arlequin, a *chevalier*, and Mezzetin, an Italian count. They proceed to argue about the merits of the play. In Regnard's *Critique de l'Homme à bonnes fortunes* which was performed at the same theatre in 1690, the main part of the discussion of the play is between two noblemen (one of them the inevitable foolish *marquis*) and two ladies, a *Baronne* and a *Comtesse*; this time the middle classes are represented both by a *pédant*, who is an admirer of Regnard's comedy, and by M. Nivelet, described as a *procureur-fiscal*, who has lost part of his cloak in the crush in the *parterre*.

For his last comedy, *Le Légataire universel*, performed at the Comédie Française in 1708, Regnard composed another *Critique* which is also in the tradition of Molière's *Critique de l'École des Femmes*. The action takes place in the theatre, when at the end of a performance *Le Légataire universel* is announced for two days ahead. An original figure in the little play is that of an apothecary, M. Clistorel, who is furious at having been put on the stage in Regnard's comedy. The other actors are the conventional ones—a *chevalier*, a *marquis*, a countess, a *financier* (a sign that we are now in the eighteenth century?), and the inevitable poet who criticizes the comedy. In the following year Lesage also wrote a *Critique* for his *Turcaret*; it took the unusual form of a prologue and an epilogue to the play, and the characters too are quite out of the ordinary. Instead of the conventional members of the aristocracy and a jealous writer, they consist of the two main personages from Lesage's novel, *Le Diable boiteux*—the devil, Asmodée, and Don Cléofas. This exception to the traditional form of these little plays does not disprove our contention that in general, from the time of Molière onwards, they mirror the importance of the aristocratic section of the theatre audience in our period.

The stress in various contemporary documents on the difference made to theatre audiences by the presence of the court in Paris or its absence also points in the same direction. It is noteworthy that in their leases of the Hôtel de Bourgogne the Confrères de la Passion, in both 1632 and 1639, inserted a clause to prevent the actors who were hiring the theatre from claiming a reduction in rent if the King and court left Paris.[1] In his *Théâtre Français* Chappuzeau tells us that established authors were reluctant to have new plays performed out of the season, which ran from All Saints' Day to the following Easter, 'lorsque toute la cour est rassemblée au Louvre ou à Saint-Germain'.[2] Or later still in the century, in the preface to his unsuccessful tragedy, *Démétrius*, which was performed at the Comédie Française in June 1689, Aubry attributes its failure to 'la saison . . . et les conjonctures des temps présents [a reference to the War of the League of Augsburg], qui ont éloigné de la cour et de la ville le plus grand nombre des personnes dont le goût fait ordinairement le destin des ouvrages de cette nature'.[3]

The vast majority of plays produced in this period received their first performance in the different Paris theatres; it was only rarely that they were first performed before the court, and even then they had to derive their main success and reward from the more mixed theatre audiences of the capital. However much one may be willing to concede that middle class and even plebeian elements were present in those audiences, it still remains true, especially given the social structure of seventeenth-century France, that the upper classes, from the *grands seigneurs* and their ladies downwards, exercised an influence on drama which was out of proportion even to the fairly considerable numbers which they furnished to the theatre audience of the time. That influence can be felt in a dozen different ways, even though it cannot always be clearly defined.

In an earlier chapter we have suggested that the sweeping transformation which occurred in French drama in the period of Richelieu, from about 1630 onwards, may well have been due less to any sudden change in the social composition of Paris theatre audiences than to the influence exercised on drama by the development of polite society in the salons of the time and the increased refinement which this brought about. In putting forward this theory we are not endeavouring to propose a complete solution to the problem of why this revolution which

[1] Soulié, *Recherches sur Molière*, pp. 164, 151. [2] p. 59.
[3] Aubry's tragedy was never published. The quotation comes from C. and F. Parfaict, *Histoire du Théâtre Français*, vol. xiii, p. 141.

transformed French drama should have taken place. No doubt the influence of polite society in one field—that of the new stress on the *bienséances*, both of subject-matter and language—is clear enough; but that French drama should rapidly have moved from a state of complete freedom which it is now fashionable to call 'baroque' to a state of rigid regimentation, not only in such matters as the unities and *vraisemblance*, but in all manner of trivial technical details, that is something which it is simply not possible to explain. Even if one accepts the highly dubious proposition that in this short period of years there was a revolution in the social composition of Paris theatre audiences, one still is not in a position to explain why, for instance, this should have led to a gradual acceptance of such rules as the unities. Again, to attribute these changes to the rationalism of the age, to a Cartesianism *avant la lettre*, is not really to advance one much towards an explanation; the unities can be rejected, as well as imposed, in the name of reason.

It is certain that in the 1630's and 1640's a considerable influence on drama was exercised by a number of writers like Chapelain and Sarrazin, La Mesnardière and Abbé d'Aubignac, who had the ear of aristocratic patrons of the theatre and especially Richelieu. In documents of the seventeenth century one finds all manner of eulogistic references to the *doctes* or, as they are more frequently called, the *savants*; it is their taste, playwrights argue, to which one must attempt to conform. Clearly the *savants* did exercise a tremendous influence on the contemporary theatre; whatever the underlying reason may have been, it was through their efforts that there was imposed on drama a rigid set of rules which certainly transformed the French theatre in the 1630's and 1640's. Yet, great as their influence was, it never extended beyond certain limits. There was, to begin with, as Professor Jacques Scherer has shown in his admirable *Dramaturgie classique*,[1] a considerable gap between dramatic theory and the actual practice of the playwrights of the time. The latter did not write for a handful of *savants*; however much and however often they may pay tribute to the taste of this small minority, in the nature of things they were interested in drawing a wider audience to the theatre. In their prefaces and other writings, as we have seen, they contrive to find numerous *savants* among their more aristocratic spectators or even in the occupants of the *parterre*; or else they declare that after all what is required of the spectator to appreciate a play is merely a certain natural common sense and good taste which the majority of their audience possess, even if they are not *savants*.

[1] Paris, 1950.

Corneille, for instance, possibly in an unguarded moment and no doubt even exaggerating his ideas slightly (he was not unfond of paradox), argued that, since the main object of a playwright was to bring as many spectators as possible to the theatre to see his plays, he must strive first and foremost to please 'la cour et le peuple':

Il faut, s'il se peut, y ajouter les règles, afin de ne déplaire pas aux savants, et recevoir un applaudissement universel; mais surtout gagnons la voix publique; autrement notre pièce aura beau être régulière, si elle est sifflée au théâtre, les savants n'oseront se déclarer en notre faveur, et aimeront mieux dire que nous avons mal entendu les règles, que de nous donner des louanges quand nous serons décriés par le consentement général de ceux qui ne voient la comédie que pour se divertir.[1]

A generation later, in the preface to his *Bérénice*, while stoutly affirming that his tragedy *does* conform to the rules, Racine appeals to the great mass of his audience, to people who are not, like professional critics and scholars, immersed in the details of the rules, and addresses to them the argument that the supreme test of his play is whether or not it has given them pleasure. Some people, he says, held that a play with such a simple action as *Bérénice* could not be in accordance with the rules:

Je m'informai s'ils se plaignaient qu'elle les eût ennuyés. On me dit qu'ils avouaient tous qu'elle n'ennuyait point, qu'elle les touchait même en plusieurs endroits, et qu'ils la verraient encore avec plaisir. Que veulent-ils davantage? Je les conjure d'avoir assez bonne opinion d'eux-mêmes pour ne pas croire qu'une pièce qui les touche et qui leur donne du plaisir puisse être absolument contre les règles. La principale règle est de plaire et de toucher. Toutes les autres ne sont faites que pour parvenir à cette première. Mais toutes ces règles sont d'un long détail, dont je ne leur conseille pas de s'embarrasser. Ils ont des occupations plus importantes. Qu'ils se reposent sur nous de la fatigue d'éclaircir les difficultés de la *Poétique* d'Aristote; qu'ils se réservent le plaisir de pleurer et d'être attendris.

Similarly Molière's spokesman in the *Critique de l'École des Femmes* declares that nothing would be easier than to prove that *L'École des Femmes* is as much in accordance with the rules as any play in existence; but to the poet Lysidas, who declares that the comedy violates all the rules, he makes the eloquent retort:

Vous êtes de plaisantes gens avec vos règles dont vous embarrassez les ignorants, et nous étourdissez tous les jours. Il semble, à vous ouïr parler, que ces règles de l'art soient les plus grands mystères du monde; et cependant

---

[1] Dedication to *La Suivante* (Paris, 1637).

ce ne sont que quelques observations aisées que le bon sens a faites sur ce qui peut ôter le plaisir que l'on prend à ces sortes de poèmes; et le même bon sens qui a fait autrefois ces observations, les fait aisément tous les jours, sans le secours d'Horace et d'Aristote.

Once again the appeal is directed, over the heads of the *savants*, to the general theatre-going public, both to the aristocratic or wealthy spectators in the boxes and on the stage, and to the humbler occupants of the *parterre*, whose taste is praised in turn in the *Critique de l'École des Femmes*. That the rules have their place, Molière does not deny; but, he insists, 'je voudrais bien savoir si la grande règle de toutes les règles n'est pas de plaire, et si une pièce de théâtre qui a attrapé son but, n'a pas suivi un bon chemin'.[1] Once again, as with Racine, the stress is all on the higher rule of giving pleasure, an aim summed up by Molière so far as comedy is concerned in the words used in the same scene, 'faire rire les honnêtes gens'—that is, the cultured and polished members of society who were not, of course, *savants*.

The theorists might build up an elaborate system of rules; but although they enjoyed a tremendous reputation and exercised a tremendous influence, their power must not be exaggerated. They were after all only a tiny minority, even among the small theatre-going public of the age. Their influence was counterbalanced not only by the exigencies of dramatic technique, but also by the general taste of the time, a taste which was moulded by the court and the polite society of Paris. The members of this restricted circle were seldom *savants*, either by training or outlook. Few of the aristocrats and even fewer of the ladies who frequented the *salons* and the theatres of seventeenth-century Paris were versed in the Classical tongues, without which no one in that age could have any claim to learning. Nor were they distressed by this lack of knowledge. On the contrary, any show of learning was regarded in such circles as mere pedantry, and in that polished society nothing could be more contemptible than a pedant. Clitandre's onslaught on 'le savoir obscur de la pédanterie' in *Les Femmes savantes* expresses admirably the attitude of the aristocratic members of society in that period towards learning, or as they would call it, pedantry:

> Il semble à trois gredins, dans leur petit cerveau,
> Que pour être imprimés, et reliés en veau,
> Les voilà dans l'État d'importantes personnes;
> Qu'avec leur plume ils font les destins des couronnes;

[1] Sc. 6.

Qu'au moindre petit bruit de leurs productions
Ils doivent voir chez eux voler les pensions;
Que sur eux l'univers a la vue attachée;
Que partout de leur nom la gloire est épanchée,
Et qu'en science ils sont des prodiges fameux,
Pour savoir ce qu'ont dit les autres avant eux,
Pour avoir eu trente ans des yeux et des oreilles,
Pour avoir employé neuf ou dix mille veilles
A se bien barbouiller de grec et de latin,
Et se charger l'esprit d'un ténébreux butin
De tous les vieux fatras qui traînent dans les livres;
Gens qui de leur savoir paraissent toujours ivres,
Riches, pour tout mérite, en babil importun,
Inhabiles à tout, vides de sens commun,
Et pleins d'un ridicule et d'une impertinence
A décrier partout l'esprit et la science.[1]

To people with such a contempt for pedantry, to judge literature by so-called rules, the creation of pedants and the standards of pedants, was unthinkable. For them the only approach to a play was the one recommended by Racine or Molière, to see whether or not it gave them pleasure. Judgements in such matters were for them founded not on reason, for that was the instrument of the pedants, but on the natural taste of the individual. It was for the 'honnêtes gens' to decide for themselves, not whether a work was in conformity with the rules, for they had no means of studying Aristotle and his commentators, but whether it possessed those indefinable qualities—that *je ne sais quoi* of which contemporary writers constantly speak—which a work of literature must have if it is to give pleasure.

The influence of the *savants* and the limits of their influence can be perceived in this history of the development of the different dramatic genres in the course of the seventeenth century. The emergence of Classical tragedy with Mairet's *Sophonisbe* was no doubt a direct result of the establishment, through the efforts of the *savants*, of strict rules; the same is true of the gradual disappearance in the second half of the century of the type of drama which had dominated the Paris stage for the greater part of the first half of the seventeenth century—tragicomedy, which with its romanesque plots could only with difficulty be made to adapt itself to the unities. Yet if for the best part of two centuries tragedy was to remain conditioned in its form by the rules established in the period between 1630 and 1650, it was in these very

[1] Act IV, Sc. 3.

years that comedy, an almost insignificant genre in France in the opening decades of the seventeenth century, began to come to the fore.
Often despised by the *savants* as an allegedly plebeian form of entertainment, certainly regarded as inferior to tragedy (see Molière's
defence of his art in the *Critique de l'École des Femmes*), it remained
largely unaffected by the rules, or at least if Molière, for instance, can
conform fairly closely to the rules in one comedy, he had no compunction about ignoring them in the next.

Comedy thus retained throughout the seventeenth century a freedom
denied to tragedy. It offered, in the works both of Molière and his
predecessors and contemporaries, an extraordinary range of types, to
suit the diverse tastes of contemporary theatre audiences. It ranged
from farce and farcical comedies to comedies of intrigue, comedies of
manners, and comedies of character; all of these different elements are
often present together in individual plays, but in varying proportions.
It merged with the ballet in the *comédies-ballets* created by Molière; it
took in singing and even dancing as part of its field. And if comedy
took on such varied forms, it was not the only companion of tragedy in
the Paris theatres in the second half of the century. Even apart from the
development of the new genre of opera, there arose a new type of
play—the *pièce à machines*—which with its spectacular effects enjoyed
an enormous popularity and secured a success equalled by few straightforward plays. An examination of the volumes of Lancaster's *History*
shows what a wide variety of plays were produced in our period to suit
the tastes of the ordinary theatre-goer of the time; if seldom entirely
absent, the influence of the theorists, of the *savants*, is scarcely very
prominent in a great many of them.

If in the first half of the century tragi-comedy and even for a short
period the pastoral play tended to predominate over tragedy and
comedy, these became by the second half of the century the two leading
dramatic genres. Tragedy, it was universally agreed, required for its
characters persons of royal blood or otherwise illustrious. It is true that
early in the century Alexandre Hardy produced a sort of *tragédie bourgeoise* in his *Scédase* which treats of the misfortunes of ordinary
mortals. It is even true that in the *épître dédicatoire* of *Don Sanche* Corneille quotes the example of this tragedy and denies that Aristotle demanded that the characters in tragedy should be of kingly or illustrious
birth. He then goes on to argue that, since the aim of tragedy is to
arouse pity and fear, that end may be achieved more easily by portraying characters whose situation is close to that of the average spectator:

Or s'il est vrai que ce dernier sentiment [fear] ne s'excite en nous par sa représentation que quand nous voyons souffrir nos semblables, et que leurs infortunes nous en font appréhender de pareilles, n'est-il pas vrai aussi qu'il y pourrait être excité plus fortement par la vue des malheurs arrivés aux personnes de notre condition, à qui nous ressemblons tout à fait, que par l'image de ceux qui font trébucher de leurs trônes les plus grands monarques, avec qui nous n'avons aucun rapport qu'en tant que nous sommes suscepti- bles des passions qui les ont jetés dans ce précipice: ce qui ne se rencontre pas toujours?

He thus concludes that it is possible to 'faire une tragédie entre des personnes médiocres, quand leurs infortunes ne sont pas au-dessous de sa dignité'. However, if we are tempted to see in Corneille a forerunner of Diderot and Beaumarchais, we are soon disillusioned, for in making the point that tragedy does not necessarily require kingly or illustrious heroes, he is simply preparing the way to define his *Don Sanche*, in which illustrious persons are presented in a non-tragic light, as a 'comédie héroïque'.

The conventional view of the characters suitable for comedy was, on paper at least, equally rigid. If tragedy was concerned with the mis- fortunes which befell kings and princes, comedy treated of people of more modest origins who were fit subjects for laughter. The classical view on this question was summed up by Chapelain when he wrote:

Dans la tragédie, qui est la plus noble espèce des pièces de théâtre, le poète imite les actions des grands dont les fins ont été malheureuses et qui n'étaient ni trop bons ni trop méchants. Dans la comédie, il imite les actions des per- sonnes de petite condition, ou tout au plus de médiocre, dont les fins ont été heureuses.[1]

This fits in admirably with the contemporary social scene in seven- teenth-century France; yet, in actual practice, writers of comedies did not by any means always limit their choice of characters in this way. Molière rather scandalized some of his contemporaries by making fun of foolish *marquis* in a number of his plays. 'Le marquis aujourd'hui est le plaisant de la comédie', he declares in *L'Impromptu de Versailles*, 'et comme dans toutes les comédies anciennes on voit toujours un valet bouffon qui fait rire les auditeurs, de même, dans nos pièces de main- tenant, il faut toujours un marquis ridicule qui divertisse la compagnie.'[2] 'Personne', wrote Rapin, not without some exaggeration,

---

[1] *Discours de la poésie représentative* in *Opuscules critiques*, pp. 129–30.
[2] Sc. I.

n'a aussi porté le ridicule de la comédie plus loin parmi nous que Molière, car les anciens poètes comiques n'ont que des valets pour les plaisants de leur théâtre, et les plaisants du théâtre de Molière sont les marquis et les gens de qualité. Les autres n'ont joué dans la comédie que la vie bourgeoise et commune, et Molière a joué tout Paris et la cour.[1]

His enemies even hinted that it was a crime bordering on *lèse-majesté* to make fun of people who danced attendance on *Le Roi Soleil*. In one of the pamphlets of the controversy aroused by the success of *L'École des Femmes* Donneau de Visé wrote:

Lorsqu'il joue toute la cour et qu'il n'épargne que l'auguste personne du Roi, . . . il ne s'aperçoit pas que cet incomparable monarque est toujours accompagné des gens qu'il veut rendre ridicules. . . . C'est pourquoi Élomire devrait plutôt travailler à nous faire voir qu'ils sont tous des héros, puisque le Prince est toujours au milieu d'eux et qu'il en est comme le chef, que de nous en faire voir des portraits ridicules.[2]

Yet Molière's example was followed by many of his contemporaries and successors. Even before his return to Paris in 1658, comedies had, of course, been written which made fun of provincial *hobereaux*, for instance, Gillet de La Tessonnerie's *Le Campagnard*, published in 1657. Now Molière added fatuous representatives of the court nobility to the list of comic types, and his example proved infectious.

The surprising thing is that in comedy seventeenth-century French playwrights showed on the whole a much broader interest in the contemporary social scene than did their successors in the following century. In seventeenth-century comedy almost all classes of society, from the peasants to the aristocracy, are brought on to the stage. Molière offers in his plays an extraordinarily wide range of social types, which, if it excludes one important section of the community, the *financiers*, takes in almost everyone from the peasants to the court aristocracy. The social atmosphere of his comedies varies from that of the world of the peasants to Célimène's salon. True, there were purists even then who objected to the presentation on the stage of such lowly personages as peasants. La Bruyère, for instance, did not allow his sympathy with the hard lot of the poorer peasants of his day to run away with him when it came to the question of exhibiting such people on the stage. 'Le paysan ou l'ivrogne', he declares, 'fournit quelques scènes à un farceur;

il n'entre qu'à peine dans le vrai comique: comment pourrait-il faire le fond ou l'action principale de la comédie?'[1] Such sentiments did not prevent playwrights, either before or after Molière, from bringing peasants on to the stage; at the end of the century Dancourt made frequent use of such characters in his comedies, even if his peasants smack rather of the *banlieue*.

The choice of characters in comedy was thus somewhat confused in our period. On the one hand, comedy was traditionally regarded as treating of the medium and lower ranks of society, just as tragedy dealt with the great and their misfortunes. Yet the practising playwrights of the age did not always take this rather narrow view. Besides bourgeois characters, representatives of the lower orders, including peasants and servants with their often barbarous speech, make frequent appearances in seventeenth-century comedy. At the same time we have seen how Molière not only introduced on to the stage the new type of the foolish *marquis*, but could also produce in *Le Misanthrope* a comedy which deals entirely with aristocrats of both sexes and is set in a seventeenth-century salon. There was thus a marked tendency as the century wore on for comedy to take in the upper classes of society. Plays like *Tartufe*, *L'Avare*, and *Les Femmes savantes* deal with upper middle class households, on the verge of the aristocracy. Thus an extraordinary variety of social types is presented in seventeenth-century comedy, and yet we perhaps already see foreshadowed the more restricted social field of the comedy of the next century.

Contemporary writers attach great importance, not only to the influence of the upper classes in general on drama, but particularly to that of the ladies and their salons. The ladies played their part as patrons of playwrights, witness the paragraph on Mme du Tillet and her pet dramatist, Boyer, in Somaize's *Dictionnaire des Précieuses*:

Toxaris [Mme du Tillet] est une précieuse du quartier de Léolie [Marais] qui voit toutes les précieuses de son quartier, et l'amour qu'elle a pour les vers et surtout pour les jeux du cirque [the theatre] est connu de tous ceux qui la visitent; elle en est même protectrice, et ne voit pas seulement les auteurs, mais même Bavius [Boyer] est logé dans sa maison. C'est un homme qui fait fort bien des vers et qui a du mérite; mais, ô temps malheureux! ô modes étranges! les applaudissements s'achètent à force de lectures, il les faut briguer, et Quirinus [Quinault] a amené cette coutume ridicule de mendier les approbations, et l'a si bien établie qu'il faut que les autres la suivent.

[1] *Caractères*, chap. i, no. 52.

Bavius, malgré sa fierté naturelle, y a été contraint, et Toxaris a bien fait son devoir de vanter ses ouvrages.[1]

There is a long and interesting, if naturally satirical, account of this whole business in Donneau de Visé's *Nouvelles nouvelles* (1663). Since this work has never been reprinted, it would seem worth while reproducing the passage in full.

Je ne puis néanmoins estimer les gens qui font tout ce qu'ils peuvent afin que les femmes les mettent en réputation, et qui aiment mieux devoir les applaudissements que l'on leur donne au bien qu'elles publient d'eux qu'au mérite de leurs œuvres; et pour moi je n'ai point de plus grand divertissement que celui de voir ou de me représenter un de ces auteurs lisant ses ouvrages au milieu de quatre ou cinq femmes qui, sans ecouter ces [*sic*] raisons, condamnent et lui font changer ce qui leur déplaît; qui lui font retrancher ce qu'elles n'aiment pas, et lui font ajouter ce qui leur vient en la fantaisie. Tout cela étant fait, si la pièce qui leur a été lue est à leur gré, elles l'envoient de maison en maison chez toutes leurs amies pour en faire des lectures, avec une recommandation et un certificat de la bonté de sa pièce. Elles le produisent après elles-mêmes dans les compagnies; elles l'y mènent; elles font son compliment; elles parlent de la bonté de son ouvrage; elles en racontent le sujet, et rendent ce pauvre auteur si confus et si surpris des louanges qu'elles lui donnent qu'encore qu'il ait beaucoup d'esprit, il n'y peut répondre que par une infinité de révérences. N'est-ce pas là un sot personnage, et le rôle que joue cet auteur, ne doit-il pas faire une plaisante vision à l'esprit de ceux qui se le représentent? Pour ce qui est des femmes, elles ont raison d'agir de la sorte car, ou les ouvrages qu'on leur fait voir les divertissent, quand ils sont bons, ou elles se divertissent aux dépens de l'auteur, lorsqu'ils ne valent rien; mais ce qui est de plus à remarquer, est que la connaissance que la plupart de ces sortes d'auteurs ont de ces femmes de qualité qui mettent beaucoup de leurs confrères en réputation, est une connaissance éloignée, recherchée, mendiée et que fait faire le plus souvent quelqu'un des domestiques qu'un auteur viendra trouver vingt fois pour le prier de parler de lui à sa maîtresse, lequel, après avoir été bien importuné, lui en parle avantageusement, et lui en dit du bien jusqu'à ce qu'il lui fasse souhaiter de le voir. Il est enfin (après avoir bien brigué cette connaissance) introduit dans sa ruelle où il lit sa pièce en présence de trois ou quatre amies, d'où s'ensuit tout ce que j'ai déjà dit, à quoi l'on peut ajouter que les galants de ces dames, sans en avoir rien vu, publient sur leur rapport que c'est la plus belle chose du monde. Les amis de ces galants le disent aussi pour les obliger et voilà ce qui met présentement les auteurs au monde. Voilà d'où vient que l'on en voit qui sont en grande réputation après leur coup d'essai, cependant que d'autres, vieillis dans l'étude, après avoir fait cent beaux ouvrages, ne sont ni connus ni estimés,

---

[1] *Dictionnaire des Précieuses*, ed. C. Livet (Paris, 1856), 2 vols., vol. i, p. 232.

faute d'avoir eu connaissance de ces femmes, qui donnent la vogue à de certains auteurs, et qui font réussir tout ce qui part d'eux.[1]

Charged with venomous exaggeration as it is, this passage does none the less offer a vivid picture of the influence of the women of the aristocracy on the fate of plays and the fame enjoyed by authors.

There are numerous references in the writings of the time to the influence of the women of polite society both on literature in general and drama in particular. In the preface to his *Œdipe* Corneille explains how he has been compelled to omit the more revolting side of the legend which 'ferait soulever la délicatesse de nos dames, qui composent la plus belle partie de notre auditoire, et dont le dégoût attire aisément la censure de ceux qui les accompagnent'.[2] In his book on the theatre Abbé de Pure declares that it is 'les dames qui aujourd'hui décident du mérite de ces choses'.[3] In particular, both in this century and the next, the prominent place occupied by love in tragedy is blamed on the ladies. 'Que dites-vous de ce caractère d'amour et de tendresse, qui est d'ordinaire d'un caractère badin, qu'on mêle dans toutes les pièces', Father Rapin wrote to Bussy in 1672, 'au lieu que les tragédies des Grecs, et même celles des Latins, ne roulent que sur de grands sentiments qui font l'héroïque qui en est l'âme, le magnifique et le grand?' Bussy offers the conventional answer: 'Il est encore certain que les sentiments de tendresse poussés trop loin ont je ne sais quoi de fade qui dégoûte dans les tragédies. Cet abus s'introduit pour plaire aux dames, qui veulent de l'amour dans tout ce qu'on leur présente, et qui ne sont pas satisfaites, si cet amour ne va pas dans l'excès.'[4]

When he came to write his *Réflexions*, Rapin penned a denunciation of the place occupied by love in French tragedy. The English, he says, 'aiment le sang dans leurs jeux, par la qualité de leur tempérament; ce sont des insulaires, séparés du reste des hommes'. In France playwrights are compelled to introduce 'des sentiments doux et tendres' into their tragedies in order to flatter the taste of their compatriots for such things. 'C'est ce qui oblige nos poètes à privilégier si fort la galanterie sur le théâtre et à tourner tous leurs sujets sur des tendresses outrées, pour plaire davantage aux femmes, qui se sont érigées en arbitres de ces divertissements, et qui ont usurpé le droit d'en décider.' In his view it is the Spaniards who were first responsible for introducing this degenerate tendency into drama; it explains why modern tragedy is inferior to that

---

[1] *Nouvelles nouvelles*, vol. iii, pp. 161–5.
[2] *Œdipe, Avis au Lecteur.*   [3] *Idée des Spectacles*, p. 168.
[4] Bussy-Rabutin, *Correspondance*, vol. ii, pp. 147, 156.

of the Ancients, who relegated love to comedy. 'C'est dégrader la
tragédie de cet air de majesté qui lui est propre', he concludes, 'que d'y
mêler de l'amour qui est d'un caractère toujours badin et peu conforme
à cette gravité dont elle fait profession.'[1]

This contemporary tendency to put most, if not all, of the blame for
this state of affairs on to women is not altogether convincing. Apart
from the obvious fact that the majority of male spectators seem to have
shared their taste for love themes in drama, it is clear that the explanation is lacking in profundity in that it is not related to the complex
realities of contemporary social and political life. The heroic tragedy
created by Corneille in the first half of the seventeenth century belongs,
as has often been pointed out, to a society in which the aristocracy was
still struggling against the attempt of the Crown to impose its absolute
authority upon France. It was an age of civil wars, conspiracies, and
general unrest, following upon the even greater upheaval of the Wars
of Religion in the previous century. The aristocracy's will to self-
assertion had not yet been curbed as it was to be after the collapse of the
Fronde and the assumption of power by Louis XIV in 1661. Even
Richelieu, for all his ruthless determination to impose the royal authority
on the country, did not succeed in quelling permanently the turbulence
of the aristocracy, as the civil wars of the Fronde were soon to prove.
This atmosphere of conspiracy and revolt, of controversy on political
problems, all of it completely alien to the France which lived under the
absolutism of Louis XIV, was that in which Corneille and his fellow
playwrights worked, and it is clearly reflected in the love of *gloire* and
self-assertion to be found in the tragedies of that part of the century.[2]

Even so we have to bear in mind that the power of the nobility was
already in decline. The court of the French kings, now permanently
established in Paris and its immediate environs, had made the capital
the centre of all social life. The aristocracy was drawn as if by a magnet
to Paris; the great nobles built their mansions there and began to indulge in the pleasures of the social life offered by the salons of the age.
They were ceasing to be semi-feudal barons and already aspiring towards the new ideal of the *honnête homme*, with its stress on the social
virtues and its elevation of women to a privileged position. Political
themes predominate over everything else in the tragedies of Corneille.
The dignity of tragedy requires, he declared, 'quelque grand intérêt
d'état, ou quelque passion plus noble et plus mâle que l'amour, telles

[1] *Réflexions*, vol. ii, p. 147.
[2] See P. Bénichou, *Morales du Grand Siècle* (Paris, 1948).

que sont l'ambition ou la vengeance, et veut donner à craindre des malheurs plus grands que la perte d'une maîtresse'. He clearly rejects the type of tragedy which was already becoming fashionable in France when he was writing his *Discours*, the tragedy which has love as its sole theme; and yet he does not altogether banish love from tragedy. 'Il est à propos d'y mêler l'amour', he goes on, 'parce qu'il a toujours beaucoup d'agrément, et peut servir de fondement à ces intérêts, et à ces autres passions dont je parle; mais il faut qu'il se contente du second rang dans le poème, et leur laisse le premier.'[1] Thus in his own tragedies from *Horace* onwards love plays a quite important, if secondary, role; indeed a study of Corneille's sources for these plays shows how he deliberately introduced a love theme into the material which he drew from history or legend. Sometimes the love theme appears indeed to be dragged in by the hair (his martyr-play, *Polyeucte*, is an obvious example) and at times (in the same tragedy, for instance) it seems almost to take first place.

Tragedies in which a political theme—'les grands intérêts'—predominated, continued to be written in the second half of the century, but new types of play also became fashionable, the kind of tragedy in which the love theme is blended in more or less equal proportions with a political theme, or even, with writers like Quinault and Racine, for instance, tragedies in which love is the dominant passion. This concentration on the portrayal of love in tragedy is clearly no accident. Since the Fronde the nobility's political aspirations had been killed stone dead. After the failure of their last revolt there was nothing for it but to adapt themselves to the new political conditions created by Mazarin and consolidated by Louis XIV and his ministers. The only forms of activity now open to a nobleman were the army (for those of the appropriate age), a life of dancing attendance on the King at the Louvre or Versailles, of court intrigue directed towards his own and his family's advantage, and the social life of the salons. The heroic tragedy of the earlier part of the century now appeared out of touch with reality. Not that Corneille did not continue to have his ardent supporters, but they belonged to an earlier generation and the spirit of the age was now moving in another direction. The salons with their light badinage in verse, their portraits and their *questions d'amour*, had created a demand for a psychological type of tragedy in which love, if it did not always hold the first place, was always prominent. Hence the lamentations of worthy critics like Rapin who compared the trends in

[1] *Discours du poème dramatique* in *Œuvres*, vol. i, p. 24.

contemporary tragedy with the model which they had derived from the Ancients.

The very instrument of language used by the playwrights of the age was forged in the salons by the *honnêtes gens*. There is no need to retell the story of how in the course of the seventeenth century polite society remoulded the French language and fashioned it in accordance with its own outlook and prejudices. Not that we can trace the influence of these changes with equal clarity in all forms of drama: it is obvious that comedy always enjoyed considerable licence in its use of language and indeed in its whole treatment of the *bienséances*. True, there were comedies and comedies, and there were also farces in which licence always remained greater. It would be idle to expect with a comedy like *Le Misanthrope*, which portrays exclusively characters drawn from the ranks of the aristocracy, either that the *bienséances* would be violated or that the language of the play, vigorous as it often is, would ever seriously depart from the established rules of polite usage. Yet Molière and his fellow writers of comedy retained considerable liberty in matters of language, both in their farces and in the more farcical scenes of their comedies, and indeed in the majority of their plays. In seventeenth-century comedy peasants speak like peasants, or at any rate as Paris audiences of the time thought peasants spoke, and servants and other low-born creatures use crude and ungrammatical language. Themes are treated which do not conform to the *bienséances* and there is no hesitation in employing terms condemned by Vaugelas and the purists. Although, when set alongside Restoration drama, French plays of the middle and later seventeenth century seem of unbelievable propriety, at times a rather surprising latitude is allowed in these matters. In the last scene of a late seventeenth-century comedy, Boursault's *Mercure Galant* which enjoyed considerable success at the Comédie Française in 1683, a foolish poet, called M. Beaugénie, appears on the scene and reads to the assembled company—male and female—a riddle in verse of his own composition, which, he assures his hearers, 'fera du bruit dans plus d'une ruelle'. It is not easy to imagine how the refined audience which frequented the Comédie Française in the 1680's could be expected to approve of the following lines being read out on the stage:

> Je suis un invisible corps
> Qui de bas lieu tire mon être;
> Et je n'ose faire connaître
> Ni qui je suis ni d'où je sors.

> Quand on m'ôte la liberté,
> Pour m'échapper j'use d'adresse;
> Et deviens femelle traîtresse,
> De mâle que j'aurais été.[1]

In tragedy we find a very different attitude to language. There the instrument at the playwright's disposal was the restricted vocabulary of polite society, purged of all realistic, plebeian, or provincial terms— 'des paroles qui n'ont rien de bas et de vulgaire, une diction noble et magnifique', to use the words of Rapin.[2] Racine, it is said, made use of only two thousand words in his eleven tragedies; it was with an extraordinarily limited and abstract vocabulary that he succeeded in producing some of the greatest French poetry ever written.[3]

We may conclude then that the Paris theatre-going public of the great Classical age of French drama was numerically a severely restricted one, given the size of the capital and its attractions for provincials and foreigners. The short run enjoyed even by the most successful plays of the period makes this point clear enough. Socially that audience appears to have been much more mixed than has sometimes been suggested. The middle classes were certainly strongly represented there, and there was probably even a sprinkling of plebeian spectators, although this point is not easily established in precise terms. On the other hand, the more aristocratic sections of society—so important in the France of Louis XIV—were certainly strongly represented in the theatre audiences of the time, and it is their outlook rather than that of the middle layers of society which is most clearly reflected in the drama of the age. Lip-service is paid by many playwrights of the period to the importance of pleasing the *savants*, but in their franker moments they recognize that, in order to be successful, a play must appeal to a wider circle, to 'les honnêtes gens', few of whom (especially the ladies) could claim to be learned. Thus the drama of the age was strongly influenced by the aristocratic outlook of the society in which it was produced. It is certainly not a learned drama, written to please a tiny group of scholars and critics; at the same time, especially in comedy and farce, it contains a down-to-earth element which, though often attributed by contemporaries to the influence of the lower and

---

[1] The key to the riddle is 'Un vent échappé par en bas'.

[2] *Réflexions*, vol. ii, p. 109.

[3] Professor Jean Pommier challenges this view in a chapter of his *Aspects de Racine* (Paris, 1954), but although he establishes some interesting points of detail, he will never convince anyone brought up on Shakespeare that the vocabulary used by Racine in his tragedies was anything but severely restricted.

middle sections of society, suited equally well the not too squeamish or refined taste of the aristocratic spectators, both male and female. On the whole, one arrives at the curious paradox that the seventeenth century, when absolutist and aristocratic standards were most firmly established in France, allowed the playwright a greater freedom and range, especially in comedy, than did the eighteenth century, for all its revolt against those standards.

3. From Marivaux to Beaumarchais

*T*HE pages which follow treat of the changes which took place in Paris theatre audiences and the influence which these exercised on drama in the three-quarters of a century which elapsed between the death of Louis XIV and the Revolution of 1789. If the first date is an entirely arbitrary one, chosen purely and simply for the sake of convenience in planning this book, the collapse of the Ancien Régime in 1789 does mark the end of an epoch. It might perhaps be argued that, so far as the more restricted world of the theatre is concerned, 1791 is a more important landmark than 1789, since it was in that year that the National Assembly decreed *la liberté des théâtres* and so abolished the monopoly of the privileged theatres, especially the Comédie Française. However, although 1789 is the closing point of this investigation, this date has not been interpreted too literally. Indeed researches into the nature of theatre audiences have been continued with profit right through the Revolutionary period, as the changes which took place in that field during the great upheaval occasionally throw interesting light on the state of affairs before 1789.

Compared with the second half of the seventeenth century, this period of seventy-five years does not in retrospect appear a brilliant theatrical age, at least so far as the production of new plays was concerned. This was not for lack of enthusiasm for the drama among the population of eighteenth-century Paris. Theatres of various kinds flourished; theatre-going was a fashionable entertainment, and amateur theatricals enjoyed an extraordinary vogue both at the court, with Mme de Pompadour and later Marie Antoinette, and in less exalted circles. Despite the ban still imposed upon them by the Church the doings of actors and actresses were news, even if only material for the *chronique scandaleuse*. To the end of the Ancien Régime a successful play still remained the most rapid road to fame for a young writer.

None the less few French plays of the eighteenth century have held the stage down to our own day. As in the previous period, tragedy remained *the* dramatic genre in the eyes of serious theatre-goers and of the critics in general; and yet not a single tragedy out of a total of very nearly two hundred which were performed at the Comédie Française between 1715 and 1789 can be said to be still living today. Although many of them, particularly a number of those of Voltaire, had considerable success both at the time and well into the nineteenth century, they are quite dead today so far as the stage is concerned. Conscientious historians of eighteenth-century French drama patiently plough their way through the tragedies not only of Voltaire, but also of Crébillon and Houdart de La Motte, Lagrange-Chancel and Piron, Marmontel and Guimond de La Touche, Saurin and La Harpe, Ducis and Marie-Joseph Chénier; but they seldom have the courage to invite their readers to follow their example. The second half of our period saw the emergence of a new genre, the *Drame*; while this possesses considerable historical interest and also proved highly influential abroad, especially in Germany, it produced only one outstanding work, and that of the second class, Sedaine's *Le Philosophe sans le savoir*. Only in comedy did the eighteenth century produce plays which still continue to delight audiences in the twentieth century—the graceful and penetrating comedies of Marivaux and the two gay, complicated, and swift-moving masterpieces of Beaumarchais.

Yet that does not prevent the eighteenth century in France from being one of the great ages of the drama. A theatre like the Comédie Française was by no means wholly dependent on new plays; it had at its disposal the rich repertoire bequeathed to it by the previous century. It had too a succession of great actors and actresses who gave life to the masterpieces of an earlier age and even to the more mediocre productions of the eighteenth century. Though Paris still retained its dominant position in the theatrical life of France, it no longer entirely dwarfed the provinces as it had done for the greater part of the seventeenth century. The eighteenth century saw a great revival of provincial theatres. Both in garrison towns and in the great commercial cities new theatres arose. On the eve of the Revolution Arthur Young found large and prosperous theatres in such towns as Bordeaux and Nantes. These new provincial theatres had their importance in the history of French drama in our period; for example, they showed themselves more hospitable towards the new genre of the *Drame* than did the Paris theatres, particularly the Comédie Française. None the less Paris still continued to play the most important part in the theatrical life of France, as was natural with the capital of a highly centralized country,

MOREAU LE JEUNE *Hommages rendus à Voltaire sur le Théâtre Français le 30 mars 1778*

drawing to itself and the neighbouring Versailles all the wealthiest and most aristocratic sections of society. The best actors and writers were settled in the capital, or strove to leave the provinces and to gain a foothold there.

The history of the different Paris theatres in the eighteenth century is considerably less obscure than in the previous age, but even so it has its complications. It is true that the history of the theatre which concerns us most is extremely clear. The Comédie Française continued to enjoy a virtual monopoly of all plays with any literary pretentions, its only rival, and that both on a small scale and for only part of the period, being the Théâtre Italien. Not only did it possess a monopoly of the extensive repertoire of plays inherited from the previous century, but with rare exceptions all the professional playwrights of the time strove to have their works performed there. Until 1770 it remained in occupation of the theatre in the Rue des Fossés-Saint-Germain (now known as the Rue de l'Ancienne Comédie) into which it had moved in 1689. When this building became too dilapidated for further use, the actors moved to the Tuileries until their new theatre was ready. The construction of the building which occupied the site of the present Comédie Française, Salle Luxembourg, was a long-drawn-out business, and it was not until 1782 that it was ready for occupation. It was in this new theatre that the actors found themselves when the Revolution broke out.

In contrast to this simple and straightforward story the history of the Théâtre Italien in our period appears somewhat involved. The Italian actors were recalled to France by the Regent in 1716. At first they gave performances in Italian, but when the first novelty of their return to Paris after an absence of nearly twenty years had worn off, these soon ceased to appeal to the theatre-going public. They thereupon revived some of the French plays which they had performed during the years before their expulsion from France, and they also sought to attract new French writers. Among the authors who wrote for them was Marivaux. Most of his plays were first produced by the Italian actors, to whom (and especially to the actress Silvia Benozzi) he owed a considerable part of such success as he enjoyed as a playwright with his own contemporaries. In these years the Italian actors specialized in parodies of plays which were successful at the Comédie Française (much to the indignation of Voltaire who disliked having his tragedies made fun of) and also gave considerable prominence to ballet. Eventually, however, in 1762, their theatre having ceased to prosper, the Italian actors were merged with the Opéra-Comique. So popular was the latter side of the entertainment offered in this theatre that seven years later the performance of French plays was completely abandoned. Another revolution occurred in 1780: it was now the turn of Italian plays to be dropped, and French actors were reinstated, along with plays in French. This change was prompted in part by the growing demand, both among playwrights and the general public, for a second theatre which would compete with the Comédie Française. It is of interest that not only comedies, but also a number of *drames* were performed under this new system. In 1783 the company abandoned the old buildings of the Hôtel de Bourgogne which the Italian actors had taken over in 1680 on the foundation of the Comédie Française; the new theatre into which they moved gave its name to the Boulevard des Italiens, despite the fact that by this time the company had lost all its Italian connexions. For a considerable part of the period from 1715 to 1789 the Théâtre Italien offered playwrights some sort of alternative to the Comédie Française. In the two decades from 1720 onwards a writer like Marivaux had most of his best plays performed there, and in the last ten years before the Revolution it did offer hospitality to both comedies and a certain number of *drames*, including some of the plays of Louis-Sébastien Mercier.

For the sake of completeness some mention should be made of the Théâtres de la Foire, which were given a decided impetus by the expulsion of the Italian actors in 1697 and fought a determined battle against the monopoly of the Comédie Française and the Opéra in the opening years of the eighteenth century. These theatres, often short-lived because of the successful legal proceedings instigated by the privileged theatres, attracted all classes of society. 'La belle assemblée: que de dames!' exclaims Don Cléofas in the *Critique de Turcaret* when he sees the audience assembled in the Comédie Française for the first performance of Lesage's comedy. 'Il y en aurait davantage', replies Asmodée, in words which are peculiarly ironical since Lesage was soon to abandon the Comédie Française and become one of the most prolific writers for these despised theatres, 'sans les spectacles de la Foire; la plupart des femmes y courent avec fureur. Je suis ravi de les voir dans le goût de leurs laquais et de leurs cochers.' Despite their popularity it cannot be maintained that these little theatres contributed anything of importance to the drama of the century, and in this study their place can only be a modest one. Gradually the Théâtres de la Foire wore down the resistance of the Comédie Française (and also that of the Italians after their return in 1716). In course of time they evolved a genre of their own, the *opéra-comique*. By an agreement with the Opéra the actors of these theatres were allowed to sing on the stage. The spectacle which they offered consisted of comic songs (*vaudevilles*), with a sprinkling of prose to link together the passages in verse. We have seen how the success of this new genre led in 1762 to an amalgamation of the Théâtre Italien with the Opéra-Comique which in the end entirely submerged the Italian element in the new theatre.

The Opéra-Comique was not the only theatre to emerge from the somewhat obscure and complicated history of the Théâtres de la Foire. Gradually by about 1760 a number of small permanent theatres were established in Paris, in addition to the 'official theatres'—the Comédie Française, Théâtre Italien, and Opéra. By 1789 the fashionable promenade, the Boulevard du Temple, boasted as many as six theatres. These small theatres undoubtedly enjoyed a considerable vogue, but once again their contribution to literature was nil. Their chief interest from our point of view is that they offered some competition to the official theatres, until finally, in 1791, the National Assembly abolished all theatrical monopolies and threw the theatre world open to unrestricted competition—a policy which incidentally was to be reversed by Napoleon, who in 1807 suddenly reduced the number of Paris theatres to a mere handful.

This sketchy account of a highly complicated subject will suffice to bring out the importance of the Comédie Française throughout the period from the death of Louis XIV to the Revolution. Endowed as it was with a monopoly of performances of all plays of any importance which had survived from the previous period, and with a near-monopoly of all new plays with serious literary pretensions, it is primarily in its audience that one must seek to examine the changes in taste which occurred in the period between 1715 and 1789.

(i) *The Size of the Audiences*

The registers preserved in the Archives of the Comédie Française and published in an abridged form by Lancaster offer us a fairly precise notion of the number of people who were in the habit of attending the theatre in eighteenth-century Paris. It is true that, given the time and the other resources required, one ought to make similar calculations for the Théâtre Italien from 1716 to the Revolution, with the help of the registers preserved in the Bibliothèque de l'Opéra; but, as we have seen, such information, while of considerable interest both in itself and for purposes of comparison with the Comédie Française, would have relatively little bearing on the history of French drama in our period.

For the other theatres which existed in Paris in this period we possess absolutely no information.

Even when we confine our inquiries to the Comédie Française there are still considerable difficulties. It is unfortunate that Lancaster chose to break off his publication of the records of this theatre at the completely arbitrary date of Easter 1774; it would have been interesting to see in detail what effect the move to the new theatre in 1782 had on the fortunes of the theatre and to have been able to follow through to 1789 and preferably to the closing of the theatre in 1793 the fortunes of the Comédie Française. All that it has been possible to do is to find out how many spectators attended one or two of the new plays put on at the theatre after 1782; here is an unfortunate gap which it has proved impossible to fill.

There is another difficulty about the interpretation of the figures for spectators at the Comédie Française in the second half of the century. One of the main grievances of Beaumarchais and his fellow playwrights of the so-called Bureau de Législation Dramatique (the ancestor of the Société des Auteurs et Compositeurs Dramatiques) was that the sums of money which they received from the actors of the Comédie Française were based on 'la recette à la porte' and took no account of the money which was received from the boxes hired out on a yearly basis (*petites loges*) or even for life (*abonnements à vie*).

The earliest mention of the *petites loges* seems to occur in the volume of Abbé de La Porte's *Spectacles de Paris* which appeared in 1757. 'Les comédiens', he writes of the Comédie Française, 'ont fait construire des loges au-dessus des deuxièmes balcons et des deux premières loges des secondes, et les louent à l'année. L'année précédente ils avaient fait rétrécir le passage qui descend à l'amphithéâtre pour former de chaque côté une petite loge.'[1] The origin of the *abonnements à vie* can be stated more precisely. In his collection of documents entitled *Les Trois Théâtres de Paris*[2] Des Essarts reproduces the 'Articles de l'acte de société passé entre les Comédiens Français ordinaires du Roi, en exécution de l'arrêt du Conseil du 18 juin 1757'; this document bears the date 9 June 1758. In order to speed up the payment of their debts the actors agree in article XL

qu'il sera abonné le nombre de cinquante places ou droits d'entrée au spectacle, à raison de 3,000 liv. pour chacune desdites places, dont chaque abonné

---

[1] (Paris, 1757), p. 52. As this volume, published in 1757, covers the period 1 Jan.–31 Dec. 1757, the date of these changes was presumably 1756, and 'l'année précédente' 1755.   [2] (Paris, 1777), p. 110.

jouira sa vie durant, sans pouvoir céder ni subroger audit droit qui que ce soit, sinon à forfait, et toujours sur la tête et la vie durant du premier abonné.

If the number of seats affected by the institution of these *abonnements à vie* was limited to fifty, the number of *petites loges* which were rented by the year seems gradually to have reached much more substantial proportions. In his *Histoire administrative de la Comédie Française*, Bonnassies gives the following details:

L'abonnement de ces petites loges, rue des Fossés, était de 500 l. par an. ....
Néelle, le caissier de la Comédie en 1760, se vante, dans un mémoire ms. qui existe aux Archives du théâtre, d'avoir augmenté d'un cinquième, puis d'un sixième le produit des loges à l'année, en établissant un tarif nouveau. Cette série de places rapportait annuellement rue des Fossés 60,000 l.; aux Tuileries et à l'Hôtel de Condé 200,000 l.[1]

This question comes up again and again in the controversy which broke out in the 1770's over payments to authors. In 1775 an obscure dramatist, Lonvay de la Saussaye, argued in a *Mémoire à consulter*[2] that, in determining whether or not his recently performed play, *Alcidonis*, still remained his property, the actors of the Comédie Française must take into account, not merely the receipts from tickets sold at the door, but also 'le produit des petites loges louées à l'année, par un abus qui s'est introduit depuis quelque temps'. When the actors agreed to allow 300 livres a performance under this heading, Lonvay de la Saussaye was still not satisfied. He asked for a statement of the actual receipts from the 'petites loges louées à l'année'. 'J'appris', he tells us, 'que leur nombre se multipliait tous les jours, non seulement aux dépens des loges publiques, mais encore de l'orchestre et même du parterre.' The actual receipts, he estimated, came to 800 livres a day.[3]

Another writer of the time who fell out with the Comédie Française

[1] p. 239. (I have been unable to track down the document in question at the Archives de la Comédie Française.)

[2] *Mémoire à consulter et consultation pour le sieur Lonvay de la Saussaye contre la troupe des Comédiens Français ordinaires du Roi* (Paris, 1775), pp. 15–16. (Bibliothèque de la Ville de Paris, 104376.)

[3] There are other interesting details about the *petites loges* in the same work (pp. 40–41): 'C'est une mode récente que celle des petites loges. Elles se sont multipliées depuis plusieurs années à un point qui n'est presque pas croyable. A présent elles remplissent l'avant-scène, le dessus des balcons, le fond de la salle. Elles empiètent sur les côtés du second et du troisième. On les a établies des deux côtés du parquet. Elles occupent presque tout le pourtour du parterre.

'Cette multiplication a été même assez prodigieuse pour effrayer le public, qui ne peut plus trouver de place au spectacle. Un certain nombre de particuliers sont les maîtres de toute la salle, où le reste des citoyens et des étrangers ne savent plus comment pénétrer. ...

'Le loyer des petites loges se paie d'avance par quartiers. On sent combien cette recette was Louis-Sébastien Mercier. In *Du Théâtre, ou Nouvel Essai sur l'art dramatique*, which appeared in 1773, he attributes the indolence of the actors of the Comédie Française and their unwillingness to put on new plays to lack of competition and to the guaranteed income of over 200,000 livres a year which they derived from the *petites loges*.[1] It was shortly after this, as a result of his disagreement with the Comédie Française over the payments due to him for the *Barbier de Séville*, that the redoubtable Beaumarchais entered the lists. In his *Compte rendu aux auteurs dramatiques*[2] (1780) he relates how he challenged the figure of 300 livres per day for receipts from the *petites loges* which was allowed in the account presented to him for the first thirty-two performances of the *Barbier*, and asks why the actors did not credit playwrights with 800 livres for each performance, since this was the average amount brought in by the *petites loges* over the year.

That, at any rate by the 1770's, the annual income from the *petites loges* had reached a very large sum is abundantly proved by the figures given in an official document entitled *État général des recettes de la Comédie Française, tant à la porte qu'à cause de l'abonnement des petites loges pendant les années 1776 à 1777, 1777 à 1778 et 1778 à 1779*:[3]

Année	Nombre de représentations	Recette journalière	Petites loges	Total
1776–7	314	438,380.15	245,100	683,480.15
1777–8	342	515,819	248,400	764,219
1778–9	317	448,706.15	255,900	704,606.15
	973	1,402,906.10	749,400	2,152,306.10

It is clear from these figures that in an average year the *petites loges* at this period of the century accounted for a good third of the total receipts of the Comédie Française. In the new theatre, occupied in 1782, there were 513 *petites loges* against 1,400 seats hired by the performance.[4]

doit diminuer la recette journalière qui se faisait jadis tout entière à la porte. Ce ne sont pas seulement les personnes qui ont leur loge, qui profitent de cet avantage. La plupart des loges sont louées par quart. Ceux qui ont l'espérance de voir, à leur tour, la septième ou la huitième représentation, ne font point de dépense extraordinaire pour voir les premières. D'autres curieux qui payeraient leurs places, s'en procurent de gratuites dans les loges de leurs amis. On se les prête les uns aux autres.' (On this last point see also Cailhava, *Les Causes de la décadence du Théâtre*, n.p., n.d., p. 32 n.)

[1] (Amsterdam, 1773), p. 367 n.
[2] *Œuvres complètes* (Paris, 1876), ed. E. Fournier, p. 608.
[3] Archives Nationales, o¹ 845 (Archives de la Maison du Roi).
[4] L. P. de Bachaumont, *Mémoires secrets pour servir à l'histoire de la République des*

The practical consequence of this state of affairs from the point of view of determining how many spectators attended the Comédie Française from 1715 onwards is to introduce an element of considerable doubt into the value of any calculations based on the number of spectators who bought tickets for individual performances. It is a relatively simple, if tedious, task to work out from Lancaster's second volume on the Comédie Française how many spectators paid for admission to that theatre in any given year. But unfortunately, in addition to the difficulty already discussed above that we have no means of determining the number of spectators who were admitted free,[1] we encounter from the middle of the 1750's onwards the much more serious problem that increasingly large numbers of spectators did not buy tickets at the door for single performances, but hired boxes, for the year or even for life, and are consequently completely missed out of Lancaster's tables of numbers of spectators present at each performance at the Comédie Française.[2]

If follows then that the only complete figures of paying spectators which we have for the period are those for the years from 1715 to 1755; even if we ignore the question of the number of spectators admitted free (and it seems reasonable to do so), we are still faced with the fact that, from 1755 onwards, figures of paying spectators extracted from the registers of the Comédie Française become increasingly incomplete as more and more people availed themselves of the possibility of hiring boxes by the year. These figures still have, of course, a considerable interest, but the fact remains that they give only the number of spectators who bought tickets for a particular performance, and leave entirely out of account the number of people who made use of their own or other people's *petites loges* on that particular day.

It is not by any means an easy task to establish exactly what was the total capacity of the three different theatres occupied by the Comédie Française in our period. Lancaster estimates that the theatre in the Rue des Fossés-Saint-Germain, which remained in use until 1770, could accommodate over 2,000 people, a result arrived at by adding together the highest recorded attendances for the different parts of the house,

Lettres en France de 1762 jusqu'à nos jours (London, 1777–89), 36 vols., vol. xx, p. 163 (7 Apr. 1782).
[1] See above, p. 50.
[2] In the fairly brief introduction which he wrote to his *Comédie Française, 1701–1774*, Lancaster makes no mention of this problem. I raised this point in reviewing his book for the *Modern Language Review* (1953, p. 347), but, so far as I am aware, it has not been discussed elsewhere.

although the largest total attendance of paying spectators on any one day in the life of this theatre was 1,586.[1] We have seen, however, that in the last fifteen years or so of the life of this theatre, an increasing amount of space was occupied by the *petites loges*, which must have reduced to some extent the number of places to be filled on any given day by the ordinary sale of tickets. We do not appear to have any precise information about how many spectators the theatre in the Tuileries occupied between 1770 and 1782 could hold, though since the accommodation offered there seems to have been roughly the same as in the theatre which the actors had just vacated, one may assume that the total capacity of the auditorium was roughly the same.[2] The largest number of spectators who paid for admission to the Tuileries theatre recorded in the four years covered by Lancaster's *Comédie Française, 1701–1774*, was 1,479 at the first performance of De Belloy's *Gaston et Bayard* on 24 April 1771.

We have what at first sight appears to be detailed and completely reliable information about the seating capacity of the new theatre to which the Comédie Française at last moved in 1782. On the authority of the *Mercure*, Lancaster gives the total number of seats (the spectators in the *parterre*, rechristened the *parquet*, were also seated now) as 1,400, with, in addition, the *petites loges*.[3] Bachaumont gives the same total, and adds that there were 513 *petites loges* which were let at 500 livres each a year. The same source also furnishes complete details about the number of seats in the various parts of the house: *Orchestre* 180, *Premières loges* and *balcons* 188, *Galerie tournante* 120, *Deuxièmes loges* 64, *Parquet* 500, *Troisièmes loges* 48, and *Amphithéâtre des troisièmes loges* 300.[4] Unquestionably these figures add up to 1,400; and yet, if one consults the Registers of the Comédie Française for this period, one finds that, when new plays were highly successful, noticeably more than 1,400 people paid for admission at the door. At the first performance of the *Mariage de Figaro* on 27 April at least 1,555 spectators paid for admission.[5] Nor was this an altogether exceptional figure during the

---

[1] *Comédie Française, 1701–1774*, p. 594. One wonders whether this figure of over 2,000 is not too high. It is obtained by adding together the highest attendances in the different parts of the house which were recorded between 1690 and 1752; in this long period of time quite a number of changes were no doubt made in the internal arrangement of the theatre.

[2] *Comédie Française, 1701–1774*, pp. 594, 830, and *French Tragedy in the Reign of Louis XVI and the Early Years of the French Revolution* (Baltimore, 1953), p. 8.

[3] *French Tragedy in the Reign of Louis XVI*, pp. 8–9.

[4] *Mémoires secrets*, vol. xx, p. 163 (7 Apr. 1782).

[5] Two tickets for *petites loges* at 24 francs and two at 7 frs. 10 s. were also sold, but how many spectators these represented it is impossible to say. This page of the Registers is re-

triumphant first run of Beaumarchais's comedy: out of the first 49 performances (the fiftieth was a charity performance and the Registers do not give any details about the number of tickets sold) no fewer than 27 attracted over 1,400 spectators. Beaumarchais was not the only playwright of the last decade of the Ancien Régime to draw such crowds to the theatre, although he undoubtedly did so more continuously than anyone else with his *Mariage de Figaro*. The first performance of Collin d'Harleville's comedy, *L'Optimiste*, in February 1788, was seen by 1,548 spectators who paid at the door, and although the play reached 22 performances only by the end of June, it was seen by over 1,400 spectators on four occasions altogether. It will thus be seen that what appears to be at first sight precise and reliable information turns out in the end to be slightly misleading; it is clear that the number of seats available for those spectators who did not possess *petites loges* must have been well over 1,400, as there were no doubt people present on these occasions who were admitted free. It is, however, fairly clear that from the 1750's onwards the *petites loges* gradually absorbed more and more space in the theatres occupied successively by the Comédie Française until finally, in the new theatre opened in 1782, only about three-quarters of the available seats could be occupied by the ordinary ticket-holders.

One would naturally imagine that the growth in the number of people who, from about 1755 onwards, hired *petites loges* would have brought about a marked decline in the number of spectators who bought tickets at the door, especially as writers like Mercier and Lonvay de la Saussaye allege that more and more space inside the theatre was given up to the profitable *petites loges*. In actual fact that was not the case. Indeed the total yearly figures of attendances at the Comédie Française for the period from 1715 to 1774 offer some curious surprises. First, it is quite clear that the years from 1715 to 1750 were very lean ones for the Comédie Française in comparison with both the previous and the following periods. The average attendance for the years from the foundation of the theatre down to 1715 was rather less than 140,000 paying spectators a year. After 1715 came a decided slump; in only four of the years down to 1750 did the total number of spectators who paid for admission reach even the earlier average of 140,000. On no fewer than seven occasions it fell below 100,000, and in the worst year (1741–2) it reached only 84,000. The average total attendance for the

produced in A. Joannidès, *La Comédie Française de 1680 à 1900: Dictionnaire général des pièces et des auteurs* (Paris, 1901), pl. 8. The first performance in the new theatre on 9 Apr. 1782 attracted at least 1,455 paying spectators (see Joannidès, pl. 7).

thirty-four years from 1715 to 1750 (we have no figures for the 1739–40 season, as the register for that year is missing) fell to about 117,000.

The division of our period at 1750 is not completely arbitrary, since the middle of the century saw a marked increase in the number of spectators paying for admission to the Comédie Française. Already in the season 1749–50 the number of paying spectators had risen well

YEARLY TOTALS OF SPECTATORS AT THE COMÉDIE FRANÇAISE FROM EASTER 1681 TO EASTER 1771 (FIVE YEAR AVERAGES)

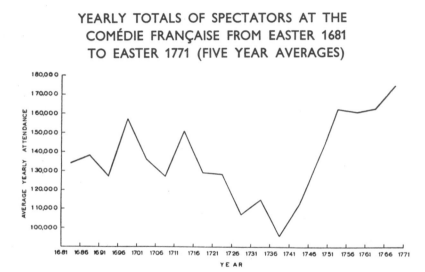

The full figures from 1681 to 1774 are given in the Appendix. As the figure for 1739–40 is not available, the average for 1736–41 is calculated from the total for the other four years of this period

above the average for the years since 1715 to reach 140,000. The rise continued for the rest of the twenty years which the Comédie Française spent at the theatre of the Rue des Fossés-Saint-Germain. Only twice did the total number of spectators who paid for admission fall below 150,000, and in the season 1769–70, the last spent in the old theatre, it reached 191,000. The average for these twenty years is not only far higher than that for the period 1715–50, but it was also well above that for the first thirty-four complete years of the existence of the Comédie Française. The average number of persons paying for admission in the years from 1750 to 1770 came to nearly 165,000. The rise in the number of paying spectators continued when the Comédie Française moved to the Tuileries in 1770. In the first four seasons at this temporary abode (Lancaster's figures do not take us any further) the average number of paying spectators came to over 180,000.

These figures are in many respects puzzling. It is difficult to account for the slump in the fortunes of the Comédie Française in the period between 1715 and 1750. It is not easy to attribute it to economic factors, since it is generally agreed that the worst period of depression in eighteenth-century France was the last ten years or so of the reign of Louis XIV. Yet while it is true that the total attendance at the Comédie Française in the two black seasons between Easter 1708 and Easter 1710 dropped to 128,000 and 114,000, and that it fell even lower to just under 107,000 in the season 1711–12, the last three years of the reign of Louis XIV were exceptionally prosperous. The average number of spectators in the three years from Easter 1712 to Easter 1715 (Louis died in September of the latter year) rose to over 170,000.

The argument that in the following period the Comédie Française had to contend with fierce competition from other theatres does not take us very far either. It is true that since the expulsion of the Italian actors in 1697, the only rivals of the Comédie Française were the Théâtres de la Foire; and undoubtedly the return of the Italians in 1716 was not without its effect. The total number of spectators in the season 1715–16 had already fallen to 133,000, and with the return of the Italians in May 1716 the total attendance of the new theatrical year reached only 104,000. The *Lettres historiques sur les trois spectacles de Paris* of Nicolas Boindin, which appeared in 1719, contain some interesting remarks on the difficulties facing the Comédie Française at this period of the century. He makes, for instance, the following observations on the state of that theatre in February 1718:

> Le 15 du même mois on ne joua point faute de spectateurs.
> Ils fermèrent aussi leur théâtre le 18 parce qu'ils jugèrent bien que M. le duc de Lorraine, qui arriva ce jour-là à Paris,[1] attirerait tout le monde à sa rencontre.[2]

He also records that in his address to the audience at the last performance of the 1717–18 season the actor Fontenay spoke of the 'triste situation' of the company, and declared: 'Nous sommes contraints quelquefois de fermer le théâtre. Nos plus belles représentations, rendues

---

[1] Leopold, Duke of Lorraine from 1697 to 1729.

[2] Pt. i, p. 23. Reference to Lancaster's *Comédie Française 1701–74* shows that there was no performance on that date. He states (p. 658) that the theatre was closed on 6 May and 16 June 1717 because of Peter the Great's visit, and again on 4 Sept. 'for lack of spectators'.

avec toute leur dignité et toute leur magnificence, ont presque été désertes.'[1] Boindin agrees that the lamentations of the Comédie Française are justified: 'En effet, nous voyons depuis un temps la Comédie Française absolument déserte.' This state of affairs he attributes to the competition of the Théâtres de la Foire.[2]

Yet, although the Italian actors and the Foire may have been responsible for the slump in attendances at the Comédie Française in the opening years of the reign of Louis XV, the interesting thing is that the worst years in the period 1715–50 (those in which the total of paying spectators fell below 100,000) occurred for the most part considerably later than this. The lowest figures were recorded for the following seasons: 1721–2, 1727–8, 1736–7, 1737–8, 1740–1, and 1741–2.[3] In other words the worst years lay in the period 1736–42 (no doubt the missing register for 1739–40 would confirm this impression). In any case competition from other theatres, particularly the Opéra-Comique, was extremely fierce in the second half of the century when figures for attendances were rising steeply. In 1765, in his *Lettres sur l'état présent de nos spectacles*, La Dixmerie laments the state of abandonment in which the Comédie Française was left as a result of the competition of less exalted theatres:

On étouffe les portiers de l'Opéra-Comique, et les *Blaise le savetier*, les *Sancho-Pança*, les *La Bride*, les *Mère Bobi* et tant d'autres personnages du même ordre ont entièrement fait oublier les *Orosmane*, les *Rhadamiste*, les *Alceste*, les *Phèdre* et les *Armide*. . . . Enfin, le gros du public a déserté le théâtre de Molière pour courir à celui de Pantalon. *Zaïre* ne fait plus verser de larmes qu'à des yeux russes, et ce sont les Anglais qui viennent admirer les beautés du *Misanthrope*. . . .[4]

Nor was La Dixmerie consoled by the striking success enjoyed by De Belloy's *Siège de Calais* in February and March of that very year: it was for him merely the exception that proves the rule. 'Le concours excité par la tragédie du *Siège de Calais*', he declares, 'semble démentir une partie de ma première lettre. Jamais, dira-t-on, le Théâtre Français ne fut suivi avec plus d'activité. Je répondrai qu'une affluence momentanée ne prouve rien contre un abandon trop réel et trop constant.'[5] Yet, how-

[1] Pt. i, p. 28.   [2] Pt. i, pp. 35–37.

[3] Writing in 1772, Collé speaks of the bad effect of the collapse of Law's System on the theatres: 'Dans mon adolescence je les ai vus désertés après la banqueroute des billets de banque et des actions de la Compagnie des Indes' (*Journal et mémoires*, ed. H. Bonhomme, Paris, 1868, 3 vols., vol. iii, p. 367).

[4] *Lettres sur l'état présent de nos spectacles* (Amsterdam and Paris, 1765), pp. 4–8.

[5] Ibid., p. 83.

ever fierce may have been the competition which the Comédie Française had to face in this period of the century, the fact remains that the number of paying spectators was steadily rising; the average attendance for the five years from Easter 1760 to Easter 1765 was well over 160,000, and this leaves out of account the spectators who occupied *petites loges*.[1]

However one may attempt to explain this state of affairs, it is clear that in the period from 1715 to 1750 the Comédie Française failed to prove as attractive to the inhabitants of the capital and visitors to it as it had done during the second half of the reign of Louis XIV. Indeed, given the increase in population which no doubt took place in this period, the attendance at the theatre over the whole of these thirty-five years can only be regarded as poor. And yet it was a period by no means devoid either of great actors and actresses or of successful new plays; it was the age of Adrienne Lecouvreur, of Voltaire's greatest tragedies, of Nivelle de La Chaussée's *comédies larmoyantes*.

The great rise in attendances at the Comédie Française in the years from 1750 onwards is equally difficult to account for. There was much more competition in these years, not only from the Comédie Italienne and the Opéra-Comique (merged in 1762), but also from the smaller theatres which gradually sprang up on the Boulevards. True, the population of Paris was no doubt increasing, but this could scarcely account for the fact that in the best years of the period 1750–74 the number of spectators who paid for admission was approximately double the number who paid for admission in the worst years of the previous period, while the average attendance rose by nearly 50,000 a year. Nor do these figures of paying spectators tell the whole truth, as they do not include the considerable numbers of people who hired *petites loges*. We can, however, conclude with certainty that, after a lean period of some thirty years, the Comédie Française began about the middle of the century to attract much larger audiences, larger indeed than those which frequented the theatre in the reign of Louis XIV.

[1] Contemporary accounts of theatre audiences can sometimes be misleading. One might gather from Rousseau that in 1758 the Comédie Française could only count on an average daily audience of 300. 'Ceux qui ne vont aux spectacles que les beaux jours, où l'assemblée est nombreuse, trouveront cette estimation trop faible', he adds; 'mais ceux qui, pendant dix ans, les auront suivis, comme moi, bons et mauvais jours, la trouveront sûrement trop forte' (*Lettre à D'Alembert sur les spectacles*, ed. M. Fuchs, Geneva, 1948, p. 127). Rousseau's experience was not up to date; what had been true of the attendances at the Comédie Française during the decade 1740–50 had ceased to be true by the time he was writing. The average attendance for the five years 1753–8 was over 160,000, compared with less than 120,000 for the five years 1743–8.

What of the number of spectators attracted to the theatre during the first run of new plays? Did it reflect the slump in the fortunes of the Comédie Française in the first half of the century from the Regency period onwards, and the increased attractions of the theatre after the middle of the century? A number of plays in the period 1715–50 succeeded in reaching 25 or 30 performances and drawing to the theatre during their first run some 25,000 or more spectators. Voltaire scored several such successes with his tragedies: in November 1718 his first play, *Œdipe*, began its phenomenally successful run and had been given 30 times by January of the following year, in which period close on 25,000 spectators had paid for admission.[1] In 1725 his tragedy, *Hérode et Mariamne*, attracted in its revised form just over 24,000 paying spectators to the theatre in its first run of 28 performances. In 1732 a more illustrious tragedy, *Zaire*, reached 31 performances in its first run during which nearly 27,000 spectators paid for admission. His greatest box-office success was his *Mérope*, which was given 29 times between February 1743 and March 1744 and attracted close on 30,000 spectators to the theatre.[2] Only one other tragedy in this period came into the same category: Houdart de la Motte's *Inès de Castro*. Its first 32 performances, given between April and August 1723, were attended by nearly 28,000 paying spectators.[3] Amongst all the comedies produced in the period only three came into the same class of successes: two plays of Destouches, *Le Glorieux*, which, when first put on in 1732, reached 30 performances, and attracted nearly 25,000 spectators, and his *Philosophe marié*, which did even better five years earlier, running to 32 performances and drawing over 29,000 spectators, and finally Fuzelier's one-act play, *Momus fabuliste*, which was given 30 times and was seen by over 30,000 spectators.

Far below these eight exceptionally successful plays which attracted between 24,000 and 30,000 spectators came the average successful plays of the period, those which reached 20 or 25 performances and which some 15,000 to 20,000 spectators paid to see. Among these figured a

[1] Voltaire continued to draw money from this play for four more performances in Mar. and Apr. 1719 and eight in Aug. 1720. (Lancaster, *French Tragedy in the Time of Louis XV and Voltaire* (Baltimore, 1950), 2 vols., vol. i, p. 54.) If we include the four performances given in Mar. and Apr. 1719, the total of paying spectators rises to nearly 27,000.

[2] The play was naturally a great financial success; it brought Voltaire over 6,000 livres, the highest sum recorded for any tragedy up to that date (Lancaster, *French Tragedy in the Time of Louis XV*, vol. i, p. 217).

[3] The author received payment for another ten performances in Feb. 1724 and three more in Mar. 1725; another 9,000 spectators paid to see these performances.

number of tragedies: Danchet's *Nitétis* (1723) (25 performances—over 18,000 spectators); Piron's *Gustave Wasa* (1733) (20 performances—16,000 spectators); Voltaire's *Alzire* (1736) (20 performances—nearly 20,000 spectators); Marmontel's first play, *Denis le Tyran* (1748) (22 performances—19,000 spectators); and Voltaire's *Sémiramis*, performed in the same year (21 performances—18,000 spectators). Among comedies Pellegrin's *Nouveau Monde* (1722) just comes into this category if we include all the performances down to August 1724 which brought in royalties—a total of 29, which attracted only some 16,000 spectators. Legrand's *Impromptu de la folie*, which was given 25 times when it was first put on in 1725, attracted just under 16,000 paying spectators, but the most popular comedies of the period were those of a serious character: La Chaussée's *Préjugé à la mode* (1735) (20 performances—17,000 spectators) and his *École des Mères* (1744) (27 performances—nearly 20,000 spectators); Gresset's *Le Méchant* (1747) (24 performances—18,000 spectators); and finally Mme de Graffigny's 'pièce dramatique,' *Cénie* (25 performances—nearly 20,000 spectators).

After these there comes a group of plays, some of them quite well known, which were far from being scorned by contemporary audiences during their first run, but which achieved only a modest success, attracting between 10,000 and 13,000 paying spectators to the Comédie Française. Several comedies of Legrand came into this category—for instance, *Plutus* (16 performances—13,000 spectators), *Le Galant Coureur* (22 performances—10,000 spectators), and *Le Philanthrope* (17 performances—13,000 spectators). Houdart de la Motte's tragedy *Romulus* reached 21 performances and drew nearly 13,000 spectators to the theatre. Slightly later Piron's *École des Pères* (22 performances—12,000 spectators) and La Chaussée's *Mélanide* (22 performances—11,000 spectators) came into the same class. Not a single comedy of Marivaux ever achieved even this distinction during its first run at the Comédie Française. Voltaire could thus write without altogether grotesque exaggeration in his notebooks for the period 1735–50: 'Dans notre nation on n'aime pas véritablement la littérature. Une pièce réussit pleinement, 5 à 6,000 personnes la voient dans Paris, 1,200 la lisent, non sic à Londres.'[1]

It is, of course, scarcely surprising that in the period between 1715 and 1750 a successful new play should have attracted to the Comédie Française only a slightly larger number of the permanent or temporary inhabitants of the capital than had been the case in the last thirty-five

[1] *Voltaire's Notebooks*, ed. T. Besterman (Geneva, 1952), 2 vols., p. 316.

years of the reign of Louis XIV; total yearly attendances throughout the first half of the reign of Louis XV had been considerably lower than in the earlier period. With the revival in the fortunes of the Comédie Française in the second half of the eighteenth century one would naturally expect that new plays would bring to the theatre larger numbers of spectators than ever before. Curiously enough, this can scarcely be said to have happened in practice. In speaking of the success of La Harpe's tragedy, *Warwick*, in 1763, Grimm wrote in the *Correspondance littéraire*: 'Elle aura vraisemblablement quinze représentations, et c'est aujourd'hui le plus haut degré de gloire auquel un poète puisse prétendre.'[1] His estimate of the play's success proved quite correct; its 15 performances brought just under 14,000 spectators to the theatre. A very similar picture is offered by La Dixmerie two years later in his *Lettres sur l'état présent de nos spectacles*; he contrasts the phenomenal run of up to 100 performances enjoyed by the worthless productions of the Théâtres de la Foire with the much smaller number achieved even by successful plays at the Comédie Française: 'Il a paru depuis quinze ans sur la scène française plus d'un ouvrage digne d'y reparaître dans tous les temps. Vingt représentations, au plus, ont épuisé le concours du public.'[2] In the same year Collé compares the longer runs enjoyed by successful new plays earlier in the century with the much shorter ones which were customary by this date: 'Il y a quarante ans les drames qui réussissaient avaient des vingt-cinq, trente représentations; dix ou douze représentations étaient des chutes.'[3]

It is as well perhaps to confront these gloomy generalizations with figures derived from the Registers of the Comédie Française. It is a curious fact that not a single play of the period from 1750 to 1774, the point at which Lancaster's second volume on the Comédie Française breaks off, was actually seen by as many as 30,000 paying spectators during its first run. If one takes the first two years of its life on the stage, we find that Voltaire's tragedy, *L'Orphelin de la Chine*, was given 33 times and attracted nearly 32,000 spectators; but what may be properly described as its first run—the 17 performances given in 1755—attracted only some 17,000 people to the theatre. Similarly his *Tancrède* reached 28 performances by the end of 1761, and brought to the Comédie Française 26,000 spectators, but the 13 performances given in 1760 attracted only some 12,000.

Only one play of this period of nearly twenty-five years succeeded

[1] F. M. Grimm (ed.), *Correspondance littéraire, philosophique et critique*, ed. M. Tourneux (Paris, 1877–82), 16 vols., vol. v, p. 416.   [2] p. 9.   [3] *Journal*, vol. iii, p. 57.

in attracting over 25,000 spectators to the theatre in one straight run; this was the *Iphigénie en Tauride* of Guimond de La Touche which between July 1757 and February 1758 reached 27 performances and attracted well over 27,000 spectators to the theatre (one of these performances was given free so that there are no records of the number of spectators present). It is perhaps significant that this new play enjoyed its first run before the innovation of *petites loges* can have absorbed any considerable part of the auditorium, for such a success was never again achieved down to 1774. A few other plays, it is true, were seen by just over 20,000 spectators: De Belloy's tragedy, *Zelmire* (1762) (24 performances and nearly 21,000 spectators), Sedaine's *Philosophe sans le savoir* (1765) (28 performances—21,000 spectators), and Barthe's comedy, *Les Fausses Infidélités* (1768), which achieved an almost identical success. What would have been unquestionably one of the most successful plays of the century—De Belloy's *Siège de Calais*—had its first run cut short by the internal quarrels of the Comédie Française, and was not revived there until 1769, four years after it was first given. It ran in 1765 for 19 performances, one of which was given free; the other 18 attracted nearly 19,000 spectators.

Most other successful plays of the period, even quite famous ones, did much less well than that. Palissot's satirical comedy, *Les Philosophes*, which is often rashly described as one of the most successful plays of the whole of the eighteenth century, was only given 14 times in 1760 and attracted fewer than 13,000 spectators. The counterblast of the *philosophes*, Voltaire's *L'Écossaise*, did rather better than this, with its 21 performances and its total of getting on for 18,000 spectators. Five other plays of these years were seen by between 15,000 and 18,000 spectators during their first run: Favart's comedy, *L'Anglais à Bordeaux* (1763) (16 performances—17,000 spectators); Poinsinet's *Le Cercle* (1764) (18 performances—15,000 spectators); Beaumarchais's first *drame*, *Eugénie* (1768) (23 performances—17,000 spectators); Saurin's adaptation of Moore's *Gamester*, *Beverley* (1768) (15 performances—15,000 spectators); and Ducis' mangled version of *Romeo and Juliet* (1772) (19 performances—16,000 spectators). Plays which appeared quite honourably at the Comédie Française in these years had an even shorter first run or drew fewer spectators. Collé's comedy, *Dupuis et Desronais* (1763), was given only 17 times and was seen by less than 15,000 spectators, while Goldoni's *Bourru bienfaisant* (1771) reached only 13 performances and attracted less than 12,000 paying spectators.

Of the period which follows it is impossible to speak in such detail, as Lancaster's published analysis of the records of the Comédie Française stops short at Easter 1774. For the fifteen years down to the Revolution all that can be offered is the results of some soundings. The triumphant success which stands out in this period and towers above all other popular plays before 1789 was the *Mariage de Figaro*. Between 27 April 1784 and 11 February of the following year the play was given 73 times. In 1787, after the hundredth performance, Beaumarchais received from the actors the unheard-of sum of 59,510 l. 14 s. 10 d.[1] The number of spectators attracted to the Comédie Française during the first run proper of 73 performances (or rather of the first 72, as we have no figures for the attendance at the fiftieth performance, which was given 'au profit des mères nourrices') was approximately 97,000—over three times as many spectators as had been present in the theatre during the first run of such well-known successes of the century as *Œdipe*, *Inès de Castro*, *Le Philosophe marié*, *Zaïre*, *Mérope*, and *Iphigénie en Tauride*.

There seems, however, no doubt that the success of the *Mariage* was exceptional even in the last two decades or so of the Ancien Régime and that it must have attracted to the Comédie Française tens of thousands of people who were not normally in the habit of frequenting that theatre. The success of *Le Barbier de Séville* nine years earlier was much more in line with what had been customary up to that time even for a very successful play; its 27 performances during its first run drew 24,000 paying spectators to the theatre. And if we take a play performed after the *Mariage de Figaro*, on the very eve of the Revolution, Collin d'Harleville's comedy, *L'Optimiste*, we find that between February and July 1788 the play was given 22 performances which attracted to the theatre some 24,000 spectators. There seems no question that the *Mariage de Figaro* achieved a success which was altogether exceptional, and that no other play of the last two decades of the Ancien Régime achieved anything remotely approaching its extraordinary popularity. Even so, it is an interesting side-light on the relative smallness of the theatre-going public of eighteenth-century Paris that for all its phenomenal popularity the *Mariage de Figaro* should have taken three years to reach its hundredth performance at the Comédie Française.

We have seen what are the difficulties in the way of forming any precise notion as to the size of the audience at the Comédie Française in

---

[1] A receipt for this sum, signed on his behalf by Gudin de la Brenellerie, is preserved in the Archives of the Comédie Française.

the period from 1715 to 1789. Not only have we no means of estimating how many people were admitted free, but in the last thirty years or so of the period the growing popularity of the *petites loges*, which in the new theatre taken over in 1782 accounted for approximately a quarter of the available seats, prevents us from knowing exactly how many paying spectators attended any particular performance in these years. It is therefore impossible to make a straightforward comparison between attendances at any given play or in any particular year with those of the earlier period.

None the less various interesting points can be clearly established. There is no question that in the first half of our period—from 1715 to 1750—the Comédie Française fell on lean days, and that attendances in these years fell well below the average for the latter part of the reign of Louis XIV. On the other hand, the successful new plays of these years drew on the whole rather larger audiences to the theatre than in the earlier period, though their reception still confirms the impression which we had earlier reached that the potential theatre audience of those days was a small one, even for the most popular plays. It seems to have been revivals of the older plays of the repertoire which attracted exceptionally poor audiences. It is notorious, for instance, that in 1746 the Duc d'Aumont, in his capacity as *Gentilhomme de la Chambre*, forbade the actors to perform any of Molière's five-act comedies until further notice.[1] On 10 May of that year *L'École des Femmes* attracted a mere 35 spectators to the theatre, and *Tartufe*, a few days later, only 32. On two occasions in June this latter comedy drew 91 and 84 spectators, while at another performance in this month *Le Misanthrope* was seen by only 170. In July *L'École des Femmes* was seen by a mere 99 spectators, and *Tartufe* by 145. In the same month Racine's *Plaideurs*, played along with *Le Médecin malgré lui*, was seen by only 31 spectators. The Duke's order is dated 11 July 1746, and was made the day after *Tartufe* had attracted only 145 spectators. It was not long observed, but its very existence does give some notion of the poor audiences which were often attracted by the great masterpieces of the seventeenth century in the period with which we are concerned.

There is no question that in the years between 1750 and the outbreak of the Revolution the Comédie Française became considerably more popular with theatre-goers. Indeed, as we have seen, the magnitude of this growth in popularity is masked by the fact that the average annual

[1] G. Monval, 'Ordre d'un gentilhomme de la Chambre portant "défense des pièces de Molière" ', *Le Moliériste* (1879), pp. 146–7.

attendances fail to take account of the thousands of people who made use of their own or other people's *petites loges* in the course of the years from 1755 onwards. If the process whereby the *petites loges* came to occupy about a quarter of the available seats was a gradual one, it is clear that we must add something like a third to the figures for spectators who bought tickets at the door if we are to get anything like a true picture either of the average annual attendance after, say, 1770, or, of course, the number of spectators present at the first run of a new play. In the last four years for which we can derive figures from Lancaster's *Comédie Française, 1701–74*, the average number of tickets bought at the door in each year was over 180,000; this might well represent a total attendance of some 240,000 if we try to take into account the occupants of the *petites loges*. This would have to be compared with an average annual attendance of some 117,000 for the period from 1715 to 1750, and rather less than 140,000 for the years from 1680 to 1715.

Yet if total annual attendances at the Comédie Française rose very sharply from 1750 onwards, this increase can scarcely be said to be reflected in the number of spectators who came to the theatre during the first run of successful new plays—a useful measuring-rod for the potential audience of a theatre. We can safely leave out of account the quite exceptional number of spectators who flocked to see *Le Mariage de Figaro*. The 27,000 who came to see Guimond de La Touche's *Iphigénie* in 1757 must represent a fairly accurate picture of the total number of people who saw the play, as the new system of *petites loges* was just beginning to get under way. Yet if we add a reasonably generous allowance of one third to cover the spectators in the *petites loges* to the total number of spectators who were present at the first run of very successful plays performed after this date, such as Sedaine's *Philosophe sans le savoir*, Beaumarchais's *Barbier de Séville*, and Collin d'Harleville's *L'Optimiste*, we arrive at totals only of between 28,000 and 32,000 spectators. Yet such figures had been achieved by successful plays in the first half of the century—by *Zaïre* and *Mérope*, *Inès de Castro* and *Le Philosophe marié*—even though in these years the total annual attendance at the theatre was much smaller. Indeed, at the beginning of its history the Comédie Française had reached equally large figures with one *dancourade*, *Les Vendanges de Suresnes*, and some 25,000 spectators with Boursault's *Ésope*.

In other words, even at the end of the Ancien Régime a very successful new play only attracted what is by modern standards an extraordinarily small number of theatre-goers. An increase undoubtedly took place, from 1750 onwards, in the total number of people who frequented the Comédie Française in any given year; but this rise in the total number of spectators did not have anything like the effect one might have imagined on the number of people able and willing to support even the most successful new play, unless it enjoyed the quite phenomenal vogue of the *Mariage de Figaro*. From the middle of the eighteenth century onwards the popularity of the Comédie Française did undoubtedly grow, but it remains clear that on the eve of the Revolution the number of people who could be attracted by a highly successful play was not very substantially greater than it had been a century earlier in the opening decades of the life of that theatre.

(ii) *The Middle Classes and the Theatre*

The eighteenth century is associated in everyone's mind with the so-called 'rise of the middle classes'. The expansion of trade and to a smaller extent of industry (an Industrial Revolution still lay far in the future so far as France was concerned) led to a growth both in the economic power of the middle classes and in their awareness of their importance in the life of the country. It is broadly agreed that the clash between their power and aspirations and the existing absolutist and aristocratic régime was one of the main causes of the French Revolution. Inevitably the rise of the middle classes had its effects in the realm of the arts—in painting as in literature, in drama as well as in the novel. In the theatre it led, we are told, to the rise of new types of drama—first, in the 1730's and 1740's, the sentimental, moralizing comedies of Destouches and the *comédies larmoyantes* of Nivelle de La Chaussée, and later a completely new genre, the *Drame*, which flourished from about 1760 down to the Revolution.

All this is no doubt broadly speaking true, but it requires some amplification and, as we shall see, some modifications of detail. This is not the place to expatiate on the economic and social history of France, but it is perhaps worth bearing in mind that the 'rise of the middle classes' was not some sudden eighteenth-century phenomenon. The middle classes had been 'rising' for a very long time, through the centuries since the Middle Ages. So far as the theatre is concerned, the presence of a strong bourgeois contingent in the audiences of Corneille, Molière, and Racine has already been established. Indeed there is no particular reason to think that the proportion of bourgeois in the audiences which saw the first performance of Diderot's *Père de famille* or Sedaine's *Philosophe sans le savoir* was any higher than at the *première* of *Le Misanthrope* or *Andromaque*.

Here, however, bare numbers would not take us very far, even if they could be precisely calculated, which would presuppose, of course, both that the term 'bourgeois' could be defined exactly and that the spectators had been required to declare their precise social status on entering the theatre. The audiences of seventeenth-century and eighteenth-century Paris were part and parcel of the society of the age. Their composition inevitably reflected the changes which were constantly taking place in the world outside the theatre. Even if the proportion of bourgeois spectators was no higher in 1760 than it had been in 1660, those of 1760 belonged to a France which subtle changes both in social relationships and in general outlook on the world had made vastly different from what it had been a century earlier. The French middle classes thirty years before the Revolution had acquired for themselves a place in the life of the country which was very much more important than that occupied by their ancestors at the beginning of the personal reign of Louis XIV. In business and the professions they were conscious of the leading part which they had come to play in the life of the country. If they had not yet shaken off their feeling of inferiority in face of the aristocracy, they were well on the way to doing so.

Yet the bourgeois were only part of the theatre audiences of eighteenth-century Paris. Not only were they confronted in the actual physical theatre with representatives of a higher social class; they still continued to be influenced by the taste and outlook of their betters. Even in the decades immediately prior to the Revolution the Comédie Française was not the scene of a bitter class war of bourgeois against aristocracy of the kind which was to take place in the world outside in 1789. The traditional canons of taste continued to hold sway in the theatre, subtly modified, but certainly not destroyed by the social transformations taking place in the world of which the theatre was only a tiny fragment.

There are, curiously enough, relatively few references in the documents of the time to the presence of the middle classes in the Paris theatres of the eighteenth century. The heroine of a novel published in 1740 is made to compare the audiences of the Opéra and the Comédie Française and to find at the latter theatre 'une assemblée nombreuse et brillante, mais ayant pourtant en gros un air un peu plus bourgeois que celle de l'Opéra, quoique composée à peu près des mêmes personnes'. At the Comédie Française, she declares, 'il perce une petite nuance de roture qui est imperceptible à l'Opéra'.[1] The splenetic Collé, in his denunciations of the *comédies larmoyantes* of Nivelle de La Chaussée, exclaims: 'Le moindre et le plus plat bourgeois veut à présent de la noblesse en tout, et une décence pédante, qui est la plus grande ennemie de la gaieté.'[2] We learn from Grimm that before the Opéra-Comique was merged with the Théâtre Italien in 1762, 'la bonne compagnie n'allait guère à ce théâtre'. The audiences of the Opéra-Comique had consequently, so Grimm alleges, lower standards than those of the Comédie Française:

> C'étaient alors messieurs les maîtres des comptes d'un côté, et messieurs les maîtres bouchers de la Pointe-Saint-Eustache de l'autre, qui décidaient du sort des pièces nouvelles. Ces deux maîtrises n'étaient pas toujours d'accord dans leurs décisions; les maîtres bouchers sifflaient souvent des tirades que messieurs les maîtres des comptes trouvaient, sur la parole de l'*avocat* Marchand,[3] remplies de sel et de finesse.[4]

Louis-Sébastien Mercier also has something to say about the presence of bourgeois in the theatre. In protesting against the way in which in comedies performed at the Comédie Française the nobleman is glorified at the expense of the bourgeois, he has some interesting remarks to make on the absence of reaction of middle-class spectators to this state of affairs. 'Comment', he asks,

> a-t-on ensuite avili sur ce même théâtre l'ordre de la bourgeoisie? Pourquoi le marquis, le comte y sont-ils toujours légers, sémillants, et le bourgeois toujours plat et bête? Dans telle pièce l'officier donne des croquignoles au marchand; et le parterre, composé de boutiquiers, n'en rit pas moins de toutes ses forces.[5]

Despite his hostility towards the nobility and all his protests against the predominance of aristocratic taste in the contemporary theatre, Mercier does not offer a very flattering picture of the intelligence of some bourgeois theatre-goers of his time:

> Le bourgeois parisien s'amuse du spectacle; mais lorsqu'il a payé, il croit être quitte envers tout le monde. J'atteste que j'en ai entendu un, qu'en style populaire on appelle *un bon bourgeois*, qui louait à outre-mesure les comédiens du Théâtre Français, en ce qu'il s'imaginait que ces acteurs produisaient de

---

[1] Bridard de la Garde, *Lettres de Thérèse* (The Hague, 1739–40), 3 vols., vol. iii, pp. 20–21.

[2] *Journal*, vol. i, p. 408 (Mar. 1754).

[3] Jean-Henri Marchand (d. 1785), author of various satirical pamphlets and of *Le Vidangeur sensible* (see below, p. 258).

[4] *Correspondance littéraire*, vol. viii, p. 136 (Aug. 1768).

[5] *Tableau de Paris* (Amsterdam, 1783–9), 12 vols., vol. vii, p. 62.

leur fond tout ce qu'ils déclamaient en public. Ce fut moi qui lui appris qu'il y avait des auteurs dont ils répétaient de mémoire les phrases et les idées. Il avait cru bonnement que Molé imaginait son rôle et que Préville était un Molière.[1]

Earlier, in his polemical work, *Du Théâtre*, he had some interesting observations to make on the tribulations of persons of moderate means who sought to visit the Comédie Française of his day:

Il nous faudrait une salle de spectacle qui ne fût pas construite uniquement pour la commodité des riches, et où le bon bourgeois, le marchand, l'artisan pussent amener leur famille à un prix modéré. Mais qu'arrive-t-il? De dix parties faites d'aller à la Comédie, neuf viennent à manquer, parce que la difficulté d'avoir des places honnêtes, l'embarras, le tumulte, la gêne font payer trop cher le plaisir qu'on se proposait d'avoir. Les comédiens y gagneraient, s'ils savaient contenter la bourgeoisie, cet ordre nombreux et qui paie; mais MM. les comédiens ont pour 200,000 livres de petites loges louées à l'année, et ils vous jettent les honnêtes gens qui n'ont pas six livres à donner,[2] dans des coins éloignés, où l'on voit mal, où l'on entend à peine, où il sent mauvais. Quoi de plus indécent et de plus cruel que ce parterre étroit, toujours tumultueux, où au moindre choc on tombe les uns sur les autres, et qui devient insupportable et très pernicieux à la santé pendant les chaleurs de l'été? Des monopoles font augmenter le prix et le nombre des billets, de sorte que les trois quarts du temps on y étouffe après avoir payé trois fois la valeur de la place. . . . De là le dégoût que presque tous les hommes faits ont conçu pour le théâtre. Si l'on y était assis commodément et à peu de frais, on préférerait sans doute le spectacle national à tout autre, on n'irait plus chez Audinot, chez Nicolet et autres farceurs, chez lesquels on rit de pitié, il est vrai, mais où du moins on est assis à son aise pour son argent.[3]

Despite the comparative rarity of such references in eighteenth-century documents, there can be no question that, as in the previous century, middle-class spectators were the backbone of the *parterre*. This part of the theatre continued to house a high proportion of the audience. Of the 19,000 spectators who bought tickets for the first run of De Belloy's *Siège de Calais* in 1765, nearly half stood in the *parterre*. Later in the same year *Le Philosophe sans le savoir* was seen during its first run by 21,000 spectators who paid for tickets at the door; just over half of them stood in the *parterre*. Ten years later, in the Tuileries theatre, of the 24,000 people who bought tickets for the first run of the

---

[1] *Tableau de Paris*, vol. xi, pp. 103–4.
[2] Six livres was the price of a seat in the first row of boxes.
[3] pp. 347–8 n.

Barbier de Séville just under half were spectators in that part of the house.

It is not an altogether easy task to compare these figures with those for the earlier period in the history of the Comédie Française from 1680 to the death of Louis XIV. We have seen how in these years the raising of prices during the first run of new plays tended to diminish the proportion of the audience in the *parterre*. However, from 1753 onwards, as Lancaster points out,[1] no distinction between new and old plays was made in fixing prices for admission. On the other hand the gradual increase in the number of *petites loges* inevitably reduced the importance of the *parterre*; if in the 1760's and 1770's its occupants still accounted for nearly half the total number of spectators who bought tickets at the door for separate performances, they formed considerably less than half the total audience, if we allow for the persons who made use of their *petites loges*. Thus, if we assume that in 1775 the *petites loges* accounted for about a quarter of the seats in the theatre, we might have to raise from 24,000 to 32,000 the total number of spectators who attended the theatre during the first run of the *Barbier de Séville*; less than 12,000 of these stood in the *parterre*. In the new theatre opened in 1782, while the prices for the now seated *parterre* were raised at one jump from 1 livre to 2 livres 8 sous, we know quite definitely that the 500 seats in that part of the theatre formed only a quarter of the total accommodation, if we count in the 513 *petites loges*.[2]

However, these developments which tended to reduce the importance of the *parterre* at the Comédie Française did not take place until the last decades of the Ancien Régime. For the greater part of our period contemporary writers continue to pay that same deference to the taste of the *parterre* which had become traditional by the end of the seventeenth century. It is true that, in private, writers were not always without their complaints about its taste. When in 1725 Voltaire's comedy, *L'Indiscret*, was performed at the Comédie Française, he felt, as he wrote in a letter to the Marquise de Bernières, that the play was more successful with the spectators in the boxes than with those in the *parterre*:

Dancourt et Legrand ont accoutumé le parterre au bas comique et aux grossièretés, et insensiblement le public s'est formé le préjugé que des petites pièces en un acte doivent être des farces pleines d'ordures, et non pas des

---

[1] *Comédie Française 1701–1774*, p. 595.

[2] The *parterre*, though still reserved for men only, had ceased to be the cheapest part of the theatre. The third row of boxes cost only 2 livres and the *paradis* 1 l. 10 s.; both of these were open to men and women. Together they seem to have provided seats for something like 350 people.

comédies nobles où les mœurs soient respectées. Le peuple n'est pas content quand on ne fait rire que l'esprit. Il faut le faire rire tout haut, et il est difficile de le réduire à aimer mieux des plaisanteries fines que des équivoques fades, et à préférer Versailles à la rue Saint-Denis.[1]

Although Voltaire might on occasion complain about the bad taste of the *parterre*, he constantly recognized the importance of gaining its applause. In 1732 he had his tragedy, *Ériphyle*, performed by amateurs before its first appearance at the Comédie Française. 'En attendant que je sois jugé par le parterre, j'ai fait jouer la pièce chez Mme de Fontaine-Martel', he writes at the beginning of February, and again in April, on the eve of his play's first performance: 'C'est ce jour-là que le parterre jugera *Ériphyle* en dernier ressort.'[2] Two years later he writes of his latest tragedy, *Alzire*: 'C'est une pièce fort chrétienne, qui pourra me réconcilier avec quelques dévots; j'en serai charmé, pourvu qu'elle ne me brouille pas avec le parterre.'[3] A few days later he speaks again of 'ce tribunal dangereux'.[4] 'Messieurs les critiques', he exclaims in a letter of 1738 addressed to Thieriot on his comedy, *L'Enfant prodigue*, 'j'en appelle au parterre.'[5]

Voltaire attached so much importance to gaining the approval of the spectators in this part of the theatre that at the first performances of his new plays he took care to organize a *claque* in order to ensure their success. Collé relates in his Journal Duclos's story of how, in 1748, in order to secure applause for his *Sémiramis*, Voltaire bought all the tickets for the *parterre*, which had been reduced to four hundred for the occasion. According to Duclos, 'malgré cette précaution, deux ou trois jeunes gens de ce parterre acheté avaient battu des mains *en bâillant tout haut*, ce qui avait fait beaucoup rire tout le monde, excepté Voltaire.'[6] A somewhat less highly coloured version of the facts is given in the memoirs of Voltaire's secretary, Longchamp. According to him it was the hostility of the supporters of his rival, Crébillon, which compelled Voltaire to have recourse to

un moyen à la vérité peu digne de lui, mais dont il crut avoir besoin, et qui en effet ne lui fut pas inutile: ce fut de prendre au bureau un nombre de billets de parterre qu'il distribua, outre les siens, à des personnages de sa connais-

---

[1] *Correspondence*, ed. T. Besterman, vols. 1–10 (Geneva, 1953–4), vol. i, p. 321. Mathieu Marais gives a rather different account of the play's reception: 'Elle a déplu et à la chambre basse [the *parterre*] qui y a trouvé peu de règles du théâtre, et à la chambre haute [the boxes], qui s'y est trouvée trop bien dépeinte.' See *Journal et mémoires*, ed. M. F. A. de Lescure (Paris, 1863–8), 4 vols., vol. iii, p. 356.

[2] *Correspondence*, vol. ii, pp. 273, 303.   [3] Ibid., vol. iii, p. 327.

[4] Ibid., p. 334.   [5] *Œuvres complètes*, vol. xxxv, p. 58.   [6] Vol. i, pp. 1–2.

sance, qui en donnèrent à leurs amis. MM. Thieriot, Dumolard, Lambert, le chevalier de La Morlière, le chevalier de Mouhy, l'abbé de La Mare, etc., dont il connaissait le dévouement, s'acquittèrent fort bien de cette commission. J'en eus pour ma part des billets à distribuer, et je les mis en de bonnes mains, c'est-à-dire capables de bien claquer et à propos. Il fallait sans doute être armés et prêts à la défense contre des agresseurs connus et nombreux. Le jour de la première représentation arrivé, les champions de part et d'autre ne manquèrent pas de se trouver sur le champ de bataille, armés de pied en cap; j'y tenais de pied ferme mon rang de fantassin. Chaque parti se promettait bien la victoire; aussi fut-elle disputée et la lutte pénible. Dès la première scène des mouvements excités dans le parterre, des brouhahas, des murmures se manifestèrent; on crut même entendre quelques coups de sifflet obscurs et honteux; mais dès le commencement aussi les applaudissements balancèrent au moins tous ces bruits, et ils finirent par les étouffer. La pièce se soutint, la représentation se termina très bien, et le succès ne parut point équivoque.[1]

This account has the ring of truth, whereas there seems a certain element of exaggeration in Collé's version of the story, as in the remarks which he made about *Sémiramis* in the following year in speaking of Voltaire's *claque* for his next play, *Nanine*. 'Cet auteur', he declares,

prend actuellement un parti singulier pour attirer du monde à ses pièces; il paie la comédie au public; il donne les deux tiers du parterre et des loges à ses nièces, ou à quelques autres femmes de sa connaissance; enfin, les comédiens ont assuré à Dutartre que la réussite de *Sémiramis* lui avait coûté huit cents livres de son argent, au delà du produit des quinze représentations qu'elle a eues.[2]

As these fifteen performances brought Voltaire 3,415 livres,[3] one has difficulty in taking literally every word of Collé's story. However, he makes similar comments about Voltaire's next tragedy, *Oreste*, performed at the Comédie Française in 1750. Despite the badness of the play, he declares,

le parterre soudoyé fit son devoir d'applaudir, et tâcha de gagner son argent; en sorte qu'aidé de ses fanatiques, soutenu par sa cabale et son manège, je ne doute pas que Voltaire ne fasse traîner sa pièce huit ou dix représentations, peut-être même ne lui fasse une petite fortune injuste, comme il l'a procurée

---

[1] *Mémoires sur Voltaire et sur ses ouvrages par Longchamp et Wagnière, ses secrétaires* (Paris, 1826), 2 vols., vol. ii, pp. 210–11.

[2] *Journal*, vol. i, p. 81 (June 1749).

[3] Lancaster, *Tragedy in the Time of Louis XV*, p. 337.

à *Sémiramis* (en payant s'entend). Je ne serais point étonné qu'elle eût quinze ou dix-huit représentations comme cette dernière rapsodie.[1]

The organization of a *claque* seems to have been one of the occupations of that adventurer, the so-called 'chevalier' de La Morlière, whom we have already encountered among the supporters of Voltaire at the first performance of *Sémiramis*. In 1762, according to a letter of Favart,[2] he ended up in the prison of Pierre-Encise at Lyons for his activities in this direction which had apparently become a form of blackmail. Favart describes him as

le chef et le capitaine des cabales contre les pièces nouvelles; il est prouvé qu'il avait à sa solde plus de cent cinquante conspirateurs. Il mettait tous les auteurs à contribution, et celui qui n'avait pas le moyen de lui payer le tribut qu'il exigeait pour faire réussir un ouvrage, pouvait compter sur une chute inévitable. La cabale qu'il a excitée contre la comédie de Palissot[3] a fait ouvrir les yeux sur ses menées, et lui a attiré une juste punition. On peut dire qu'en cette occasion La Morlière a joué de malheur, parce que la pièce de Palissot n'avait pas besoin d'être poussée pour choir.[4]

Playwrights themselves, however, continued to organize *claques* to secure the success of their works. In his *Correspondance littéréraire* for 1776 La Harpe has great fun in describing the methods used by Dorat to bolster up his plays. 'C'est de lui que M. d'Alembert a fort bien dit', writes La Harpe, 'que le parterre était à ses ordres et *à ses frais*. Il entreprend un succès comme une affaire d'argent, paie trois cents billets par représentation, remplit sept ou huit loges de ses protecteurs et protectrices.' After the fourteen performances of his tragedy, *Régulus*, which was given together with his comedy, *La Feinte par Amour*, in 1773, 'M. Dorat me dit lui-même', says La Harpe, 'qu'il se trouvait redevable aux comédiens de sept cents livres. Je lui répondis en riant: *Monsieur, encore deux ou trois succès comme celui-là, et vous etes ruiné.*' His comedy, *Le Malheureux imaginaire* (1776), brought the following comment from La Harpe: 'Au surplus, de compte fait avec les comédiens, sa dernière pièce lui coûte 92 louis; je le sais des comédiens eux-mêmes qui en rient à ses dépens.' La Harpe quotes with glee the following epigram:

---

[1] *Journal*, vol. i, pp. 123–4 (Jan. 1750). *Oreste* was given nine times in its first run.

[2] In the *Mémoires secrets* for 13 Aug. 1762 (vol. i, p. 115) Bachaumont speaks of the Chevalier being imprisoned at Saint-Lazare, but does not give any reason.

[3] *Les Méprises*, performed at the Comédie Française on 7 June 1762. It was given only once.

[4] C. S. Favart, *Mémoires et correspondance littéraires, dramatiques et anecdotiques*, ed. A. P. C. Favart (Paris, 1808), 3 vols., vol. ii, p. 21.

Le plus bavard de nos rimeurs français
Se plaignait fort d'un censeur téméraire
Qui lui niait sa gloire et ses succès,
En démentant les *bravo* du parterre.
Quelqu'un lui dit pour le réconforter:
'Ne craignez rien; d'une gloire enviée,
On aurait tort de vous rien disputer.
Elle est à vous, vous l'avez bien payée.'

He is not content with one epigram. Another follows:

Des petits vers pour Iris, pour Climène,
Dans les boudoirs m'avaient fait quelque nom.
Désir me prit de briller sur la scène;
Mais j'y parus sans l'aveu d'Apollon.
Là comme ailleurs s'achète la victoire.
A beaux deniers l'on m'a vendu la gloire.
Mieux eût valu, ma foi, qu'on m'eût berné.
Que m'ont servi tant de prôneurs à gages?
De mes succès où sont les avantages?
Un seul encore, et je suis ruiné.[1]

The amusing thing is that, two years later, Meister made in his *Correspondance littéraire* exactly the same charge against La Harpe. He alleged that the eleven performances of his tragedy, *Les Barmécides*, brought him in just over 600 livres,

sur lesquelles il redevait plus de moitié à la Comédie pour des billets donnés à ses amis. . . . Les admirateurs de M. de La Harpe reparaissaient à chaque représentation des *Barmécides* au parterre; et s'y trouvant toujours également à leur aise, on les a nommés assez plaisamment *les pères du Désert*.[2]

This did not prevent La Harpe from continuing to refer with contempt to the existence of *claques* in the *parterre*. In 1779, in commenting on the dismissal from the Comédie Française of Mlle Sainval and the 'ragging' of the other leading lady, Mlle Raucourt, he contrasts the hubbub created by the admirers of Mlle Sainval with the absence of reaction from the *parterre* when Mlle Clairon had left the theatre. 'Quelle est la raison de cette différence?' he asks. 'C'est que Mlle Clairon n'avait d'amis que dans la bonne compagnie qui ne fait point de bruit au spectacle, et que Mlle Sainval a su mieux que personne mettre en œuvre une foule de polissons soudoyés qui composent aujourd'hui

---

[1] *Correspondance littéraire* (Paris, 1801–7), 6 vols.; vol. ii, pp. 14–15, 62–63.
[2] Ibid., vol. xii, p. 166. See Bachaumont, *Mémoires secrets*, vol. xii, p. 97 (28 Aug. 1778) for exactly the same story.

un tiers du parterre, et s'en rendent quelquefois les maîtres.'[1] In the little play, *Molière à la nouvelle salle*, which he wrote for the opening of the new theatre in 1782, he introduced a scene between Molière and a character called M. Claque, who has lost his job as the organizer of hired applause and, with it, 'vingt écus par mois'.[2]

At the same period in the century Mercier has some interesting remarks to make on the subject in the chapter 'Cabale' in his *Tableau de Paris*. In earlier days, he declares, there used to be 'des cabales contre la pièce; aujourd'hui il y en a pour'. A play which is a failure at the first performance, succeeds at the second. 'L'arrêt du parterre inflexible est cassé deux jours après par un parterre bénévole, qui met une espèce de gloire à ressusciter l'auteur.' He quotes the example of the success of the *Barbier de Séville*, and adds the further remark:

> Le cabaleur en chef qui jadis ameutait tout un parterre, n'existe plus. Ce rôle singulier, et que j'ai vu dans ma jeunesse, s'est effacé et ne figure plus dans nos spectacles. Il se forme bien quelques petits pelotons d'auteurs infortunés et envieux; mais tous les accès de la jalousie ne font plus rien contre une pièce qui recèle de vraies beautés.[3]

It is interesting that Meister also accuses Beaumarchais of packing the *parterre* with his friends, this time at the fourth performance of the *Mariage de Figaro*. 'Il avait eu soin de le garnir de tous ses amis', he writes, 'à qui il avait annoncé que ce jour verrait éclore la cabale la plus violente contre son innocent ouvrage.'[4] After all, in his first comedy, produced nine years earlier, Beaumarchais had revealed a considerable knowledge of the practical side of organizing a play's success when he made Figaro relate to the Count his own experiences as a playwright:

> En vérité, je ne sais comment je n'eus pas le plus grand succès, car j'avais rempli le parterre des plus excellents travailleurs; des mains . . . comme des battoirs; j'avais interdit les gants, les cannes, tout ce qui ne produit que des applaudissements sourds; et d'honneur, avant la pièce, le café m'avait paru dans les meilleures dispositions pour moi. Mais les efforts de la cabale . . .
> Le Comte: Ah! la cabale! monsieur l'auteur tombé!
> Figaro: Tout comme un autre: pourquoi pas? Ils m'ont sifflé; mais si jamais je puis les rassembler . . .[5]

No doubt many of these stories about hired *claques* and the *parterre*

---

[1] *Correspondance littéraire*, vol. iii, p. 4.   [2] Sc. 8.
[3] *Tableau de Paris*, vol. vii, pp. 116–17.
[4] *Correspondance littéraire*, vol. xiii, p. 522.
[5] *Barbier de Séville*, Act I, Sc. 2.

being filled with the author's friends are highly exaggerated, even though they must contain an element of truth. Yet they all show the importance of giving satisfaction to this highly vocal body of men who, at least until 1782, stood squashed together for hours on end at the first performances of a new play. Writers continued to lavish praise on the taste of this section of the audience as their predecessors had done in the previous century, particularly in prologues to comedies. The most interesting example is to be found in D'Allainval's *L'École des Bourgeois*, first performed at the Comédie Française in 1728. Though struck out of the acting versions of this play since 1770, the prologue throws considerable light on the attitude of playwrights of the time to their audiences. The characters are the ones traditional in works of this kind since Molière's *Critique de l'École des Femmes*: the author, a pedant (in this case a tutor), two noblemen, and a *Marquise* and her sister. In the opening scene the Chevalier expresses surprise that the author, who is all agog for the performance of his new play, should not have opened his mouth during dinner, either to speak or to eat. 'Qui diable reconnaîtrait un auteur à ces deux traits?' he asks, and then exclaims: 'Tu as l'air d'un homme à qui on va lire son arrêt.' To this the author replies, in words full of flattery for the spectators of the *parterre*: 'N'attends-je pas le mien du parterre? Ciel! combien de juges!' he exclaims; and the Chevalier interjects: 'Qui n'y viennent point pour dormir, ni pour opiner du bonnet.' 'J'y vois de toutes parts des gens d'esprit', declares the trembling author;

de ce côté, c'est un avocat qui a pâli toute la journée sur des questions épineuses de jurisprudence; là, c'est un officier qui vient de perdre son argent; ici c'est un homme désespéré de l'infidélité de sa maîtresse. Ils viennent à la Comédie pour faire trêve, l'un à ses travaux, les autres à leurs chagrins. Ils me regardent tous avec un air farouche et effrayant, et je crois les entendre me dire: Fais-moi rire, je viens ici pour cela.

In the second scene of the prologue the various characters assemble to hear the author read his play, and to give their verdict on it. Here d'Allainval gives an original turn to his prologue. The Chevalier is made to speak ironically of the conventional form employed in such little plays: 'Encore, prologue? Hé, la comédie, je t'en conjure. Nous devinons ton prologue. Il va venir un marquis dire du mal de ton *École des Bourgeois* et un raisonneur de tes amis la défendre. Tous les prologues sont montés sur ce ton-là.' Here the contents of the prologue are rather different. The author tries hard to read his play to the assembled company, but he is never able to get beyond the title and

the word, *prologue*, as he is constantly interrupted by the foolish remarks of all those present. The Chevalier, for instance, claims to be a
connoisseur in such matters: 'Je m'en pique, et cela m'est naturel, car
personne n'a peut-être jamais moins étudié, ni moins lu que moi.'

Finally the author, frustrated in his attempts to read his play, treats
his hearers to a fable in verse, *Le Singe joueur de gobelets*. The monkey
summons all the animals to see it perform its tricks, and the description
of its audience provides an entertaining picture of the different classes
of spectator who frequented the boxes, stage, and *parterre* of the
Comédie Française in the first half of the eighteenth century:

> Dans les loges devaient briller
> L'aimable et tendre Philomèle,
> La charmante Serine et Perruche la belle.
> Sur le théâtre on verrait s'étaler
> Et jouer de la prunelle
> Sire Lion, Milord Rhinocéros,
> Le Seigneur Éléphant, et tel autre gros dos.
> Aux renards, troupe connaisseuse,
> Le parterre fut assigné.

Before facing this audience, the monkey is invited to give a private
performance:

> Une heure avant le rendez-vous donné,
> Chez la Grue et sa sœur, engeance curieuse,
> Notre singe fut attiré.
> Deux étourneaux étaient près d'elles,
> Ainsi qu'un noir hibou, commensal des donzelles

—a transparent disguise for the two ladies, the two noblemen, and the
tutor who formed the author's audience. When the monkey is ready to
perform its tricks, all the members of its audience bombard it with
foolish criticisms. The fable then ingeniously concludes:

> De cet accueil Messer Bertrand surpris,
> Leur dit, serrant sa gibecière:
>   (*L'auteur remet sa pièce dans sa poche*)
> 'C'est aux renards qu'il m'importe de plaire.
> Voilà l'heure à peu près qu'ils doivent s'assembler.
> Je n'oserais compter sur leur suffrage;
>   Mais on n'ira pas me siffler
> Avant que de mes tours on ait vu l'étalage.'
> Avec un ris moqueur leur ayant dit cela,
>   Le singe fait la gambade et s'en va.
>   (*L'auteur sort.*)

In the brief final scene we are shown the effect of the author's lesson on his hearers:

BÉLISE: L'impertinent! Je n'irai point à sa pièce pour le punir.

LA MARQUISE: Moi, j'irai; mais je ne l'écouterai point; je contrôlerai toutes les femmes des loges, afin d'empêcher celles avec qui je serai d'entendre la comédie.

LE CHEVALIER: Allons, Acaste, allons au parterre. Morbleu, singe, mon ami, tu m'y entendras parmi les renards.

Another example of a prologue of the time which offers the same flattery of the *parterre* is Boissy's *L'Auteur superstitieux*, which preceded his comedy, *La Critique*, performed at the Théâtre Italien in 1732. In it we are shown Clitandre, the writer, Arlequin, his lackey, and his friend, Damon. Clitandre is filled with anxiety about the fate of his play. Damon rushes off to take his place in the *parterre*, while Clitandre exclaims:

> Allez vite; en un jour de combat et de guerre
> On ne saurait avoir trop d'amis au parterre.[1]

He himself hurries off to the theatre, only to return in haste two scenes later:

ARLEQUIN: Qu'avez-vous?

CLITANDRE: Un fauteuil, vite; je n'en puis plus!
Mes sens, jamais mes sens ne furent plus émus.
J'entre à la comédie, admire mon étoile!
Dans le moment fatal qu'on lève la toile,
Du monde que je vois je suis épouvanté;
J'entends mugir les flots du parterre agité:
Je regarde en tremblant tous ces juges sévères,
Que ne sauraient fléchir ni brigues, ni prières.
De mon supplice alors je crois voir les apprêts;
Tous les cris que j'entends me semblent des sifflets.

In the last scene he receives a letter from his beloved to say that her father has given his consent to their marriage; so, despite the loss of a lawsuit and his anxiety over the still unknown fate of his play, he cheers up again:

> Ah! mon procès perdu m'est d'un mauvais augure.
> Mais voyons au plus tôt cet objet ravissant,
> Et nous visiterons le parterre en passant.

It is true that in an earlier scene of this same prologue Boissy puts

[1] Sc. 5.

into the mouth of a character, Chrisante, who is described as 'homme singulier', a violent and colourful attack on the behaviour of the spectators in the *parterre*.[1] When he is asked by Apollo what complaint he has to make about the theatre public, he launches into a long diatribe:

> Aux spectacles, ses flots, ses vertiges fréquents,
> Ses battements de mains donnés à contretemps;
> Toutes ses moucheries,
> Ses bâillements, ses crachements
> Aux endroits les plus beaux, les plus intéressants;
> Son ridicule étrange
> De recevoir avidement
> La plus insipide louange,
> Et d'applaudir toujours le banal compliment
> Qu'on lui retourne incessamment:
> Sa rage opiniâtre
> De crier presque à tout moment:
> 'Place aux dames! place au théâtre!
> Parlez plus haut! L'habit noir, chapeau bas!
> Paix! Monsieur l'abbé, haut les bras!
> Annoncez! Bis! La capriole!'
> Et pour tout dire, enfin, l'insupportable rôle
> Qu'il fait, dès qu'au parterre il se trouve pressé,
> Ce qui révolte l'âme, et fait hausser l'épaule
> A tout homme de goût, à tout homme sensé.

Apollo takes a much more favourable view of the behaviour of the audience, at least of what he calls 'le vrai public':

> Vous peignez là la multitude,
> Mère du tumulte et du bruit,
> Que n'arrête aucun frein, que l'exemple séduit,
> Qu'entraîne la coutume ou l'aveugle habitude,
> Et non le vrai public que la raison conduit,
> D'où part ce grand corps de lumière,
> Qui me guide moi-même, et sans cesse m'éclaire:
> Ce public, en un mot, avec choix assemblé,
> Tel qu'on le voit paraître
> Aux jeux d'un théâtre réglé,
> Quand il écoute en sage, et qu'il prononce en maître
> Ses arrêts qui le font si dignement connaître,
> Et dont nul, avant vous, n'a jamais appelé.[2]

---

[1] Sc. 3.

[2] The same passage, with very slight changes, occurs again in Boissy's *L'Apologie du Siècle ou Momus corrigé* (Sc. 5), which was first performed in 1734.

The passages which we have just quoted throw interesting light on the composition of the *parterre* in our period. In the prologue to *L'École des Bourgeois* d'Allainval specifically mentions among the spectators in that part of the theatre 'un officier qui vient de perdre son argent'. No doubt, as in the seventeenth century, the less well-to-do type of noblemen, especially officers, continued to frequent the *parterre*, except perhaps if they came to the theatre in feminine company. References to their presence are not common in the period, though in 1769 Collé alleges that at the second performance of Longueil's *drame*, *L'Orphelin anglais*, a friend of the author, in order to ensure the play's success, 'jeta beaucoup de gens dans le parterre, entre autres quarante officiers irlandais du régiment de Fitz-James', with the result that 'la pièce fut portée aux nues'.[1]

More characteristic of the general social level of the occupants of this part of the theatre whom d'Allainval mentions in his prologue is 'un avocat qui a pâli toute la journée sur des questions épineuses de juris-prudence'. Certainly in our period there seems to have been no social degradation involved in standing in the *parterre*. In *La Nouvelle Héloïse* Saint-Preux is made the mouthpiece for one of Rousseau's favourite theories that men should be kept apart from women in social life. The French, he declares, are 'le seul peuple du monde où les hommes se tiennent debout au spectacle, comme s'ils allaient se délasser au parterre d'avoir resté tout le jour assis au salon'.[2] In the 1780's an English traveller, Thomas Pennington, observes that, al-though one has to stand there, he had often seen in the *parterre* 'well-dressed people, in bags, ruffles, etc. with whom I had dined at the table d'hôte, at half-a-crown a head'.[3] When Dr. Burney visited Paris in the 1760's, he wrote to his twelve-year-old daughter Fanny: 'I am just come from the Comick Opera, which is here called the *Comédie Italienne*, where I have been extremely well entertained, but am so tired with standing the whole time, which every one in the pit does, that I can hardly put a foot to the ground, or a hand to the pen.'[4]

French writers of the period, illustrious or unimportant, comfort-ably off as well as poor, seem to have made no difficulties about stand-ing in the *parterre*. There is the famous anecdote about the voice from

[1] *Journal*, vol. iii, p. 218 (Jan. 1769).

[2] *La Nouvelle Héloïse*, ed. D. Mornet (Paris, 1925), 4 vols., vol. iii, pp. 197–8.

[3] *Continental Excursions; or Tours into France, Switzerland and Germany in 1782, 1787 and 1789* (London, 1809), 2 vols., vol. i, p. 287.

[4] *The Early Diary of Frances Burney*, ed. A. R. Ellis (London, 1907), 2 vols., vol. i, p. xlvii.

the *parterre* which in 1750 destroyed the effect of a vital scene in Marmontel's *Cléopâtre*: 'Cléopâtre mourait sur le théâtre de la piqûre d'un aspic; ce reptile automate, imaginé par le célèbre Vaucanson, s'élançait en sifflant sur le sein de cette reine infortunée; au même instant l'on entendit crier une voix du parterre: "Je suis de l'avis de l'aspic"; c'était la voix de Piron.'[1] Much more respectable personages than Piron frequented the *parterre* in the eighteenth century. In his Journal for 1750 Collé relates how he attended at the Théâtre Italien the first performance of a new comedy which he wrongly suspected was by the Abbé de Voisenon: 'Je le rencontrai dans le parterre', he declares, 'et lui demandai le nom de l'auteur de la pièce.'[2] Nor was it considered an insult for an author to offer a ticket in the *parterre* to one of his acquaintances. In 1754 Collé received a free ticket from Crébillon for the first performance of his *Triumvirat*: 'Crébillon m'avait fait avoir un billet de parterre, mais on y avait laissé entrer tant de monde que j'y étouffais.' He was indeed compelled to go out at the third act and to return to the second performance, but there is no trace of ill-feeling in his Journal.[3]

An author might himself go to the *parterre* to stimulate enthusiasm for his new play. In 1751 the Vicomte de Grave, an army captain, had performed at the Comédie Française his tragedy, *Varron*, which reached sixteen performances. According to Lekain, who had an important part in the play, 'L'auteur étant au parterre, le jour de la première représentation, fit seul le succès de son ouvrage, en s'écriant au dénouement, qui n'est autre chose qu'un tour de passe-passe: "Ah! que cela est ingénieux!"'[4] More often, however, an author would send his friends to do their duty by him in the *parterre*. Rousseau of Toulouse, so Raynal informs us, 'le jour de la représentation de sa pièce[5] envoya un billet de parterre à un de ses amis et lui écrivit assez plaisamment ces mots d'une prière bien connue: *In manus tuas commendo spiritum meum*'.[6]

In 1760 Diderot appears to have led the Encyclopaedist troops in the *parterre* of the Comédie Française in the battle for the success of Voltaire's *L'Écossaise*. Under the title of 'Relation d'une grande bataille', Fréron gives in his *Année littéraire* a long account of the struggle which raged in the *parterre* of the Comédie Française, and

[1] Meister in *Correspondance littéraire*, vol. xiv, p. 72.
[2] *Journal*, vol. i, p. 261 (Dec. 1750).   [3] Ibid., p. 445 (Dec. 1754).
[4] Lekain, *Mémoires* (Paris, 1801), p. 20 n.
[5] *L'Esprit du jour*, performed at the Théâtre Italien in 1754.
[6] *Nouvelles littéraires* (in Grimm, *Correspondance littéraire*), vol. ii, p. 187.

furnishes not only a colourful description of the army of the *Philosophes*, but also a portrait of their leader: 'Le redoutable Dortidius était au centre de l'armée; on l'avait élu général d'une voix unanime. Son visage était brûlant, ses regards furieux, sa tête échevelée, tous ses sens agités, comme ils le sont lorsque, dominé par son divin enthousiasme, il rend ses oracles sur le trépied philosophique.'[1] If, even after reading Fréron's article, one is still not very clear as to whether Diderot did stand in the *parterre* on this occasion,[2] the point is presumably established by a letter of Fréron to Malesherbes,[3] in which he exclaims: 'Quoi, . . . il sera permis à ce tartuffe de Diderot, à ce bas flatteur Grimm, d'aller au parterre de la Comédie le jour de la première représentation de l'*Écossaise*, exciter leur cabale et lui donner le signal de l'applaudissement!'

If professional men and writers frequented the *parterre* of the eighteenth-century Paris theatres, they were joined there by the rising generation of schoolboys and students. Louis-Sébastien Mercier gives a vivid account of the interest aroused in the pupils of the higher forms of the Collège des Quatre Nations when they frequented the theatre some thirty years before the Revolution. It was in 1757, when he was seventeen, that he began to haunt the Comédie Française: 'J'entrais le premier au parterre, j'en sortais le dernier. Nous formions comme une phalange de jeunes littérateurs.' After the theatre Mercier and his companions made their way across the road to the Café Procope where plays and all manner of theatrical matters were discussed. At the Comédie Française, he tells us, he and his companions could indulge their hatred of kings—or at least French kings. 'Quand on donnait le *Brutus* de Voltaire', he writes,

on ne jouait guère que pour les banquettes et pour la phalange littéraire, car nous n'aimions pas les rois. Louis XV passait parmi nous pour un imbécile parce qu'il n'aimait ni la poésie ni Voltaire; mais nous étions transportés de joie lorsque nous apprenions que Frédéric faisait ses réponses en vers. Le grand homme! Voltaire était le dieu du café.[4]

So long as the Comédie Française remained in the Faubourg Saint-Germain, the schoolboy and student population appears to have con-

---

[1] *Année littéraire*, 1760 (vol. v), p. 210.
[2] He seems to have done so in the previous year, for on 4 June 1759 he wrote to Sophie Volland: 'J'irai ce soir à la comédie nouvelle. . . . Je serai dans le parterre, vers le fond et dans le milieu; c'est de là que mes yeux vous chercheront' (*Lettres à Sophie Volland*, ed. A. Babelon, Paris, 1938, 2 vols., vol. i, p. 30).
[3] 31 July 1760 (Bibliotheque Nationale, Ms. fr. 22191, f. 272).
[4] 'Sur la tragédie de *Brutus*' in the newspaper *Bien Informé* (6 pluviôse, an VII).

tributed a by no means negligible proportion of the spectators of the *parterre*; when the theatre moved to the Tuileries in 1770, the loss of a considerable part of these spectators gave rise to lamentations amongst contemporary dramatic critics.[1] As early as 1761, Grimm, partly inspired no doubt by the cool reception accorded to the *Père de Famille* of his friend Diderot, composed for his *Correspondance littéraire* his 'Très humbles remonstrances au parterre de la Comédie Française pour l'ouverture du théâtre', in which he complained that the taste of this section of the audience had undergone a decline:

> On dit que vous aviez autrefois parmi vous tout ce qu'il y avait de bons esprits dans la nation; qu'alors vous aviez un instinct si prompt et si sûr, un tact si juste et si vif pour saisir le beau et le vrai, pour rejeter le mauvais et le faux, que vos arrêts en ont acquis une espèce d'infaillibilité. Si par hasard votre corps n'était plus composé de cette élite des meilleurs esprits; si ces lumières et cette finesse de goût avaient disparu parmi vous, au moment où la philosophie a fait le plus de progrès en France, il faudrait pour votre honneur et pour la gloire de la nation vous défier un peu de vos décisions, et moins présumer de votre crédit, afin de vous épargner de la confusion.[2]

It is, however, from 1770 onwards that complaints about the poor taste of the spectators in the *parterre* become more insistent. The removal of the Comédie Française from the Faubourg Saint-Germain to the Tuileries did not apparently please the actors, who found themselves performing before a new public. 'Quelques-uns d'entre eux', wrote Bachaumont in the summer of 1770, just after the move,

> prétendent que ce n'est plus le même public auquel ils ont affaire; que le parterre moderne ne sent que les masses, et ne saisit pas les morceaux de détail qui constituent l'acteur; qu'au moyen de cet engourdissement et de cette froideur, ils doivent éprouver insensiblement la même langueur; et que, n'étant plus échauffés par l'encouragement soutenu d'un public éclairé, ils courent risque de perdre leur talent ou de le dénaturer, et de tomber dans le mauvais goût.[3]

Four years later Bachaumont complains about the constant addition to the theatre of new *petites loges*, at the expense of the *parterre*; the actors, he adds, care little about the spectators in that part of the house, except for 'le sieur Lekain qui regrette toujours le faubourg Saint-Germain, à raison du parterre d'alors, dont il prisait fort les critiques et les éloges'.[4]

---

[1] See pp. 219–23.   [2] Vol. iv, p. 361.
[3] *Mémoires secrets*, vol. xix, p. 203 (30 July 1770).
[4] Ibid., vol. xxvii, p. 207 (14 Apr. 1774).

In the 1770's La Harpe joins in these lamentations in the *Correspondance littéraire* which he composed for the Grand Duke Paul of Russia. 'Tout ce qu'on appelle bonne compagnie', he writes in 1775,

retiré dans de petites loges, n'a plus l'expression de son avis et se contente de rire tout bas des extravagances du parterre, qui est aujourd'hui si mal composé qu'à peine sur cent hommes en trouverait-on trois ou quatre instruits et bien élevés. Ce parterre est mené comme on veut avec vingt ou trente billets achetés, et le plus mauvais acteur s'y fait applaudir comme Lekain.[1]

We have seen that contemporaries alleged that La Harpe himself knew how to organize a *claque* of his own! Two years later, in discussing the reception at the Comédie Française of De Belloy's posthumous tragedy, *Gabrielle de Vergy*, with its horrific last act, he relates an anecdote which throws some light on the spectators of this part of the theatre:

Un homme du parterre qui ne savait pas de qui était *Gabrielle*, comme cela arrive quelquefois dans notre parterre, qui n'est pas toujours composé de gens fort instruits, dit à son voisin: *Monsieur, quel est l'auteur de cette tragédie?* — *Monsieur, il est mort.* — *Oui, mais je vous demande son nom.* — *Monsieur, il s'appelle Desrues.* La plaisanterie est sanglante.[2]

In this same year Bachaumont gives an account of disturbances at the Comédie Française which do not show the *parterre* in a very creditable light. When the actor Monvel failed to turn up to perform his part in *Horace*, it was finally decided to put on a different play:

Cependant le parterre témoignait son humeur; en vain a-t-on voulu le calmer par un discours préparatoire; cela ne s'est terminé qu'en offrant de rendre l'argent aux mécontents. Un d'eux a poussé l'indécence jusqu'à faire ses ordures au milieu de l'assemblée, escorté et soutenu par quelques polissons comme lui.[3]

La Harpe continued to make disparaging remarks about the *parterre* of the Tuileries theatre. In 1780 he relates in his *Correspondance littéraire* how he had read at the Academy two acts of his tragedy, *Philoctète*, adapted from Sophocles, but he declares that for the present he has no intention of having his play performed, as the taste of the Academy and that of 'le parterre d'aujourd'hui' are too different. At present 'la corruption du goût est si générale et si honteuse' that the simplicity and eloquence of Greek tragedy would simply not be appreciated. Perhaps, he adds, when the Comédie Française is installed in its new theatre, in which all spectators will be seated, a new public will

---

[1] Vol. i, p. 255.
[2] Vol. ii, p. 135. Desrues was a murderer, executed in 1777.
[3] *Mémoires secrets*, vol. x, p. 12 (18 Jan. 1777).

be formed; it is possible that this may be 'une réforme utile qui ramène au moins la décence, si elle ne ramène pas le goût que les *petits spectacles* ont achevé de perdre; mais il faut attendre ce moment et voir les effets qu'il produira'.[1] In the following year he expresses his indignation at De Rosoi's *Richard III* being performed at this theatre as many as six times, 'au grand scandale des honnêtes gens, révoltés qu'une farce si plate et si barbare fût tolérée. Mais, comme on a dit quelque part, le parterre des Tuileries joue de son reste, et il faut bien le laisser faire: son règne, dit-on, ne sera pas encore bien long.'[2]

The new theatre on the Left Bank was at last opened after Easter 1782. The effects of the long-awaited revolution which provided seats for the spectators in the *parterre* (still reserved for men only) are interpreted rather differently by contemporary writers. Goldoni suggests that young men who had been accustomed to paying 20 sous to stand in the *parterre* would now think twice before paying 48 sous for a seat in the same part of the theatre, while many of those who had been in the habit of paying higher prices would have no objection to paying less for what was quite a reasonable seat. More important, the new prices must rule out the *cabales* of earlier periods:

C'était le parterre autrefois qui jugeait les pièces nouvelles; ce parterre n'est plus le même. Les auteurs[3] donnaient des billets pour faire réussir leurs ouvrages, les jaloux en donnaient pour les faire tomber; le redoublement du prix doit diminuer les soutiens des uns, et la cabale des autres: est-ce un bien? est-ce un mal? Je m'en rapporte à la recette des comédiens, mais elle est si considérable et si assurée par les loges louées à l'année, qu'ils ne peuvent pas s'apercevoir du plus ou du moins de bénéfice.[4]

Mercier definitely regrets the change in the seating arrangements. The *parterre*, he declares, has lost its old influence on the fate of plays and has become completely passive. 'On l'a fait asseoir, il est tombé dans la léthargie. . . . Autrefois un enthousiasme incroyable l'animait, et l'effervescence générale donnait aux productions théâtrales un intérêt qu'elles n'ont plus. Aujourd'hui le calme, le silence, l'improbation froide ont succédé au tumulte.' Yet this decline in the authority of the *parterre* has, in Mercier's eyes, more deep-rooted causes than the mere change of theatre and the new seating arrangements; he joins with those who lament the decline in the quality of the spectators in that part of the house and sighs for the good old days. 'Le parterre ancien, beaucoup

---

[1] Vol. iii, pp. 132–3.   [2] Vol. iii, p. 251.   [3] The text has 'acteurs'.
[4] *Mémoires pour servir à l'histoire de sa vie et à celle de son théâtre* (Paris, 1787), 3 vols., vol. iii, p. 247.

mieux composé, peuplé d'amateurs,' he declares, 'non seulement jugeait la pièce, mais encore il devinait les forces et les ressources de l'auteur.'[1] These lines appeared in 1783; six years later Mercier repeats the same lament: 'Nos parterres sont maintenant composés de manière à ne plus mériter la prépondérance qu'ils avaient sur le sort des ouvrages du temps de Corneille et de Racine.'[2]

In his *Éléments de littérature* Marmontel also discusses the influence of the changes in the *parterre* of the new theatre on that section of the audience. 'Il paraît moins tumultueux', he declares, 'mais plus difficile à émouvoir.' Perhaps because the price of the new seats is too high to attract 'cette foule de jeunes gens dont l'âme et l'imagination n'avaient besoin, pour s'exalter, que d'entendre de belles choses', perhaps because in general the taste for 'les beautés simples' has been lost, one can no longer win success by such means.[3] A very different view is put forward by Fleury in his memoirs. The object of providing seats for the *parterre*, he declares, was to make it less rowdy and, by raising the price of tickets, to restrict it to 'des gens bien élevés'. Yet this did not prevent the spectators in that part of the theatre from showing their feelings as before. 'Le parterre assis n'en siffla pas moins très bien et très fort M. Imbert', whose one-act play, *L'Inauguration du Théâtre Français*, was performed at the opening of the new theatre in 1782. Fleury proceeds to develop an ingenious theory to explain why it is always the *parterre* which gives the signal for catcalls or applause:

On va au parterre pour n'être ni chez soi, ni chez les autres. Une loge est un salon, dont la plus jolie femme qui s'y trouve est la maîtresse; on lui doit des égards, des attentions, on se doit à soi-même de paraître de bonne compagnie; siffler nuit à l'harmonie du visage, applaudir peut déranger l'ensemble de la parure. Les parterriens, eux, sont les enfants perdus du spectacle, ils se doivent à l'esprit de corps. Payer un carton de six francs, c'est entrer dans l'aristocratie; payer un carton de quarante sous, c'est faire acte de popularité; dans les deux cas, c'est prendre l'esprit de l'argent déboursé. Il y aurait un seul moyen d'amortir le tumulte du parterre, ce serait d'y admettre des femmes; la galanterie imposerait la décence, mais aussi peut-être imposerait-elle la froideur.[4]

Whether or not the *parterre* became less rowdy after the move to the new theatre, and whatever may have been the effect of the steep rise in

---

[1] *Tableau de Paris*, vol. vii, pp. 64–65.   [2] Ibid., vol. ix, p. 170.

[3] *Éléments de littérature* in *Œuvres* (Paris, 1819–20), 7 vols., vol. iv, p. 833.

[4] *Mémoires*, ed. J. B. P. Lafitte (Paris, 1836–8), vol. ii, pp. 288–90. Women do not appear to have been admitted to the *parterre* of the Comédie Française until about the end of the last century.

price on the composition of this section of the audience at the Comédie
Française, there is a good deal of agreement among contemporary
writers that the taste of the spectators in that part of the theatre had
undergone a considerable decline. Critics of the time address similar
reproaches to the *parterre* of the Théâtre Italien. In 1784, for instance,
Meister reports that the latter theatre has put on with success Mercier's
drame, *La Brouette du vinaigrier*, and declares that the taste of the
parterre there has been corrupted by the 'théâtres du boulevard'. 'Leur
parterre, presque aussi bien composé que celui des théâtres du boulevard', he writes ironically, 'l'a reçue avec transport; il l'a reçue pour
ainsi dire comme un hommage que des comédiens pensionnaires du roi
rendaient à la noble école où s'est formé son goût.'[1] Two years later
La Harpe describes how at the same theatre Desfontaines's comedy,
La Dot, after being rejected by the court at Fontainebleau as too indelicate, was applauded 'précisément dans les endroits qui avaient déplu
davantage à la cour'. La Harpe holds that on this occasion the court was
right: 'Notre parterre, gâté par les spectacles des boulevards, n'a pas
à beaucoup près l'oreille aussi délicate qu'autrefois.'[2]

That in the last twenty or thirty years of the Ancien Régime there
was a decline in the prestige of the *parterre* of the two main Paris
theatres is abundantly clear from the documents which we have already
quoted. This question links up, as we shall see, with changes in the
social composition of the audience which appear to have taken place
in the last few decades before the Revolution. There is evidence to
show that a slightly more plebeian element found its way into the
parterre of the two main theatres in these years; the surprise which this
caused to writers of the time furnishes in its turn interesting evidence
that this was a new phenomenon, that for many a long year the Théâtre
Italien and especially the Comédie Française had been in the main the
preserve of the wealthier and more cultured sections of society. It is
therefore time to examine the place occupied by the plebs in the theatre
audiences of eighteenth-century Paris.

(iii) *The Plebs and the Theatre*

According to Pixerécourt in his *Rapport: Observations sur l'état où se
trouvaient les théâtres avant la Révolution*[3] the Ancien Régime tolerated

---

[1] *Correspondance littéraire*, vol. xiv, pp. 61–62.

[2] *Correspondance littéraire*, vol. v, p. 94.

[3] Published by E. Estève in his article 'Observations de Guilbert de Pixerécourt sur les
théâtres de la Revolution', *Revue d'histoire littéraire de la France* (1916), pp. 546–61.

two kinds of theatres: 'Ceux dont l'éclat ne permet la fréquentation qu'aux riches sont consacrés à perpétuer la flatterie; ceux que l'on abandonne au peuple ne creusent pour lui que le précipice de la débauche. Telle était la situation des théâtres de la France avant la Révolution.'[1] After describing conditions at the Comédie Francaise, the Opéra, and the Opéra-Comique, he goes on: 'Si des grands théâtres nous passons à ceux que fréquentait le peuple, à ceux que les dédains du gouvernement semblaient lui délaisser par une insultante pitié pour sa misère, quel cloaque de saletés! quelle boue d'impures inepties!'[2]

Despite the exaggerations of its Revolutionary phraseology this description of the divisions in the theatrical world of eighteenth-century Paris seems broadly speaking true. If the 'grands théâtres' were for the most part the preserve of the wealthier and more cultured sections of the community, there did exist other theatrical entertainments in the Théâtres de la Foire and, later in the century, in the Théâtres des Boulevards, for the delectation of the masses. Here the low prices of seats allowed the lower and middle classes of society to find dramatic entertainments of sorts; if these were denounced in terms almost as violent as those of Pixerécourt by the writers and critics of the century, this did not make of them a purely plebeian entertainment. On the contrary, to the anger of the privileged theatres and in particular that of the Comédie Francaise, members of the aristocracy, not only the roués, but apparently respectable ladies, insisted on swelling the crowds which frequented them.

Already in 1709, as we have seen, Lesage had denounced in his *Critique de Turcaret* the taste of the ladies for such spectacles. Sixty years later Bachaumont writes of the popularity enjoyed by Audinot's theatre: 'La modicité des places, dont les plus chères sont à 24 sous, met tout le monde à portée de se régaler de cette foire, en sorte que la duchesse et le savoyard s'y coudoient sans distinction.'[3] Throughout our period the Comédie Française, the Opéra, and the Théâtre Italien strove their hardest to prevent their 'better-class' clients from going to these rival theatres. At the beginning of 1769 Grimm notes, for instance, in his *Correspondance littéraire*:

Aujourd'hui on prétend qu'on va forcer les farceurs du boulevard et de la foire de mettre toutes les places indistinctement à vingt-quatre sous; on se flatte qu'en confondant ainsi les gens du monde avec la populace, on dé-

[1] p. 549.   [2] p. 551.
[3] *Mémoires secrets*, vol. xix, pp. 49–50 (24 Feb. 1769).

goûtera la bonne compagnie d'y aller, et qu'on la ramènera forcément s'ennuyer à la Comédie Française et à l'Opéra.[1]

If we turn to the Journal of Papillon de La Ferté, the *Intendant des menus* at this period, we find that it was the Maréchal de Richelieu, one of the four *Gentilshommes de la Chambre* responsible for the running of the privileged theatres, who had persuaded the government to issue an edict reducing the prices of seats at all the smaller theatres to 24, 12, and 6 sous. The aim of the operation is made quite clear: 'On espère par ce moyen en chasser la bonne compagnie.'[2] The measure did not have the desired effect. Two years later Bachaumont describes the tremendous vogue of Audinot's theatre, with its child actors and 'beaucoup de polissonneries'. The audience attracted to it was by this account a very mixed one: 'Les filles se sont portées en foule de ce côté-là et beaucoup de libertins, d'oisifs, de freluquets avec elles. Ce monde en a attiré d'un autre genre. Les femmes de la cour, qui en cette qualité se croient au-dessus de tous les préjugés, n'ont pas dédaigné d'y paraître, et ce théâtre est la rage du jour.'[3]

If such entertainments were far from being scorned by the upper ranks of society, they were none the less primarily intended for the lower orders. The authorities seem to have looked with a benevolent eye on the establishment of new theatres of this type since they could serve to keep the populace out of mischief. Thus, when a new theatre was set up near the Louvre in 1769, Bachaumont declares that the police authorities were in favour, because 'le peuple de cette partie de la ville éloignée des deux boulevards était affamé de spectacles; par cet arrangement la populace de tous les quartiers pourra s'en repaître et se délasser agréablement de ses travaux sans perdre un temps précieux à courir au loin pour trouver des parades et des farces'.[4] Writers of the time do not take such an indulgent attitude, denouncing in terms as violent as those later used by Pixerécourt the moral corruption produced by these theatres. In 1773 Mercier backs up his demand for a new type of drama suited to the outlook and aspirations of the masses with a bitter attack on the dramatic entertainments so far provided for 'le petit peuple'. 'On empoisonne son âme de ces sales turpitudes', he declares, 'dont le peuple sent lui-même la grossièreté; et la police protège un pareil scandale, qui suffirait seul à avilir une nation!'[5] He re-

[1] Vol. viii, p. 232.
[2] *Journal*, ed. E. Boysse (Paris, 1887), p. 242.
[3] *Mémoires secrets*, vol. vi, pp. 6–7 (7 Oct. 1771).
[4] Ibid., vol. xix, p. 126 (30 Oct. 1769).
[5] *Du Théâtre*, p. 212 n.

turns to the attack in his *Tableau de Paris*, where he blames the actors of the Comédie Française for clinging to their monopoly of all plays with any literary pretensions and compelling the masses to see nothing but corrupting rubbish: 'Le peuple est condamné à n'entendre que l'expression du libertinage et de la sottise. Et voilà où aboutit la police des spectacles chez un peuple renommé pour ses chefs-d'œuvre dramatiques.' The plays of the popular theatres not only corrupt; they also cause workmen to waste their time:

Les parades qu'on représente extérieurement sur le balcon comme une espèce d'invitation publique, sont très préjudiciables aux travaux journaliers, en ce qu'elles ameutent une foule d'ouvriers qui, avec les instruments de leur profession sous le bras, demeurent là, la bouche béante, et perdent les heures les plus précieuses de la journée.[1]

Bachaumont joins in the chorus of denunciation of these plebeian entertainments. 'Ces boulevards', he declares in 1782, 'sont le repaire de tous les mauvais sujets de Paris, l'école de tous les vices, et leurs spectacles des gouffres où va s'engloutir le gain des artisans, des ouvriers, des manouvriers, de tout le peuple en un mot, et se perdre l'innocence des enfants des deux sexes.'[2] In the same year a letter addressed to the *Journal de Paris*[3] protests against this corruption, and asks 'pourquoi, après avoir érigé des théâtres pour le peuple, on s'obstinerait à l'amuser avec le spectacle des plus mauvaises mœurs, à le faire rire par de sales équivoques, par des tableaux licencieux, quand il est possible de faire tourner ses amusements au profit de son instruction'. Three years later the Archbishop of Paris, Mgr Leclerc de Juigné, joined in the attack on these plebeian theatres. 'L'indigence paraissait devoir préserver le peuple de ce péril', he declares, 'mais n'a-t-on pas encore imaginé pour lui ces spectacles grossiers, ces farces indignes d'une nation honnête ... où de pauvres artisans ... vont consumer un temps qui devrait appartenir au commerce et aux arts ?'[4]

Such were the entertainments provided for the masses in eighteenth-century Paris. Neither the Comédie Française nor the Théâtre Italien was considered by contemporaries to be suitable for the more lowly tastes of the plebs. A manuscript *Mémoire sur les spectacles inférieurs*, dated April 1764, defends these more humble places of entertainment

[1] Vol. iii, p. 25.

[2] *Mémoires secrets*, vol. xx, p. 252 (15 May 1782).

[3] 10 Aug. 1782 (quoted in F. Gaiffe, *Le Drame en France au XVIIIe siècle*, Paris, 1910, pp. 84–85).

[4] *Mandement ... qui permet l'usage des œufs*, 5 Feb. 1785; Bibliothèque Nationale, E. 3687 (5).

against the attempts of the privileged theatres to have them closed down, on the grounds that only these modest amusements are within the capacity and the purse of the *peuple*. 'Le Théâtre François', the anonymous author declares,

a une dignité qui ne convient point au peuple. Il n'entend rien ni à l'italien ni à la sublimité des nouvelles ariettes.[1] Ces deux spectacles sont d'un prix auquel il ne peut atteindre. L'entrée même en est interdite à ceux qui ne sont pas mis d'une certaine façon. Il faut donc un ordre inférieur de divertissements pour amuser les gens du peuple et les empêcher de mal faire.

If these plebeian theatres were shut down, the result would not be increased receipts for the Comédie Française, since ordinary people have neither the taste nor the money to go there.

Celui qui remplit une place à 4 ou à 6 ou 8 sous chez Nicolet ne voudrait pas (même pour un pareil prix) assister à une représentation du *Misanthrope*, encore moins à celle de *Britannicus*, et si on lui fermait la porte de Nicolet, il préférerait sans hésiter celle du cabaret à celle de la Comédie Française, où tout serait trop élevé pour son goût et trop cher pour sa bourse.

The same is true of women, so the author argues: 'Si la vanité fait dépenser à quelques-unes 40 s. pour briller à des places distinguées chez Nicolet, elle ne leur donne pas le goût nécessaire pour se déterminer à être confondues dans la foule pour entendre une bonne pièce.' It is impossible, he declares, to imagine that the actors of the Comédie Française should be given a complete monopoly of plays in French in the Paris theatres so long as no woman can gain admission to their theatre without paying 30 s.—and that 'pour ne les entendre presque point et les voir encore moins'. The argument concludes: 'Ces prix annoncent qu'ils ne veulent jouer que pour les riches. A la bonne heure, mais qu'ils n'empêchent donc pas que d'autres jouent pour ceux qui n'ont que fort peu à sacrifier à leur plaisir. L'amusement de ceux-ci est peut-être encore plus nécessaire au bon ordre.'[2]

No doubt a good deal of this is special pleading; it was not, for instance, the case that the Théâtres des Boulevards catered only for the masses, and it may also have been true that a certain number of spectators at the 'grands théâtres' came from the lower orders of society. In the long article which he devoted to the *parterre* in his *Éléments de littérature*, published in 1787, Marmontel speaks of the spectators in that part of the theatre as consisting of 'les citoyens les moins riches, les

---

[1] Of the Opéra-Comique, which was now fused with the Théâtre Italien.
[2] Bibliothèque Nationale, Ms. fr. 9557.

moins maniérés, les moins raffinés dans leurs mœurs'. It is a matter for astonishment, he declares, that plays should be so well judged by the *peuple*; but the explanation is that 'dans le *parterre* tout n'est pas ce qu'on appelle peuple, et . . . parmi cette foule d'hommes sans culture, il y en a de très éclairés'. It is this cultured minority which is followed by the mass of spectators in this part of the theatre. Moreover, 'au petit nombre d'hommes instruits qui sont répandus dans le *parterre*, se joint un nombre plus grand d'hommes habitués au spectacle, et dont c'est l'unique plaisir'. Through long practice these people have developed a sound, instinctive taste in matters concerning the theatre.

Le *parterre* est donc habituellement composé d'hommes sans culture et sans prétentions, dont la sensibilité ingénue vient se livrer aux impressions qu'elle recevra du spectacle, et qui, de plus, suivant l'impulsion qu'on leur donne, semblent ne faire qu'un esprit et qu'une âme avec ceux qui, plus éclairés, les font penser et sentir avec eux.[1]

It must be said that Marmontel's stress on the plebeian character of the majority of the spectators in the *parterre* is unusual in the writings of the time. Indeed, what is far more customary is to find exactly the opposite interpretation—namely that the 'grands théâtres' and particularly the Comédie Française were beyond the purse and the tastes of the masses. In his *Projet pour rendre les spectacles plus utiles à l'état* (published in the *Mercure* in 1726) Abbé de Saint-Pierre suggests that Paris ought to have a second company of French actors whose theatre prices would be half the existing ones. If this were done, he argues, 'la nation se polirait de plus en plus jusques parmi le peuple', and 'les habitants médiocrement riches' could partake of the pleasures of the theatre. Clearly he considered that the high cost of theatre-going prevented many people from indulging in such an eminently moral entertainment.[2]

Forty years later we find Voltaire stressing once again the smallness of the reading and theatre public. 'Le public, en fait de livres,' he wrote in 1765, 'est composé de quarante ou cinquante personnes, si le livre est sérieux, de quatre ou cinq cents, lorsqu'il est plaisant, et d'environ onze ou douze cents, s'il s'agit d'une pièce de théâtre. Il y a toujours dans Paris plus de cinq cent mille âmes qui n'entendent jamais parler de tout cela.'[3] This was when he was telling his compatriots some home truths, but three years later, in a letter to Horace Walpole, he argues that Paris

---

[1] *Œuvres*, vol. iv, pp. 830–2.
[2] *Œuvres diverses* (Paris, 1728–30), 2 vols., vol. ii, pp. 191–3.
[3] *Œuvres complètes*, vol. iii, p. 77.

is superior to Athens in everything concerning the theatre. 'Nous avons plus de trente mille âmes à Paris qui se plaisent aux beaux-arts, et Athènes n'en avait pas dix mille.' What is more important, 'le bas peuple d'Athènes entrait au spectacle, et il n'y entre pas chez nous, excepté qu'on lui donne un spectacle gratis, dans des occasions solennelles ou ridicules.'[1] The fact that the *canaille* did not set foot in the theatres of Paris, except on the rare occasions of a free performance to celebrate some royal birth or marriage, was obviously a telling point in his eyes.

Three years earlier, in the *Correspondance littéraire*, Grimm had made a similar comparison between the theatre audiences of the ancient world and of modern Paris:

La tragédie était chez les anciens une institution politique, un acte de religion; chez nous, c'est une affaire d'amusement pour faire passer quelques heures de la journée aux désœuvrés dont les capitales et les grandes villes sont remplies. En Grèce et à Rome, le peuple assistait aux spectacles en corps. . . . Ce n'est point le peuple qui fréquente chez nous les spectacles; c'est une coterie particulière de gens du monde, de gens d'arts et de lettres, de personnes des deux sexes à qui leur rang ou leur fortune a permis de cultiver leur esprit: c'est l'élite de la nation à laquelle se joint un très petit nombre de gens qui tiennent au peuple par leur état ou par leur profession.[2]

This last point is important. Grimm, we see, does not entirely exclude the lower orders from the 'grands théâtres' of his day; but he does regard their presence as merely an unimportant exception to the general rule that the spectators are drawn from the middle and upper ranks of society.

While Grimm obviously regarded this as a normal and healthy state of affairs, a few years later Louis-Sébastien Mercier was to denounce in passionate terms this virtual exclusion of *le peuple* from the enjoyment of all serious drama. In *Du Théâtre, ou Nouvel Essai sur l'art dramatique* (1773) he shocked most of his contemporaries by demanding both that the *peuple* should be admitted to the theatre and that the subject-matter and form of plays should be adapted to its outlook. He protests against the fact that 'nos pièces, pour la plupart, sont vides de sens, eu égard à un peuple nombreux', and are merely written for 'une compagnie particulière à laquelle les poètes ont eu le dessein de plaire exclusivement'.[3] French plays can be neither appreciated nor understood by the masses.

[1] Ibid., vol. xlvi, p. 82.   [2] Vol. vi, pp. 170–1.
[3] p. v.

Le poète coupable et dédaigneux a élargi encore ces distances inhumaines que nous avons mis [*sic*] entre les citoyens. Il devait plutôt les rapprocher, mais il se serait cru homme du peuple, s'il se fût avisé à écrire pour le peuple; il en a été puni en méconnaissant la vraie nature et cette vraisemblance, mère charmante de l'illusion, et cet intérêt qui remue tous les cœurs.[1]

In a passage of the windy rhetoric in which his works abound, Mercier challenges the prevailing prejudice against the plebs in the theatre. 'Et pourquoi fermez-vous votre théâtre au peuple, nation orgueilleuse ou avare? Si vous jugez le spectacle utile, de quel droit en privez-vous la partie la plus nombreuse de la nation? Pourquoi la renvoyez-vous sur les boulevards entendre des pièces licencieuses où triomphent le vice et la grossièreté?'[2]

Mercier's campaign for a drama which would at once deal with ordinary people and appeal to ordinary people was answered by La Harpe's *Réflexions sur le Drame* which sets out to refute his *Nouvel Essai sur l'art dramatique*. In it La Harpe explicitly agrees with Mercier's statement that the masses are exluded from the serious theatre of the day; this he considers not only inevitable, but a positive good. 'Pourquoi donc', he retorts to Mercier's plea for the *peuple*, 'veut-il absolument que nos tragédies soient pour le peuple, répète-t-il sans cesse ce mot de peuple, nous reproche-t-il amèrement de ne pas travailler pour le peuple, de mépriser le peuple?' No, La Harpe retorts, he does not despise the people; but surely the pleasure which can be derived from the arts is one which requires a certain degree of education to which in the present state of most European nations the people cannot attain. 'Est-ce le peuple qui vient à nos spectacles? Il n'en a ni le temps, ni le moyen.' If Mercier replies, he continues, that the masses ought to have both the time and the means, then his answer is simple:

Mais alors chargez-vous de changer le gouvernement et la police. Faites que les choses soient ou puissent être autrement qu'elles ne sont. Faites que les trois quarts et demi des habitants d'une grande ville ne soient pas nécessairement occupés d'un travail qui est leur unique ressource pour subsister. Faites que, sur un temps qui leur suffit à peine pour travailler, ils prennent le moment de s'instruire. Faites que sur le salaire dont ils se nourrissent, ils prennent de quoi payer une place au spectacle; et quand vous aurez fait cela, il sera faux encore qu'il faille composer des tragédies pour le peuple.

It is true, he concedes, that on the occasions when the Comédie Française offers a free performance, people of all ranks of society show themselves capable of tears at the spectacle of a tragedy; but 'quoique le

---

[1] pp. ix–x.   [2] p. 212.

peuple . . . pleure à la tragédie qu'il voit une fois en dix ans, il aimera toujours mieux un spectacle plus analogue à ses goûts, à ses mœurs, à son ton, et il préférera Taconet[1] jouant le savetier à Lekain jouant Mahomet, et peut-être préférera-t-il à tous deux le cabaret et la guinguette'.[2]

In his *Lycée* La Harpe could only account for the obstinate admiration which the English showered on that barbarian Shakespeare by the popular nature of the London theatres and the obvious explanation that 'partout le goût du peuple est grossier'. In the London theatres Shakespeare 'est éminemment le poète du peuple, dont il sut saisir et flatter tous les goûts, d'autant plus aisément que c'étaient les siens propres, quoique d'ailleurs son génie naturel, qui n'était pas vulgaire, l'élevât quelquefois au niveau des plus grands esprits'. In France conditions were very different. There theatrical entertainments 'ne furent long-temps à la portée que de leurs juges naturels, les classes de la société qui ont le plus de moyens d'éducation et d'instruction'. It was only when the government allowed the establishment of *les petits spectacles* for the people that the rot set in.[3]

Pixerécourt views the awakening of the masses to the pleasures of the serious theatre from a very different angle, but he too maintains that they had virtually no place in the audience of theatres like the Comédie Française before the Revolution. The emancipation which the great upheaval brought about in the world of the theatre, freeing all the masterpieces which had once been the monopoly of the Comédie Française for performance in any theatre, proved, he declares,

que le peuple, quoique sans éducation, avait le sentiment des beautés; qu'il n'était point étranger aux pensées sublimes des grands maîtres; qu'ainsi le théâtre était un grand mobile d'instruction; et que les applaudissements qu'il prodiguait aux meilleurs ouvrages dramatiques étaient la plus amère critique de l'espèce de mépris que l'ancien régime avait semblé faire de son intelligence, mais sous lequel, bien plutôt, il dérobait la crainte qu'elle lui inspirait.[4]

As early as the spring of 1790 the Comédie Française tried to salve its uneasy conscience about the relatively small social groups from which it drew its audiences, by promising to add to the existing auditorium more than 600 cheaper seats. In the speech which one of

---

[1] A well-known actor of the Théâtre de la Foire (1730–74).
[2] *Œuvres* (Paris, 1778), 6 vols., vol. i, pp. 175–7.
[3] *Le Lycée, ou Cours de littérature ancienne et moderne* (Paris, 1818), 14 vols., vol. xii, pp. 133–9.
[4] Estève, 'Observations de Guilbert de Pixerécourt', p. 552.

the actors delivered at the opening of the 1790–1 season he declared that it was their intention to 'procurer à la classe des citoyens les moins aisés la facilité d'assister à la représentation de nos chefs-d'œuvre'. In practice, however, nothing came of the plan. Instead of adding new seats to their theatre the actors finally reduced the prices of the cheaper tickets; in March 1791 prices in the *parterre* were reduced from 48 to 36 sous, and in the gallery from 4 l. 16 s. to 3 livres.[1]

The marked change which came over the audience in the leading Paris theatres whenever, both in the seventeenth and eighteenth centuries, a free performance was given to celebrate some public event, is one more proof of the relatively small section of the community from which the spectators were normally drawn. In his series of articles entitled *Sur l'instruction publique* (1791–2) Condorcet refers contemptuously to the free performances which had been given under the Ancien Régime, as an 'espèce d'aumône qu'on donne au peuple, et qui lui fait plutôt envier que partager les plaisirs du riche'.[2] Generally this more plebeian audience was given fairly popular plays, as Helvétius pointed out in *De l'Esprit*: 'Dans les journées de réjouissances publiques, où le spectacle s'ouvre *gratis*, les comédiens, ayant alors d'autres spectateurs à amuser, donneront plutôt *Dom Japhet* et *Pourceaugnac* qu'*Héraclius* et le *Misanthrope*.'[3] Most of the plays performed at the Comédie Française on such occasions in the eighteenth century were in fact comedies. Scarron's *Dom Japhet d'Arménie* was given in 1714 to celebrate the return of peace and again in 1729 for the birth of the Dauphin.[4] *Monsieur de Pourceaugnac* was given, along with Dancourt's *Trois Cousines*, to celebrate the return of peace in 1739. *Le Bourgeois gentilhomme* was given in 1682, 1704, and 1721, and among other Molière plays performed in the eighteenth century were *L'Avare* (1707, 1751), *Le Festin de Pierre* (in Thomas Corneille's version, 1727), and *L'École des femmes* (1749). Regnard's *Joueur* was performed free in 1725 and 1770 and his *Légataire universel* in 1752. The only serious eighteenth-century comedy given on one of these occasions seems to have been Destouches's *Philosophe marié*, performed in 1753 to celebrate

---

[1] C. G. Étienne and A. Martainville, *Histoire du Théâtre Français depuis le commencement de la Révolution jusqu'à la réunion générale* (Paris, 1802), 4 vols., vol. i, p. 95; vol. ii, pp. 48–49.

[2] *Œuvres*, ed. A. C. O'Connor and F. Arago (Paris, 1847–9), 12 vols., vol. vii, p. 366.

[3] *De l'Esprit* (Paris, 1758), discours ii, chap. iv.

[4] For the 1729 free performance see the *Mercure*, Sept. 1729, p. 2020. Where no source is given for the information about these free performances, it is derived from Lancaster's *Comédie Française, 1680–1701*, and *Comédie Française, 1701–1774*.

a royal birth. From this time onwards the choice seems to have turned to more serious plays. In 1757 Guimond de la Touche's tragedy, *Iphigénie en Tauride*, was given at a free performance presumably because it was then in its first run,[1] while in 1765 the actors received a royal command to give a free performance of De Belloy's patriotic tragedy, *Le Siège de Calais*. Two tragedies of Voltaire were given later in the century—*Zaïre* in 1778 to celebrate the birth of a daughter to Marie Antoinette,[2] and *Adélaïde du Guesclin*, along with Collé's *Partie de Chasse de Henri IV*, for the birth of the Dauphin in 1781.[3]

Contemporary accounts of these occasions make it quite clear that they drew to the Paris theatres an audience markedly more plebeian than did normal performances. The *Mercure* in 1721 states, in describing a performance of *Le Bourgeois gentilhomme* 'orné de chants, de danses et de la cérémonie turque', that half the seats of the Comédie Française had been filled by midday and that before two the theatre was crammed. 'On avait observé dès le commencement', we are told, 'de laisser entrer aux loges, au théâtre et à l'amphithéâtre les femmes, les enfants et les hommes âgés et incommodés, renvoyant au parterre les jeunes gens et le bas peuple.' The performance, the writer adds with a certain amount of surprise, passed off

sans la moindre contestation ni le moindre accident, et ce qu'il y a de particulier, c'est que cette populace assemblée fut non seulement attentive pendant toute la représentation, mais encore elle applaudit très juste et très sensément aux meilleurs endroits de la pièce... Cette assemblée n'était ni brillante, ni auguste par la parure, ni par la qualité des personnes qui la composaient, mais on peut dire qu'elle était fort singulière, et en quelque manière respectable, par les bonnes gens qu'on voyait livrés à la joie, et par le plaisir de la surprise qu'on remarquait en eux. Cette diversité d'expression répandue sur tous les visages, pour signifier la même chose, était véritablement digne de la curiosité des meilleurs esprits.[4]

The writer obviously belonged to the school which considered that on such occasions the much more plebeian audience exhibited a surprising understanding of the plays which were performed. Bachaumont, in describing the free performance of the *Siège de Calais* in 1765, declares that it was followed 'avec une attention surprenante de la part

---

[1] Curiously enough, almost a hundred years earlier, in 1660, at a free performance to celebrate the return of peace the Hôtel de Bourgogne had also performed a tragedy—Thomas Corneille's *Stilicon*, then in its first run (Loret, *Muse historique*, 21 Feb. 1660).

[2] Bachaumont, *Mémoires secrets*, vol. xii, pp. 205–6 (24 Dec. 1778).

[3] *Journal de Paris*, 25 Oct. 1781.

[4] *Mercure*, Aug. 1721, pp. 102–3.

des spectateurs', though he adds significantly: 'On ne doute pas qu'il n'y eût là des gagistes qui les avertissaient d'applaudir aux endroits désignés.'[1] Thirteen years later the same source assured its readers that at the free performance of Voltaire's *Zaïre* 'toute l'assemblée a été dans le plus grand silence, et a parfaitement goûté les beautés de sentiment de cet ouvrage'.[2] In announcing the free performance which was given by the Opéra to celebrate the birth of the Dauphin in 1781, Bachaumont tells us that many people were disgusted at the thought of the newly constructed theatre being 'souillée dans sa fraîcheur par toute cette canaille dégoûtante'.[3] Some days later there is an account of how the performance opened with frantic expressions of joy at the glad news: 'A cette violente explosion de la joie générale a succédé l'attention la plus soutenue, et telle que les auteurs désiraient (*sic*) qu'elle fût pour tous les ouvrages dans la nouveauté.' This remark is slightly qualified by what follows: 'La crainte de perdre un seul beau mouvement faisait modérer les témoignages de la satisfaction, ou plutôt cette populace, étonnée de tout ce qu'elle voyait et entendait, en était comme suspendue dans ses facultés. Cependant, revenue à elle, elle a beaucoup applaudi certains morceaux.'[4]

As might be expected from an enthusiastic advocate of drama for the people, Louis-Sébastien Mercier takes a very favourable view of the reactions of this plebeian audience. 'Ce qu'il y a de plus étonnant', he declares in the *Tableau de Paris*, 'c'est que cette populace applaudit aux beaux endroits, aux endroits délicats même, et les sent, tout comme l'assemblée la mieux choisie.' He adds in a footnote: 'On a contesté le fait; j'en appelle à l'expérience. Les grands traits n'ont jamais passé sans applaudissements.'[5] A less partial witness, Framery, advocating in 1790 the introduction of special popular theatrical performances on Sundays and holidays, takes the same view: 'Le peuple a plus d'intelligence qu'on ne le croit. Toutes les fois qu'on a donné gratis des tragédies ou des pièces du haut comique, il ne s'est jamais trompé sur les endroits qui méritaient d'être applaudis.'[6]

A rather different view—and one which because of its *nuances* is perhaps nearer the truth—is contained in an anonymous letter which appeared in the *Journal de Paris* in 1781 after the free performances of

[1] *Mémoires secrets*, vol. ii, p. 167 (12 Mar. 1765).
[2] Ibid., vol. xii, p. 206 (24 Dec. 1778).
[3] Ibid., vol. xviii, p. 97 (23 Oct. 1781).
[4] Ibid., p. 107 (28 Oct. 1781).
[5] Vol. iii, p. 11.
[6] *De l'Organisation des spectacles de Paris* (Paris, 1790), p. 224.

Adélaïde du Guesclin and *La Partie de chasse*, to celebrate the birth of the Dauphin. 'Il est doux', the writer declares, 'de voir le bonheur ramener, pour ainsi dire, l'égalité et faire participer le pauvre aux jouissances des riches.' But, he argues, while it is true that on these occasions the populace admires what it sees and hears, it is 'peu sensible à la beauté des choses qu'on lui fait entendre et bien moins encore au mérite de l'art qui les a fait imaginer'. Appreciation of any of the arts can only be the prerogative of 'une raison exercée'. The applause of the *peuple* at such performances does not always come in the right places; in any case on these occasions regular theatre-goers put in an appearance out of curiosity, and it is often they who give the signal for applause.

In the course of this letter an interesting objection is raised, only, of course, to be speedily refuted. 'Me dira-t-on que le goût du théâtre s'est aujourd'hui si fort répandu que parmi le plus bas peuple on trouve des gens qui le fréquentent et s'y connaissent? Dès lors, ces gens-là cessent d'être peuple; ce n'est pas d'eux dont il est ici question; ils sont sortis de la classe où le sort les avait cachés.'[1]

This last remark is highly significant. If all the evidence which we have discussed about the specially plebeian audience which frequented the leading Paris theatres on such exceptional occasions as those on which free performances were given proves that in general the normal theatre audience of the time contained at most a mere sprinkling of representatives of the poor and even modest classes of the capital, this statement is one of several which would seem to indicate that in the last two or three decades of the Ancien Régime there was a noticeable increase in the proportion of the humbler classes of society who found their way to the privileged theatres, even to the Comédie Française. This is an interesting factor for a study of the audience both between, say, 1760 and 1789, when the plebeian element grew larger, and also for the earlier period, perhaps even the preceding hundred years or so, when, we may infer, such plebeian spectators were altogether exceptional. The very surprise with which this new phenomenon is greeted by writers in the last decades before the Revolution suggests that for a considerable period up to that time the Paris theatre audiences had been drawn from a relatively narrow section of society—from the aristocracy and the more cultured section of the middle classes.

We have already seen how there were numerous complaints about the decline in the taste of the *parterre* after the Comédie Française had

[1] 12 Nov. 1781.

abandoned in 1770 its old theatre in the Rue des Fossés Saint-Germain for its temporary home at the Tuileries. Many contemporaries attribute this decline to a change in the social composition of this section of the audience which was brought about by the removal from the Left Bank. 'Quand la Comédie Française était dans le pays latin', wrote Mercier in his *Tableau de Paris*,

le parterre était beaucoup mieux composé qu'il ne l'est aujourd'hui. Ce parterre savait former des acteurs. Ceux-ci, privés de l'utile censure que les étudiants exerçaient, se pervertissent devant un parterre grossier, parce qu'on n'y voit plus que les courtauds de boutique de la rue Saint-Honoré, ou les petits commis de la douane et des fermes.[1]

Writing in his *Censeur dramatique* in 1797, Grimod de la Reynière speaks with nostalgic affection of 'le parterre du Faubourg Saint-Germain, si renommé dans toute l'Europe pour la pureté de son goût et l'équitable sévérité de ses arrêts, qui a formé tous les grands écrivains et tous les grands comédiens de ce siècle'. He too considers that the removal of the Comédie Française to the Tuileries in 1770 had had results, and that the change in the composition of the *parterre* led to the emergence of scarcely any good actors. Nor did the return of the Comédie Française in 1782 to the Faubourg Saint-Germain improve matters: 'Les temps étaient changés: le goût du spectacle, devenu trop général pour que les spectateurs fussent choisis comme autrefois, et la nouvelle position du parterre, joint à l'exhaussement des prix, l'avaient entièrement dénaturé.'

In 1797, he argues, if the Comédie Française were to return once more to its original quarters on the Left Bank, it would be impossible to re-create the old atmosphere:

Le Faubourg Saint-Germain n'est plus ce qu'il était autrefois, c'est-à-dire le quartier le plus éclairé de Paris. Le voisinage du pays latin, source de toutes les lumières, est nul depuis la destruction de l'Université et la dissémination de l'instruction publique sur les différents points de la ville. La destruction de la magistrature a porté aussi un coup funeste à cette portion de Paris. Les entours du Théâtre Français étaient peuplés de magistrats, de jurisconsultes, de jeunes légistes, qui, avec les étudiants de l'Université, composaient la majorité de ce parterre célèbre qui a régné avec tant de gloire pendant près de quatre-vingt-dix années.[2]

He returns more than once to praise of the taste of the *parterre* in the

---

[1] Vol. i, p. 147.

[2] *Le Censeur dramatique, ou Journal des principaux théâtres de Paris et des départements* (Paris, 1797–8), 4 vols., vol. ii, pp. 120–1.

years down to 1770 when the Comédie Française was still in the Faubourg Saint-Germain:

> On ne peut se dissimuler que le parterre d'alors ne renfermât une foule d'hommes instruits, dont la majeure partie, fréquentant le théâtre depuis bien des années, étaient un répertoire vivant de tous les usages et de tous les événements dramatiques. Ces respectables habitués, indulgents pour la jeunesse qui venait se former à leur école, se faisaient un plaisir de l'éclairer et de l'instruire, et cette jeunesse, ardente et docile, recevait avec avidité ces notions et ces conseils. Accoutumée à respecter la vieillesse et à honorer l'expérience, elle s'éclairait dans ces conversations instructives et amusantes, et devenait elle-même capable de juger. Tous ces avantages ont disparu avec l'ancien parterre du Faubourg Saint-Germain, qu'on ne saurait trop louer, ni trop regretter.[1]

The appearance in the theatres of Paris, even at the Comédie Française, of at any rate a noticeable number of people from the lower ranks of society, in particular of skilled workers, is described by Rétif de la Bretonne in *La Mimographe*, which appeared in the very year that the Comédie Française migrated to the Tuileries. He declares that, although Rousseau's estimate of an average daily attendance of only three hundred at the Comédie Française was right for the period when the *Lettre à D'Alembert* appeared,[2] the daily audience must nearly have trebled since then:

> Jamais le goût du théâtre ne fut si vif, si général. Les ouvriers, qui buvaient le dimanche, quelquefois le lundi, et qui par là se trouvaient hors d'état de travailler le mardi, vont aujourd'hui à la comédie. Ils en retirent cet avantage que, lorsqu'ils buvaient, ils perdaient tout le jour; au lieu qu'à présent ils travaillent courageusement le matin et ne donnent au spectacle que quelques heures de l'après-midi, temps le moins précieux, surtout en hiver, où l'on est obligé de se servir de chandelle. En raisonnant d'après l'expérience, je sais que le sage spectacle de notre capitale produit depuis quelques années un bien réel parmi les ouvriers des professions qu'on nomme *honnêtes*; ceux qui le fréquentent sont les plus habiles et en général, c'est d'eux que les maîtres sont le plus contents. L'usage des plaisirs des honnêtes gens leur élève l'âme et leur fait acquérir cette urbanité que le séjour de la ville ne donne pas seul; les pièces de théâtre ébauchent ce que la conversation de quelques personnes éclairées, qui suivent nos spectacles, achève à leur égard.[3]

What Rétif calls 'ce goût des spectacles devenu trop commun' appeared

---

[1] *Le Censeur dramatique*, vol. ii, p. 216 (see also pp. 313–20).
[2] For a discussion of this point see above, p. 177 n.
[3] *La Mimographe, ou Idées d'une honnête femme pour la réformation du théâtre national* (Amsterdam, 1770), p. 239 n.

to him to have two disadvantages: first, a reduction in the consumption of alcohol, and, second, that 'les grands dédaigneront peut-être de le partager avec le peuple. Alors plus de chefs-d'œuvre à espérer dans le dramatisme; plus de grands acteurs, dans le mimisme; la comédie retournerait sur les tréteaux; car qui voudrait écrire pour le peuple ?'[1]

Louis-Sébastien Mercier, as we have already seen, was certainly willing to do so. He too refers in his *Nouvel Essai sur l'art dramatique*, which appeared in 1773, to the fact that workmen now make their appearance in the Paris theatres, and even at the Comédie Française:

On a remarqué que les artisans, qui autrefois allaient s'enivrer et s'empoisonner au cabaret, vont aujourd'hui à la comédie. Un fat rira de cette observation; moi, je suis enchanté que ces ouvriers contractent l'habitude des plaisirs honnêtes qui élèvent l'âme. Rien ne doit paraître indifférent à l'écrivain, qui doit porter son attention sur tous les états et se réjouir de tout bien commencé.[2]

Even Mercier, however, excludes from his enthusiasm for the *peuple* a considerable proportion of the population of eighteenth-century Paris. Though he declares that the spectators at free performances show an astonishing ability to understand and appreciate the plays presented to them, he maintains that on such occasions 'on donne entrée à la plus vile populace, laquelle est fort au-dessous de ce que j'appelle le peuple'.[3]

Other writers of the time bear witness to this change in the theatre audience. It is true that one cannot give much weight to Voltaire's outburst in 1774: 'Notre parterre de la Comédie n'est rempli que de clercs de procureurs et de garçons perruquiers';[4] for one thing he had not set foot in Paris for some twenty-five years. More importance can be attached to the complaints of Meister in the same year: 'On a remarqué depuis dix ans un changement très sensible dans les jugements du parterre des différents spectacles. Presque tout y réussit, et rien n'y est délicatement senti.' Meister refuses to accept the conventional explanation that, so far as the Comédie Française was concerned, this change was due to its move to the Tuileries, because it was already visible, he declares, before 1770, and in any case the other theatres had not moved, but had none the less experienced similar changes. The real explanation,

---

[1] *La Mimographe*, p. 241.
[2] *Du Théâtre, ou Nouvel Essai sur l'art dramatique*, p. 209 n.
[3] Ibid., p. 202 n.
[4] *Œuvres complètes*, vol. xlix, p. 184.

says Meister, is that they have been brought about by the growth in luxury:

En effet, le parterre était composé, il y a quinze ans, de l'honnête bourgeoisie et des hommes de lettres, tous gens ayant fait leurs études, ayant des connaissances plus ou moins étendues, mais en ayant enfin. Le luxe les a tous fait monter aux secondes loges, qui ne jugent point, ou dont le jugement, au moins, reste sans influence; c'est le parterre seul qui décide du sort d'une pièce. Aujourd'hui cet aréopage est composé de journaliers, de garçons perruquiers, de marmitons; qu'attendre de pareils sujets? et peut-on se méprendre à la cause des disparates de leurs jugements?[1]

Writing in 1783, La Harpe makes the same contrast between the select spectators at the Comédie Française in former days and the more plebeian audience of the present time. In discussing the reasons for the great success of Ducis's version of *King Lear*, he declares that

la principale, c'est que nos spectacles ne sont plus ce qu'ils ont été, une assemblée choisie d'amateurs et d'hommes plus ou moins instruits: c'est le rendez-vous d'une foule désœuvrée et ignorante, depuis que le peuple des petits spectacles n'a eu besoin, pour envahir les grands, que de payer un peu plus cher un plaisir dont on lui a donné le goût et qui n'était pas fait pour lui.[2]

The *Correspondance secrète* of Métra explains the success of the *Mariage de Figaro* in the following year by its attraction for large numbers of members of the lower orders; Beaumarchais's predecessors, it declares,

ont toujours eu l'intention de faire rire les grands aux dépens des petits; ici, au contraire, ce sont les petits qui rient aux dépens des grands, et le nombre des petits étant très considérable, on ne doit point s'étonner de ce concours prodigieux de spectateurs de tout état que *Figaro* appelle. On dirait qu'ils viennent se consoler de leur misère en s'amusant des ridicules de ceux qui en sont les instruments.[3]

Certainly, as we have seen, Beaumarchais's comedy drew to the Comédie Française vast numbers of people who cannot have been in the habit of going there in the ordinary way.

This point is also made in a letter attacking the same play which is attributed to Suard. In it Beaumarchais is offered ironical congratulations on his success in drawing to the Comédie Française members of the lowest ranks of the society of the day:

Le bruit de votre nom et de vos succès a retenti jusqu'aux Halles et au

---

[1] Grimm, *Correspondance littéraire*, vol. x, pp. 340–1.
[2] *Correspondance littéraire*, vol. iv, p. 75.
[3] F. Métra, *Correspondance littéraire secrète* (London, 1787–90), 18 vols., vol. xvii, p. 215.

port Saint-Nicolas. Il n'y a pas un gagne-denier ou une blanchisseuse un peu renforcée qui n'ait vu au moins une fois le *Mariage de Figaro*, et qui n'en ait retenu quelques traits facétieux qui égaient à chaque instant leurs conversations . . .

Un grand nombre de ces bonnes gens, qui ne connaissaient pas même le nom du Théâtre Français, ont voulu voir votre comédie; et comme ils n'y ont rien compris d'abord, ils y sont retournés. Le plaisir et l'instruction qu'ils y ont trouvés les ont conduits naturellement aux théâtres des boulevards où ils aiment à revoir Figaro sous toutes les formes, et toujours avec son esprit et son ton.[1]

No doubt one cannot take literally such an obviously hostile account of the success of the *Mariage de Figaro*, but, for all their exaggeration, Suard's remarks must have contained some element of truth; they certainly fit in with other contemporary evidence on the subject.

In his memoirs the actor Fleury describes how, at the last performance given by the Comédie Française in September 1793 before the arrest of the actors, the audience recalled the select company which frequented the theatre under the Ancien Régime. 'Jamais la salle n'avait été ni plus brillante ni mieux composée.' Not only were the ladies there in force:

Parmi les hommes j'apercevais bien quelques têtes à cheveux noirs et crépus, mais nous avions en grande majorité de belles lignes de têtes poudrées, de ces têtes dignes et respectables qui, depuis vingt ans, avaient suivi et protégé la Comédie Française, restes précieux de l'ancien parterre du Faubourg Saint-Germain.[2]

In 1797, as we have already seen, Grimod de la Reynière looks back to the good old days when the three privileged theatres were frequented by a small *élite*—'par un petit nombre d'amateurs, d'hommes instruits, de jeunes gens studieux et tourmentés du besoin d'apprendre'. By contrast the audiences of 1797 are, he declares, completely inept:

Il suffit d'assister à nos jeux scéniques pour en être convaincu. Ces spectateurs, également étrangers aux connaissances préliminaires que le goût de la comédie nécessite et suppose, ignorant jusqu'aux premiers éléments de la grammaire et de la versification, ne savent point distinguer la prose des vers, le comique de la farce, l'enflure du sublime, le pathétique du larmoyant . . . *Madame Angot*[3] seule est en possession, et a le droit de leur plaire.

No doubt there is a very large element of exaggeration in these words;

<hr />

[1] Grimm, *Correspondance littéraire*, vol. xiv, pp. 117–18.
[2] Vol. iv, p. 424.
[3] The type of the *parvenue* who was the subject of various popular plays from 1795 onwards.

indeed I have even heard the late Jean-Jacques Olivier, in the library of the Comédie Française, speak in almost identical terms of the spectators who frequent that theatre in the 1950's! Perhaps more interesting, though at times equally exaggerated, is the description which Grimod de la Reynière gives of the new spectators in the *parterre* of the main Paris theatres. First, there are considerable numbers of soldiers.

Ensuite des êtres à peine sortis de l'enfance, qui seraient mieux placés a l'école qu'au théâtre, et dont la conversation obscène ne décèle qu'une corruption précoce. En troisième lieu, des ouvriers de la dernière classe du peuple, dont le langage grossier atteste toute la rusticité, et qui goûteraient bien mieux les plaisirs de la courtille que ceux du Théâtre Français. Enfin, quelques commis, classe autrefois assez éclairée, mais qui n'est plus guère aujourd'hui que le réceptacle d'une foule d'automates, dont un tiers sait à peine écrire, et qui, pour se soustraire aux dangers des combats, ont acheté le droit d'entraver les affaires publiques, en obstruant de leur insolente inutilité nos innombrables administrations.[1]

All the evidence shows that it was several decades before the Directoire that representatives of the lower orders began to seep into the *parterre* of the leading Paris theatres and even into the Comédie Française. It is probably a fair assumption that their numbers, at any rate before 1789, were not as large as some contemporary writers appear to maintain. One would, no doubt, have to distinguish, both for the last decades of the Ancien Régime and for the earlier period, between the audiences of the Comédie Française on the different days of the week, some of which were more fashionable than others. Year after year, in the introduction to his *Spectacles de Paris*, from 1754 onwards, Abbé de La Porte informs his readers: 'Les trois jours où il y a le plus de monde à la Comédie Française, sont le lundi, le mercredi et le samedi. C'est pour ces jours-là qu'on réserve les meilleures pièces ou les pièces nouvelles. Les autres jours, le spectacle est moins fréquenté, excepté les dimanches, où il y a aussi beaucoup de peuple.' In the *Tableau de Paris* Mercier tells us that on Sundays and saints' days a different audience frequented the Paris theatres:

Les gens du bon ton ne sortent pas ces jours-là, fuient les promenades, les spectacles, et les abandonnent au peuple. Les spectacles donnent ce qu'ils ont de plus usé; les acteurs médiocres s'emparent de la scène; tout cela est bon pour des parterres moins difficiles, et pour qui les pièces les plus anciennes sont toujours des pièces nouvelles. Les acteurs chargent ces jours-là plus

---

[1] *Le Censeur dramatique*, vol. i, pp. 4–7.

que de coutume, et obtiennent de grands applaudissements. Les bourgeois aisés sont partis dès la veille pour leur petite maison de campagne.[1]

Scarron's *Dom Japhet d'Arménie*, Bachaumont states in 1777, is the sort of play which is revived during Shrovetide 'pour amuser les bourgeois et le peuple, qui vont par extraordinaire au spectacle ces jours-là'.[2]

What sort of people were the new and more plebeian spectators who began in the last decades of the eighteenth century to find their way to the Comédie Francaise and the other privileged theatres? Rétif and Mercier seem to suggest that they were mainly skilled workmen. Other writers of the time do not give us much additional information; they generally remain in the realm of vague generalities. In his post-humous work, *De l'Homme*, which appeared in 1773, in speaking of the need for recreation, Helvétius exclaims: 'Avec quel plaisir l'ouvrier et l'avocat quittent-ils, l'un son atelier, et l'autre son cabinet pour la comédie! S'ils sont plus sensibles à ce spectacle que l'homme du monde, c'est que les sensations qu'ils y éprouvent, sont moins émoussées par l'habitude, sont pour eux plus nouvelles.'[3] If this passage is interesting because it puts on exactly the same level both the workman and the lawyer as spectators, Helvétius does not tell us what sort of workman he had in mind nor what sort of theatre. Nor does Diderot in his *Éléments de physiologie*, written in the 1770's, when he relates the story of a workman who was in the habit of attending the theatre in his leisure hours and who was afflicted by a violent fever: 'Alors cet homme se met à réciter des scènes entières de pièces dont il n'avait pas le moindre souvenir dans l'état de santé; il y a bien pis, c'est qu'il lui en est resté une malheureuse disposition à versifier. Il ne sait pas le premier mot des vers qu'il débitait dans sa fièvre, mais il a la rage d'en faire.'[4] Both Meister in the *Correspondance littéraire* and Bachaumont relate a significant incident which occurred in 1784 at the Théâtre Italien before the first performance of a satirical comedy, *Les Docteurs modernes*, which was directed against Mesmer and his followers. The programme began with a performance of Mercier's *drame, La Brouette du vinaigrier*. This play was interrupted in the middle of the second act by 'un coup de sifflet très fort et très prolongé' from the middle of the *parterre*. The miscreant was arrested. 'Il s'est trouvé', says Bachaumont,[5]

[1] *Tableau de Paris*, vol. iv, p. 96.
[2] *Mémoires secrets*, vol. x, p. 39 (16 Feb. 1777).   [3] Section viii, chap. xxii.
[4] *Œuvres complètes*, ed. J. Assézat and M. Tourneux (Paris, 1875–7), 20 vols., vol. ix, p. 367.
[5] *Mémoires secrets*, vol. xxvii, p. 18 (17 Nov. 1784). Meister (*Correspondance littéraire*, vol. xiv, p. 77) describes the man as 'un imbécile de laquais'.

que c'était un homme du peuple qui n'avait jamais vu le spectacle, et à qui quelque mesmériste avait donné de l'argent et un sifflet pour qu'il fît usage du dernier au milieu de la pièce des *Docteurs modernes*. Son peu d'usage, son ignorance si l'on jouait deux pièces, ou si l'on n'en jouait qu'une seule, l'avaient fait se méprendre et siffler trop tôt. Sa bonne foi lui a servi d'excuse, et il a été relâché.

Apparently even in 1784 it was still possible for a member of the lower orders to have singularly little knowledge of what normally went on inside one of the leading theatres of the capital.

From the available evidence—fragmentary and inadequate as it is—two conclusions may reasonably be drawn. The first is that in the last two or three decades of the Ancien Régime the *parterre* of the privileged theatres, including the Comédie Française, did begin to attract a certain proportion of the lower classes. These men, if we are to believe writers like La Harpe, graduated to theatres like the Comédie Française from the *théâtres des boulevards* where they first acquired a taste for drama. That such spectators were ever numerous before 1789 or that they exercised any real influence on the type of plays performed at the Comédie Française, one may beg leave to doubt. The presence of these humbler spectators in theatres like the Comédie Française in the closing decades of the Ancien Régime is chiefly interesting for the light which it throws on the composition of the *parterre* in the eighteenth century as a whole. The surprise, indeed at times the indignation, with which their presence in the theatres of the time is mentioned by contemporary writers shows very clearly that in the eighteenth century (and possibly for at least a considerable part of the seventeenth) the *parterre* of the Comédie Française and other theatres of that class was not accustomed to house anything but a solid bourgeois audience, with perhaps a sprinkling of noblemen. No doubt it was not impossible, even before, say, 1760, for an occasional representative of the lower orders to have the necessary taste and money to acquire a ticket to the *parterre* of the Comédie Française; but all the evidence we possess would seem to indicate that this was very exceptional. The vast majority of the spectators in the *parterre* in the eighteenth century would seem to have been men of some standing and culture—lawyers, schoolmasters, writers, students, and schoolboys, in a word, 'intellectuals' and members, present or future, of the liberal professions, with, of course, a sprinkling of army officers, drunk or sober. That was the *parterre* before which the tragedies of Voltaire, the comedies of Marivaux and Beaumarchais came up for judgement.

(iv) The Aristocracy and the Theatre

So far we have concerned ourselves with the representatives of the middle and lower ranks of society in the theatres of eighteenth-century Paris. To complete our picture of theatre audiences of the time we must also take into account the place occupied in the theatres of this age by the representatives of the upper classes of a society in which blue blood still retained an importance difficult to grasp today. Until the privileges of the aristocracy vanished in the blood and smoke of the Revolution of 1789 French society still continued to be dominated by the royal family, the princes of the blood and the countless lords and ladies who inhabited Versailles and Paris. There were too—often by now inter-married with the survivors of the old feudal nobility—the judges of the *Parlements*, the high civil servants, the bankers and tax-farmers whose wealth gave them considerable standing in the society of the eighteenth century. Moreover, in this more civilized, polished, and tolerant age polite society adopted into its ranks and even idolized the writers and thinkers who often came from quite humble homes. The playwrights of the time moved for the most part quite freely and naturally in this society, at once exclusive and yet open to men of talent; their taste, indeed their whole outlook on the world were inevitably moulded in the pattern of that society. In the workaday world solid merchants, bankers, and industrialists might be continually increasing their wealth and power, but for the writer who moved in high society and who owed his success and his very bread and butter to his ability to please this more restricted circle, 'the rise of the middle classes' can often have meant very little. It was Monsieur le Duc or Madame la Comtesse, even Louis XV or, later, Marie Antoinette, whose taste they endeavoured to please.

Little more than a dozen years before the Revolution we find Voltaire upbraiding Shakespeare for daring to introduce into a tragedy such a monstrous phrase as 'Not a mouse stirring'. In his *Lettre à MM. de l'Académie Française* in which he denounced Shakespeare and his translator, Le Tourneur, he exclaims: 'Oui, monsieur, un soldat peut répondre ainsi dans un corps de garde; mais non pas sur le théâtre, devant les premières personnes d'une nation, qui s'expriment noblement, et devant qui il faut s'exprimer de même.'[1] M. de Voltaire retained to the end a fine sense of what one owed to the proprieties and to the 'best people'. We find in his writings, not only constant references to

---

[1] *Œuvres complètes*, vol. xxx, p. 363.

the *parterre* of the Comédie Française, but also frequent allusions to the importance of the aristocratic sections of the contemporary theatre-going public. In 1752, in a letter from Potsdam to Mme Denis, he penned a vivid description of a first night in the Paris of his day:

> C'est un grand jour pour le beau monde oisif de Paris qu'une première représentation: les cabales battent le tambour; on se dispute les loges; les valets de chambre vont à midi remplir le théâtre.[1] La pièce est jugée avant qu'on l'ait vue. Femmes contre femmes, petits-maîtres contre petits-maîtres, sociétés contre sociétés; les cafés sont comblés de gens qui disputent; la foule est dans la rue en attendant qu'elle soit au parterre.[2]

The *parterre* comes into the picture, of course, but here it is almost over-shadowed by the spectators of the boxes and the stage. Another characteristic account of the theatre audience of the time is to be found in a letter in which Grimm describes to Voltaire the début of a new actor at the Comédie Française in 1770; although the new-comer had no great success, he writes, 'on n'aurait pas trouvé la place d'une épingle dans la salle, et l'assemblée était formée de tout ce qu'il y a d'illustre et de considérable en France'.[3]

Until the abolition of seats on the stage at the Comédie Française in 1759 this part of the theatre drew to it, along with a sprinkling of writers who had presumably the privilege of free admission, the male members of the most aristocratic and wealthy sections of the community. In a memoir which he drew up shortly before the abolition of seats on the stage Lekain asks his fellow actors:

> Ne nous paraît-il pas, à nous-mêmes, de la dernière absurdité de voir figurer sur notre théâtre les pères de la Grèce et de Rome avec nos jeunes colonels, nos élégants sénateurs, nos opulents financiers, et leurs plus riches intendants?
>
> Sera-ce une loi toujours sacrée parmi nos vétérans, que le danger de Joas, sur son trône, excite des éclats de rire indécents, quand les ministres du Très-Haut, confondus avec les soldats d'Athalie et nos élégants français, se battent tous ensemble, les uns pour enlever un dépôt si précieux, les autres pour le sauver?[4]

When these seats had at last been abolished and the stage was left free

---

[1] In order to reserve seats on the stage for their masters.
[2] *Œuvres complètes*, vol. xxxvii, p. 381.
[3] Ibid., vol. xlvii, p. 276.
[4] 'Mémoire qui tend à prouver la nécessité de supprimer les banquettes de dessus le théâtre de la Comédie Française, en séparant ainsi les acteurs des spectateurs' (20 Jan. 1759), in *Mémoires*, p. 48.

to the actors, Collé gives in his Journal an amusing picture of the contrast between the new state of affairs and the old:

L'illusion théâtrale est actuellement entière; on ne voit plus César prêt à dépoudrer un fat assis sur le premier rang du théâtre, et Mithridate expirer au milieu de tous gens de notre connaissance; l'ombre de Ninus heurter et coudoyer un fermier général, et Camille tomber morte dans la coulisse sur Marivaux et sur Saint-Foix qui s'avancent ou se reculent pour se prêter à l'assassinat de cette Romaine par la main d'Horace, son frère, qui fait rejaillir son sang sur ces deux auteurs comiques.[1]

The abolition of these seats on the stage must have been a severe blow to the members of the upper classes who liked to disport themselves there, even if their behaviour was not always as fatuous as that described almost exactly a century earlier by Molière in *Les Fâcheux*. This part of the theatre was apparently favoured by the Princes of the Blood. They and their womenfolk, so Riccoboni tells us in 1738,[2] had the right to occupy any of the boxes in the first row, even though it was already let to some private individual; but he adds, in a sentence which brings vividly to life the importance of rank in the society of the Ancien Régime: 'Les princes du sang vont le plus souvent se placer sur le théâtre; et alors les acteurs suspendent la scène, tous les spectateurs se lèvent par respect, et les princes vont occuper la première place qui leur est cédée par celui qui y était assis.'

The important place occupied in the Paris theatre audience by the aristocratic and wealthy sections of the community is underlined in 1769 by Mme Riccoboni in the preface to her *Nouveau Théâtre anglais*. The crudity of so much English drama is to be explained, she maintains, by a fundamental difference in the theatre audiences of London and Paris:

A Paris les grands et les riches suivent assidûment les spectacles. A Londres les personnes distinguées vont rarement à la comédie; l'emploi de leur temps et l'heure de leurs repas ne leur permettent guère d'être libres quand elle commence. C'est donc à la bourgeoisie, même au peuple, que l'on est obligé de plaire.[3]

These remarks got Mme Riccoboni into hot water with her old friend Garrick. She wrote to defend her views after she had learned that in a letter to a mutual friend he had complained about these reflections on

[1] Vol. ii, p, 172.
[2] In his *Réflexions historiques et critiques sur les différents théâtres de l'Europe* (Paris, 1738), p. 137.
[3] *Le Nouveau Théâtre anglais* (Paris, 1769), 2 vols., vol. i, pp. viii–ix.

English theatre audiences. Her information, she points out, came from her English friends who had all given her this explanation of the difference between English and French plays. English noblemen, she declares, are scarcely depicted in a flattering light on the London stage: 'Le sot, le fat ou le malhonnête homme mêlé dans l'intrigue est presque toujours un lord; semble-t-on travailler pour une classe que l'on s'applique à dégrader, que l'on expose à la risée? Est-ce un moyen de l'attirer?' How different, she adds, is the state of affairs in the Paris theatres: 'Ici les premiers du royaume font leur séjour habituel du théâtre: les dames ont de petites loges à l'année, la comédie est le rendez-vous de la bonne compagnie.' 'Elle ne divertit guère', she continues,

mais elle occupe beaucoup. On disserte, on prône, on juge, on cabale: mille fainéants titrés n'ont d'autre ressource contre l'ennui que les chauffoirs des trois spectacles. . . . Aussi les auteurs remplissent-ils la scène de comtes, de marquis; ils n'osent faire parler les bourgeois; la nature et la plaisanterie sont bannies de leurs pièces, et comme il est très *ignoble* de rire, ils cherchent à faire pleurer.[1]

We must leave it to historians of English drama to judge between Garrick and Mme Riccoboni on the question of London theatre audiences, but we are left in no doubt as to the importance of the aristocratic section of the audience in the Paris theatres only twenty years before the Revolution.

Since the upper classes of society continued until 1789 to provide so many spectators for the privileged theatres, it followed that these had to be situated reasonably near the fashionable quarters of Paris. In 1772 Grimm speaks with scorn of a proposal to build a new theatre for the Comédie Italienne 'à l'extrémité du Marais et de la rue Boucherat, vis-à-vis le Pont-aux-Choux, c'est-à-dire à une lieue du quartier du Palais-Royal, et à deux lieues du Faubourg Saint-Germain. Il faut convenir que nos faiseurs de projets sont admirables dans leurs enfantements.'[2] The same point emerges from a study of the places in eighteenth-century Paris at which the posters of the Comédie Française, Théâtre Italien, and Opéra were put up. An admirable article by M. François de Dainville[3] shows that in 1753 not a single one of the

[1] Garrick, *Private Correspondence* (London, 1831–2), 2 vols., vol. ii, p. 561.

[2] *Correspondance littéraire*, vol. x, p. 65.

[3] 'Les lieux d'affichage des comédiens à Paris en 1753', *Revue d'histoire du théâtre* (1951), pp. 248–53.

175 sets of theatre posters displayed in Paris was placed in the plebeian quarters of the Faubourg Saint-Marcel and the Faubourg Saint-Antoine; nearly all of them were to be found in the old aristocratic quarters—the Marais and the region near the Louvre and Palais Royal —and the now rising aristocratic districts of the Faubourg Saint-Germain and the Faubourg Saint-Honoré. The fifty posters which were placed at the entrance to mansions[1] were nearly all to be found in these two faubourgs which were inhabited by noblemen and *Parlementaires*.

Yet another proof of the importance of the aristocracy and the wealthier section of society in general for the theatres of the time is to be found in the effect which the Revolution had on the fortunes of the privileged theatres. In 1790 we find La Harpe declaring in his *Correspondance littéraire*: 'La révolution a ruiné tous les spectacles, soit par la diversion fréquente des grands intérêts publics qui arrachent à tout amusement, soit par l'émigration de tant d'habitants de Paris, et de la classe la plus riche. L'Opéra menace de faire retraite; les Italiens de faire banqueroute. Les Comédiens Français ont emprunté des sommes considérables.'[2] By 1790 the break-up of the old society and the emigration of so many nobles and wealthy people brought the total receipts of the Comédie Française down to below 500,000 l., from an average of nearly a million in the closing years of the Ancien Régime. It is significant that the greater part of the fall was due to the decline in the income from the *petites loges*, which, because of their expense, were chiefly occupied by members of the upper classes of society. The income from this source had dropped by 1790 from 800 l. a day to 300 l.[3]

It was, of course, inevitable that, despite the importance of the upper-class section of the spectators in the Paris theatres of the time, the more mixed audiences of the capital should at times take a different view from the court as to the merits of individual plays. In 1774 John Moore noted the frequent clashes between the taste of the court and of the Paris theatre audiences. 'Obedient to the court in every other particular', he wrote,

the French disregard the decisions pronounced at Versailles in matters of taste. It very often happens that a dramatic piece, which has been acted before the royal family and the court with the highest applause, is afterwards

---

[1] This was so much regarded as a privilege that in 1753 a bill-poster was sent to prison for failing to put up the posters on the house of the Duc de Gesvres.

[2] Vol. v, p. 349.

[3] J. Bonnassies, *Les Auteurs dramatiques et la Comédie Française aux XVIIe et XVIIIe siècles* (Paris, 1874), pp. 116–17.

damned with every circumstance of ignominy at Paris. In all works of genius
the Parisians lead the judgment of the courtiers and dictate to their monarch.[1]

The same observation is made nine years later by both Meister and
Mercier. The former declares in the *Correspondance littéraire*: 'Paris se
plaît souvent à réformer les jugements de la cour en matière de goût;
on l'a dit il y a longtemps: *Fontainebleau est le Châtelet, et le parterre de
Paris est le Parlement qui casse souvent ses sentences.*'[2] Mercier extends
this decline in the influence of court taste far beyond the theatre; he is
obviously writing not many years before the upheaval of 1789, in a
France very different from what it had been a hundred years earlier at
the high point of absolutism:

> Le mot de *cour* n'en impose plus parmi nous comme au temps de Louis
> XIV. On ne reçoit plus de la cour les opinions régnantes; elle ne décide plus
> des réputations, en quelque genre que ce soit; on ne dit plus avec une emphase
> ridicule *La cour a prononcé ainsi.* On casse les jugements de la cour; on dit
> nettement: Elle n'y entend rien, elle n'a point d'idées là-dessus, elle ne saurait
> en avoir, elle n'est pas dans le point de vue.
>
> La cour elle-même, qui s'en doute, n'ose pas prononcer affirmativement
> sur un livre, sur une pièce de théâtre, sur un chef-d'œuvre nouveau, sur un
> événement singulier ou extraordinaire. Elle attend l'arrêt de la capitale;
> elle-même a grand soin de s'en informer, afin de ne pas compromettre son
> premier avis, qui serait cassé *avec dépens.*[3]

It ought, however, to be observed that in the last years of the Ancien
Régime, from the time that Marie Antoinette allowed the spectators to
applaud at court performances (a thing hitherto unheard of), the situation changed somewhat, if we are to believe what Meister has to say on
the subject in 1786. Playwrights, he declares, look upon the Paris
theatre public as the 'juge en dernier ressort des jugements portés par le
public de la cour'; but since applause has been permitted at theatrical
performances at court, there has been a great change, and now 'il est
bien rare que le public de Paris ne confirme pas les arrêts prononcés par
la cour'.[4]

Earlier in the century clashes between the taste of Paris and the
court seem sometimes to have been the other way round. In 1717
Crébillon's tragedy, *Sémiramis*, was criticized in Paris and applauded

---

[1] John Moore, *A View of Society and Manners in France, Switzerland and Germany*
(London, 1779), 2 vols., vol. i, p. 86.

[2] Vol. xiii, p. 367.

[3] *Tableau de Paris*, vol. iv, p. 153.

[4] *Correspondance littéraire*, vol. xiv, p. 483.

at Court. 'Le public', wrote a contemporary journal,[1] 'en se partageant sur le sujet de *Sémiramis*, a suivi le train ordinaire. La ville avait critiqué, il était dans la règle que la cour approuvât; ce sont deux espèces de républiques, composées d'hommes différents; ils se moquent les uns des autres.' Sometimes the court rejected plays which had been successful in Paris for reasons which are very understandable; it is not surprising, for instance, that Marivaux's little one-act comedy, *L'Île des Esclaves*, should not have gone down well at court in 1725, since it depicts an imaginary island where the former slaves are now masters, and the former masters have become slaves.[2] It is interesting that nearly sixty years later, in 1782, Laignelot's tragedy, *Agis*, which according to Bachaumont had been very successful in Paris partly because of its apparent allusions to the Parlement Maupeou,[3] should not have been a success at Versailles. 'Le ton républicain de cette tragédie', Bachaumont declares, 'n'était pas fait pour être agréable en pareil lieu.'[4]

It would be naïve to imagine that even in such an age of refined politeness as the eighteenth century the level of taste of the French upper classes was necessarily high. A novelist of the 1760's describes, no doubt with considerable satirical exaggeration, how the best people liked to 'do' the Comédie Française, the Opéra, and the Théâtre Italien in one evening:

Nos coquettes et nos petits-maîtres seraient au désespoir de ne se pas montrer presque en même temps à tous les spectacles à la fois. L'on fait un léger acte de comparution à la Comédie Française pour envier les grâces de la charmante Gaussin; l'on y minaude avec l'éventail ou le chapeau, car les minauderies sont des deux sexes. Nos jeunes fats y lorgnent les beautés; c'est un mérite aujourd'hui de se parer d'une lorgnette. Bientôt l'on en sort; on vole à l'Opéra pour l'un des grands chœurs, et de là on passe aux Italiens où l'on arrive à temps pour le ballet. On ne serait pas sur le bon ton si l'on n'agissait ainsi. Il n'est que du bourgeois et tout au moins de la prude et du philosophe de pouvoir assister à une représentation entière.[5]

The satirists of the time give a very unflattering picture of the behaviour of the ladies who frequented the *petites loges*. In *Le Tableau de Paris*

[1] *L'Europe savante*, Jan. 1718, pp. 136 f. (Quoted in C. and F. Parfaict, *Histoire du Théâtre Français*, vol. xv, p. 257.)

[2] T. S. Gueullette, *Notes et souvenirs sur le Théâtre-Italien au XVIIIᵉ siècle*, ed. J. E. Gueullette (Paris, 1938), p. 105.

[3] It was given twelve times at the Comédie Française during its first run.

[4] *Mémoires secrets*, vol. xx, p. 232 (6 May 1782).

[5] É. de Sainte-Colombe, *Les Plaisirs d'un jour, ou la Journée d'une provinciale à Paris* (Brussels, 1764), pp. 195–6.

Mercier quotes a picturesque description of their outlook taken from a
work called *Les Vues simples d'un bon homme*:[1]

Si le public se plaint de voir les comédiens disposer ainsi de la salle, une
petite maîtresse s'écrie: 'Comment! l'on veut m'astreindre à entendre une
comédie tout entière, pendant que je suis assez riche pour n'en écouter
qu'une scène? Oh, c'est une tyrannie! Il n'y a plus de police en France:
puisque je ne peux pas faire venir la comédie chez moi, je veux au moins avoir
la liberté d'y arriver à sept heures, d'y paraître en simple déshabillé, comme
lorsque je sors de mon lit. Je veux y apporter mon chien, mon bougeoir, mon
vase de nuit; je veux jouir de mon fauteuil, de ma dormeuse, recevoir l'hommage de tous mes courtisans, et m'en aller avant que l'ennui me saisisse. Me
priver de tant d'avantages, c'est attenter à la liberté que donnent le bon goût
et la richesse.'

Mercier then proceeds to add his own highly unfavourable picture of
the behaviour of this section of the audience to his general indictment
of the actors for creating the *petites loges*:

Il faut donc, quand on est femme, avoir dans une *petite loge* son épagneul,
son coussin, sa chaufferette, mais surtout un petit fat à lorgnette, qui vous
instruit de tout ce qui entre et de tout ce qui sort, et qui vous nomme les
acteurs. Cependant la dame a dans son éventail une petite ouverture, où est
enchâssé un verre, de sorte qu'elle voit sans être vue.[2]

Plays did not need to be of the very highest merit to enjoy the favour
even of the royal family and the court. Bachaumont relates how Scarron's not over-refined comedy, *Dom Japhet d'Arménie*, which formerly
had been reserved for the delectation of the bourgeois and plebs who
came to the theatre *par extraordinaire* in Shrovetide, suddenly won
great favour with Marie Antoinette and the other members of the royal
family when it was put on at the Comédie Française in 1777 during this
season:

Cette pièce a fait une fortune extraordinaire cette année:[3] et elle a fort
réjoui la reine et la famille royale. On y a joué le divertissement qu'on appelle
la Cavalcade; on l'a enrichi de tableaux pittoresques, analogues aux courses,
qui sont aujourd'hui la fureur des princes et de nos jeunes seigneurs, ce qui
fait le spectacle, et est réellement fort amusant; en sorte que *Dom Japhet*
dure encore pendant le carême.[4]

In the chapter entitled *Attrapes* in the *Tableau de Paris* Mercier also

---

[1] Paris, 1776 (attributed by Barbier to J. H. Marchand).
[2] *Tableau de Paris*, vol. ii, p. 188.
[3] It was given eight times.
[4] *Mémoires secrets*, vol. x, p. 39 (16 Feb. 1777).

deals with this topic, in comparing the crude practical jokes perpetrated by people in the streets during Shrovetide with some of the things which happened on the stage of the Comédie Française, in such plays as *Dom Japhet d'Arménie* and Molière's *Monsieur de Pourceaugnac*:

Les comédiens français, ces jours-là, ne manquent point de donner *Dom Iaphet d'Arménie* et autres *scarronnades*, et les spectateurs s'amusent fort d'un pot de chambre vidé sur la scène, d'un apothicaire en attitude, et d'un malade dévoyé qui court à la garde-robe avec les grimaces du moment. La canaille rit dans les carrefours et le beau monde sur les banquettes de velours de l'orchestre et de l'amphithéâtre. Préville, comédien du roi, joue la dégoûtante mascarade tout aussi bien et avec autant de feu que le polisson des rues, et leurs gestes licencieux sont à peu près les mêmes.[1]

The contemporary vogue among high society of *parades*—smutty little farces at which the ladies used their fans to hide their blushes (or their smiles)—was paralleled throughout the period, as we have seen, by the interest taken by members of the upper classes of both sexes in the plays of the Théâtres de la Foire and, later in the century, the Théâtres des Boulevards. These entertainments, although theoretically reserved for the lower orders, also had their appeal for polite society. In 1779, for instance, at the little theatre of the Variétés-Amusantes an actor named Jeannot scored a tremendous success—142 performances —in a farce called *Les Battus paient l'amende* by a very minor playwright called Dorvigny. After describing the success of this 'farce de la foire', La Harpe adds: 'On la rejoue après souper, pour la bonne compagnie. On fait même venir Jeannot dans les maisons particulières pour de l'argent.'[2] Bachaumont declares that this play is 'la fureur du jour', adding:

Non seulement le peuple y court en foule mais la ville et la cour. Les plus grands en raffolent, les graves magistrats, les évêques y vont en loge grillée; les ministres y ont assisté; le comte de Maurepas[3] surtout, grand amateur de farces. On a même prétendu que celle-ci était de sa composition; et cette anecdote n'a pas peu contribué à en soutenir et augmenter la vogue.[4]

'La ville et la cour', writes Meister, have flocked to see the play: 'Dans le même temps où l'on voyait une si grande affluence de monde à la cent douzième représentation des *Battus paient l'amende*, il n'y avait pas

---

[1] Vol. v, p. 144.
[2] La Harpe, *Correspondance littéraire*, vol. ii, p. 412.
[3] The leading minister of Louis XVI at this period of the reign.
[4] *Mémoires secrets*, vol. xiv, p. 137 (2 Aug. 1779).

deux loges de louées pour la première représentation de *Rome sauvée*, de
M. de Voltaire,[1] et à la troisième la salle était déserte.'[2] In his little play,
Molière à la nouvelle salle, performed shortly after the opening of the
new theatre of the Comédie Française in 1782, La Harpe denounces the
taste in drama of the upper classes of his day as being just as plebeian as
that of the lower orders:

THALIE: Le Boulevard l'emporte.
MOLIÈRE: Oui, pour le peuple.
THALIE: Non; hommes de tous les rangs,
        Et la Ville et la Cour, les petits et les grands,
        Tout y court; autrefois la bonne compagnie,
                Donnant et l'exemple et le ton,
        Entraîna par degrés toute la nation
                Vers le spectacle du génie;
        Mais chacun a son tour, et le peuple aujourd'hui
        Rend les honnêtes gens aussi peuple que lui.[3]

With all their faults, and although they were certainly outnumbered
by the more bourgeois section of the theatre audience of the time, the
aristocratic spectators continued throughout our period to exercise a
surprising influence on the content and form of French drama. Admirers of Shakespeare in eighteenth-century France—Louis-Sébastien
Mercier, for instance—spoke of him as a national poet who addressed
himself to a very broad cross-section of his fellow countrymen, in contrast to a writer like Corneille. Shakespeare, says Mercier,[4] is admired
by Englishmen because he

a su trouver le secret de parler à tous les individus qui composent cette nation
respectable.·. . . Shakespeare est pour les Anglais un poète bien plus national
que Corneille ne l'est pour nous. Ce n'est point à Paris qu'il faut le juger,
à Paris où l'on fait tout pour les riches, où l'on n'a même d'idées que
pour eux. C'est à Londres, où chaque homme a son existence propre et
personnelle.

He quotes with appropriate enthusiasm the following lines from
Grosley's *Londres*:[5] 'J'ai vu des gens du peuple pleurer à la vue de
Shakespeare, dont la statue très belle et parlante leur rappelait les
scènes de ce poète, qui leur avaient déchiré l'âme.' French drama, he

---

[1] The play was given three performances when it was revived in this year.
[2] Grimm, *Correspondance littéraire*, vol. xii, pp. 253–4.
[3] Sc. 1.
[4] *Du Théâtre, ou Nouvel Essai sur l'art dramatique*, p. 206.
[5] (Lausanne, 1770), 3 vols., vol. i, p. 356. They occur in a description of the statues in
Westminster Abbey.

continues, may be much more correct than English, but it is infinitely less interesting: 'L'éloquence de la scène anglaise est celle du peuple, et voilà pourquoi elle a de la véhémence, de la franchise et un singulier intérêt. . . . Voilà de quoi étonner nos petits rimailleurs français, qui croient posséder le goût par excellence, en rejetant le goût populaire.'[1]

Mercier is, of course, scarcely a disinterested witness here, as he was an ardent propagandist for a type of drama which would appeal to the masses. Yet it is interesting to find Mme de Staël, in the opening years of the nineteenth century, making the same point about French tragedy and for that matter French poetry in general. In *De l'Allemagne* she too has an axe to grind, but if what she says about other countries is somewhat exaggerated, what she has to say of French poetry and drama is no doubt true. French poetry, she maintains, is the only one which does not reach the masses. In their own countries the poems of Tasso, Calderon, Camoens, Goethe, and Bürger are known and often sung by everybody. 'Shakespeare est autant admiré par le peuple en Angleterre que par la classe supérieure.' French poets are no doubt admired by all cultured people both in France and in the rest of Europe, 'mais ils sont tout à fait inconnus aux gens du peuple et aux bourgeois même des villes, parce que les arts en France ne sont pas, comme ailleurs, natifs du pays même où leurs beautés se développent'.[2] In speaking of the theatre, she repeats that Shakespeare's plays appeal equally to all classes in England, whereas 'nos plus belles tragédies en France n'intéressent pas le peuple. . . . Nous possédons peu de tragédies qui puissent ébranler à la fois l'imagination des hommes de tous les rangs.'[3]

Our period inherited from the seventeenth century the tradition that the main characters of a tragedy must be of high birth, preferably of royal blood. It was inevitable that this predilection for characters of exalted rank in tragedy should come in for criticism in the second half of the century when more equalitarian attitudes were penetrating into drama. In his *Essai sur le genre dramatique sérieux*, which was published in 1767 along with his first *drame*, *Eugénie*, Beaumarchais roundly declares that the preference for kings and princes in tragedy is a matter of vanity, and that the use of such characters merely reduces the interest which the ordinary spectator takes in tragic heroes. 'Que me font à moi, sujet paisible d'un état monarchique du dix-huitième siècle, les révolutions d'Athènes et de Rome?' he asks. 'Quel véritable intérêt

[1] *Du Théâtre, ou Nouvel Essai sur l'art dramatique*, p. 207 n.
[2] *De l'Allemagne* (Paris, 1874), p. 156.
[3] Ibid., p. 200.

puis-je prendre à la mort d'un tyran du Péloponnèse? au sacrifice d'une jeune princesse en Aulide? Il n'y a dans tout cela rien à voir pour moi, aucune moralité qui me convienne.'[1] Six years later Mercier takes up the same theme in even more energetic language in his *Nouvel Essai sur l'art dramatique*. He denies that as tragic heroes kings are any more interesting than ordinary mortals: 'Ils m'intéresseront comme hommes, mais non comme rois. En mettant bas sceptre et couronne, ils ne m'en deviendront que plus chers.' A young and unfortunate prince can arouse tears of pity, but not because he is a prince. 'Quoi! toujours au théâtre d'autres objets que mes semblables?' asks Mercier. 'Eh! Si l'on veut peindre des rois, représentez donc leur ambition comme la source des malheurs du peuple.' It is only as tyrants that kings should be depicted, if tragedy is to have a truly moral aim.[2]

The gap between the heroes of tragedy and the ordinary spectator during the Ancien Régime is stressed by Pixerécourt in a violently demagogic passage which throws interesting light on the pre-Revolutionary audience at the Comédie Française:

Une seule classe dans la tragédie était plus rapprochée de la classe des auditeurs, c'était celle des confidents. Et quelle école? Ou ministres complaisants des attentats et des passions des grands personnages; ou flatteurs mercenaires, leur aplanissant, comme Œnone, les sentiers du crime; ou despotes subalternes, renchérissant, comme Altémore, sur la perfidie d'un Avogare;[3] ou spectateurs insignifiants, comme Corasmin,[4] des emportements de leurs maîtres, tels étaient les modèles offerts par les poètes tragiques aux gens de cour qui peuplaient le Théâtre Français; et la dégradation était au point que les hommes d'une classe plus inférieure encore, jetés pour leurs 30 sous au milieu du parterre, en étaient venus peut-être à envier le sort de ces confidents qu'un sourire de leurs idoles payait de leurs bassesses.[5]

This picture of French tragedy before the Revolution as entirely monopolized by tragic heroes of illustrious birth is not wholly accurate, even if we leave aside for the moment such *tragédies bourgeoises* as Landois's *Silvie* or Saurin's *Beverley* which may properly be considered in connexion with the new genre of the *Drame*. We have, for instance, the example of De Belloy's *Siège de Calais* which scored a phenomenal success during its first run at the Comédie Française in 1765, and would no doubt have beaten all records there if its performance had not been

---

[1] *Théâtre complet*, ed. R. d'Hermies (Paris, 1952), p. 39.
[2] *Du Théâtre ou Nouvel Essai sur l'art dramatique*, pp. 42–44.
[3] In de Belloy's *Gaston et Bayard*.
[4] In Voltaire's *Zaïre*.
[5] Estève, 'Observations de Guilbert de Pixerécourt', p. 550.

brought to an end by a quarrel among the actors. The play, it is true, contains a number of characters of high birth—Edward III, Godefroy d'Harcourt, a baron who had gone over to the English, and Aliénor, the daughter of the governor of Calais. But the heroes of the play, headed by Eustache Saint-Pierre, the Mayor of the besieged town, and his son, are the burghers of Calais. Their loyalty to the French King is contrasted with the treachery of some of the barons. Aliénor exclaims:

> Harcourt trahit son prince, et d'Artois l'abandonne;
> Un maire de Calais raffermit sa couronne! . . .
> Quelle leçon pour vous, superbes potentats!
> Veillez sur vos sujets dans le rang le plus bas:
> Tel qui sous l'oppresseur loin de vos yeux expire,
> Peut-être quelque jour eût sauvé votre empire.[1]

Edward III sees in another light the same lowly origins of the Mayor when he prepares to win him over to his side by lavish promises:

> Sur ce maire employons mon heureuse industrie.
> Je connais le vulgaire; il chérit peu sa vie
> Lorsqu'en un sort obscur il la voit consumer;
> Mais s'il peut être grand, il commence à l'aimer.
> Je sais ses préjugés, et l'art de les détruire;
> Tel brave les tourments qu'un bienfait peut séduire;
> Et les rois ont toujours un charme impérieux
> Sur ces derniers humains, nés et nourris loin d'eux.[2]

Even forty years later, Petitot was still astonished at the author's boldness in choosing such heroes for a tragedy. 'L'adresse avec laquelle l'auteur a traité son sujet laisse à peine deviner', he declares, 'combien il était difficile, en mettant des bourgeois sur la scène, de les élever à toute la hauteur de la tragédie.' Indeed he adds significantly that this was all the more difficult in view of the aristocratic nature of at least part of his audience: 'Il ne fallait pas moins d'art pour mettre l'héroïsme du côté de la bourgeoisie, la trahison du côté de la noblesse, c'est-à-dire pour opposer Eustache Saint-Pierre au comte d'Harcourt, sans choquer la première classe de la nation.'[3]

In the following year another dramatist, Lemierre, chose a plebeian hero for a tragedy in putting on to the stage the legend of William Tell. *Guillaume Tell* reached only seven performances during its first run. A revised version of the play was put on twenty years later, but although

---

[1] Act IV, Sc. 4.   [2] Act V, Sc. 1.
[3] *Répertoire du Théâtre Français*, ed. C. B. Petitot (Paris, 1803–4), 23 vols., vol. v, p. 246.

the play was given a fair number of times during the Revolution, it cannot be said ever to have enjoyed a striking success. Here there is no question of a contrast between the treachery of the great nobles and the patriotism of the lower orders, but once more the tragic hero is a man of modest origins. Gessler's *confident* describes William Tell in the following terms:

> Sa fortune est obscure,
> Sa force est le seul bien qu'il tient de la nature;
> C'est un de ces humains qui, courbés dans leurs champs,
> De la terre avec peine arrachent les présents;
> Mais dans son sort obscur, seigneur, dans sa bassesse,
> Il s'est fait remarquer longtemps par son adresse;
> Une flèche, dit-on, sous son coup d'œil certain,
> Frappa toujours le but au sortir de sa main.[1]

When Tell, having successfully passed through the ordeal of shooting an apple on his son's head, explains that he had kept his second arrow in order to shoot Gessler if anything had gone wrong, the latter exclaims in his fury to his *confident*: 'Un tel excès d'audace en un rang aussi bas!' To this the latter replies:

> Il est de ces mortels dans les plus vils états,
> De ces séditieux aigris par leur bassesse,
> Qui, pour se distinguer, n'ont que la hardiesse;
> Plus leur sort est obscur, plus leur rang est abject,
> Plus ils osent franchir les bornes du respect.[2]

In the 1760's even Voltaire, the High Priest of Classical tragedy, seemed eager to break with the convention which required the principal characters of tragedy to be of high birth. Here he was no doubt influenced by the vogue of the *Drame*. In the preface to his tragedy, *Les Scythes* (1767), he makes a transparent allusion to Diderot and his dramatic theories,[3] while he speaks of his next tragedy, *Les Guèbres*, as a 'tragédie plus que bourgeoise'.[4] In the preface to *Les Scythes* he declares that his aim is to offer a contrasting picture of the ancient Scythians and Persians (in reality, the Swiss and the French), adding: 'C'est une entreprise un peu téméraire d'introduire des pasteurs, des laboureurs, avec des princes, et de mêler les mœurs champêtres avec celles des cours.' He underlines his own boldness in the following terms: 'Qui voit-on d'abord paraître sur la scène? Deux vieillards

---

[1] Act III, Sc. 1.   [2] Act IV, Sc. 5.
[3] *Œuvres complètes*, vol. vi, p. 269 (it should be added that he does not invoke Diderot's example on this particular point).   [4] Ibid., p. 483.

auprès de leurs cabanes, des bergers, des laboureurs. De qui parle-t-on ? D'une fille qui prend soin de la vieillesse de son père, et qui fait le service le plus pénible. Qui épouse-t-elle ? Un pâtre qui n'est jamais sorti des champs paternels.' Later in the preface he puts forward the heretical view that 'tous les états de la vie humaine peuvent être représentés sur la scène tragique', though he is careful to add a prudent reservation to this sweeping statement: 'en observant toujours toutefois les bienséances, sans lesquelles il n'y a point de vraies beautés chez les nations policées, et surtout aux yeux des cours éclairées'.[1] He obviously had no intention of admitting into his definition of tragedy the 'farces monstrueuses' of Shakespeare which violated the Classical *bienséances*.

Les Scythes was performed at the Comédie Française in 1767, but reached only four performances; it was given five times more in 1770 and then vanished for ever from the repertoire. *Les Guèbres*, completed two years later, could not be performed in Paris because of its attack on religious intolerance. In the preface to this latter tragedy Voltaire assures the reader that, in order to drive home the moral lesson of the play,

on a choisi des personnages dans l'ordre commun. On n'a pas craint de hasarder sur la scène un jardinier, une jeune fille qui a prêté la main aux travaux rustiques de son père, des officiers dont l'un commande dans une petite place frontière, et dont l'autre est lieutenant dans la compagnie de son frère; enfin un des acteurs est un simple soldat.

These characters, he maintains, are more likely to produce a profound impression than 'des princes amoureux et des princesses passionnées: les théâtres ont assez retenti de ces aventures tragiques qui ne passent qu'entre des souverains, et qui sont de peu d'utilité pour le reste des hommes'. He almost apologizes for introducing an Emperor into his play, but points out that he does not appear until the very last scene, and then only to 'prononcer une loi telle que les anciens les feignaient dictées par les dieux'—in less enigmatic language, to proclaim the necessity for religious toleration.[2]

While it is true that in *Les Guèbres* all the main characters are of lowly origins, Voltaire can never have seriously expected the play to be performed at the Comédie Française, although he would no doubt dearly have liked to achieve such a *tour de force*. It is, in fact, little more than a pamphlet in dramatic form. *Les Scythes*, which was, as we have seen, performed in Paris, is, despite the preface, not nearly

---

[1] *Œuvres complètes*, vol. vi, pp. 267, 270.
[2] Ibid., vol. vi, pp. 491–2.

as unconventional in its choice of characters as Voltaire claims in his preface. His two Scythians, father and son, are no doubt of modest origins, but the heroine, Obéide, is the daughter of an exiled Persian general and court dignitary, while she is pursued by Athamare, who is no less a personage than the nephew of Cyrus and king of Ecbatana. Despite the revolutionary principles of the preface, the tragedy still remains mainly confined to persons of high rank.

What is more, important sections of the theatre-going public of the time were undoubtedly hostile to the introduction of any but illustrious personages into tragedy. It is true that De Belloy's *Siège de Calais* scored a phenomenal success at the Comédie Française in 1765, but Collé assures us that the 'gens de qualité' were hostile to it because of its bourgeois hero. The Comte d'Ayen is alleged to have declared that such a tragedy 'n'était bonne que pour des cordonniers', though later the courtiers were compelled to eat their words when they found that the play was so popular with Louis XV that it was given no fewer than three times in a month at Versailles. Even so, their real opinion, according to Collé, was extremely hostile: 'N'est-ce point qu'ils ont été révoltés de ce que les héros de cette pièce n'étaient que de plats bourgeois? Ils ont trouvé insolent que des *vilains* fussent des héros et que le seul traître de la pièce fût un seigneur de la plus grande maison.'[1]

The spectacle of the burghers of Calais on the stage of the Comédie Française did not inaugurate a rush of tragedies with bourgeois heroes; it was not indeed until the Revolution that such characters were to become common in tragedies performed in the different Paris theatres.[2] To say that, before 1789, they were exceptional would be an understatement. Indeed we find in tragedies of the second half of the eighteenth century examples of exactly the opposite process: the ennobling of characters of humble birth to raise them to the dignity of tragic heroes. For instance, in his *Spartacus* (1760) Saurin makes his hero into the son of a German prince. 'J'ai craint, je l'avouerai,' he declares in his preface, 'ce vers de Racine:

> Spartacus, un esclave, un vil gladiateur!

J'ai craint nos préjugés et notre délicatesse.'

In the shocked comments on Shakespeare made by many French critics of the eighteenth century one of the chief charges levelled against him is that he lacked any notion of the dignity of tragedy.

---

[1] *Journal*, vol. iii, p. 22 (Mar. 1765).
[2] Lancaster, *French Tragedy in the Reign of Louis XVI*, p. 159.

Instead of confining himself to portraying people of exalted birth he brought on to the stage a motley *canaille* of artisans, soldiers, and grave-diggers. Shakespeare also offended against other canons of the aristo-cratic taste of eighteenth-century France. He had no respect for the sacred rule of the *bienséances* in either the themes or the language of his plays. The low manners and speech of the vulgar characters whom he introduced into his tragedies even infected those of their betters and completely destroyed the solemn, dignified tone of tragedy. Instead of rigorously excluding all comic elements and all realistic and trivial scenes from his tragedies, Shakespeare wallowed in them and thus completely destroyed the atmosphere of tragedy. Judged by the aristo-cratic standards of taste of eighteenth-century France, his plays were bound to seem to all but a handful of the critics of the time the very antithesis of tragedy; despite their flashes of genius they appeared to be the outpourings of an ignorant barbarian whose only thought was to pander to the low instincts of the mob.

With only minor and generally timid modifications the *bienséances* continued to reign in French tragedy down to the Revolution. The *style noble* which likewise reflects the influence of polite society on French drama under the Ancien Régime was to keep its tyrannical hold over tragedy until the Romantic revolution of the 1820's. Playwrights like Voltaire deplored the excessive place given to love in French tragedy, especially compared with English drama; love, Voltaire main-tained, must either have the first place (as in his *Zaïre*) or be entirely banished (as in *Mérope*). Again and again in his prefaces and cor-respondence he blames the ladies for the preponderant place occupied by love in tragedy. A typical comment is to be found in one of his letters of the 1750's: 'Vos premières loges sont composées de personnes qui connaissent mieux l'amour que l'histoire romaine. Elles veulent s'attendrir, elles veulent pleurer, et avec le mot d'*amour* on a cause gagnée avec elles.'[1] One may beg leave to doubt whether an interest in this particular passion is confined to women, and whether amongst women it was in the eighteenth century the ladies of the aristocracy who attached most importance to its presence in tragedy, but certainly Voltaire lays the blame at their door.

As regards eighteenth-century French comedy there is a constant stream of complaints from the middle of the period onwards that, whereas Molière took in all classes of society in his plays, playwrights have tended to confine their attention more and more exclusively to the

[1] *Œuvres complètes*, vol. xxxix, p. 293.

portrayal of characters drawn from the upper ranks of society. The constant recurrence in so many eighteenth-century comedies of *Marquis*, *Comtesses*, and *Chevaliers*, with an occasional *Conseiller* or *Président* or perhaps a *Fermier général*, seems a striking anomaly in an age when the whole aristocratic façade of society was so soon to tumble into ruin. It is a curious form of the 'aristocratic reaction' which took place in many other fields in France in the second half of the eighteenth century, whether in an effort to squeeze the last penny in feudal dues out of the peasantry or to achieve and preserve a complete monopoly of all the higher posts in the state and the church.

Complaints and protests against this state of affairs came thick and fast from the middle of the century onwards. The earliest seems to have arisen out of the failure of the visit to London made in 1749 by a company of French actors led by Jean Monnet. According to a letter attributed to one of the actors, a certain Desormes,[1] a number of Englishmen who had been in France told him that they had been bored by the most popular modern French comedies, and wanted to see nothing but those of Molière. 'Ne serait-ce pas, Monsieur,' he continues, 'que les comédies d'aujourd'hui sont trop fines, trop dénuées d'action et ne portent que sur quelques nuances passagères affectées aux personnes du grand monde? Au lieu que Molière a peint des vices et des ridicules généraux qui conviennent à toutes les nations et à tous les états.' In 1758 the *Journal encyclopédique* makes a similar complaint about the narrow field depicted by contemporary authors of comedies. 'Pourquoi', it asks, 'les auteurs dramatiques ne choisissent-ils plus leurs modèles que parmi les géns du haut ton, ou parmi les courtisans? Des sujets bourgeois fourniraient des caractères plus saillants.'[2]

But this is as nothing compared with Rousseau's outburst in *La Nouvelle Héloïse*, which began its highly successful career three years later. Tragedy, Saint-Preux is made to declare during his visit to Paris, deals with subjects remote from the experience of ordinary people, while comedy, which ought to depict the manners of the nation for whom it is written, confines itself nowadays to reproducing 'les conversations d'une centaine de maisons de Paris'.

Hors de cela, on n'y apprend rien des mœurs des Français. Il y a dans cette grande ville cinq ou six cent mille âmes dont il n'est jamais question sur la

---

[1] Fréron, *Lettres sur quelques écrits de ce temps* (London, 1752), vol. ii, pp. 272 f. Quoted in M. and P. Fuchs, 'Comédiens français à Londres, 1738–1755', *Revue de littérature comparée* (1933), p. 64 n.

[2] *Journal encyclopédique*, Feb. 1758 (quoted in Gaïffe, *Le Drame*, p. 91).

scène. Molière osa peindre des bourgeois et des artisans aussi bien que des marquis; Socrate faisait parler des cochers, menuisiers, cordonniers, maçons. Mais les auteurs d'aujourd'hui qui sont des gens d'un autre air, se croiraient déshonorés s'ils savaient ce qui se passe au comptoir d'un marchand ou dans la boutique d'un ouvrier; il ne leur faut que des interlocuteurs illustres, et ils cherchent dans le rang de leurs personnages l'élévation qu'ils ne peuvent tirer de leur génie.

What is more, Saint-Preux is made to argue, that is what the theatre-going public wants:

Les spectateurs eux-mêmes sont devenus si délicats qu'ils craindraient de se compromettre à la comédie comme en visite, et ne daigneraient pas aller voir en représentation des gens de moindre condition qu'eux. Ils sont comme les seuls habitants de la terre; tout le reste n'est rien à leurs yeux. Avoir un carrosse, un suisse, un maître d'hôtel, c'est être comme tout le monde. Pour être comme tout le monde, il faut être comme très peu de gens. Ceux qui vont à pied ne sont pas du monde: ce sont des bourgeois, des hommes du peuple, des gens de l'autre monde, et l'on dirait qu'un carrosse n'est pas tant nécessaire pour se conduire que pour exister.

It is for this handful of fops, Saint-Preux declares, that the Paris theatres exist; this explains why the sphere of drama becomes ever more restricted and the modern theatre never puts off 'son ennuyeuse dignité'.

On ne sait plus montrer les hommes qu'en habit doré. Vous diriez que la France n'est peuplée que de comtes et de chevaliers, et plus le peuple y est misérable et gueux, plus le tableau du peuple y est brillant et magnifique. Cela fait qu'en peignant le ridicule des états qui servent d'exemple aux autres, on le répand plutôt que de l'éteindre, et que le peuple, toujours singe et imitateur des riches, va moins au théâtre pour rire de leurs folies que pour les étudier, et devenir encore plus fou qu'eux en les imitant.

Here, of course, we find the author of the *Lettre à D'Alembert* renewing his onslaught on the immorality of the theatre; he even goes so far as to accuse Molière of having corrected the court by infecting 'la ville' with its vices.[1]

It can well be imagined that a dozen years later Mercier would join in this attack on the narrow range of both comedy and tragedy. In a string of rhetorical questions he asks whether a playwright should simply follow in the tracks of his predecessors:

Ira-t-il réveiller les cendres des rois? Ne verra-t-il à peindre dans le monde que ces têtes à diadèmes? Ou, parmi ses concitoyens, s'arrêtera-t-il, comme

[1] *La Nouvelle Héloïse*, vol. ii, pp. 340–3.

poète du beau monde, sur les marquis élégants qui dans la comédie remplacent les rois, et qui prétendent donner à la société le ton qu'elle doive suivre? Agira-t-il comme s'il n'y avait que ces deux espèces d'hommes sur la terre?[1]

In his analysis of the weaknesses of modern comedy he declares that irony has become the favourite instrument of the playwright 'parce qu'elle est celle du beau monde; et ce beau monde est composé de trois à quatre cents fats qui ne savent comment exister'. Authors of comedies do not depict such useless creatures in order to make them blush, but in order to 'perfectionner leur ton licencieux et frivole et pour le distribuer en détail au reste de la nation'. Instead of copying the manners of a hundred or so households, the comic writer ought to study the great mass of mankind. He concludes with a violent on-slaught on the corruption of the aristocracy of his day:

La comédie doit-elle étaler nécessairement le ridicule des grands, leur langage, leurs manières, leur jargon, leur morale? Nous faut-il sur la scène des sybarites, des railleurs élégants, des originaux vicieux, des persifleurs, des hommes de cour? Oui, je le dirai hautement, il en faut si l'on veut étendre une corruption générale; il nous faut alors des marquis, des comtes, de petits ducs, avec leur langage fade, leur sourire dédaigneux, le ton apprêté de leur mollesse.[2]

Mercier returns to the attack in the preface to his *drame*, *Molière*, first published in 1776. He complains that since the death of his hero the field of comedy, which he had enlarged, has greatly contracted: 'On n'a plus voulu y admettre que certains hommes choisis et distingués par leurs titres et leur naissance, c'est-à-dire, les seuls que le poète était censé pouvoir fréquenter décemment.' The playwrights who fol-lowed Molière have replaced 'le vaste tableau de la nation' which is to be found in his comedies by 'de jolies miniatures, brillantes, pointil-lées et froides'. Whereas Molière gave to comedy 'un front populaire', they have degenerated into mannerism and affectation: 'Les marquis modernes, en expulsant les bourgeois, chassèrent le naturel et la sim-plicité.' Taking up the complaint that Molière had exhausted the great comic types, he adds that in their impotence his successors have even declared that the populace no longer has the colourful and picturesque character which it once possessed. 'De là naquirent ces copies rebattues qui vont encore en s'affaiblissant; le trait original s'éloigna et disparut.'[3]

Mercier comes back again to the subject in his *Tableau de Paris*. Since

---

[1] *Du Théâtre, ou Nouvel Essai sur l'art dramatique*, p. 16.
[2] Ibid., pp. 78–80.
[3] *Théâtre complet* (Amsterdam, 1778–84), 4 vols., vol. iii, pp. 223–4.

Molière, he declares, comedy has lost its gaiety and naturalness by ceasing to depict the bourgeois: 'Le poète, pour faire imaginer qu'il fréquentait la noble compagnie, n'a plus voulu faire parler que des ducs, des comtesses et des marquises; il a raffiné à tout propos le style et les idées, et il a créé des expressions recherchées.' Indeed, he goes on to claim, not only did the bourgeois not appreciate and understand this new jargon, neither did the 'gens du monde': 'C'est de l'esprit d'auteur, a-t-on dit; c'est lui qui parle, et non ses personnages. Il a voulu faire sa comédie pour les premières loges, et il n'a pas même réussi devant elles.'[1]

Looking back at eighteenth-century comedy from the other side of the Revolution of 1789, Pixerécourt joins in the chorus of reprobation which was earlier directed against the aristocratic 'monopoly' of comedy:

La comédie ne marchait pas de son côté d'un pas plus ferme vers la morale publique. Le *Misanthrope*, le *Tartufe* étaient déserts.[2] Le jargon entortillé et décousu des hautes sociétés; les pointes émoussées des sentiments factices; les petits sarcasmes de l'instant; les portraits au pastel de quelques ridicules; cinq actes de jeux de mots, et pas une scène de comique, encore moins d'instruction; des maîtres roués, les femmes ou trompées ou perfides, sans regrets comme sans remords, des soubrettes à prétentions, des valets de bonne compagnie: telle était la manière dont on paraphrasait le *Castigat ridendo mores*.[3]

It was frequently held against authors of comedies in our period that they did not know at first hand the high society which it was, or should have been, their aim to depict. Raynal criticizes severely Panard's one-act play, *Les Tableaux*, which was performed at the Théâtre Italien in 1747, because, he maintains, its portrayal of a Paris household is not true to life. 'C'est tout au plus celle des faubourgs ou de certains quartiers habités uniquement par le même peuple que l'auteur paraît assez bien connaître. Il semble que M. Panard n'ait jamais vu des palais et des hôtels que les façades ou les jardins, et qu'il n'ait jamais percé dans l'intérieur pour y voir ceux qui les habitent.'[4] It is interesting that Collé, writing in his Journal on the death of Panard in 1765, should have complained that this playwright had confined himself too much to bour-

---

[1] *Tableau de Paris*, vol. iv, pp. 110–11.
[2] Though it is true that these comedies were given less frequently at the Comédie Française in the second half of the eighteenth century than in the first, there is considerable exaggeration here.
[3] Estève, 'Observations de Guilbert de Pixerécourt', pp. 550–1.
[4] *Nouvelles littéraires* in Grimm, *Correspondance littéraire*, vol. i, p. 102.

geois society, not to mention that he had spent too much of his time in taverns in the company of drunken actors and writers: 'Le peintre des mœurs doit tâcher de voir tout le monde, depuis le prince du sang jusqu'au quincailler', he maintains. In a day when literary patronage was still far from dead, Collé held that a playwright should endeavour to have some first-hand knowledge of men of both high rank and great wealth: 'Il ne faut les voir que passagèrement, et ne point vivre avec eux: dans le peu de temps que l'on les voit, les beaucoup étudier pour en accroître son talent, et les faire servir, d'un autre côté, honnêtement à l'accroissement de sa petite fortune.'[1]

At the same date, Collé severely castigated Bret for his comedy, *Le Mariage par dépit*, the one performance of which at the Comédie Française did not get beyond the second act. 'Il n'a nullement le ton du grand monde', he complains, 'et au contraire il met souvent à sa place le ton trivial et bas des sociétés bourgeoises qu'il voit, et même le ton de province, qui n'est point goûté à Paris.'[2] This gradation of blame from 'bourgeois' to 'provincial' is an interesting commentary on the hold of the high society of Paris over French drama less than a quarter of a century before the Revolution.

Poinsinet's attempt to portray high society and its foibles in his little comedy, *Le Cercle ou la Soirée à la mode*, performed at the Comédie Française in 1764, also aroused the sarcasm of contemporary critics who declared that his play showed the author's lack of knowledge of such circles. 'On voit à chaque ligne', says Grimm,[3] 'que M. Poinsinet n'a pas vécu dans la meilleure compagnie du royaume.' Bachaumont is equally critical: 'On trouve le petit Poinsinet bien peu délicat, bien bourgeois, pour tracer les mœurs du grand monde, et nous rendre les formes fragiles de pareils personnages.' A few days later he renews this criticism: 'L'on sent que l'auteur n'a vu la bonne compagnie que de loin; il n'y a pas cette touche fine et légère, qui désigne l'homme du grand monde.'[4]

This monopoly of comedy by characters drawn from high society extended to a marked degree even into the new genre of the *Drame*. Its predecessors in the first half of the century—the serious, moralizing comedies of Destouches and the *comédies larmoyantes* of Nivelle de La Chaussée—had portrayed characters drawn from the upper classes

---

[1] *Journal*, vol. iii, pp. 35–36 (June 1765).
[2] Ibid., p. 33.
[3] *Correspondance littéraire*, vol. vi, p. 89.
[4] *Mémoires secrets*, vol. xvi, p. 218 (2 and 8 Sept. 1764).

of eighteenth-century French society. It is true that in such wholly uncomic plays as *Mélanide* (1741) and *La Gouvernante* (1747), La Chaussée depicts the misfortunes and sufferings of people drawn from contemporary society, and not, as in tragedy, the calamities which befall heroes and heroines drawn from remote countries and ages and of illustrious birth; but his characters are taken from the upper ranks of the society of his day. The same tendency continues to be visible in the *Drame* in the second half of the century.

It is nearly fifty years ago since Félix Gaiffe, in his masterly work, *Le Drame en France au XVIIIᵉ siècle*, put forward his well-known definition of the new dramatic genre: 'un spectacle destiné à un auditoire bourgeois ou populaire et lui présentant un tableau attendrissant et moral de son propre milieu'.[1] This definition, like any other, invites critical comment. After our examination of the theatre audiences of eighteenth-century Paris it is impossible to accept the notion that any play of the time, which was written for performance at either of the two privileged theatres, the Comédie Française and the Théâtre Italien, could conceivably have been written exclusively for 'un auditoire bourgeois ou populaire'. The high society of the capital played far too prominent a part in the theatrical life of eighteenth-century Paris right down to 1789 for this first half of the definition to go unchallenged. It may, of course, be argued, and it will be in the pages which follow, that the more aristocratic taste of the audiences of the privileged theatres and particularly the Comédie Française tended to compel writers in the new genre to have their plays performed either in the provinces or even in the humble Théâtres du Boulevard. Yet aristocratic taste was by no means uniformly hostile to the *Drame*. Louis XV, it is true, would have nothing to do with the new genre. Bachaumont tells us that in settling the list of plays to be performed before the court at Fontainebleau in 1769, the King 'a rayé de sa main le *Philosophe sans le savoir, Eugénie* et *Beverley*, par la raison que ces drames tristes et lugubres ne convenaient point à son âge, qui n'avait besoin que de choses agréables et gaies'.[2] But Saurin's *Beverley, tragédie bourgeoise* was performed by high-born amateur actors in the houses of the aristocracy before being given at the Comédie Française. In his dedication to the Duc d'Orléans, the first Prince of the Blood, the author declares: 'Une pièce honorée des larmes et du suffrage de Votre Altesse ne pouvait manquer de réussir.' The Duc d'Orléans and his actors gave hospitality not only to *Beverley*, but also to Collé's *Partie de chasse de*

[1] p. 93. [2] *Mémoires secrets*, vol. xix, p. 91 (30 June 1769).

Henri IV, while *L'Honnête Criminel* of Fenouillot de Falbaire was performed at the house of Mme de Villeroi.[1]

The second half of Gaiffe's definition—that the *Drame* offered the bourgeois or plebeian audience 'un tableau attendrissant et moral de son propre milieu'—cannot be accepted either without serious qualifications. It is no doubt true that the *Drame* offers a broad picture of eighteenth-century French society from the aristocracy down to the lower orders of town and country. Gaiffe admits the presence of noblemen in such plays, but reduces their importance to modest proportions: 'Outre que ces gentilshommes ne jouent pas toujours le rôle le plus important ni le plus sympathique, partout le milieu est dominé par les idées, les sentiments, les manières de la bourgeoisie, et les plus humbles classes de la société y figurent en bonne posture. . . .'[2]

Bourgeois in spirit the *Drame* may be, whether its aim was to depict contemporary life or to portray events from past history. Collé's *Partie de chasse de Henri IV* depicts the worthy peasants of the time as well as the King and his courtiers. When it was first performed at the Comédie Française in 1774, it drew from the pen of Mlle de Lespinasse the indignant outburst:

> Oh! la détestable pièce! que l'auteur est bourgeois, et qu'il a un esprit commun et borné! que le public est bête! que la bonne compagnie est de mauvais goût! . . . Si vous saviez comment ce public a applaudi! Molière ne pourrait pas prétendre à un plus grand succès. Il n'y a de noble que les noms et les habits: l'auteur fait parler les gens de la cour et Henri IV du ton des bourgeois de la rue Saint Denis. Il est vrai qu'il donne le même ton aux paysans.[3]

Yet, however bourgeois in outlook the *Drame* may be, the fact remains that the characters actually portrayed in plays of this type are very often much more exalted in social rank than Gaiffe's definition would lead one to believe.

As early as 1742 Landois, in the prologue to his *Silvie*, had made a plea for the introduction into drama of characters whose lives had 'un peu plus de rapport avec celle des spectateurs'.[4] Fifteen years later, in his *Entretiens sur le Fils Naturel*, Diderot claimed for domestic tragedy that it portrayed characters drawn from a world close to that of the average spectator, and not from a more or less remote past:

---

[1] Gaiffe, *Le Drame en France*, p. 205.
[2] Ibid., p. 97.
[3] *Lettres*, ed. G. Isambert (Paris, 1876), 2 vols., vol. i, p. 201.
[4] Sc. 3 (p. 10).

Elle est plus voisine de nous. C'est le tableau des malheurs qui nous environnent. Quoi! vous ne concevez pas l'effet que produiraient sur vous une scène réelle, des habits vrais, des discours proportionnés aux actions, des actions simples, des dangers dont il est impossible que vous n'ayez tremblé pour vos parents, vos amis, pour vous-même?[1]

Yet if we look closely at the *drames* which were successfully performed at the Comédie Française between 1760 and the Revolution, we find that they most frequently depict characters drawn from the upper classes of society: if not always from the aristocracy, at least on the fringe of it. Like other authors of *drames* Diderot himself was content to take his characters from the same restricted social groups depicted in the great majority of the comedies of his day.

In his *Fils Naturel* he portrays people of wealth with carriages and servants, of whom at least one, Clairville, is a nobleman. If, when at last produced at the Comédie Française in 1771, this play did not get beyond one performance, the *Père de Famille*, after only a modest success in 1761, was given on several occasions every year between its revival in 1769 and 1789 (108 times in all) and, incredible as it may seem to the modern reader, was given there as late as 1839. Gaiffe takes the picture of family life presented in the *Père de Famille* as an illustration of the startling contrast offered in the *Drame* between the corruption of the aristocracy and the solid moral standards of the middle classes and peasants.[2] But Diderot's hero, M. d'Orbesson, is clearly presented to us as a nobleman. His aristocratic brother-in-law, M. le Commandeur d'Auvillé, is indeed portrayed in an unfavourable light, but he is by no means the only representative of the nobility in the play. M. d'Orbesson is depicted as a landowner with an *intendant*.[3] What is more striking still is the way in which his son, Saint-Albin, is depicted as a nobleman in the important scene in which M. d'Orbesson endeavours to dissuade him from pursuing further his passion for Sophie. 'Quelle est donc la femme qui me convient?' asks Saint-Albin. 'Celle', replies D'Orbesson, 'qui par son éducation, *sa naissance*, son état et sa fortune, peut assurer votre bonheur et satisfaire à mes espérances.' To this Saint-Albin retorts: 'Il me faut une compagne honnête et sensible, qui m'apprenne à supporter les peines de la vie, et non une femme riche *et titrée* qui les accroisse.' The point is stressed again in the long speech of D'Orbesson: 'Lorsque je me félicite d'avoir un fils qui répond à *sa naissance* qui

---

[1] *Œuvres complètes*, vol. vii, p. 146.
[2] *Le Drame en France*, p. 368.
[3] Act II, Sc. 1.

le destine aux meilleurs partis, et à ses qualités personnelles qui l'appel-
lent aux grands emplois, une passion insensée, la fantaisie d'un instant
aura tout détruit.' 'Vous avez', he goes on, '*un nom*, des parents, des
amis, les prétentions les plus flatteuses et les mieux fondées; et vous êtes
malheureux?' Another remark of Saint-Albin in this scene underlines
yet again his noble rank: 'Vous avez vu Sophie! ... Si je la quitte *pour
un rang*, des dignités, des espérances, des préjugés, je ne mériterai pas de
la connaître.'[1] No doubt the inspiration behind the *Père de Famille* is
thoroughly bourgeois, but not only do its main characters belong to the
upper classes of eighteenth-century French society; they all belong unquestionably to the aristocracy.

Le Philosophe sans le savoir, the most long-lived of the *drames*
produced in the last decades of the Ancien Régime, is even more
interesting for this clash between bourgeois outlook and aspirations
and the choice of aristocratic characters. This play is no doubt, to use
Gaiffe's words, 'l'œuvre de la bourgeoisie enrichie et éclairée'. Yet he
concedes that there is something artificial about the portrayal of the
merchant in the person of M. Vanderk. 'Sedaine a été pris entre son
sujet et sa thèse. La thèse tendait à la glorification de la bourgeoisie
philosophe: l'épisode du duel exigeait que les adversaires fussent de
condition.'[2] Vanderk *fils* is a naval officer, and we gradually learn that
his father is of noble birth. After fighting a duel in his youth, he had
been forced to flee the country, had become the partner of a Dutch
merchant and had married the love of his youth, the daughter of a
nobleman of his native province. His son-in-law occupies 'une des
premières places de la robe'. Even his warm praise of the merchant and
his calling—one of the *poncifs* of eighteenth-century French literature
—is modified by his final words on the question: 'Il n'y a peut-être que
deux états au-dessus du commerçant ...: le magistrat, qui fait parler les
lois, et le guerrier, qui défend la patrie.'[3] It is difficult to decide to what
extent Sedaine's rather curious choice of a nobleman as a representative
type of the merchant of his day is due to the technical requirements of
the plot of his play which demanded for the duel a character of noble
birth, or to the prevailing tendency in comedy to depict characters
drawn from the upper classes of contemporary society, but it is none
the less clear that the portrayal of Vanderk is considerably modified by
the social origins which Sedaine gives his hero.

[1] Act II, Sc. 6.
[2] *Le Philosophe sans le savoir*, ed. F. Gaiffe (Paris, n.d.), pp. 10–11.
[3] Act II, Sc. 4.

In the first of Beaumarchais's two *drames*, *Eugénie* (1767),[1] the scene of the action was finally shifted to England, but here there is no question of bourgeois characters: the characters, on the contrary, are members of the English aristocracy. The heroine's father is 'le Baron Hartley', her brother goes under the name of 'Sir Charles', while her lover and bogus husband is 'le Lord Comte de Clarendon'. It is true that his second and much less successful *drame*, *Les Deux Amis ou le Négociant de Lyon* (1770),[2] brings us back to France and indeed to the commercial life of Lyons. Beaumarchais assured a correspondent:

J'aurais été bien trompé dans mes vues si le commerçant que j'ai cherché à montrer dans le plus beau jour en cet ouvrage n'était pas satisfait du rôle digne et honnête que je fais jouer à un homme de son état. . . . Je souhaite qu'elle plaise aux négociants, cette pièce qui a été faite pour eux et en général pour honorer les gens du tiers état.[3]

The praise of the merchant put into the mouth of his hero, Aurelly, is more fulsome still than that in Sedaine's play:

Je fais battre journellement deux cents métiers dans Lyon. Le triple de bras est nécessaire aux apprêts de mes soies. Mes plantations de mûriers et mes vers en occupent autant. Mes envois se détaillent chez tous les marchands du royaume; tout cela vit, tout cela gagne, et, l'industrie portant le prix des matières au centuple, il n'y a pas une de ces créatures, à commencer par moi, qui ne rende gaiement à l'état un tribut proportionné au gain que son émulation lui procure. . . . Et tout l'or que la guerre disperse, Messieurs, qui le fait rentrer à la paix? Qui osera disputer au Commerce l'honneur de rendre à l'état épuisé le nerf et les richesses qu'il n'a plus? Tous les citoyens sentent l'importance de cette tâche: le négociant seul la remplit. Au moment que le guerrier se repose, le négociant a l'honneur d'être à son tour l'homme de la patrie.[4]

Yet who are the characters in this play written 'pour honorer les gens du tiers état'? A *fermier général* who is no Turcaret, but, as the list of characters rather naïvely informs us, an 'homme du monde estimable'; a member of the wealthy class of *receveurs généraux des fermes*, who as the younger son of a provincial nobleman began his career as an army

---

[1] Historians of the theatre sometimes fail to distinguish between the merits of this play, which are negligible, and its contemporary success, which was considerable. It was given 23 times in 1767 and had reached 94 performances by 1789. It was given four times at the Comédie Française as late as 1863, making 192 performances in all.

[2] It reached twelve performances in 1770, but, after two more in 1783, it disappeared for ever from the Comédie Française.

[3] *Théâtre complet: Lettres relatives à son théâtre*, ed. M. Allem (Paris, 1934), pp. 543–4.

[4] Act II, Sc. 10.

officer; and finally the merchant, who is not only a 'riche négociant de Lyon', but has just acquired *lettres de noblesse* (presumably, like Beaumarchais himself, he might have said of his noble rank: 'Personne n'oserait me la disputer, car j'en ai la quittance!'). Even if Beaumarchais transports his spectators to the despised provinces and shows his main characters at grips with commercial and financial problems, the persons he depicts remain well within the orbit of the upper classes of the society of his day.

The same is on the whole true of the characters portrayed in Saurin's *tragédie bourgeoise, Beverley*, adapted from Moore's *Gamester*.[1] There is no precise description of the social position of the main characters, but it is made clear that, but for his incurable vice of gaming, the hero would lead a rich and comfortable existence. In the course of the play he receives 300,000 livres from Cadiz, and with this money he proposes to buy back

> cet antique héritage
> Par mes pères transmis jusqu'à moi d'âge en âge,
> Que j'ai vendu presque pour rien.

From the scenes in Act IV in which he challenges Leuson, his sister's fiancé, to a duel, it is clear that both have been army officers. On the whole it may be said that Saurin slightly ennobled the hero of his *tragédie bourgeoise* in the process of adapting Moore's play.[2] His subject is indeed modern, but scarcely specifically bourgeois.

Another *drame* which scored a modest success when it was first performed at the Comédie Française in 1769 and had reached thirty-eight performances by 1789, was the Marquis de Longueil's *L'Orphelin anglais*. The setting of this play is the London of Edward III. The principal characters are two carpenters, Thomas Frick and his son-in-law, Thomas Spencer, along with Mistriss Molly, their daughter and wife. The setting of Act I stresses that the milieu depicted is that of

---

[1] Lancaster discusses Saurin's play in his *French Tragedy in the Time of Louis XV* as if it were a straightforward tragedy, but in his dedication Saurin speaks of it as belonging to 'un genre qui, quoique très inférieur au genre héroïque, ne laisse pas d'avoir des beautés qui lui sont propres'. In his *Discours de réception* Condorcet declared that 'à ces ouvrages [his tragedies and comedies] M. Saurin fit succéder un drame, et eut la gloire, unique jusqu'ici, d'avoir laissé au théâtre des pièces dans chacun des trois genres qui partagent la scène française' (*Œuvres*, vol. i, p. 408).

[2] In the English play Beverley and his family are shown in lodgings; in Saurin's they still inhabit his mansion, though it is stripped of all its rich furnishings. In Act IV of Moore's play Beverley draws his sword on Lewson, but there is no question of their having been officers. There is a reference in Act I of the *Gamester* to the way Beverley has squandered his wife's fortune and 'his own large estate', but not to 'cet antique héritage ...'.

artisans: 'Le théâtre représente l'arrière-boutique d'un menuisier; on y voit plusieurs ouvrages finis, les plus recherchés, et composés avec autant de grâce que d'élégance; d'autres sont à part, et moins bien que les premiers.' Although it is made clear that the two carpenters are highly skilled men, working for an aristocratic clientèle and producing very expensive work, we seem for once to be confronted in an eighteenth-century *drame* with characters drawn rom the middle or even lower ranks of society. Yet this impression is almost destroyed in Act II when the virtuous nobleman, Lord Kiston, a foil to his wicked sister, Lady Lallin, appears on the scene to inform Thomas Spencer, an orphan who had been adopted by Thomas Frick and had finally married his daughter, that he is 'le fils et l'héritier du Comte de Glocester; par conséquent Lord dès votre naissance'. The question now arises whether the King will consent to recognize Mistriss Molly, a mere commoner, as the lawful spouse of such a powerful vassal as Thomas Spencer has become, or whether he will declare the marriage null and void. After much anguished uncertainty everything is straightened out in the last scene of the play, when the King, touched by Molly's self-sacrifice, recognizes her as 'Lady Spencer'. Despite the relatively humble milieu presented at the beginning of the play two of the main characters are suddenly pushed up into the aristocracy.

The same tendency is visible up to a point in another *drame* presented at the Comédie Française in these years, *Le Fabricant de Londres* of Fenouillot de Falbaire, despite the author's clearly expressed purpose of producing a play with thoroughly bourgeois characters. In his preface, written after his play's one and only performance in 1771, the author explains his purpose in writing it:

Quand nous sortons du spectacle, après la représentation d'une belle tragédie, nous rencontrons rarement des princes fugitifs, des rois détrônés, qui puissent profiter de l'attendrissement que nous venons d'éprouver. Mais nous voyons chaque jour enlever et vendre les effets de citoyens malheureux, qui auraient besoin de notre commisération, auxquels nous pourrions accorder d'utiles secours, et dont une pitié généreuse préviendrait la ruine.

After recalling a recent touching incident when 'un prince connu par sa bienfaisance et son humanité' paid the debts of an unfortunate man whose goods were being carried off to be sold as he happened to pass by, Fenouillot de Falbaire declares that his aim is to encourage similar acts of generosity and underlines the thoroughly bourgeois theme of his *drame*:

J'ai voulu mettre sur la scène une famille bourgeoise, tombante dans cet état d'infortune, et . . . je me suis proposé d'en présenter un tableau simple, naturel et tout à fait vrai. Je me suis dit: Je commencerai par peindre l'intérieur de la maison de mon fabricant, je tâcherai de faire aimer ceux qui l'habitent; et quand j'aurai bien familiarisé mon spectateur avec tous mes personnages, qu'il aura, pour ainsi dire, vécu quelque temps avec eux dans l'intimité domestique, je lui montrerai le désastre de cette même maison, et il en sera plus vivement affecté.

The hero of *Le Fabricant de Londres*, Vilson, is a cloth-maker who employs six workmen and two clerks. When the play opens, his normally prosperous business is threatened with catastrophe through the failure of a Norwich banker. This calamity happens on the very day that he embarks upon a second marriage, and he thus ruins not only himself and his two children, but also his wife and mother-in-law who give everything they possess to avert the catastrophe. Yet into this straightforward bourgeois tragedy the author works two aristocratic subplots. First we learn early in the play that Vilson's fiancée, Fanni, and her mother have turned down the pressing offer of marriage made by a nobleman who rejoices in the name of Lord Orsey; while already in the second act there appears upon the scene a Scottish nobleman, Lord Falkland, now a widower, who is searching feverishly for a long-lost daughter and her (unmarried) mother. As in the first act the spectator has been told the touching story of how Vilson's mother-in-law had been seduced by the said Lord Falkland before he was compelled by his father to marry a noblewoman, he is prepared for a touching reunion later in the play. This is postponed until the last act, when Falkland, who has been told that the two women he is seeking are dead, meets near Westminster Bridge the unfortunate Vilson, who has decided to save his wife and children from poverty by drowning himself and thus leaving Fanni free to marry Lord Orsey. 'Faisons du moins encore une bonne action avant que de mourir!' exclaims Falkland; he promises to pay Vilson's debts, and at that very moment the latter's wife and mother-in-law appear upon the scene. Lord Falkland is thus happily reunited with his former love and his daughter. In a splendid final scene Vilson throws himself at the feet of his benefactor, who has now become his father-in-law:

Falkland, le retenant, et l'embrassant encore.
    Appelle-moi ton père . . . Oui, je le suis, je veux l'être. Je te charge du bonheur de ma fille, et vous vous unirez tous deux à moi, pour rendre heureuse enfin . . . (*Il se rejette dans les bras de Madame Sonbridge*) une amante, une épouse dont je causai si longtemps les peines et les douleurs.

In his essay on drama Louis-Sébastien Mercier makes an eloquent
defence of characters of humble birth on the stage against the prevailing
prejudice:

Mais voir les conditions humaines les plus basses, les plus rampantes!
ajoutera-t-on encore, les mettre sur la scène! un tisserand! un ouvrier! un
journalier! Et pourquoi pas? Homme dédaigneux, approche; que je te juge à
ton tour. Qui es-tu? qui te donne le droit d'être hautain? Je vois ton habit,
tes laquais, tes chevaux, ton équipage; mais toi, que fais-tu? ... Tu souris, je
t'entends; tu es homme de cour, tu consumes tes jours dans une inaction
frivole, dans des intrigues puériles, dans des fatigues ambitieuses et risibles.
Tu ruines tes créanciers pour paraître un homme *comme il faut*.

We may spare the reader half a page of the best Mercier vituperation
and jump to the conclusion:

Verge avilie du despotisme, un tisserand, son bonnet sur la tête, me paraît
plus estimable et plus utile que toi. Si je te mets sur la scène, ce sera pour la
honte. Mais ces ouvriers, ces artisans peuvent y paraître avec noblesse; ce sont
des hommes, que je reconnais tels à leurs mœurs, à leurs travaux. Et toi, né
pour l'opprobre du genre humain, plût à Dieu que tu fusses mort à l'instant
de ta naissance![1]

The campaign for bourgeois and even plebeian characters in drama
aroused the satirical criticisms of contemporaries. In the preface to *Le
Roué vertueux, poème en prose en quatre chants, propre à faire, en cas de
besoin, un Drame à jouer deux fois par semaine*, Coqueley de Chasse-
pierre, the lawyer of the Comédie Française, ironically asks:

Car enfin, comment veut-on qu'un honnête bourgeois de Paris, un philosophe, un académicien, une marquise, si l'on veut, prenne plus d'intérêt aux
malheurs de Cinna, de Britannicus, de Thyeste ou de Sémiramis, qu'à ceux
de son menuisier, qui a boisé sa chambre, qui laisse une femme et des enfants
dans la plus affreuse misère, et qu'on a cent fois vu venir chez soi? Notre
cœur a son optique, ainsi que notre œil, et les objets le frappent moins en
raison de la distance où ils sont de lui.

In a parody of the best sentimental, rhetorical prose of the time, he
exclaims:

Oh! divine Philosophie! pourquoi nous avoir laissés si longtemps dans
l'erreur? Oh! humanité! est-il donc quelque chose qui puisse vous être
étranger? Tous les hommes ne sont-ils pas égaux à vos yeux? Est-il des rangs,
des conditions, des lois même, pour le cœur? Le maçon, le vidangeur, le
menuisier, le galérien, ne sont-ils donc pas des hommes? Eh, quelle femme de

---

[1] *Du Théâtre, ou Nouvel Essai sur l'art dramatique*, pp. 137-8.

qualité ne rougirait pas de refuser ses larmes aux malheurs qui accableraient la famille d'un de ces individus, et qui viendraient déchirer son cœur *paternel*?[1]

Another ironical attack on the portrayal on the stage of characters drawn from the lower orders appeared in a pseudo-*drame*, published in 1777 by another lawyer, Jean-Henri Marchand.[2] The hero of *Le Vidangeur sensible*, the scene of which is set in London, bears the appropriate name of William Sentfort. The aim of the author, according to the *Avertissement de l'éditeur*, was to 'jeter une sorte de ridicule sur les dénouements trop noirs et trop atroces, et sur les personnages trop bas qu'on voudrait introduire au théâtre'. The *Dissertation sur le Drame* which follows contains an ironical defence of the new genre and of the choice of the lowly character who is the hero of the play. 'J'ai pensé', declares the author, 'qu'on verrait sans dégoût, et même avec plaisir, dans un vidangeur toutes les vertus qui distinguent l'honnête homme, le bon citoyen.' Why should people disapprove of such a person being brought on to the stage? 'C'est un citoyen comme un autre, c'est un homme qui s'emploie à procurer la propreté et la salubrité nécessaires dans une grande ville.' In the concluding paragraph the author ironically declares: 'Ceux qui ont prétendu qu'on pourrait faire paraître dans un drame les gens de la plus vile populace, seront satisfaits puisque mon principal héros est un vidangeur, et que je me suis permis de tout peindre, jusqu'à un combat à coups de poings.'[3]

It is, however, interesting that after all Mercier's outcry about the imperative necessity of introducing characters of humble rank into drama and after all the ridicule which such a notion inevitably aroused in the society of pre-Revolutionary France, his application of the theory in his own *drames* is extraordinary timid. Several of his plays have as their principal characters men and women drawn from the upper classes of the society of the day, even indeed from the despised aristocracy. The characters of *Natalie* and *Les Faux Amis* are certainly drawn from the upper classes, while in *Zoé* all the four main characters are of noble birth. In *Jenneval*, Mercier's version of Lillo's *London Merchant*, we come slightly lower down the social scale, but the main characters of his *drame* are of solid bourgeois stock. The principal characters of *Le Déserteur* are more mixed: we have a soldier who has risen from the ranks, and his son, the deserter, who in civil life has become manager of the business of a manufacturer's widow, with a

---

[1] *Le Roué vertueux* (Lausanne, 1770), pp. 7, 9.
[2] In collaboration with Nougaret, according to Gaiffe (*Le Drame en France*, p. 576).
[3] *Le Vidangeur sensible*, ed. L. Faucou (Paris, 1880), pp. 24–27.

daughter whom he is on the point of marrying. There is also an empty-headed young nobleman who chases anything in petticoats, but in the end magnanimously tries to save the deserter's life.

In *Le Juge* an important part is played by a real peasant and his wife and family; the main theme of the play is their struggle to preserve their land against the selfish schemings of the lord of the manor. M. de Leurye, the latter's judge, appears as a thoroughly bourgeois character until, by one of those ridiculous *coups de théâtre* in which Mercier delights, he is suddenly transformed into the son of the lord of the manor whose schemings he has just thwarted. This device which brings about the inevitable recognition scene is a favourite one with Mercier, as with many other eighteenth-century dramatists; it can, as we shall see, almost nullify the picture of bourgeois or even plebeian life which he offers in his plays.

La Brouette du Vinaigrier certainly seems to promise a plebeian hero. It is true that the action takes place in the house of a wealthy business man, but there, sure enough, we meet the vinegar-merchant, complete with his wheelbarrow. 'On ne manquera pas', Mercier declares in his preface, 'même avant que d'avoir lu la pièce, de dire: "*La Brouette du Vinaigrier*! quel sujet! ... Les personnages de ce drame sont trop bas!" J'ai prévu le reproche, et je l'ai bravé.' This is scarcely true, as he proceeds to admit in the next few lines. In the forty-five years during which he has plied his wares, the vinegar-merchant has amassed a very considerable fortune which he wheels on to the stage in time to convince his son's prospective father-in-law that he is a worthy suitor for his daughter. 'Me voilà donc réconcilié avec le *bon goût*', Mercier exclaims. 'Ma brouette ... peut se présenter en bonne compagnie; elle aura l'air de ces gens qu'on reçoit sous des habits mesquins, parce que l'on sait qu'il ne tient qu'à eux d'être vêtus autrement. Voilà donc ma brouette anoblie, ou je ne m'y connais pas.'[1] He cannot have it both ways: if his vinegar-merchant, along with his wheelbarrow, is ennobled by his accumulated wealth, then he ceases to belong to the lower orders.

At first sight, at least, *L'Indigent* is the most plebeian of Mercier's *drames*. The play opens with a startling picture of sordid toil and poverty. 'Le théâtre', so the stage directions run,

représente une misérable salle basse sans cheminée. Les tabourets sont dépaillés. Les meubles sont d'un bois usé. Un morceau de tapisserie cache un grabat. On voit d'un côté un métier de tisserand, au-dessous d'un vitrage

---

[1] *Théâtre complet*, vol. iii, p. 216.

vieux, dont la moitié est réparée avec du papier. On aperçoit dans un petit cabinet, dont la porte est entr'ouverte, le pied d'un petit lit.

In these poverty-stricken surroundings, unheated in the depth of winter, live and toil Joseph, a weaver, and his sister, Charlotte, a lace-maker. It is four in the morning, and Joseph is labouring away at his loom, while his sister is snatching an hour or two's sleep. As if to emphasize their poverty, a noisy carousal is going on in another part of the house which has been rebuilt to lodge a rich and extravagant young man. The weaver and his sister, we learn, come from the country and slave away night and day to earn enough money to secure the release of their white-haired father who is imprisoned for debt. Yet the whole effect of this sordid poverty is very nearly cancelled out when, later in the play, the rich young man whose revels have disturbed Charlotte's sleep and who, incidentally, tries to seduce her, turns out to be Joseph's cousin and the brother of Charlotte, who is the heiress to half a very large fortune. They can thus return to the country with Joseph's father, now released from prison, to live a life of rustic happiness, with ample money to indulge their typically eighteenth-century passion for *bienfaisance*. If the play opens with a startling contrast between the honest, toiling poor and the hard-hearted and debauched rich, it ends in a typical *sensiblerie*; in the process the portrayal of the tribulations of the poorer classes of Mercier's day has vanished entirely from sight.

From the very beginning the whole attempt to depict in the *drame* or *tragédie bourgeoise* characters drawn from the middle and lower ranks of contemporary society had met with fierce opposition, as was natural in the aristocratic society of the day. In the prologue to the very first play of this kind, Landois's *Sylvie*, which was given two performances at the Comédie Française in 1742, the author deals with 'le grand reproche . . . d'avoir traité un sujet *bas*'.[1] *Sylvie* certainly met with a somewhat cold reception, and later those critics who reflected the aristocratic taste of Paris were to adopt the same disdainful attitude towards plays deal-ing with ordinary people. Grimm, in the *Correspondance littéraire*, speaks contemptuously of Beaumarchais's second *drame*, *Les Deux Amis*, written, as we have seen, 'en l'honneur du tiers état'. If part of his criticism is directed, not unfairly, against the literary defects of the play, it is clear that it reflects also the aristocratic prejudices of at least an important section of the audience at the Comédie Française:

Quand on veut faire passer à la meilleure compagnie de France une

[1] Sc. 3.

journée tout entière dans la maison d'un receveur des fermes, avec un commerçant brise-raison et un fermier général fat et suffisant, on a encouru, *ipso facto*, la peine des sifflets et l'on doit se louer toute sa vie de l'indulgence de ses juges, qui ont bien voulu bâiller tout bas quand ils pouvaient siffler tout haut.[1]

In the preface to the *Mariage de Figaro* Beaumarchais himself denounces the aristocratic prejudice aroused by his earlier play:

Entre autres critiques de la pièce, j'entendis, dans une loge auprès de celle que j'occupais, un jeune *important* de la Cour qui disait gaiement à des dames: 'L'auteur, sans doute, est un garçon fripier, qui ne voit rien de plus élevé que des commis des fermes et des marchands d'étoffes; et c'est au fond d'un magasin qu'il va chercher les nobles amis qu'il traduit à la scène française.'— Hélas! Monsieur, lui dis-je en m'avançant, il a fallu du moins les prendre où il n'est pas impossible de les supposer. Vous ririez bien plus de l'auteur, s'il eût tiré deux vrais amis de l'Œil-de-bœuf ou des Carrosses? Il faut un peu de vraisemblance, même dans les actes vertueux.[2]

It is characteristic that the courtier should place Beaumarchais's characters very much lower down the social scale than they really are; the two main characters of *Les Deux Amis* are men of substance, a wealthy merchant and a high official in the tax farm.

Speaking more generally of this whole question in his *Lettre modérée sur la chute et la critique du 'Barbier de Séville'*, Beaumarchais refers to his two plays in ironical terms as 'deux tristes drames, productions monstrueuses, comme on sait, car entre la Tragédie et la Comédie, on n'ignore plus qu'il n'existe rien'. He adds:

Pour moi, j'en suis tellement convaincu, que si je voulais aujourd'hui mettre au théâtre une mère éplorée, une épouse trahie, une sœur éperdue, un fils déshérité, pour les présenter décemment au public je commencerais par leur supposer un beau royaume où ils auraient régné de leur mieux, vers l'un des archipels ou dans tel autre coin du monde; certain, après cela, que l'invraisemblance du roman, l'énormité des faits, l'enflure des caractères, le gigantesque des idées et la bouffissure du langage, loin de m'être imputés à reproche, assureraient encore mon succès.

He offers ironical submission to the traditional interpretation of the functions of the two existing forms of drama: 'Présenter des hommes d'une condition moyenne accablés et dans le malheur, fi donc! On ne doit jamais les montrer que bafoués. Les citoyens ridicules et les rois malheureux, voilà tout le théâtre existant et possible, et je me le tiens pour dit; c'est fait, je ne veux plus quereller avec personne.'[3]

[1] Vol. viii, p. 442. [2] *Théâtre complet*, pp. 176–7.
[3] *Théâtre complet*, p. 119.

Such criticisms of the *Drame* are to be encountered in the most surprising places. When in 1771 *Le Fabricant de Londres* received its one and only performance at the Comédie Française, Condorcet—the future revolutionary, Condorcet—wrote to Turgot: 'On a donné avant-hier, aux Français, une tragédie bourgeoise de M. de Falbaire; elle est lourdement tombée. Les mœurs insipides de la petite bourgeoisie y étaient peintes avec une vérité dégoûtante.'[1] It is true that when, a month later, he sent a copy of the play to Turgot, he speaks less harshly of it: 'Les deux derniers actes m'ont paru n'être pas sans intérêt. Il est vrai que je n'y suis pas difficile, et que mon âme s'attendrit aisément, soit sensibilité, soit mobilité.'[2] It is also true that in his *Discours de réception* at the Academy in 1782, in speaking of the *Beverley* of his predecessor, Saurin, he endeavours to deal impartially with the new type of drama, and even concedes that its moral lesson is more direct and therefore more useful than that of tragedy. He concludes that Saurin's play is 'un drame intéressant et moral, une pièce qui n'est point une tragédie mise sous des noms vulgaires, un ouvrage qui n'est pas né de l'impuissance de faire parler avec noblesse les héros et les grands hommes'.[3] None the less his first spontaneous reaction to the sort of characters depicted in Fenouillot de Falbaire's *drame* still remains highly significant.

In 1775 Fréron, writing of Mercier's *Brouette du Vinaigrier*, offers the ironical advice:

Je conseillerais à M. Mercier de mettre ainsi sur le théâtre tous les corps de métiers dont cette capitale abonde et de nous donner, en drames bien relevés et bien pathétiques, *Le Sac du Charbonnier, L'Auge du Maçon, La Tasse du Quinze-Vingt, Le Chaudron de la Vendeuse de Châtaignes, La Chaufferette de la Marchande de Pommes, Le Tonneau de la Ravaudeuse, La Hotte du Crocheteur, La Sellette du Décrotteur*, etc. etc.[4]

Five years later, when the Comédie Française performed the *drame héroïque* of a certain D'Ussieux, entitled *Les Héros français ou le Siège de Saint-Jean-de-Losne*, which portrayed the resistance of the *échevins* of this little town in Burgundy to the siege of 1636, Meister comments ironically in the *Correspondance littéraire*: 'Ce sont des héros bourgeois, des héroïnes bourgeoises, des tyrans bourgeois, et leur prose boursouflée a paru plus bourgeoise encore, grâce au ton tragique et déclamatoire avec lequel les acteurs ont tâché de la faire valoir.' At least the

---

[1] *Correspondance inédite de Condorcet et de Turgot*, ed. C. Henry (Paris, 1883), p. 36.
[2] Ibid., p. 43.   [3] *Œuvres*, vol. i, pp. 410–11.
[4] *Année littéraire* (1775), vol. vii, p. 13.

failure of the play, he declares, proves 'que nous ne sommes pas encore aussi barbares qu'on nous l'a reproché quelquefois'.[1] A sympathetic reference to Mercier and his *Brouette du Vinaigrier* in Bachaumont in 1784 underlines the fact that he and his *drames* were not in favour with high society in Paris and Versailles: 'S'il n'est pas le poète des gens de la cour et du grand monde, il est celui des bonnes mœurs, de l'honnêteté et des partisans de la vertu rigide.'[2]

This resistance in France to the new genre was predicted by Lessing in his *Hamburgische Dramaturgie* as early as 1767 in the famous words: 'Die Nation ist zu eitel, ist in Titel and andere äußerliche Vorzüge zu verliebt; bis auf den gemeinsten Mann, will alles mit Vornehmern umgehen; und Gesellschaft mit seines gleichen, ist so viel als schlechte Gesellschaft.'[3] Lessing, it will be noticed, attributes this opposition to the *Drame* less to high society itself than to those people beneath it in rank who try to ape their betters and consequently would rather see them on the stage than their equals; the point had been made even earlier by Rousseau in his *Nouvelle Héloïse*.[4] Yet at least two writers, speaking from this side of 1789, attribute the failure of the *Drame* in the first place to the resistance of the upper classes of French society before the Revolution. Pixerécourt maintains that it would be quite wrong to believe that the lack of success of this new genre was wholly due to its literary defects.

Erreur. Il présentait des scènes populaires, il déplut à l'orgueil. . . . Enfin il apportait, pour ainsi dire, les vertus privées à la barre de l'opinion des grands; et les gens du *bon ton* lui refusèrent *les honneurs de la séance*. Le mauvais goût fut le prétexte de l'exclusion, le but du genre fut le tacite et le véritable motif.[5]

Garat's reflections in his memoirs on the relative unpopularity of the *Drame* are perhaps more precise and reliable. After defending Diderot's dramatic theories, he goes on:

On ne voulait pas que la tragédie pût être populaire, lorsque la nature et les passions font naître tant d'événements tragiques parmi le peuple; on ne voulait pas voir que, dans ses rapports avec la tragédie, le peuple n'est plus ce qu'il était il y a cent ans; qu'il s'est élevé à toute la hauteur du cothurne; que par l'indépendance de la fortune, par la noblesse des sentiments et du langage les classes populaires un peu distinguées peuvent désormais, comme les grands, parler sur les théâtres la langue des Corneille, des Racine et des Vol-

[1] Vol. xii, p. 433.
[2] *Mémoires secrets*, vol. xxvi, p. 242 (13 Oct. 1784).
[3] *Sämtliche Schriften*, ed. K. Lachmann (Stuttgart, 1886–1907), 23 vols., vol. ix, p. 240.
[4] See above, p. 245.
[5] Estève, 'Observations de Guilbert de Pixerécourt', p. 551.

taire. Les poétiques excluaient le tiers état de la scène tragique, précisément comme l'aristocratie, des dignités sociales. C'était le même préjugé sur la scène et dans le monde.[1]

This passage is all the more significant since the author betrays the limits of his own attitude to the *peuple* in the amusingly revealing phrase, 'les classes populaires *un peu distinguées*'.

The amount of truth contained in these statements is not easily calculated, when we come to examine in detail the attitude of the Paris theatres, and particularly of the Comédie Française, to the new genre. It seems fairly clear that the actors of this last theatre were not too well disposed towards it, partly because it did not fit in with their style of acting.[2] How far their coldness towards the *Drame* was due in part to the reluctance of their audience to applaud the new genre is not easily established. A study of the plays—new and old—performed at the Comédie Française in the decades between 1760 and 1789 does not lead to altogether clear-cut results. In these years the serious comedies of Destouches and the *comédies larmoyantes* of Nivelle de La Chaussée continued to be both regularly and frequently performed, as did similar plays of Voltaire such as *L'Enfant prodigue*, *Nanine*, and *L'Écossaise*. Indeed in the thirty years from 1761 to 1790 these three plays were given more often than such famous tragedies as *Zaïre* and *Mérope*, though not even the most often performed of them, *L'Enfant prodigue*, had quite the success of Voltaire's last important tragedy, *Tancrède* (1760). The 1760's saw the successful performance of four plays of the new genre—the *Père de Famille*, the *Philosophe sans le savoir*, *Eugénie*, and *Beverley*—all of which were to remain in the repertoire of the Comédie Française until 1789 and beyond. Their success was eclipsed, from 1774 onwards, when Collé's historical *drame*, *La Partie de chasse de Henri IV*, could at last be performed at the Comédie Française after the death of Louis XV; by 1789 it had been given there no fewer than 140 times, a success which was surpassed in this period only by the triumphant *Mariage de Figaro*. Yet, if it would be an exaggeration to suggest that in the 1770's and 1780's the actors of the Comédie Française were deliberately hostile to the *Drame*, it is certainly the case that, apart from Collé's play, no work of this type established itself in this theatre with anything like the success of those first given in the 1760's.

It is certainly a matter of historical fact that the actors of the Comédie

---

[1] *Mémoires historiques sur la vie de M. Suard, sur ses écrits et sur le XVIII⁰ siècle* (Paris, 1820), 2 vols., vol. ii, p. 17.

[2] Gaiffe, *Le Drame en France*, pp. 120–2.

Française treated Sedaine so badly that they drove away to the Théâtre Italien perhaps the most able dramatist of the time who had taken up the new genre. From 1769, when the Théâtre Italien gave up the performance of French plays until they were reinstated at the beginning of 1780, the Comédie Française had a complete monopoly of the performance of all new plays with any literary pretensions whatsoever. In this period the Théâtre Italien produced a large number of *opéras-comiques*, including several by Sedaine, in which the influence of the *Drame* was very clearly visible. From 1780 onwards, with the reintroduction of French plays, the Théâtre Italien performed its quota of *drames*, both new and old. Hitherto Louis-Sébastien Mercier had been obliged to content himself with the faint consolation of having his *drames*, all of which were scorned by the Comédie Française, performed in one of the Théâtres des Boulevards; it was at the Théâtre des Associés in 1776 that *Jenneval* and *La Brouette du Vinaigrier* were first performed in Paris.[1] However, in the 1780's most of these despised productions were put on by the Théâtre Italien. His favourite play, *Natalie*, was a failure, but *Jenneval*, *Le Déserteur*, *L'Indigent*, *La Brouette du Vinaigrier*, and *L'Habitant de la Guadeloupe* were all well received and established themselves in the repertoire of this theatre.[2] Indeed in 1787 even the Comédie Française consented to put on one of his *drames*, *La Maison de Molière*, which was given thirty-one times before the closing of the theatre in 1793.

It seems clear, however, that it was in the provinces, where in the second quarter of the century there had begun, both in the great commercial centres and in garrison towns, a considerable revival in theatrical activity,[3] that the *Drame* scored its greatest successes in the last decades of the Ancien Régime. After speaking of the resistance which the new genre encountered from the more aristocratic taste of the capital, Pixérécourt adds: 'En général le Drame fut mieux accueilli en province qu'à Paris; c'est qu'en province on était moins dépravé que dans la capitale, et c'est une preuve de plus de la vérité de mon observation.'[4] In his essay, *Du Théâtre*, Mercier rebuked his fellow playwrights for their concentration on the capital and their neglect of the provinces. 'Il y a autant de goût au moins dans la province qu'à Paris', he affirmed;

[1] L. Béclard, *Sébastien Mercier: sa vie, son œuvre, son temps d'après des documents inédits* (Paris, 1903), pp. 686–7.
[2] Ibid., pp. 692–704.
[3] M. Fuchs, *La Vie théâtrale en province au XVIIIe siècle* (Paris, 1933), vol. i, p. 34.
[4] Estève, 'Observations de Guilbert de Pixerécourt', p. 551.

il y est même plus droit, moins gâté et plus raisonnable. On y sait entendre encore et reconnaître la voix du sentiment. Les âmes n'y ont pas reçu l'empreinte de ce dédain superbe qui se refuse à admirer pour le triste plaisir d'une censure qu'enfante l'orgueil. Dans la province il y a généralement plus de mœurs, et c'est là qu'un poète dramatique doit s'étudier surtout à plaire.[1]

Paris critics like La Harpe might continue to sneer at the successes won in the provinces by the works of the *dramaturges*; but the success which their plays enjoyed there is highly significant from our point of view. Plays which were scorned by the actors of the Comédie Française or which, if accepted there, met with little or no success, often had an enthusiastic reception in the provinces. It was not until three years after its publication in 1758 that the *Père de Famille* was performed at the Comédie Française, and it was only in 1769 that it was successful enough to establish itself in the repertoire of that theatre for fifty years and more. Yet in December 1760, some two months before his play was given at the Comédie Française, the happy author could write to Sophie Volland: 'On joue à présent à Marseille *Le Père de Famille*. Je suis désolé de ne pouvoir vous envoyer la gazett equi fait mention de son succès. Toutes les têtes en sont tournées. . . . Si ces gens-là ont parlé d'après l'impression, il faut qu'elle ait été bien violente. Jamais aucune pièce n'a été louée comme elle est là.'[2] According to Grimm, the play was performed successfully, not only in Marseilles but also in Toulouse, Bordeaux, and Lyons, before it reached the Comédie Française.[3]

Beaumarchais's *Eugénie* was received in the provinces with considerable favour, but, what is more interesting, his second *drame*, *Les Deux Amis*, with its picture of commercial life, though it had a cool reception at the Comédie Française, was successful outside Paris. It would be wrong to suggest that the play was a total failure at the Comédie Française since at the twelve performances given between January and March 1770 nearly 9,000 spectators paid for admission; but this could certainly not count as much of a success, especially as the play was not revived until thirteen years later and was then given only twice. Yet in October 1770 we find Beaumarchais writing, in a letter to a theatre-manager in Bordeaux who was about to put on his latest play: 'Elle a été jouée à Lyon, à Marseille et à Rouen avec le plus grand succès.'[4]

---

[1] *Du Théâtre*, pp. 368–9.
[2] *Lettres à Sophie Volland*, vol. i, pp. 207–8.
[3] *Correspondance littéraire*, vol. iv, p. 353.
[4] *Théâtre complet: Lettres relatives à son théâtre*, p. 543.

The popularity of the *drames* of Mercier in the provinces contrasts sharply with their rejection by the Comédie Française and their belated success at the Théâtre Italien in the 1780's. In 1777 a letter from Bordeaux relates the triumphant reception given to such plays as *La Brouette du Vinaigrier*, *Le Déserteur*, and especially *Jenneval*, his first *drame*: 'Quatre cents personnes qui viennent quelquefois s'ennuyer au *Tartufe* par désœuvrement juraient dans la rue contre leur méchante étoile qui les avait conduits trop tard au guichet.'[1] In the following year, in a letter addressed to the *Journal de Paris*, Mercier replied ironically to the attacks of La Harpe: 'Je ne conteste point à M. de La Harpe ses *grands succès* sur les théâtres de la capitale; qu'il me laisse mes obscurs succès *de province*, qui ne peuvent nuire à *sa renommée de Paris*.'[2] After the success of *Le Tableau de Paris* Mercier's popularity as a dramatist rose even higher. In 1782 Restif de La Bretonne could write to him: 'L'un de ces jours un comédien de province achetait de vos pièces chez la dame veuve Duchesne, en vous maudissant: *Ils veulent les pièces de cet enragé*. N'est-ce pas une vraie bénédiction que les malédictions d'un pareil homme?'[3] Four years later, when Mercier happened to be in Rouen, the actors there took the opportunity to perform two of his plays. 'Vendredi dernier, 3 du courant', so ran the *Journal de Normandie*,

l'*Indigent* avait attiré une brillante assemblée. A la fin de la pièce le public a demandé l'auteur avec le plus vif empressement. Le s^r Bérard vint annoncer que M. Mercier était assis parmi les spectateurs. Les instances du public ayant alors recommencé avec encore plus de vivacité, M. Mercier s'est levé du parquet où il était assis et a laissé voir sa sensibilité pour un honneur qui devenait une juste récompense du talent marqué et des intentions vertueuses qui se font remarquer dans tous ses ouvrages.[4]

It lies outside the scope of this book to investigate in detail the fortunes of the *Drame* in the French provinces in the last decades of the Ancien Régime.[5] It is clear, however, that plays which were coolly received in Paris, or even kept off the stage entirely, met with a more

---

[1] *Journal des Théâtres*, 1 Dec. 1777 (quoted in Gaiffe, *Le Drame en France*, p. 202).
[2] *Journal de Paris*, 9 June 1778 (quoted in Gaiffe, ibid.).
[3] Quoted in Béclard, *Sébastien Mercier*, pp. 685–6.
[4] Quoted ibid., pp. 716–17.
[5] A detailed investigation of the question might perhaps show that, while the success of the *Drame* in the provinces was considerable, it was not so great as is sometimes held. For instance, in his 'Note sur l'histoire du théâtre à Montpellier au XVIIIᵉ siècle' (*Mélanges d'histoire littéraire offerts à Daniel Mornet*, Paris, 1951, pp. 133–40) Professor Pierre Jourda shows that comedy was distinctly more popular in this particular town than either tragedy or the *Drame*.

favourable reception in provincial towns. It seems fair to deduce from this state of affairs that the more aristocratic taste of Paris audiences, particularly those of the Comédie Française, did offer some resistance to the new genre, on aesthetic grounds no doubt in some measure (and justifiably so), but almost certainly too for social reasons, since both the aristocratic sections of the audience and those of humbler birth continued to accept the traditional view of the scope of drama which limited tragedy to the portrayal of the fate of illustrious personages and confined comedy to the portrayal of polite society. The new genre or rather genres (the *Drame* since its inception by Diderot ranged from sentimental comedy to domestic tragedy) sought to deal with the affairs of ordinary people; it was inevitable both that playwrights should show a certain timidity when it actually came to depicting on the stage even honest bourgeois, let alone the lower orders, and that the aristocratic traditions in the theatre should have militated against the success of the *Drame* at the Comédie Française. Clearly in literature in general, in the novel as well as in drama, there was a demand, in the second half of the eighteenth century, for a broader picture of contemporary society; but attempts to satisfy this demand, cautious as they were for the most part, encountered a certain amount of opposition. The relative lack of success of the *Drame* was due above all to the absence of any man of genius and great theatrical gifts among the playwrights who tried their hand at this new dramatic form. Yet it is not unfair to suggest that it was also due in some indefinable degree to the spirit of the age; in the Comédie Française, the leading theatre of the capital, as in the world of journalists and critics, there was undoubtedly considerable hostility to such experiments in drama.

Despite the changes which occurred in Paris theatre audiences in the course of the eighteenth century, despite the gradual transformation which was taking place in the decades immediately before the Revolution, down to 1789 taste in drama remained strongly influenced by aristocratic traditions which were sustained by the as yet unshaken predominance of *le monde* in the literary world of the time. Eighteenth-century taste in drama reflected to some degree the changes which are summed up in that rather overworked formula, 'the rise of the middle classes'; but it also reflected the hold over literature in general which the marriage of blue blood and wealth gave to the high society of the capital until the social upheaval of 1789, and even beyond.

Conclusion

I T lies in the very nature of the subject that this long voyage of exploration through the history of Paris theatres and their audiences in the two centuries which stretch from the end of the Wars of Religion to the Revolution of 1789 has not led to any final and clear-cut results. Yet to see assembled and tentatively interpreted such evidence as is available concerning the audiences which frequented the Paris theatres in these years is perhaps not without interest. Scrappy and at times contradictory as the documents are, they do permit one to offer at least some sort of a picture of these audiences and the changes which took place in them over these two centuries. Though the result falls far short of what had been dreamed of, the investigation has, it is hoped, brought more life to the whole question and on occasion corrected, as well as amplified, the theories put forward, with or without the backing of precise documents, in a score of earlier books and articles.

The history of Paris theatre audiences in the seventeenth and eighteenth centuries might be summarized thus. Our knowledge of the state of the theatres of the capital in the opening decades of the seventeenth century is so fragmentary that it is impossible to speak with any certainty of the kind of spectators who frequented them. In particular, there is not enough evidence either to confirm or to disprove the generally held view that in these years audiences were overwhelmingly plebeian. On the other hand the fact that in the first two decades of the seventeenth century the court was by no means as indifferent to drama as has often been supposed would suggest that there is considerable exaggeration in the stress laid upon the plebeian nature of theatre audiences in these years. If from both the aesthetic and the moral point of view the drama of these years was extremely crude, so was the taste of the court and of the aristocracy in general; there was not an unbridgeable gulf between the low tastes of the plebs and the refined and sophisticated tastes of the court, for refinement and sophistication were equally lacking on both sides. In the third decade of the seventeenth century the Paris theatre began to become both more popular and, from an aesthetic and moral point of view, more worthy of admiration; but this may have been due less to a sudden revolution in theatre audiences which made them cease to be plebeian, than to the growing refinement of the upper classes through the development of social life in the *salons*.

All these conclusions must remain highly speculative. For the period which began about 1630 and stretched through the age of Corneille, Racine, and Molière on to the period of Marivaux, La Chaussée, and Voltaire, down to, say, 1760, we are on much firmer ground, even if our information still remains fragmentary. An examination of the term 'aristocratic audience' as applied to the theatre of these hundred years or so has shown it to require some qualification. While it would seem a fair deduction from the available evidence that the lower orders of Paris society played a minor and indeed almost negligible rôle among the spectators of this period, it would appear that already in the Classical age the educated and more cultured sections of the middle classes exercised, especially from their place in the *parterre*, a very considerable influence on the fate of new plays and on the degree of popularity enjoyed by older ones. On the other hand French society of the age of Louis XIII, Louis XIV, and Louis XV was fundamentally aristocratic; and in the theatres of seventeenth- and eighteenth-century Paris the representatives of the upper classes exerted an influence on both the content and form of plays which far exceeded even their numerical importance among the audiences of the time.

French society in these two centuries was in a constant state of slow evolution, which was undoubtedly reflected in the theatre audiences of Paris, particularly in the last decades before 1789. There is evidence to show that from about 1760 onwards a more plebeian type of spectator began to infiltrate into the hitherto somewhat exclusive audiences of the two main Paris theatres, the Comédie Française and the Théâtre Italien. At the same time the educated sections of the middle classes continued to frequent the theatre, and to do so in a society in which the section of the community to which they belonged was assuming an ever greater importance. Yet until the Revolution came to destroy the society of the Ancien Régime, the upper classes of society—the court nobility, the *Parlementaires*, the bankers and tax-farmers, together with their womenfolk—what is known for convenience as *le monde*—continued to form an important part of the theatre audience and to mould to their taste the drama of the age.

Interesting as is a study of the changing theatre audiences of Paris under the Ancien Régime as an end in itself, it gains further value from the light which it throws on the evolution of French drama in these two centuries. Little is to be deduced, it is true, from the very tentative conclusions which can be arrived at from a study of Paris theatre audiences in the opening decades of the seventeenth century. In any case the drama of this period is dead, and there is little to be gained by attempting to relate it to the scraps of often contradictory information which we can manage to glean about the theatre audiences of these years. But for the age which began with Corneille and his generation of of playwrights and lasted until the Revolution, it is possible, as we have seen, to establish many interesting connections between developments in drama and those in the audiences, at once bourgeois and aristocratic, that frequented the Paris theatres in these years in which Absolutism rose to its zenith and began to sink towards its final destruction, and in which the society of the *salons* exerted a decisive influence on literature in general and drama in particular.

In the last decades of the Ancien Régime an attempt was made to found a new dramatic genre. The supporters of the *Drame* had as their aim to create a type of drama in between Comedy and Tragedy, inclining now towards sentimental and moralizing comedy, now towards domestic tragedy, one which would concern itself with the problems of ordinary people, and no longer portray merely the remote heroes and heroines of classical tragedy or the restricted aristocratic circles of so much of eighteenth-century French comedy. Something came of this demand for a new type of drama which would be more in keeping with the social realities of the France of that age; but it also encountered resistance in the aristocratic traditions which had reigned in French drama for over a century and were sustained by the still important place occupied in the Paris theatres by the representatives of high society. It needed the Revolution of 1789 to destroy the semi-feudal society of the Ancien Régime; it was only in the new society created by the Revolution and Napoleon that there at last occurred the literary revolution which swept away so many of the traditions and conventions on which French drama had lived for nearly two centuries.

APPENDIX

Yearly Totals of Spectators at the Comédie Française from Easter 1681 to Easter 1774

THESE figures, corrected to the nearest thousand, have been calculated from the data provided by H. Carrington Lancaster in *The Comédie Française, 1680–1701*, and *The Comédie Française, 1701–1774*. The difficulties involved in their interpretation are discussed above (pp. 50 and 168–71).

1681–2	135,000	1707–8	136,000	1733–4	109,000
1682–3	155,000	1708–9	128,000	1734–5	105,000
1683–4	109,000	1709–10	114,000	1735–6	110,000
1684–5	137,000	1710–11	120,000	1736–7	98,000
1685–6	134,000	1711–12	107,000	1737–8	94,000
1686–7	133,000	1712–13	173,000	1738–9	99,000
1687–8	146,000	1713–14	157,000	1739–40	—[1]
1688–9	135,000	1714–15	185,000	1740–1	94,000
1689–90	144,000	1715–16	133,000	1741–2	84,000
1690–1	131,000	1716–17	104,000	1742–3	132,000
1691–2	120,000	1717–18	122,000	1743–4	125,000
1692–3	123,000	1718–19	117,000	1744–5	114,000
1693–4	117,000	1719–20	155,000	1745–6	107,000
1694–5	117,000	1720–1	146,000	1746–7	116,000
1695–6	156,000	1721–2	98,000	1747–8	129,000
1696–7	139,000	1722–3	124,000	1748–9	119,000
1697–8	147,000	1723–4	159,000	1749–50	140,000
1698–9	193,000	1724–5	135,000	1750–1	177,000
1699–1700	137,000	1725–6	125,000	1751–2	147,000
1700–1	168,000	1726–7	109,000	1752–3	156,000
1701–2	145,000	1727–8	92,000	1753–4	165,000
1702–3	130,000	1728–9	118,000	1754–5	153,000
1703–4	138,000	1729–30	110,000	1755–6	187,000
1704–5	143,000	1730–1	106,000	1756–7	160,000
1705–6	123,000	1731–2	127,000	1757–8	155,000
1706–7	139,000	1732–3	122,000	1758–9	178,000

[1] The Register for this year is lost.

1759–60	159,000	1764–5	177,000	1769–70	191,000
1760–1	153,000	1765–6	146,000	1770–1	184,000
1761–2	151,000	1766–7	173,000	1771–2	187,000
1762–3	151,000	1767–8	166,000	1772–3	175,000
1763–4	189,000	1768–9	161,000	1773–4	187,000

Bibliography

MANUSCRIPT SOURCES

Archives de la Comédie Française. Registers and miscellaneous papers.
Archives Nationales. o¹ 845. Archives de la Maison du Roi.
Bibliothèque de l'Arsenal. MSS. 6541–5. Recueil de Jean-Nicolas de Tralage.
Bibliothèque Nationale. MS. français 4022–7. Journal de Jean Héroard.
—— MS. français 9557. Mémoire sur les spectacles inférieurs, Avril 1764.
—— MS. français 21625. Collection Delamare.
—— MS. français 22191. Correspondance de Malesherbes.
—— MS. français 25496. Du Ryer, *Arétaphile* and *Clitophon.*
—— Cinq Cents Colbert. Vol. 92.

PRINTED SOURCES

ADAM, A. *Histoire de la littérature française au XVII⁰ siècle.* 4 vols. Paris, 1948–
54.
ALLAINVAL, L. J. C. S. d'. *L'École des Bourgeois.* Paris, 1729.
ARGENSON, M. R. de V. d'. *Notes.* Ed. L. Larchey and E. Mabille. Paris, 1866.
AUBIGNAC, Abbé d'. *La Pratique du Théâtre.* Ed. P. Martino. Paris, 1927.
—— *Deux Dissertations concernant le poème dramatique en forme de remarques sur
deux tragédies de M. Corneille, intitulées 'Sophonisbe' et 'Sertorius'.* Paris, 1663.
—— *Quatrième Dissertation servant de réponse aux calomnies de M. Corneille.*
Paris, 1664.
—— *Dissertation sur la condamnation des théâtres.* Paris, 1666.
AUERBACH, E. *Vier Untersuchungen zur Geschichte der französischen Bildung.*
Berne, 1951.
BACHAUMONT, L. P. de. *Mémoires secrets pour servir à l'histoire de la République
des Lettres en France de 1762 jusqu'à nos jours.* 36 vols. London, 1777–89.
BAILLET, A. *Jugements des Savants sur les principaux ouvrages des auteurs.* 8 vols.
Amsterdam, 1725.
BARCLAY, J. *Euphormionis Lusinini Satyricon, pars secunda.* Rouen, 1628.
—— *Les Satires d'Euphormion de Lusine.* Transl. J. Tournet. Paris, 1625.
BASCHET, A. *Les Comédiens italiens à la cour de France sous Charles IX, Henri III,
Henri IV et Louis XIII.* Paris, 1882.
BASSOMPIERRE, F. de. *Journal de ma vie.* Ed. Marquis de Chantérac. 4 vols.
Paris, 1870–7.
BEAUMARCHAIS, P. A. C. de. *Œuvres complètes.* Ed. E. Fournier. Paris, 1876.

BEAUMARCHAIS, P. A. C. de. *Théâtre complet*. Ed. R. d'Hermies. Paris, 1952.

—— *Théâtre complet: Lettres relatives à son théâtre*. Ed. M. Allem. Paris, 1934.

BÉCLARD, L. *Sébastien Mercier: sa vie, son œuvre, son temps d'après des documents inédits*. Paris, 1903.

BELLOY, P. L. B. de. *Le Siège de Calais*. Paris, 1765.

BÉNICHOU, P. *Morales du Grand Siècle*. Paris, 1948.

BENSERADE, I. *Méléagre*. Paris, 1641.

BOILEAU, N. *Œuvres complètes*. Ed. C. Boudhors. 9 vols. Paris, 1934–43.

BOINDIN, N. *Lettres historiques sur les trois spectacles de Paris*. Paris, 1719.

BOISSY, L. de. *La Critique*. Paris, 1732.

—— *L'Apologie du Siècle, ou Momus corrigé*. Paris, 1734.

BONNASSIES, J. *La Comédie Française. Histoire administrative (1658–1757)*. Paris, 1874.

—— *Les Auteurs dramatiques et la Comédie Française aux XVIIe et XVIIIe siècles*. Paris, 1874.

BORDELON, Abbé L. *Les Coudées franches*. 2 vols. Paris, 1712.

BOUHOURS, D. *La Manière de bien penser dans les ouvrages de l'esprit*. Paris, 1705.

BOURSAULT, E. *Artémise et Poliante*. Paris, 1670.

—— *Le Portrait du peintre, ou la Contre-critique de l'École des Femmes*. Paris, 1663.

—— *La Comédie sans titre, ou le Mercure Galant*. Paris, 1683.

BOYER, C. *Artaxerce*. Paris, 1683.

BRIDARD DE LA GARDE, P. *Lettres de Thérèse, ou Mémoires d'une jeune demoiselle de province pendant son séjour à Paris*. 3 vols. The Hague, 1739–40.

BROSSE, de. *Les Songes des hommes éveillés*. Paris, 1646.

BROWNE, E. *A Journal of a Visit to Paris in the year 1664*. Ed. G. Keynes. London, 1923.

BRUEYS, D. A. de. *Œuvres de Théâtre*. 3 vols. Paris, 1735.

BRUSCAMBILLE [DES LAURIERS]. *Œuvres*. Rouen, 1626.

BURNEY, F. *The Early Diary, 1768–1778*. Ed. A. R. Ellis. 2 vols. London, 1907.

BUSSY-RABUTIN, R. de. *Correspondance*. Ed. L. Lalanne. 6 vols. Paris, 1858–9.

CAILHAVA, J. F. *Les Causes de la Décadence du Théâtre et des moyens de le faire refleurir, extrait de l'Art de la Comédie*. n.p., n.d.

CAMPARDON, E. *Les Comédiens du roi de la troupe française pendant les deux derniers siècles*. Paris, 1879.

—— *Les Comédiens du roi de la troupe italienne pendant les deux derniers siècles*. 2 vols. Paris, 1880.

—— *Documents inédits sur J. B. Poquelin Molière*. Paris, 1871.

CAMPISTRON, J. G. de. *Œuvres*. Paris, 1715.

CAMUS, J. P. *Les Spectacles d'horreur*. Paris, 1630.

CHAPELAIN, J. *Correspondance*. Ed. T. de Larroque. 2 vols. Paris, 1880–3.

—— *Opuscules critiques*. Ed. A. C. Hunter. Paris, 1936.

CHAPPUZEAU, S. *Le Théâtre Français*. Ed. P. L. Jacob. Brussels, 1867.

CHEVALIER [JEAN SIMONIN]. *Les Amours de Calotin*. Paris, 1664.

CHOISY, Abbé de. *Mémoires* in *Nouvelle Collection des Mémoires pour servir à l'histoire de France*, ed. J. F. Michaud and J. J. F. Poujoulat, 34 vols. Paris, 1836–9.

COLLÉ, C. *Journal et mémoires*. Ed. H. Bonhomme. 3 vols. Paris, 1868.

CONDORCET, J. A. N. de. *Œuvres*. Ed. A. C. O'Connor and F. Arago. 12 vols. Paris, 1847–9.

—— *Correspondance inédite de Condorcet et de Turgot*. Ed. C. Henry. Paris, 1883.

COQUELEY DE CHAUSSEPIERRE. *Le Roué vertueux*. Lausanne, 1770.

CORNEILLE, P. *Œuvres*. Ed. C. Marty-Laveaux. 12 vols. Paris, 1862–8.

DABNEY, L. E. *French Dramatic Literature in the Reign of Henri IV*. Austin, 1952.

DAINVILLE, F. de. 'Les Lieux d'affichage des comédiens à Paris en 1753', *Revue d'histoire du théâtre*. 1951.

DANGEAU, P. *Journal*. Ed. E. Soulié and others. 19 vols. Paris, 1854–60.

DEIERKAUF-HOLSBOER, S. W. *Vie d'Alexandre Hardy, Poète du Roi*. Philadelphia, 1947.

—— *Le Théâtre du Marais*. Vol. I. Paris, 1954.

DEPPING, G. B. (ed.). *Correspondance administrative sous le règne de Louis XIV*. 4 vols. Paris, 1850–5.

DES ESSARTS, N. T. *Les Trois Théâtres de Paris*. Paris, 1777.

DESMARETZ DE SAINT-SORLIN, J. *Les Visionnaires*. Paris, 1637.

Dictionnaire de l'Académie Française. 4 vols. Paris, 1694.

DIDEROT, D. *Œuvres complètes*. Ed. J. Assézat and M. Tourneux. 20 vols. Paris, 1875–7.

—— *Lettres à Sophie Volland*. Ed. A. Babelon. 2 vols. Paris, 1938.

DONNEAU, F. *Le Cocu imaginaire*. Paris, 1660.

DONNEAU DE VISÉ, J. *Nouvelles nouvelles*. 3 vols. Paris, 1663.

—— *Zélinde, ou la Véritable Critique de l'École des Femmes et la critique de la Critique*. Paris, 1663.

—— *Réponse à l'Impromptu de Versailles, ou la Vengeance des Marquis*. Paris, 1664.

DORIMOND. *La Comédie de la Comédie, et les Amours de Tripotin*. Paris, 1662.

ESTÈVE, E. 'Observations de Guilbert de Pixerécourt sur les théâtres de la Révolution', *Revue d'histoire littéraire de la France*. 1916.

ÉTIENNE, C. G., and MARTAINVILLE, A. *Histoire du Théâtre Français depuis le commencement de la Révolution jusqu'à la réunion générale*. 4 vols. Paris, 1802.

FAGNIEZ, G. *La Femme et la société française dans la première moitié du XVIIᵉ siècle*. Paris, 1929.

FAVART, C. S. *Mémoires et correspondance littéraires, dramatiques et anecdotiques*. Ed. A. P. C. Favart. 3 vols. Paris, 1808.

FENOUILLOT DE FALBAIRE, C. G. *Le Fabricant de Londres*. Paris, 1771.

FLEURY [J. A. BÉNARD]. *Mémoires*. Ed. J. B. P. Lafitte. 6 vols. Paris, 1836–8.

FOURNIER, E. (ed.). *Variétés historiques et littéraires*. 10 vols. Paris, 1855–63.

FRAMERY, N. E. *De l'Organisation des Spectacles de Paris*. Paris, 1790.

FRANÇOIS DE SALES, St. *Introduction à la vie dévote*. 3rd ed. Lyons, 1610.

FRANSEN, J. 'Documents inédits sur l'Hôtel de Bourgogne', *Revue d'histoire littéraire de la France*. 1927.

FRÉRON, E. C., and others. *Année littéraire*. Paris, 1754–91.

FUCHS, M. *La Vie théâtrale en province au XVIIIᵉ siècle*. Vol. I. Paris, 1933.

—— and P. 'Comédiens français à Londres (1738–55)', *Revue de littérature comparée*. 1933.

FURETIÈRE, A. *Dictionnaire universel.* 3 vols. The Hague and Rotterdam, 1690. 2nd ed., 3 vols. The Hague and Rotterdam, 1701.

——— *Recueil des Factums d'Antoine Furetière.* Ed. C. Asselineau. 2 vols. Paris, 1859.

GACON, F. *Le Poète sans fard.* n.p., 1701.

GAIFFE, F. *Le Drame en France au XVIIIe siècle.* Paris, 1910.

——— *Le Rire et la scène française.* Paris, 1932.

GARAT, D. J. *Mémoires historiques sur la vie de M. Suard, sur ses écrits et sur le XVIIIe siécle.* 2 vols. Paris, 1820.

GARRICK, D. *Private Correspondence.* 2 vols. London, 1831–2.

GASTÉ, A. (ed.). *La Querelle du Cid.* Paris, 1898.

GAULTIER-GARGUILLE. *Chansons.* Paris, 1632.

GHERARDI, E. (ed.). *Le Théâtre Italien, ou le Recueil général de toutes les comédies et scènes françaises jouées par les comédiens italiens du roi.* 6 vols. Paris, 1700.

GOLDONI, C. *Mémoires pour servir à l'histoire de sa vie et à celle de son théâtre.* 3 vols. Paris, 1787.

GRIMAREST, J. L. de. *La Vie de M. de Molière.* Ed. L. Chancerel. Paris, 1930.

GRIMM, F. M. (ed.). *Correspondance littéraire, philosophique et critique.* Ed. M. Tourneux. 16 vols. Paris, 1877–82.

GRIMOD DE LA REYNIÈRE, A. B. L. (ed.). *Le Censeur dramatique, ou Journal des principaux théâtres de Paris et des départements.* 4 vols. Paris, 1797–8.

GROSLEY, P. J. *Londres.* 3 vols. Lausanne, 1770.

GUÉRET, G. *La Guerre des auteurs anciens et modernes.* Paris, 1671.

——— *Le Parnasse réformé.* Paris, 1669.

GUEULLETTE, T. S. *Notes et souvenirs sur le Théâtre Italien au XVIIIe siècle.* Ed. J. E. Gueullette. Paris, 1938.

HARBAGE, A. B. *Shakespeare's Audience.* New York, 1941.

HARDY, A. *Théâtre.* Ed. E. Stengel. 5 vols. Marburg, 1883–4.

HELVÉTIUS, C. A. *De l'Esprit.* Paris, 1758.

——— *De l'Homme.* 2 vols. London, 1773.

HENRY IV. *Recueil de lettres missives.* Ed. Berger de Xivrey. 9 vols. Paris, 1843–76.

HÉROARD, J. *Journal sur l'enfance et la jeunesse de Louis XIII (1601–28).* Ed. E. Soulié and E. de Barthélemy. 2 vols. Paris, 1868.

JAL, A. *Dictionnaire critique de biographie et d'histoire.* Second edition. Paris, 1872.

JOANNIDÈS, A. *La Comédie Française de 1680 à 1900: Dictionnaire général des pièces et des auteurs.* Paris, 1901.

JOURDA, P. 'Note sur l'histoire du théâtre à Montpellier au XVIIIe siècle', in *Mélanges d'histoire littéraire offerts à Daniel Mornet.* Paris, 1951.

Journal de Paris. Paris, 1777 et seq.

LA BRUYÈRE, J. de. *Œuvres complètes.* Ed. G. Servois. 3 vols. Paris, 1865–78.

LACHÈVRE, F. *Les Recueils collectifs de poésies libres et satiriques.* 2 vols. Paris, 1914–22.

LA CROIX, P. de. *La Guerre comique ou la Défense de l'École des Femmes.* Paris, 1663.

LACROIX, P. (ed.). *Ballets et mascarades de cour de Henri III à Louis XIV (1581–1652).* 6 vols. Geneva, 1868–70.

LA DIXMERIE, N. B. de. *Lettres sur l'état présent de nos spectacles.* Amsterdam and Paris, 1765.

LA FONTAINE, J. de. *Œuvres.* Ed. H. Régnier. 11 vols. Paris, 1883–92.

LAGRANGE, C. V. de. *Le Registre de Lagrange (1659–1685).* Ed. B. E. and G. P. Young. 2 vols. Paris, 1947.

LA GRAVETTE DE MAYOLAS. *Lettres en vers,* in *Les Continuateurs de Loret.* Ed. Baron James de Rothschild. 3 vols. Paris, 1881–9.

LA HARPE, J. F. de. *Correspondance littéraire.* 6 vols. Paris, 1801–7.

—— *Le Lycée, ou Cours de littérature ancienne et moderne.* 14 vols. Paris, 1818.

—— *Molière à la nouvelle salle.* Paris, 1782.

—— *Œuvres.* 6 vols. Paris, 1778.

LAMARE, N. de. *Traité de la police.* 4 vols. Paris, 1705–38.

LA MESNARDIÈRE, H. J. de. *La Poétique.* Vol. I. Paris, 1639.

LANCASTER, H. C. *A History of French Dramatic Literature in the Seventeenth Century.* 9 vols. Baltimore, 1929–42.

—— *French Tragedy in the Time of Louis XV and Voltaire.* 2 vols. Baltimore, 1950.

—— *French Tragedy in the Reign of Louis XVI and the Early Years of the French Revolution.* Baltimore, 1953.

—— *The Comédie Française, 1680–1701: Plays, Actors, Spectators, Finances.* Baltimore, 1941.

—— *The Comédie Française, 1701–1774: Plays, Actors, Spectators, Finances.* Philadelphia, 1951.

LANDOIS, P. *Silvie.* Paris, 1742.

LANSON, G. *Corneille.* Paris, 1898.

LA PORTE, Abbé J. de. *Les Spectacles de Paris.* 26 vols. Paris, 1754–78.

LA TUILLERIE, J. F. *Soliman.* Paris, 1681.

LECLERC DE JUIGNÉ, A. E. L. *Mandement . . . qui permet l'usage des œufs.* Paris, 1785.

LEKAIN, H. L. *Mémoires.* Paris, 1801.

LEMIERRE, A. M. *Guillaume Tell.* Paris, 1767.

LESAGE, A. R. *Turcaret: Critique de la Comédie de Turcaret.* Paris, 1709.

—— *La Valise trouvée.* n.p., 1740.

LESPINASSE, Julie de. *Lettres.* Ed. G. Isambert. 2 vols. Paris, 1876.

LESSING, G. E. *Sämtliche Schriften.* Ed. K. Lachmann. 23 vols. Stuttgart, 1886–1907.

L'ESTOILE, P. de. *Mémoires-Journaux.* Ed. G. Brunet and others. 12 vols. Paris, 1875–96.

LONGCHAMP, S. G., and WAGNIÈRE, J. L. *Mémoires sur Voltaire et sur ses ouvrages.* 2 vols. Paris, 1826.

LONGUEIL, C. H. de. *L'Orphelin anglais.* Paris, 1769.

LONVAY DE LA SAUSSAYE and FRANÇOIS DE NEUFCHÂTEAU. *Mémoire à consulter et consultation pour le sieur Lonvay de la Saussaye contre la troupe des Comédiens Français ordinaires du Roi.* Paris, 1775.

LORET, J. *La Muse historique.* Ed. C. Livet. 4 vols. Paris, 1857–78.

LOUGH, J. 'The Earnings of Playwrights in Seventeenth-Century France', *Modern Language Review.* 1947.

—— 'French Actors in Paris from 1612 to 1614', *French Studies.* 1955.

MAGENDIE, M. *La Politesse mondaine et les théories de l'honnêteté en France au XVIIe siècle de 1600 à 1660.* Paris, 1925.

MAGNE, E. *Gaultier-Garguille, comédien de l'Hôtel de Bourgogne.* Paris, n.d.

—— *Le Plaisant Abbé de Boisrobert.* Paris, 1909.

MALHERBE, F. de. *Œuvres.* Ed. L. Lalanne. 5 vols. Paris, 1862–9.

MARAIS, M. *Journal et mémoires.* Ed. M. F. A. de Lescure. 4 vols. Paris, 1863–8.

MARCHAND, J. H. *Le Vidangeur sensible.* Ed. L. Faucou. Paris, 1880.

MARESCHAL, A. *Le Véritable Capitan Matamore.* Paris, 1640.

MARMONTEL, J. F. *Œuvres.* 7 vols. Paris, 1819–20.

MÉLÈSE, P. *Le Théâtre et le public à Paris sous Louis XIV (1659–1715).* Paris, 1934.

MERCIER, L. S. *Du Théâtre, ou Nouvel Essai sur l'art dramatique.* Amsterdam, 1773.

—— *Théâtre complet.* 4 vols. Amsterdam, 1778–84.

—— *Tableau de Paris.* 12 vols. Amsterdam, 1783–9.

—— 'Sur la tragédie de *Brutus*', *Bien Informé.* An VII.

Mercure, Le. Le Mercure galant. Paris, 1678–1714; *Le Nouveau Mercure.* Paris, 1714–21; *Le Mercure.* Paris, 1721–4; *Le Mercure de France.* Paris, 1724–91.

MÉTRA, F. *Correspondance secrète, politique et littéraire.* 18 vols. London, 1787–90.

MICHAUT, G. *Molière raconté par ceux qui l'ont vu.* Paris, 1932.

MOLIÈRE, J. B. P. de. *Œuvres.* Ed. E. Despois and P. Mesnard. 13 vols. Paris, 1873–1900.

—— *Théâtre.* Ed. A. Bret. 6 vols. Paris, 1773.

MONGRÉDIEN, G. 'Bibliographie des œuvres du facétieux Bruscambille', *Bulletin du Bibliophile.* 1926.

—— 'Chronologie des troupes qui ont joué à l'Hôtel de Bourgogne (1598–1680)', *Revue d'histoire du théâtre.* 1953.

MONNET, J. *Supplément au Roman comique.* 2 vols. London, 1772.

MONTFLEURY, A. *L'Impromptu de l'Hôtel de Condé.* Paris, 1664.

—— *Le Procès de la Femme juge et partie.* Paris, 1669.

MONVAL, G. 'Ordre d'un gentilhomme de la Chambre portant "défense des pièces de Molière" ', *Le Moliériste.* 1879.

MOORE, E. *The Gamester.* London, 1753.

MOORE, J. *A View of Society and Manners in France, Switzerland and Germany.* 2 vols. London, 1779.

ORLÉANS, CHARLOTTE ÉLISABETH D'. *Correspondance.* Transl. E. Jaeglé. 3 vols. Paris, 1890.

L'Ouverture des Jours Gras, ou l'Entretien du Carnaval. Paris, 1634.

PAPILLON DE LA FERTÉ, D. P. J. *Journal.* Ed. E. Boysse. Paris, 1887.

PARFAICT, C. and F. *Histoire du Théâtre Français depuis son origine jusqu'à présent.* Amsterdam and Paris, 1735–49.

PENNINGTON, T. *Continental Excursions: or Tours into France, Switzerland and Germany in 1782, 1787, and 1789.* 2 vols. London, 1809.

PETITOT, C. B. (ed.). *Répertoire du Théâtre Français.* 23 vols. Paris, 1803–4.

PLATTER, T. 'Description de Paris en 1599', *Mémoires de la Société de l'histoire de Paris.* 1899.

POMMIER, J. *Aspects de Racine.* Paris, 1954.

PRUNIÈRES, H. *Le Ballet de cour en France avant Benserade et Lully.* Paris, 1913.

PURE, Abbé de. *Idée des spectacles anciens et modernes.* Paris, 1668.

QUINAULT, P. *La Comédie sans comédie.* Paris, 1657.

RACAN, H. de. *Œuvres complètes.* Ed. T. de Latour. 2 vols. Paris, 1857.

RACINE, J. *Œuvres.* Ed. P. Mesnard. 9 vols. Paris, 1865–73.

RAPIN, R. *Réflexions sur l'éloquence, la poétique, l'histoire et la philosophie* in *Les Comparaisons des grands hommes de l'antiquité.* 2 vols. Paris, 1684.

RAVEN, C. E. *John Ray Naturalist. His Life and Works.* Cambridge, 1942.

RAYNAL, Abbé G. T. F. *Nouvelles littéraires* in Grimm, F. M. (ed.), *Correspondance littéraire* (q.v.).

RAYSSIGUIER, de. *L'Aminte du Tasse.* Paris, 1632.

REGNARD, J. F. *La Critique du Légataire universel.* Paris, 1708.

Remontrance au Roi . . . pour l'abrogation de la Confrérie de la Passion en faveur de la Troupe royale des comédiens. Paris, 1631.

RENAUDOT, T. *Recueil des gazettes, nouvelles, relations et autres choses mémorables de toute l'année.* 21 vols. Paris, 1633–53.

RÉTIF DE LA BRETONNE, E. N. *La Mimographe, ou Idées d'une honnête femme pour la réformation du théâtre national.* Amsterdam, 1770.

RICCOBONI, L. *Réflexions historiques et critiques sur les différents théâtres de l'Europe.* Paris, 1738.

RICCOBONI, Mme M. J. (transl.). *Le Nouveau Théâtre anglais.* 2 vols. Paris, 1769.

RICHELET, P. *Dictionnaire français.* Geneva, 1680.

RIGAL, E. *Le Théâtre Français avant la période classique.* Paris, 1901.

ROBINET, C. *Panégyrique de l'École des Femmes.* Paris, 1664.

ROCHEMONT, Sieur de. *Observations sur une comédie de Molière intitulée le 'Festin de Pierre',* in Molière, *Œuvres.* Ed. E. Despois and P. Mesnard. Vol. V.

ROLLAND DU PLESSIS, N. *Remonstrances très humbles au Roy de France.* n.p., 1588.

ROOSBROECK, G. L. van. 'Un document inconnu sur la Querelle du Cid: *L'Anatomie du Cid', Revue d'histoire littéraire de la France.* 1925.

ROTROU, J. *La Bague de l'Oubli.* Paris, 1635.

ROUSSEAU, J. J. *Lettre à D'Alembert sur les spectacles.* Ed. M. Fuchs. Geneva, 1948.

—— *La Nouvelle Héloïse.* Ed. D. Mornet. 4 vols. Paris, 1925.

SAINT-ÉVREMOND, C. de. *Œuvres.* Ed. R. de Planhol. 3 vols. Paris, 1927.

SAINT-PIERRE, Abbé C. I. de. *Œuvres diverses.* 2 vols. Paris, 1728–30.

SAINT-COLOMBE, E. de. *Les Plaisirs d'un jour, ou la journée d'une provinciale à Paris.* Brussels, 1764.

SAURIN, B. J. *Beverley.* Paris, 1768.

—— *Spartacus.* Paris, 1760.

SCARRON, P. *Le Roman comique.* Ed. E. Magne. Paris, 1937.

—— *Œuvres.* 7 vols. Paris, 1786.

SCHERER, J. *La Dramaturgie classique.* Paris, 1950.

SCHWARTZ, W. L. 'Molière's Theater in 1672–3: Light from *Le Registre d'Hubert', Publications of the Modern Languages Association of America.* 1941.

SCUDÉRY, G. de. *L'Apologie du Théâtre.* Paris, 1639.

—— *Arminius.* Paris, 1643.

SCUDÉRY, G. de. *Didon*. Paris, 1637.

SEDAINE, M. J. *Le Philosophe sans le savoir*. Ed. F. Gaiffe. Paris, n.d.

SEGRAIS, J. R. de. *Segraisiana*. Paris, 1721.

SÉVIGNÉ, Mme de. *Lettres*. Ed. L. J. N. de Monmerqué. 14 vols. Paris, 1862–6.

SKIPPON, P. *An Account of a Journey through Part of the Low Countries, Germany, Italy and France* in *A Collection of Voyages and Travels*. Vol. VI. London, 1732.

SOMAIZE, A. B. de. *Dictionnaire des Précieuses*. Ed. C. Livet. 2 vols. Paris, 1856.

SOREL, C. *De la connaissance des bons livres*. Amsterdam, 1672.

—— *La Maison des Jeux*. 2 vols. Paris, 1642.

SOULIÉ, E. *Recherches sur Molière et sur sa famille*. Paris, 1863.

STAËL, Mme de. *De l'Allemagne*. Paris, 1874.

SUBLIGNY, A. T. de. *La Folle Querelle ou la Critique d'Andromaque*. Paris, 1668.

TABARIN [ANTOINE GIRARD]. *Œuvres complètes*. Ed. G. Aventin. 2 vols. Paris, 1858.

TALLEMANT des RÉAUX, G. *Historiettes*. Ed. G. Mongrédien. 8 vols. Paris, 1932–4.

TRISTAN L'HERMITE. *Le Page disgracié*. Ed. A. Dietrich. Paris, 1898.

—— *Amaryllis*. Paris, 1653.

URBAIN, C., and LEVESQUE, E. (eds.). *L'Église et le Théâtre*. Paris, 1930.

VIANEY, J. 'Bruscambille et les poètes bernesques', *Revue d'histoire littéraire de la France*. 1901.

VIGNEUL-MARVILLE [N. BONAVENTURE D'ARGONNE]. *Mélanges d'histoire et de littérature*. 3 vols. Paris, 1725.

VILLIERS, Abbé P. de. *Entretiens sur les tragédies de ce temps*. Paris, 1675.

VIMONT, M. *Histoire de la Rue Saint-Denis*. 3 vols. Paris, 1936.

VIOLLET LE DUC, E. L. N. (ed.). *Ancien Théâtre Français*. 10 vols. Paris, 1854–7.

VOLTAIRE, F. M. A. de. *Correspondence*. Ed. T. Besterman. Vols. 1–10. Geneva, 1953–4.

—— *Notebooks*. Ed. T. Besterman. 2 vols. Geneva, 1952.

—— *Œuvres complètes*. Ed. L. Moland. 52 vols. Paris, 1877–85.

YATES, F. A. 'English Actors in Paris during the Lifetime of Shakespeare', *Review of English Studies*. 1925.

Index

REPRINTED LITHOGRAPHICALLY IN GREAT BRITAIN
AT THE UNIVERSITY PRESS, OXFORD
BY VIVIAN RIDLER
PRINTER TO THE UNIVERSITY